The Message of the Mind
in Neo-Confucianism

Neo-Confucian Studies
Sponsored by the Regional Seminar in Neo-Confucian Studies,
Columbia University

君子法天之圖

主一無適
整齊嚴肅
聖要四說
常惺惺法
其心收斂
不容一物

THE
MESSAGE
OF THE MIND
in Neo-Confucianism

WM. THEODORE DE BARY

COLUMBIA UNIVERSITY PRESS

NEW YORK

The frontispiece is the
"Diagram of the Noble Man Modeling Himself on Heaven"
by Ch'en Chen-sheng (1410–1473). See p. 227.

The jacket design is taken from the
"Diagram of Heaven, Earth, and Sagehood"
by Ch'en Chen-sheng (1410–1473).

COLUMBIA UNIVERSITY PRESS

NEW YORK   GUILDFORD, SURREY

LIBRARY OF CONGRESS

LIBRARY OF CONGRESS CATALOGING-IN-PUBLICATION DATA

De Bary, William Theodore, 1919–
The message of the mind in Neo-Confucianism / Wm. Theodore de Bary.
p.   cm. — (Neo-Confucian studies)
Based on lectures delivered at the Collège de France in May 1986.
Bibliography: p.
Includes index.
ISBN 0-231-06808-5
1. Neo-Confucianism—China.   I. Title.   II. Series.
B127.N4D399   1989
181'.09512—dc19   88-18740
CIP

Printed in the United States of America

Design by Charles Hames

Casebound editions of Columbia University Press books are Smyth-sewn
and printed on permanent and durable acid-free paper

Contents

Diagrams Illustrating the Succession to the Way and Learning of the Mind-and-Heart

Preface

The present volume has emerged from lectures delivered at the Collège de France in May 1986 which were intended as a sequel to my *Neo-Confucian Orthodoxy and the Learning of the Mind-and-Heart* (1981). In the earlier study I drew attention to key doctrines concerning the mind which linked the Neo-Confucian view of self-cultivation to the dominant political philosophy in pre-modern East Asia. The focus in that first study was on the historical process by which certain Neo-Confucian ideas and texts became institutionalized as an official orthodoxy during the late Sung, Yüan, and early Ming dynasties (thirteenth to fifteenth centuries). In the present work, I follow this development down into the nineteenth century, but with more attention to how certain core ideas and practices underwent change in the continuing discussion and debate that marked the later Confucian tradition. What we speak of as "tradition" may indeed be better understood as a sustained discourse in which the central values of Neo-Confucianism never ceased to be at issue, with two among them—the "mind" *(hsin)* and tradition *(tao-t'ung)* itself—most seriously contested.

My title "The Message of the Mind" expresses in another way something essential to the "Learning of the Mind-and-Heart." It is meant to suggest that, besides being "about" the mind, this communication was to be "by" and "of" the mind, i.e., an active involvement of the mind was required for passing the message on. Such is the intention which underlay the Neo-Confucians' frequent use of the term *hsin-fa* in this connection. *Hsin-fa* defies literal translation, and, even among free renderings, there is no single one that adequately conveys

its several meanings and uses. In *Neo-Confucian Orthodoxy* I translated *hsin-fa* as method or system of the mind-and-heart (the latter
often shortened just to "mind," once the idea had been registered that
mind always stands for heart as well, and vice versa). Subsequently I
have considered such possible renderings as "formula," "recipe," or
"secret" of the mind. At this point, however (and I will not say "finally"), I have decided on three separate translations—"message,"
"method," and, less often, "measure" to express three distinct meanings that attach to *hsin-fa* in Neo-Confucian discourse as recounted in
this book. "Message" conveys the idea that this is an instruction transmitted from the early sage-kings; in this sense *hsin-fa* is parallel to the
"transmission of the mind [of the sages]" (ch'uan-hsin) also much
discussed in Neo-Confucianism. "Method," *fa* as a way of doing or
practicing something, lends itself to the Neo-Confucian view that the
message bears with it a specific formula for moral practice *(kung-fu)* in
the conduct of life and especially of government. Lastly, "measure,"
besides connoting a step to be taken, can represent *fa* as a model or
norm, and thus suitably stand for *hsin-fa* as the "measure of the mind."
In Neo-Confucian parlance, in contrast to Buddhist, it asserts a definite
standard of moral value or judgment as inherent in, and intrinsic to, the
mind.

If one looks in standard dictionaries or histories for the meaning of
the closely related term *hsin-hsüeh* ("learning of the mind-and-heart"),
one invariably finds it identified with the teaching of Lu Hsiang-shan in
the Sung period and then with Wang Yang-ming in the Ming, or with
the so-called "Lu-Wang School of the Mind," even though no evidence
is given for such usage of the term earlier than the sixteenth century.[1]
One of the purposes of this study is to show that in fact Neo-Confucian
hsin-hsüeh originated in the Ch'eng-Chu school and primarily in reference to the "message" and "method" of the mind. Only later, with
the rise to dominance of Wang Yang-ming's teaching, was the term
appropriated for Wang's own purposes. Then, so prevalent did this new
interpretation become that virtually all modern writers have accepted it
unquestioningly, without searching behind the smokescreen of six-
teenth-seventeenth–century controversy that obscured the view of what
had gone before. Nor, given the accepted view that "School of the
Mind" was to be equated with "Lu-Wang," did anyone attend to the
continuing manifestations of this learning of the mind in orthodox and

neo-orthodox forms of Ch'eng-Chu Neo-Confucianism down into the nineteenth century.

With this anomaly we inherit a problem as to how orthodoxy itself is to be understood. The "tradition" includes phases in which new movements establish themselves as orthodox (whether in scholarly or official terms); reform movements emerge from within to challenge and take over from the old orthodoxy, and still newer formulations arise out of the attempt to reconcile conflicting claims in a mainline consensus. Hence some clarification of my own use of key terms is in order.

"Neo-Confucianism," a Western term, is applied in general to the new trends of thought emerging from the Confucian revival in the Sung, which thought of itself as renewing ancient ideals. Roughly, it covers the same ground as the term Way or Learning of the Sages (sheng-hsüeh or sheng-jen chih tao or sheng-tao), as Sung Chinese referred to this broad movement. "Orthodox Neo-Confucianism" limits it to the Ch'eng-Chu teaching which became established both in schools and government, based on the writings of Chu Hsi and, for practical purposes, mostly on his version of the Four Books. One can be quite specific about the new ideas, texts, and practices which attach to orthodoxy in this form.[2] This is not to say that such doctrines and texts go undisputed. On the contrary the very fact of their being perennially questioned and reinterpreted confirms their crucial importance in the new tradition. The "Learning of the Way (tao-hsüeh), a term antedating Chu Hsi and originally applicable to more strands of Neo-Confucian thought in the twelfth century than just Chu Hsi's alone, became more narrowly defined in the Sung History, a Yüan period compilation in which tao-hsüeh came to be identified almost exclusively with the Neo-Confucian orthodoxy of the Ch'eng-Chu school.[3]

Resisting this narrowed conception of orthodoxy, however, other Neo-Confucians in the Ming and Ch'ing insisted that one could be faithful to tradition (whether Confucian or Neo-Confucian) without keeping within the limits or conforming to the models thus officially defined. And among those who stood for a more broad-gauged tradition were some who redefined even "orthodoxy" more loosely. Thus there is need for a term which can distinguish this more liberal sense of orthodoxy from the narrower Ch'eng-Chu line, and I have used "neo-orthodoxy" for this purpose, since it allows for the incorporation of some new elements into the Ch'eng-Chu system.

Another recurrent problem in the life of the Neo-Confucian "tradition" is that presented by fundamentalism and radicalism. In the studies which follow there are several instances of thinkers who claim to be fundamentalists in their adherence either to basic values or to canonical texts. Such fundamentalism may be directed either to classical Confucianism (i.e., the "literal" sense of the Confucian classics) or to orthodox Neo-Confucianism (i.e., the basic doctrines or texts of Chu Hsi). Often these come into conflict with officially established or scholastically approved teachings, and thus have a reformist thrust as well as a traditionalist appeal. In political and social terms, the same can be true of a restorationism that, literally, claims to be rooted in tradition, and is actually radical in program. We should not be misled into thinking that fundamentalism simply equals traditionalism or is ipso facto conservative of the status quo. Rather, like modern fundamentalist movements, it may offer a direct challenge to accepted views or be quite radical in its demands for change in the established political or social order.

Finally a word about the relation of the foregoing to Neo-Confucian developments in Korea and Japan. In *Neo-Confucian Orthodoxy and the Learning of the Mind-and-Heart* I tried to show how important a correct understanding of Chinese developments was to the extensions and transmutations of Neo-Confucian thought and practice elsewhere in East Asia. It would be my hope that a better understanding of the Chinese case, such as I try to present here, would be helpful to comparative study of parallel developments in Korea, Japan, and no doubt also in Vietnam. But to pursue these possibilities is another task and awaits another time—as well as, no doubt, the work of other hands.

Acknowledgments

Much of the research for this book was done in the spring of 1985 while I was a Visiting Scholar at the Kyoto University Research Institute for Humanistic Sciences on a grant from the Japan Foundation, and then in Beijing at the Institute for the Study of World Religions of the Chinese Academy of Social Sciences, as an exchange scholar of the Committee for Scholarly Communication with the People's Republic of China. I wish to extend my thanks to both institutions for their hospitality and to my sponsors for their support.

More particularly I wish to express my debt to the late Professor and Mrs. Kaizuka Shigeki of Kyoto University; to Professors Tonami Mamoru and Yokoyama Toshio of the Institute in Kyoto for their most kind hospitality, and to Okada Takehiko, Professor Emeritus of Kyushu University, as well as to the staffs of the Tōyō Bunken Senta at Kyoto University, the Naikaku bunko and Seikadō bunko in Tokyo and the Hōsa bunko in Nagoya. In Beijing my principal host was the ever helpful Professor Ren Jiyu. While there I benefited greatly from discussions with Professors Jung Chao-tsu of the Academy and Professor Fung Yulan of Beijing University. I should like to acknowledge also the assistance of Mr. Huang Fusheng of the Institute, and the staff of the Peking University Library. In this project as in so many others Dr. Wang Chen-ku and Theresa Wang Chang of the National Central Library in Taipei have been most helpful in making rare books or scarce editions available to me.

Professor Jacques Gernet was responsible for the invitation to lecture at the Collège de France which spurred the preparation of this material for publication. I am most grateful to him and his colleagues for their most kind reception, so much in keeping with the Collège's traditional hospitality to scholars of all countries and to the cause of public education.

It has become almost routine for me to acknowledge the continuing helpfulness of my dear friends and colleagues at Columbia, Professors Wing-tsit Chan and Irene Bloom, but no thanks expressed to them in the past ever catches up with their continuing readiness to save me from mindless mistakes. My thanks also to Pei-yi Wu, and to Martin Amster, Ronguey Chu, Marie Guarino, Emma Rockwell, and Marianna Stiles for their help in the preparation of the manuscript. It has also been a special pleasure to renew my association with Joan McQuary of Columbia University Press, who assisted in the publication of *Sources of Japanese, Chinese, and Indian Traditions.*

Finally, and again as so often in the past I acknowledge the never-failing inspiration and support, through our forty-seven years together, of my wife Fanny Brett de Bary.

The Message of the Mind
in Neo-Confucianism

1

General Introduction

The concept of the mind-and-heart *(hsin)*, which for Chinese encompassed the emotions as well as the intellect, had already been much discussed in classical Confucianism before it attracted new and still greater attention in the Sung period, as Confucian thinkers reexamined and reconceived its significance for a new era. Then, so central did the mind become as a philosophical and practical concern of what we now call Neo-Confucianism that, for many of its adherents, the new teaching would often be known as the Learning of the Mind-and-Heart.

  Yet this new importance of the mind came only as the outgrowth of earlier developments, each marked by its own characterization of what was central to the new teaching, and most notably by such terms as the Way of the Sages *(sheng-tao)*, the Learning of the Sages *(sheng-hsüeh)*, and Learning of the Way *(tao-hsüeh)*. In the first two cases the sages referred to were mainly ancient sage-kings, put forward in the eleventh century as models for the rulers of the Sung dynasty and frequently evoked as symbols of an idealized social order in antiquity. In other words this Sagely Learning purported to convey to rulers what they ought to know about the wise rule and benevolent institutions of the sage-kings, as the basis for a new reform program.

  Increasingly, however, as difficulties were encountered during the Northern Sung period in implementing such a program, the emphasis in this learning shifted to the personal cultivation of the educated elite and how they might exemplify the Way of the Sages in their own conduct of life, no matter what obstacles may have arisen to the accomplishment of their political goals. In such circumstances the terms

"Learning of the Sages" or "Way of the Sages" took on more the meaning of a personal Way to the attainment of Sagehood. With the hope of social renewal now seen as lying in the moral self-reformation of the educated elite, the latter's responsibility for leadership in the society, often on the local level rather than at court, assumed more of an educational role and cultural burden than a political one.

By the time of Chu Hsi, the leading Neo-Confucian of the twelfth century, he could even think of this aim in learning as one to which any poor lad in a rural village might aspire, depending only on his readiness to undertake such a task, i.e., take responsibility both for himself and for the Way *(tzu-jen yu tao)*. In this sense it became a Way for everyman, provided only that he could measure up to the noble man's sense of a high calling, in which he would join the company of other dedicated bearers of Confucian culture.

At this point one's view of the "Way" and of the "self" acquired heightened importance, and the "Learning of the Way" took on a deeper significance for those who followed this path of intellectual, moral, and spiritual cultivation. Undertaking such a commitment amounted virtually to a religious decision; it meant dedicating oneself to a set of ultimate values such as one could live or die for. For such devotees then this Way had an absoluteness and finality to it, often expressed by quoting Confucius' "Hearing the Way in the morning, one can die content in the evening" (*Analects* 4:8), whence adherents to the "Learning of the Way *(tao-hsüeh)* became known for their total earnestness and complete dedication to its practice, though to less sympathetic observers they might appear instead to be overly serious and excessively punctilious about it.

There is significance, however, not only in this understanding of the "Way" as an ultimate value, but also in its being thought of as a form of "Learning" rather than just as a "school." The translation of *tao-hsüeh* as "Learning of the Way" may have a certain awkward ring to it in English. "School of the Way" might seem more felicitous and is certainly not inappropriate as a rendering for *tao-hsüeh* in the sense of a company of scholars, a fellowship of like-minded persons who exhibit a distinctive manner and life-style. In some contexts the "Teaching of the Way" may also convey better the sense of *tao-hsüeh* as a defined set of doctrines. Yet Chu Hsi, the teacher par excellence of *tao-hsüeh*, attached first importance to the student's self-motivation and active pursuit of learning, rather than to the passive assimilation of what is taught or to anything like indoctrination. Thus "Learning of the Way" may, in its very awkwardness, draw special attention to Chu Hsi's emphasis on the individual will to learn and the intensely personal nature of this process, as distinct from the given content of the teaching or the school as an institution.

The same consideration bears upon Chu Hsi's frequent identification of the Confucian way as "Learning for the Sake of One's Self" *(wei chi chih hsüeh)*. I have discussed this in *The Liberal Tradition in China*, but the essential point bears repeating, as it bore repetition by generations of Neo-Confucians down into the nineteenth century, for whom the crucial criterion of the learning's authenticity was its commitment to the self-fulfillment of the human person as the ultimate value in both education and government. By contrast, seen as unworthy goals were Tao-hsüeh's two major rivals as competing life commitments: the "utilitarian" pursuit of power, wealth, or prestige on one side, and the Buddhist/Taoist path on the other. Confucius and Mencius had exposed the former in their time, and Chu Hsi in his day singled out the latter as an even more subtle form of human perversion. Most of Chu Hsi's discussion of learning aims at achieving a mean between these two, which represent opposite extremes but share a common failing. In a word, they are equally selfish—in different ways but essentially for the same reason: their lack of any true concept of the self.

This conclusion was not of course self-evident, but Chu Hsi was quite prepared to argue it out. In the case of utilitarianism *(kung-li)*, its main failing lay not in mere expediency per se. Chu recognized the need in human life and given historical circumstances to adapt to less than ideal conditions and make reasonable compromises. But this is workable only if one has a clear conception of the principle that should govern and of what exceptions or concessions can be made within the limits of tolerance. Unfortunately those who pursue utilitarian advantages rarely have any notion of principle. They go after immediate advantages, often in the name of providing material gratifications for the individual or else rationalizing self-interest in high-sounding language. But, for want of any clearly defined conception of what it means to be human, or of what true fulfillment as a human person consists in, such gains and gratifications inevitably prove ephemeral. Dealing with human nature solely on the physical and appetitive level, the utilitarians end up treating men as animals—most often sacrificed to the selfish ambitions of those who hold power. Shallow appeals to self-interest, though

3

alluring, fail to recognize the full dimensions of human capability or the deep complexity of human needs and motivations. Such inducements are no more than tactics, and as the basis of a political order, simply specious. As Chu Hsi insisted:

> . . . the cultivation of what is essential and the examination of the difference between the principle of Heaven and human selfish desires are things that must not be interrupted for a single moment in the course of our daily activities . . . If one understands this point clearly, he will naturally not go so far as to drift in to the popular ways of success and profit and expedient schemes. . . . Master Ch'eng said, "one must not let the myriad things in the world disturb him. When the self is established, one will naturally understand the myriad things in the world" (*I-shu* 6:2a). When one does not know where to anchor his body and mind, he talks about the kingly way and the despotic way, and discusses and studies the task of putting the world in order, as if it were a mere trick. Is that not mistaken?[1]

Note that the crux of the problem, for both Cheng Yi and Chu Hsi, lies in "establishing the self" and "knowing where to anchor the body and mind." This problem is also at the heart of the danger perceived in Buddhism and Taoism. In the latter case, however, the error lies on the other side of shortsightedness. Chu allowed that Buddhism offered a lofty ideal in the attainment of Buddhahood and Bodhisattvahood, but, for him, this was too visionary and unreal, unconnected with the need for "establishing the self" in a human world or providing an "anchor for the body and mind" in the natural order. Indeed Buddhism foreswore all conceptions of the self in ordinary empirical terms and resisted any anchoring of the body and mind except in a Buddha-world. In Ch'an, the form of Buddhism Chu was most exposed to, the self was indefinable in rational, moral terms. One could only intuit one's nature by looking directly within, through an experience of enlightenment incommunicable in ordinary language.

When Ch'an was of a mind to express itself more philosophically, it often did so in the language of Hua-yen Buddhism, explaining the relation of this higher wisdom to the world of actuality in terms of "principle and fact" *(li, shih)*, while affirming the complete compatibility of the two (i.e., the mutual accommodation of the higher principle

4

and the world of concrete reality). Yet this view of mutual accommodation or "non-obstruction" *(wu-ai)* was predicated on the Emptiness principle: that all things were "empty" of any substantial nature or fixed identity. Hence the reality of the ordinary world could only be affirmed through its assimilation into the higher wisdom of the Emptiness view. Ordinary human experience was not valued in itself, but only insofar as it lent itself to the liberating experience of Enlightenment.

For Chu then the crucial question was whether or not one accepted the Emptiness view. Ch'eng I had made Buddhism's "selfishness" the main point of his criticism, and Lu Hsiang-shan followed by stressing the difference between moral principle and selfish gain. But Chu, though not disagreeing with that point, saw it as only a secondary issue. For one who holds to the Emptiness view, said Chu, there are no principles on the basis of which to determine what is selfish or unselfish. One who sees principle as "empty" and his true nature as indefinable will simply look within and do whatever intuition prompts him to do. If there is no recognition of the indwelling moral nature or Mind of the Way, anything goes. Yet too, if there is no objective investigation of things, some things will go wrong. One may take to be food what is actually poison.[2]

From Chu Hsi's point of view the failure here lay in not addressing the real self, real principle, or the real mind. In actuality the self came into being from birth as the product of creative forces, both cosmic and human, which left one's own life inextricably involved with others, in a web of moral relations that extended through the whole range of human experience; it left one's own nature genetically coded to respond to others in certain regular, patterned ways. Hence the proper conduct of life, dealing with these relationships according to constant norms, could only be accomplished through the making of particular value judgments according to defined principles, and not by seeing through these to some higher principle of indeterminacy [i.e., Emptiness]. Even though principle in the Hua-yen understanding could accommodate itself to such realities, it accepted, and lent its seeming sanction to, anything and everything without distinction. Thus in the end it could be as undiscriminating and expedient as utilitarianism itself. "Non-obstruction" provided no ground on which to stand against human injustice or exploitation.

Obviously we are dealing here with quite different views of reality and principle, and not, as has often been supposed, a Hua-yen view of principle and fact assimilated to a Neo-Confucian world view. Yet by Chu Hsi's time the question was almost moot. The dominant forms of Ch'an in his day chose less and less to resort to Hua-yen philosophy, and spoke rather in terms of Emptiness *(k'ung)*, Nothingness *(wu)*, No-Mind *(wu-hsin)*, or No Thought *(wu-nien)*. Responding to these alternative views, then, it was only natural that Chu should have focused on the mind as well as principle.

In fact one could even say that, from the start, the discussion of principle was inseparable from that of mind in Ch'eng-Chu thought, for reasons both philosophical and practical. Practically speaking, the Ch'engs and Chu felt themselves engaged in a struggle with Buddhism for the minds and hearts of men. Philosophically, their conception of principle as both an inner structure and a polar, directional force in all things, meant that the human mind-and-heart was not simply "empty" consciousness, but was ordered and guided in a certain direction according to the Way. All things, indeed, shared a common structure to some degree. Only the human mind-and-heart had had built into it the moral sense and reasoning power which enabled man to participate consciously and conscientiously in the creative and productive processes of Heaven-and-earth.

Since Chu Hsi's overarching concern was with self-cultivation as the key to the governing of human society *(hsiu-chi chih-jen)*, there is almost no part of his voluminous writings that does not deal with both principle and the mind-and-heart as central to that concern. But for practical purposes most of the important issues connected with the "message of the mind" or "learning of the mind" appear in two short works of Chu Hsi's in which he sought to present his definitive views on the subject. These are the *Great Learning (Ta-hsüeh)* and the *Mean (Chung yung)*, together with his prefaces and commentaries on them.

Among students of Chinese thought it is well known that the *Mean (Chung yung)* attracted attention from the early days of the Confucian revival in the Sung, and that its importance in Neo-Confucian thought was confirmed by its inclusion in the newly constituted Four Books, the key texts of Neo-Confucian education throughout East Asia in the pre-modern period.

For over 700 years after Chu Hsi's time his commentaries were inseparable from the texts themselves and became indispensable reading for students of the Four Books. And it was the particular importance Chu attached to the *Great Learning* and the *Mean* that gave them priority even over the other two, the *Analects* and *Mencius*, central though these latter already were to the Neo-Confucian enterprise. Among the four texts, Chu Hsi said, one should start with the *Great Learning*, proceed to the *Analects* and *Mencius* and only then attempt the *Mean*, which dealt with more speculative, and thus inherently more difficult, matters of the mind. Yet in later editions of the Four Books it was rare for the *Mean* to be placed last. Far more often the order was from the *Great Learning* and the *Mean* to the *Analects* and *Mencius*. In this process the status of the *Mean* was further enhanced. Thenceforth no educated man in East Asia would fail to read the *Great Learning* and *Mean*, along with Chu's commentary, and very probably before he read the *Analects* and *Mencius*.

This priority no doubt also testified to Chu's preferential and special treatment of them. He wrote prefaces to the *Great Learning* and *Mean*, as he did not do for the others, and he added special notes (in addition to the phrase by phrase commentary) to direct the reader's attention to key points. What added to the interest of these prefaces and notes was that they headlined doctrines and concepts which were of prime importance to Chu even though they were not actually found in the original text.

In the case of the *Great Learning*, Chu's preface stressed several key points: the doctrine of the innate moral nature as the Heaven-given endowment—the seed of sagehood—in all men; the importance of education to develop that nature, on all levels of society; the need for schools (as institutional structures) to promote this aim; and the desirability of a learning sequence which would provide a sound and systematic alternative to the entrancing, but for Chu Hsi ultimately stultifying, teachings of Buddhism and Taoism.

In his commentary Chu draws particular attention to the first steps in the process of self-cultivation, *ko-wu chih-chih*, most commonly rendered as "the investigation of things and extension of knowledge." He says that *ko* ("investigate") means to reach or arrive, and he indicates that this is a process by which principles in the mind are brought into contact with principles in things, and thus made present to each other. "*Chih*," he says, is to recognize or be conscious of, to project one's knowing, hoping that one's capacity to know would be used to the full (lit. "exhausted"). The same passage can be read, translating *chih* as "knowledge" instead of "knowing," but in that case it should not be understood as in "a body of knowledge" for this would set an impossible goal for the "exhausting" of learning. One would need to know every-thing, instead of, as he intended, simply to develop one's learning capacity and understanding to the full.

Chu added a special note on *ko-wu chih chih*:

"The extension of knowing lies in the investigation of things" means that if we wish to extend our knowing, it consists in fath-oming the principle of any thing or affair we come into contact with, for the intelligent mind of man always has the capacity to know and the things of this world all have their principles, but if a principle remains unfathomed, one's knowing is not fully exer-cised. Hence the initial teaching of the Great Learning insists that the learner, as he comes upon the things of this world, must proceed from principles already known and further explore them until he reaches the limit. After exerting himself for a long time, one day he will experience a breakthrough to integral comprehen-sion. Then the qualities of all things, whether internal or external, refined or coarse, will all be apprehended, and the mind, in its whole substance and great functioning, will be fully enlightened. This is "things [having been] investigated." This is "knowing having reached [its limit]."[3]

In this passage Chu Hsi seems to be saying that if one pursues study and reflection long enough his understanding will be enlarged to the point where he overcomes any sense of things or others being foreign to oneself, and he will have achieved an empathetic insight that is both integral and comprehensive *(kuan-t'ung)*. He would have developed his capacity for learning and knowing to its limit, and thus would be equally at home with himself and his world. At this point "learning for the sake of oneself" would have overcome all distinction between self and others.

In later Neo-Confucianism great importance was attached to this holistic conception of a culminating point in intellectual and moral self-cultivation. Some later scholars saw in it an "experience" of enlighten-ment remarkably close to the sudden enlightenment of Ch'an; others, seeing it as consistent with Chu's philosophy as a whole, explained it as a gradual process that was indeed more than simply cognitive but, instead of going beyond the moral and rational order, recognized the latter as having its own numinous aspect.[4]

In his preface to the *Mean* Chu also took the moral nature as his starting point but proceeded to focus more on the mind-and-heart as the embodiment of principle. He dwelt on the concept of the mind as characterized by the mind of the Way and the human mind; and on the method for cultivating the mind. Here Chu spoke in both his preface and a special introductory note about a concept not found in the original text of the *Mean:* the *hsin-fa*, as the message, method, and measure of the mind-and-heart.

For the moment I shall leave *hsin-fa* untranslated in order to explain its multiple significances as message, method, and measure of the mind. I shall also refrain from discussing earlier uses of the term *hsin-fa* in Buddhism, Taoism, and Neo-Confucianism, a matter I have dealt with in *Neo-Confucian Orthodoxy and the Learning of the Mind-and-Heart.*[5] The essential point is that although *hsin-fa* had been used earlier by Buddhists in at least two different senses ("elements of mentation" and "method of cleansing the mind"), it had by Sung times entered into cosmological discussions among Taoists and Neo-Confucians. Also, quite apart from these, it had come to represent a formula or recipe of the sage-kings for good government, based on the rectification of the ruler's mind. It was this latter usage, having nothing to do with Buddhism, that Chu Hsi picked up from Ch'eng I (or possibly from Ch'en Ch'ang-fang, 1108-48), in the intervening generation.[6]

What Chu first points to in his preface is the *hsin-fa* as a message concerning the mind transmitted from the early sage-kings to Confucius and Mencius and thence, leaping over centuries of uncomprehending scholars, to the inspired minds of the Ch'eng brothers, from whose fragmentary writings Chu Hsi was able to piece together and reconstitute the essential message. In this respect the *hsin-fa* was intimately associated with Chu's concept of the "succession to the Way" or "tradition of the Way" *(tao-t'ung)* and the "transmission of the mind," to be discussed later.

The content of that message is encapsulated in the cryptic sixteen-word injunction of the sage-king Shun to his successor the Great Yü: "The human mind is precarious: the mind of the Way is subtle. Be refined and single-minded. Hold fast the Mean."

The language Chu used to express this idea was drawn from a text of dubious authenticity, "The Counsels of Yü the Great" *(Ta Yü mo),* in a relatively late version of the classic *Book of Documents (Shu ching).* The fact that Chu, though aware of this dubiety, nevertheless drew upon this passage, suggests that, whatever its historicity, he saw it as peculiarly apt for expressing what he had in mind. In his preface and in discussions of the passage in Chu's *Classified Conversations,* he explains its somewhat cryptic language in terms of his own philosophy of human nature. Briefly summarized, this may be put as follows:

1. The "mind of the Way" *(tao-hsin)* represents the moral nature with which man is endowed by Heaven (as the opening lines of the *Mean* state). It is something like the voice of conscience, speaking for the right principles implanted in the human mind as the goodness of its nature.

2. The "human mind" *(jen-hsin)* stands for that aspect of the mind-and-heart expressive of man's psycho-physical nature, that is, for appetites and desires that could become selfish if not guided or directed by the mind of the Way.

3. To call the human mind "precarious" or "endangered" *(wei)* means, according to Chu, that it is insecure, precariously poised between selfish and unselfish desires and liable to err if not properly directed by right principles. In the delicate balance between its selfish and unselfish tendencies, selfishness or self-indulgence can be deceptively masked as legitimate self-interest or self-enjoyment, while the fine line between the two is often hard to discern. Thus to call the mind of the Way "subtle" *(wei)* means that it is difficult to perceive when right principles are mixed in the human mind with the physical desires of the individual, since the natural self-regarding tendency of the individual may becloud or distort one's perception of right principles.

4. Chu further explains in the preface that "refinement" *(ching)* means to discriminate between the two tendencies, selfish and unselfish, and not let them be confused. Hence "refined discrimination" may better express the actual meaning of *ching* in many contexts. "Single-mindedness" means to "hold on to the correctness of the original mind [of the Way] and not become separated from it." From the discussion in the school of Ch'eng I prior to Chu Hsi we know that *ching,* "discrimination," was to be applied to particular value distinctions that represent the diverse particularizations of the Way in human affairs, while "singleness" or "oneness" *(i)* was applicable to the Way or Principle in its unity. In other words, the Method of the Mind was a practice appropriate to the Neo-Confucian doctrine of the "Unity of principle and its diverse particularizations *(li-i fen-shu)*."[7]

5. "Holding fast to the Mean" had a dual significance. It meant not

being partial or one-sided in one's judgments, but rather holding to the impartiality expressed in terms of what is common or shared *(kung)*. In action it also stands for what is appropriate to the situation, neither going too far nor falling short. Elsewhere Chu expressed it as a mean in self-cultivation, by which one avoided the laissez-faire extreme of Taoist "forgetting" of moral values on the one hand, and the strained effort of the Mohist to make the moral will prevail, no matter what the circumstances (i.e., to manipulate things in a way contrary to nature), at the other extreme.

In his preface Chu explains that these two minds are only two aspects of one mind; much in the same way that someone may be spoken of as "being of two minds" about something. Here too, and in the *Classified Conversations*, Chu makes it clear that all men are of "two minds" in this sense. Even the sage possesses the human mind, as well as the Mind of the Way, but in him the latter always controls the former. At the same time even an ignorant man has the Mind of the Way as part of his innate nature, although his psycho-physical nature may obscure it at times through the influence and indulgence of selfish desires. Later Chu Hsi would be accused, from a misunderstanding on this latter point, of attributing evil to the psycho-physical "human mind" in contrast to the goodness of the moral mind or Mind of the Way. Actually Chu makes it clear that the human mind is not to be seen as evil, and that the natural feelings and appetites of the individual (including those for food, clothing, sex, etc.) are entitled to satisfaction, as long as they are not carried to the point of selfishness or partiality.

This was a problem for Chu Hsi in part because Ch'eng Yi had asserted simply that "the human mind is human desires."[8] Chu Hsi felt a need to clarify this. "The human mind cannot be taken simply as human desires. If the human mind were simply human desires, the sage [Shun] would not have spoken of it as precarious. To say that it is precarious means only that it is in danger of running after human desires."[9] Similarly, in another conversation Chu insists that the human mind cannot be viewed as evil for the same reason: if it were already evil, the sage would have had no reason to speak of the danger of its going bad.[10]

In the *Classified Conversations* Chu Hsi also quotes his contemporary Lu Hsiang-shan, this time with whole-hearted approval, for his comment on the sage-king Shun's sixteen-word dictum:

11

"If Shun had meant to say that the human mind was entirely evil, then he would have stated that it was no good, so men would shun it. His referring to it [instead] as precarious means that it was unsafe and could not be relied upon [being liable to either good or evil]. When he spoke of the need for refinement, he sought discriminating judgment so as not to allow the good to become mixed with the bad!

To this Chu adds the comment: "This is of course correct."[11]

Chu's use of the term "human desire" to represent "selfish desire" is what may, in part, have given rise to the misunderstanding. This is a case in which the expression "human desires" (jen-yü), as used by Buddhists, had already come to mean selfish desire (since, in Buddhism, all desires tend to become selfish craving and sources of delusion, unless extinguished via the Eightfold Path or transformed in the Higher Wisdom). But Chu quite consciously differentiated the legitimate natural feelings and appetites of the human mind-and-heart from the selfish desires, expressed in the term "human desires," which were seen as evil. He further stressed the point by asserting that no appetite, desire, action, or activity was in itself evil; only selfish intent rendered it such. Here then Chu meant to affirm the reality and goodness of both the moral and physical nature of man. Inasmuch, however, as he used the term jen yü in the Buddhist sense, it is understandable how later Confucians might have criticized Chu as Buddhistic for seeming to share the Buddhist's pessimistic view of human desires, even though it was Chu and his Sung predecessors who had originally articulated the more positive position from which these critics later spoke. The latter, in fact only represented a further extension of Chu's earlier line of thought.

Chu Hsi addressed the question of the human mind, Mind of the Way, and human desires in many writings and conversations over the years. It was a matter of central and constant concern to him, and not just an idea that occurred to him while writing an occasional piece or a perfunctory preface. Without attempting a more exhaustive account of the matter, however, I shall add here only the clarification Chu offers in a well-known essay included in his *Collected Writings*.[12] It is called an "Essay on the Viewing of the Mind" (*Kuan-hsin lun*). The expression translated here as "viewing the mind" is better known in Buddhist thought than Confucian; indeed, *kuan-hsin* makes no significant appearance in the Confucian classics. In this respect it somewhat resembles *"hsin-fa,"* performing an earlier function in Buddhism and then serving a later, different purpose for Chu Hsi.

In Buddhism "viewing the mind" had been understood as a kind of contemplation; it could mean either observing the phenomenal activity of the human consciousness or, in samadhi, having transcendental insight into the Buddha-mind. The first was essentially a mind-clearing operation and the second a mind-disposing one—at least to the extent that it was widely superseded in Chu's time by the Ch'an view of "No Mind" or "No Thought." In neither case did a well-defined picture of the mind emerge, but only a glimpse of ephemeral phenomena or manifest traces of a transcendent mind.

In Chu's case, however, the viewing is both analytic and synthetic (wherefore Professor Chan's translation of *kuan-hsin* as "examination of the mind"). Excerpted below, the essay shows how the question is precipitated by the implicit challenge of Buddhism, and how the sixteen-word formula provides the basis for Chu's attempt to define better the natural structure and operation of the mind:

Someone asked whether it is true that the Buddhists have a doctrine of the examination of the mind.

Answer: The mind is that with which man rules his body. It is one and not a duality, is subject and not object, and controls the external world instead of being controlled by it. Therefore, if we examine external objects with the mind, their principles will be apprehended. Now (in the Buddhist view), there is another thing to examine the mind. If this is true, then outside this mind there is another one which is capable of controlling it. But is what we call the mind a unity or a duality? Is it subject or object? Does it control the external world or is it controlled by the external world? We do not need to be taught to see the fallacy of the Buddhist doctrine.

Someone may say: In the light of what you have said, how are we to understand such expressions by sages and worthies as refined discrimination and singleness (of mind),[13] "Hold it fast and you preserve it. Let it go and you lose it."[14] "Exert the mind to the utmost and know one's nature."

Answer: These expressions and (the Buddhist doctrine) sound similar but are different, just like the difference between seedlings and weed, or between vermilion and purple, and the student should clearly distinguish them. What is meant by the precariousness of the human mind is the budding of human selfish desires, and what is meant by the subtlety of the Mind of the Way is the mysterious depth of the Principle of Heaven.[15] The mind is one; it is called differently depending on whether or not it is rectified. The meaning of the saying, "Be refined and single-minded" is to abide by what is right and discern what is wrong, as well as to discard the wrong and restore the right. If we can do this, we shall indeed "hold fast the Mean,"[16] and avoid the imbalance of too much or too little. The saying does not mean that the Mind of the Way is one mind, the human mind another, and then still a third one to make them refined and single. "Holding it fast" is another way of saying that we should not allow our conduct during the day to fetter and destroy our innate mind characterized by humanity and righteousness.[17] It does not mean that we should sit in a rigid position to preserve the obviously idle consciousness and declare that "This is holding it fast and preserving it!" As to the exerting of the mind to the utmost, it is to investigate things and study their principles to the utmost, to arrive at broad penetration, and thus to be able fully to realize the principle (li) embodied in the mind. By preserving the mind is meant "seriousness (ching) to straighten the internal life and righteousness to square the external life,"[18] a way of cultivation similar to what has just been called refinement, singleness, holding fast, and preserving. Therefore one who has fully developed his mind can know his nature and know Heaven,[19] because the substance of the mind is unbeclouded and he is equipped to search into principle in its natural state, and one who has preserved the mind can nourish his nature and serve Heaven,[20] because the substance of the mind is not lost and he is equipped to follow principle in its natural state. . . .

If these moral qualities are always borne in mind, we will see them no matter where we may go. But it does not mean that we observe the mind . . .[21]

That Chu Hsi meant clearly to distinguish his view from the Buddhist is evident from the extended discussion of the mind of the Way and human mind in his *Classified Conversations*, where he insists on the need to recognize and reckon with both:

If one solely follows the operation of the human mind-and-heart and does not recognize the Mind of the Way [as the guiding conscience], then one is bound to descend into unrestrained and deviant behavior; but if one seeks solely to preserve the Mind of the Way and do away with the human mind, then it divides the moral nature from the actual nature [the given psycho-physical constitution] as if they were two separate things, so that the Mind of the Way becomes empty and nonexistent; this then leads one into Buddhism and Taoism . . .[22]

Chu goes on to explain the indispensability to each other of the human mind and Mind of the Way. To treat the human mind simply as selfish desires leads to the suppression and extinguishing of the natural appetites, and therefore to the loss of vital instincts necessary to man's participation in the creative processes of Heaven and Earth. On the other hand, not to recognize the moral conscience in the Mind of the Way leaves these desires without the necessary direction and control.

As the question is addressed in Chu's *Classified Conversations*, he says the Buddhists consider the nature to consist in "function"; or so at least Boddhidharma had replied to the King's question about nature, saying "The nature lies in function" *(hsing tsai tso yung)*.[23] In the Ma Tsu line of Ch'an this function was expressed as "Everyday work is itself the Way." According to this view the nature of the eye lies in seeing, of the ear in hearing, of the hand in holding, of the foot in moving. . . . But, says Chu, "take for instance the hand's holding: if it seizes a knife and violently kills someone, could that be called its nature?"[24]

Similarly with the Ch'an saying that "the marvelous spiritual functioning *(miao yung)* of the Buddha-nature lies in hauling water and chopping wood."[25] This kind of "marvelous function," being indefinable and unpredictable, provides no definite criterion for what ordinary functions are to be allowed as proper or denied as improper.[26] Were the nature to be so conceived, the mind would have nothing to hold on to or to guide its activities; indeed, such is the condition of the "human mind" in itself—precarious and insecure—were it not for the moral nature, the mind of the Way, providing a standard[27] (or, as Chu elsewhere puts it, serving as a rudder for the human vessel as it steers through the turbulent and dangerous waters of life)[28]. The affirmation of moral principles in the Mind of the Way is essential to providing the standards for human conduct, so that the human mind can hold to something reliable and cease to be endangered or liable to err. The Buddhist principle of emptiness, according to this view, does not give man such a secure reliance; hence it is essential to recognize not only the substantial reality of principles, but also the inherence of such principles in the mind as are needed to give direction to human life. Indeed, without them one could not commit oneself to a life of learning as Confucius had said he did.[29]

The same passage in the *Analects* (2:4) in which Confucius speaks of committing himself to learning at age fifteen, ends with the affirmation that this life-time of learning has culminated at seventy in Confucius' achieving a sense of freedom in which he could "follow his heart's desire without transgressing the norm [lit. "measuring square"]." In other words, according to the Neo-Confucian view that principles in the mind serve as an innate standard or "measuring square," a life-time of learning and self-discipline by the aspirant to sagehood brings his conduct of life naturally and easily into accord with this intuitive sense in the mind-and-heart. Neo-Confucians often contrasted this gradual maturing life process to the sudden enlightenment of Ch'an which was premised on no such moral norm or rational measure in the mind. In that sense *hsin-fa* would be understood as "measure of the mind," symbolized by Confucius' "measuring square."

The *hsin-fa* as method was expressed in the injunction "Be refined and single-minded." Even though this language is not found in the *Mean* itself, it could easily be identified with the "solitary watchfulness" recommended in the first chapter of the *Mean*, where the insistence on spiritual realities, the reality of what is not seen or heard, could be interpreted as comparable to the subtlety of the Mind of the Way and the difficulty of perceiving principle in the midst of one's involvement with things and affairs.

In the Neo-Confucian school, diverse types of praxis were employed to maintain this "solitary watchfulness" over one's every thought, word, and deed, but especially in the interior recesses of the mind-and-heart. Two of the most common methods were "quiet-sitting" and the keeping of a daily record of self-examination. The former had an obvious resemblance to Ch'an "sitting in meditation"; the latter was a religious practice shared with Taoism, Buddhism, and popular syncretic teachings. The injunction to be "discriminating," the need for relentless moral self-scrutiny, and the insistence on constant value judgments and strict control was the way to bring the human mind completely into line with the Mind of the Way, thereby achieving perfect sincerity and integrity. It stood in marked contrast, however, to the general emphasis in meditative Buddhism on the cessation of all discriminating habits of mind in order to achieve undifferentiated unity through nondiscrimination. There were also significant practical differences between Ch'an meditation directed toward the achievement of enlightenment and Neo-Confucian quiet-sitting as an aid to the conduct of daily life. Nevertheless, as a form of praxis, quiet-sitting had no precedent in earlier Confucian moral practice, and there can be little doubt that the adoption of quiet-sitting and the intensified Neo-Confucian preoccupation with "solitary watchfulness," reflect the powerful challenge from and response to Buddhist spirituality, reinforcing the centripetal forces converging on the self as the main pole of Neo-Confucian thought. For this very reason there was controversy among later Neo-Confucians over the acceptability of quiet-sitting as a form of practice *(kung-fu)* in the Learning or Method of the Mind.

From the discussion thus far, reflecting Chu's treatment of the subject in his preface and commentary to the *Mean* and in his *Classified Conversations,* it is obvious that he had Buddhism and Taoism constantly in mind as the alternative positions to be dealt with. Much of the time, it would seem, he had in mind Ch'an Buddhism, which was certainly the alternative he had personally explored before becoming persuaded of the Confucian view. While it is sometimes thought that in the doctrinal or conceptual realm the Ch'eng brothers and Chu Hsi drew more heavily on Hua-yen Buddhism, it is significant that the leading contemporary historian of Ch'an Buddhism, Yanagida Seizan, believes that Chu Hsi's criticisms of Buddhism most often refer to Ch'an, and to a particularly radical form of Ch'an in the Southern and Western schools. This was a widely influential teaching best known in Buddhist literature through the *Platform Sutra of the Sixth Patriarch.* In discussing the thought of the eminent Buddhist synthesizer Kuei-feng Tsung-mi (780–841), and his objections to the doctrine of sudden enlightenment, Yanagida sees strong parallels between Chu Hsi's criticisms of Buddhism and Tsung-mi's strictures against this radical form of Ch'an. Moreover, in his analysis of the teaching of Wu-chu (714–774) a leading exponent of the sudden enlightenment doctrine, as found in the *Li-tai-fa-pao chi,* Yanagida says "Whether we agree with Chu

Hsi or not, the fact remains that the evidence for every one of his criticisms of Buddhism can be found in the *Li-tai-fa-pao chi.*"[30]

Some writers have tended to dismiss Chu Hsi's criticisms of Buddhism as due to misunderstandings or misrepresentations of it, and have charged him with a failure to distinguish between its so-called Hinayana and Mahayana forms. Sometimes this is also expressed as a failure on Chu Hsi's part to recognize how the Mahayana in China had developed beyond its earlier Indian formulations. Yet these assertions fall to the ground if there is such a congruence between the criticisms made by both Tsung-mi and Chu Hsi of this distinctively Chinese form of Buddhism. Tsung-mi was certainly familiar with Buddhist thought as a whole, both Indian and Chinese, and was not unaware of the Mahayana critique of Hinayana.

While much remains to be done in sorting out and evaluating specific criticisms of both Chu and Buddhism, the significance of this general issue for our discussion of Chu's method or measure of the mind would seem to lie in the fact that Chu's views so often appear to be put forward in contrast to the Ch'an view of no-mind or no-thought also criticized by Tsung-mi. If we take the alternative views of the mind presented in the *Platform Sutra*, we may cite as illustrations the famous verses attributed to Shen-hsiu (606?–706) and Hui-neng (d. 713) respectively. Shen-hsiu's verse is:

> The body is the Bodhi tree,
> The mind is like a clear mirror
> At all times we must strive to polish it
> And must not let the dust collect.

Hui-neng's alternative verse is:

> Bodhi originally has no tree
> The mirror also has no stand
> Buddha nature is always clean and pure
> Where is there room for dust?[31]

While there are significant differences between the two verses' characterization of the concept and cultivation of the mind, both affirm the essential and original purity of the mind as a mirror reflecting true reality. Whether one conceives of this as static or dynamic, or in essentialist or existentialist terms, from Chu Hsi's point of view it is a mind fundamentally characterized by emptiness and nothingness, or by the equation of Nirvana and samsara (i.e., emptiness and form), and not by the principles, both ontological and ethical, which Chu sees as constituting the basic structure of the universe no less than of the mind. Moreover, this Buddhist view of the mind fails to take into account, as Chu would have it, the reality of both the "human mind" and "human desires." Because it fails to affirm the reality of the desires, instincts, and affections that enliven the human mind, it is empty and unreal. Because it fails to provide value principles, directions, and standards for the measured expression of "human desires," these are very likely, even in the compassionate individual, to become indiscriminate and wayward (rather than Way-ward).

At this point, we are obliged, I think, to take into account another aspect of Chinese Mahayana Buddhism which is often overlooked in such discussions. The Ch'an view of the universality of the Buddha-nature, and of its direct and instantaneous realization, may be considered to manifest a strong this-worldly optimism, often thought characteristically Chinese. Yet the other major form of Chinese Mahayana Buddhism, while also emphasizing religious practice rather than doctrine, started from different assumptions. Pure Land Buddhists took a dim view of the human condition, relying on faith rather than human effort for salvation. Apparently they had not heard of native Chinese optimism and this-worldliness. Instead of glossing over human weakness they shared Tsung-mi's more sober realism and acknowledged the difficulty of coping with the corruption of this world unaided.

In Buddhist literature one of the best known expressions of this Pure Land view is found in Shan-tao's "Parable of the White Path." Here Shan-tao (613–681) likens the faint light of hope and faith in the Buddha to the White Path which lies between the raging seas of human passion, corruption, and delusion. Let me, without recounting the whole parable, quote only the most apposite portion of Shan-tao's interpretation:

The two rivers of fire and water are comparable to human greed and affection—like water, and anger and hatred—like fire. The white path between them, four or five inches wide, is comparable to the pure aspiration for rebirth in the Pure Land which arises in the midst of the passions of greed and anger. Greed and anger are powerful, and thus are likened to fire and water; the good mind is infinitesimal and thus is likened to a white path [of a few inches in width]. The waves inundating the path are comparable to the constant arising of affectionate thoughts in the mind which stain and pollute the good mind. And the flames which scorch the path are comparable to thoughts of anger and hatred which burn up the treasures of dharma and virtue. The man proceeding on the path toward the West is comparable to one who directs all his actions and practices toward the West[ern Paradise]. . . .[32]

If one considers this in relation to Chu Hsi's concepts of the mind of the Way, the human mind, and "human (i.e., selfish) desires," one notices an immediate difference between Shan-tao's view of the human affections (lit. "love") as impediments to salvation, and Chu Hsi's view of human affections as natural and a potential source of good if properly directed and cultivated. (Parenthetically, one might observe that the Mahayana formulation of the "passions as enlightenment" also allows for illusory desires to serve the purposes of salvation through the principle of adaptive means, but in that case enlightenment must also be seen in the light of emptiness, a qualification which, among other difficulties, leads Shan-tao's contemporary, Tao-ch'o [d. 645] to trust in the saving power of Amitabha rather than rely on one's own capacity to cope with the temptations, distractions, and illusions of worldly passions.)[33]

From Chu Hsi's point of view, Shan-tao's formulation would seem to deny the positive reality of the affections as expressions of man's psycho-physical nature. Moreover, since it does not see moral principles as inherent in the mind, it provides no self-direction to the mind-and-heart, but only a reliance on transcendent faith in the Buddha and the Pure Land, which leads out of the ordinary world into another realm emptied of impurities and obstructions.

Still, we cannot help being struck by the great similarity between Shan-tao's characterization of the "good mind" of faith and Chu Hsi's explanation of the Mind of the Way. The Good Mind is spoken of as infinitesimal, a path three or four inches wide in the midst of the raging fires and heaving tides of human passions. What is translated here as "infinitesimal," in reference to the path's spatiality, is the same *wei* used by Chu to describe the mind of the Way as "subtle" and "barely perceptible." In both cases the human mind-and-heart is imperiled, fraught with danger, and liable to err. In both cases it is human desires that threaten the proper direction of the mind. In this respect then, Shan-tao's view is faithful to the original Buddhist sense of the desires as selfish and in need of discipline. Though Shan-tao puts little hope now in self-discipline, he does not hesitate to face the evil in man and admit it realistically.

From this we know that not all of Chinese Buddhism sloughed off its Indian antecedents, and indeed from the later history of both Chinese Buddhism and Neo-Confucianism we are aware that traditionalists in both camps retained this classic sense of the need for self-scrutiny and self-restraint. Thus the late Ming Buddhist reformer Chu-hung and the Neo-Confucian Kuan Chih-tao (1536–1608) both criticized the libertarian views of Li Chih (1527–1602) which drew upon the more free-wheeling interpretations of the T'ai-chou school and so-called "Wild Chan."[34]

As we shall see later, seventeenth-century critics of late Ming thought, like Ku Yen-wu (1613–1682), saw in these radical, libertarian tendencies evidence of the influence on Neo-Confucianism of Ch'an Buddhism, with its individualistic approach to enlightenment and exalting of the perfect freedom of the Buddha-mind. Others in the late seventeenth and early eighteenth centuries detected Buddhist influence on the Neo-Confucian doctrine of the human desires as selfish desires, and in the repression of these desires in the name of "principle," which they also saw as a metaphysical conception influenced by Buddhism. Actually these charges gain some plausibility from the particularly rigoristic form of Ch'eng-Chu teaching propagated in the early period by Chen Te-hsiu (1178–1235), who, while adhering to Chu Hsi's teachings in all important respects, often spoke of the danger from human desires in language strikingly reminiscent of Shan-tao's parable, with its violent picture of the human passions undirected by the Buddha-mind.[35] What this probably means is that such criticisms often oversimplify the facts with regard to both Buddhism and Neo-Confucianism, overlooking the long-standing tension in Chinese thought between these opposing views of the mind-and-heart, while reducing the two teachings to just one or the other. Rarely did they achieve the balance of Chu Hsi.

To my knowledge no one before has drawn attention to the striking parallels between Shan-tao's Good Mind and Chu Hsi's Mind of the

Way, or to Chu's use of the term *jen yü* to mean selfish desires which imperil the human mind, in the same manner as Shan-tao's parable. Although there is no evidence in the indices to Chu's *Collected Writings* and *Classified Conversations* of direct influence by Shan-tao on Chu Hsi, the Parable of the White Path was well known in Pure Land Buddhism, the most popular form of Buddhism in China. Hence the possibility of indirect influence cannot be excluded. In any case, one must allow that in the Chinese tradition this more pessimistic view of the mind coexisted with the more optimistic; neither Mencius' view of human nature as good nor the Ch'an view of the Buddha-nature in all men can be taken as wholly representative of the Chinese tradition. While some interpreters see Chu Hsi as heavily influenced by Hsun Tzu's views concerning human nature, what I would emphasize rather is the carefully balanced treatment found in Chu's formulation of the human mind and Mind of the Way, with the latter characterized in terms quite similar to Shan-tao's "good mind," and with "human desires" too understood very much in a Buddhist sense, but with the human mind poised precariously between the two.

Whether or not Chu actually drew upon Shan-tao's parable, he did not, in any case, put these terms or concepts to the same uses. Nevertheless these parallels suggest certain new possibilities for understanding what Chu Hsi was about. One is that he may well have had a broader familiarity with different aspects of Chinese Buddhist thought than some critics have allowed, and this probably challenged him to engage in a more subtle and sophisticated analysis of the mind. A second implication is to bring out the special significance of the *Mean* for Chu Hsi, and of the method or measure of the mind *(hsin-fa)* propounded in his preface and notes. The program of self-cultivation found in the *Great Learning*, with its predominantly intellectual and scholarly approach to the understanding of principle *(tao wen-hsüeh)*, was supplemented and reinforced in important ways by Chu's emphasis on moral and spiritual cultivation *(tsun te-hsing)* in these new interpretations of the *Mean*.

After Chu Hsi's time the tendency developed to identify the "investigation of things and fathoming of principle" with the "Learning of Principle" *(li-hsüeh)*, while the cultivation and rectification of the mind came to be spoken of as the "Learning of the Mind-and-Heart" *(hsin-hsüeh)*. Much later still, these two types of learning were to be seen as divergent if not antithetical. But as the Neo-Confucian synthesis left

22

the hands of Chu Hsi, it was both and neither—i.e., neither one in an exclusive sense. From his point of view it would make no sense to study either mind or principle without embracing and making the most of both.

2

The Learning
of the Mind-and-Heart
in the Early Chu Hsi School

In *Neo-Confucian Orthodoxy and the Learning of the Mind-and-Heart*[1] I reported on developments in the thirteenth through fifteenth centuries which saw the rise of the new Learning of the Mind-and-Heart as an accompaniment to Neo-Confucianism's establishment as an official orthodoxy—a development which had been largely ignored in earlier histories both of ideas and institutions. By the mid-Ming, however, with the more intensive development of Neo-Confucian thought that followed from its dominance of the educational and scholarly scene, important philosophical issues surfaced which had not been so fully addressed in the phase of rapid early growth. My earlier study stopped short of this later development, recognizing it to constitute a new chapter in the history of Neo-Confucian thought. Yet as long as this later phase remained unexamined, we would be left without an adequate explanation of how such a radical change could have come about in the later way of perceiving the earlier development. This is especially true of the modern identification of the Learning of the Mind-and-Heart *(hsin-hsüeh)* with the so-called "Lu-Wang School," reserving it to that branch of Neo-Confucianism alone, while the Learning of Principle *(li-hsüeh)*, originally almost coextensive with *hsin-hsüeh*, became designated as a separate Ch'eng-Chu reservation.

By now the association of *"hsin-hsüeh* with "Lu-Wang" has become such a fixture of modern scholarly thinking that one encounters it almost everywhere in histories, textbooks, encyclopedias, and dictionaries.[2] Two brief quotations from Fung Yu-lan's *History of Chinese Philosophy* will serve to illustrate the point:

Contemporary with Chu Hsi, the greatest figure in the Rationalistic *(Li-hsüeh)* school of Neo-Confucianism, there lived another thinker who is important as the real founder of the rival idealistic *(Hsin Hsüeh)* school. This is Lu Chiu-yüan (1139–93), better known under his literary name as Lu Hsiang-shan . . . If we wish to sum up the difference between the two schools in a word, we may say that Chu's school emphasizes the "Learning of Principle" *(li-hsüeh)* . . . whereas that of Lu emphasizes the "Learning of the Mind *(Hsin-hsüeh).*[3]

A concomitant of this oversimplification has been the tendency to view principle *(li)* as opposed to mind *(hsin)*, and thus arrive at a neat dichotomy of the orthodox Ch'eng Chu school, representing the "school of principle," versus the unorthodox "Lu-Wang School of the Mind." Further confusion has arisen from the breadth of the concept of "mind-and-heart" *(hsin)* itself, as also from the inherent generality and multiple uses of the Chinese term for learning, *hsüeh*, which serves equally as a form of learning, a school of thought, or some institutionalization of it.

Some of this confusion underlies the issue raised by Ch'ien Mu in his monumental study of Chu Hsi's teaching, the *Chu Tzu hsin hsüeh-an.* After presenting his overview of Chu's "learning," Ch'ien devotes a major portion of his five-volume work to Chu's view of the mind-and-heart, and comments on the Ch'eng-Chu/Lu-Wang dichotomy as follows:

> In later times men have said that Ch'eng-Chu emphasized the nature as principle, while Lu-Wang stressed the mind as principle. Accordingly they differentiated Ch'eng-Chu as the learning of principle *(li-hsüeh)* and Lu-Wang as the learning of the mind-and-heart *(hsin-hsüeh).* This distinction has something to be said for it, but actually there was no one to match Master Chu in his ability to elucidate the similarities and differences, divergences and convergences, in the matter of mind and principle, as well as the precise connections and interactions between them. Therefore in general to say that the learning of Chu Hsi was most thoroughly, from beginning to end, a vast and fully-defined learning of the mind is not at all inappropriate.[4]

Lest this be taken as a mere passing comment of Ch'ien's rather than one truly representative of his work as a whole, it should be said that these lines introduce a major segment of Ch'ien's study (vol. 2), and the view they express is reinforced frequently elsewhere in the work. For instance:

> To say that the learning of principle is the learning of the mind may be allowable, but to say that Ch'eng-Chu and Lu-Wang can be divided into two separate lineages, is something for which I find no warrant. . . . (2:106)

> Men of later times have spoken of the learning of principle as the learning of human nature and principle. As one can see from the preceding quotations [by Chu Hsi on the mind and nature], the learning of the nature and principle (hsing-li hsüeh) is truly the learning of the mind. All understanding and effort with respect to the nature and principle depends completely on the mind, so that if you leave out the mind, there is nothing left of the learning of the nature and principle to speak of. (1:49)

> When recent scholars have discussed the similarities and differences between Chu and Lu, they have generally identified Chu with the Learning of Principle and Lu with the Learning of Mind, the error of which I have discussed above. Actually the difference between the two lies squarely in [their different views of] the learning of the mind. (1:139; see also 1:49, 59, and 2:5)

When Ch'ien Mu says, as in the first quotation above, that "the learning of Chu Hsi was most thoroughly, from beginning to end, a vast and fully-defined learning of the mind-and-heart . . . ," he speaks in terms almost exactly like those used by early followers of Chu Hsi;[5] but not in the terms of Chu himself, who referred to the new teaching most often as the Sage Learning (sheng-hsüeh) or Learning of the Way (tao-hsüeh). "Sage Learning" meant the learning which had come down from the sages, but also the "learning of sagehood," i.e., how one can achieve sagehood, as the overarching conception of the new movement and as the alternative to the ideal of attaining Buddhahood. Although Chu talked a great deal about human nature, principle, and mind, it was only after Chu Hsi's time that the terms "learning of principle" (li-hsüeh), "learning of human nature and principle" (hsing-li hsüeh), and "learning of the mind" *(hsin-hsüeh)* came into wide use to describe the essential content of the sage learning. As Ch'ien Mu has said, discussing Chu Hsi's learning of the mind as one that leads to sagehood:

> Those who have not yet reached the stage where the mind is completely identified with principle, must have a gate and a path, through which, by degrees and stages, they come to understand the substance of the mind and make judgments in practice, and through which they can hope to attain their goal—this is the essence of the learning of the mind as discussed by Chu Hsi. (2:5)

If a proper understanding of the mind-and-heart was essential to the attainment of sagehood, it was no less intimately bound up with Chu's philosophy of human nature as grounded in his cosmology of principle and material force *(ch'i)*. Of this Ch'ien Mu says:

> In this Master Chu made every effort to point out the importance of the mind. . . . Therefore when it is said that Lu-Wang represents the learning of the mind and Ch'eng-Chu the learning of principle, this distinction is not appropriate. If one said the Lu-Wang school was exclusively oriented toward the human order, while Ch'eng-Chu equally emphasized the human and cosmic orders, that might be closer to the truth."[6]

Chu Hsi apparently did not use the term *"hsin-hsüeh"* himself, but then neither did Lu Hsiang-shan, the reported progenitor of the School of the Mind, although their contemporary Yang Wan-li (1127-1206), known for his devotion to the teaching of the *Great Learning*, gave the title "Essays on the Learning of the Mind-and-Heart *(Hsin-hsüeh lun)* to a series of discussions on themes central to the developing Neo-Confucian *hsin-hsüeh:* the Confucian classics and rites as manifestations of the Way; the word in speech, writing and book-learning as means of communicating the Way of the Sages; the holistic unity of the Way joining inner self and outer world; and the roles of Yen Hui, Tseng Tzu, Tsu Ssu, Mencius and Han Yü as the transmitters of the Way and defenders of it against heterodoxy.[7] Yet, notwithstanding Yang's title, he too makes no use of the term *hsin-hsüeh* in the essays themselves.

The terms Chu Hsi himself used, which became most important in the later discussion of the learning of the mind, were the transmission of the mind *(ch'uan-hsin)*, the method of the mind *(hsin-fa)*, and by contextual association the Tradition of, or Succession to, the Way *(tao-t'ung)*. All three concepts involve a similar conception of the Way, how it is communicated, and practiced, and how these relate to the mind. First I shall deal with the concept of *tao-t'ung*.

1. *Succession to, or Tradition of, the Way (tao-t'ung)*

This concept is used to represent both the process by which the Way is perpetuated ("Succession to the Way") and its content ("Tradition of the Way"). It came down to Chu through the school of Ch'eng I but was first formulated in these terms by Chu in his preface to the *Mean (Chung-yung)*.[8]

"Why was the *Mean* written? Master Tzu-ssu wrote it because he was worried lest the transmission of the Learning of the Way *(tao-hsüeh)* be lost.[9] When the divine sages of highest antiquity had succeeded to the work of Heaven and established the Supreme Norm, the transmission of the Tradition of the Way *(tao-t'ung)* had its inception. As may be discovered from the classics, "Hold fast the Mean" is what Yao transmitted to Shun.[10] That "the mind of man is precarious" and the "mind of the Way is subtle and barely perceptible"; that one should "have refined discrimination and singleness of mind" and should "hold fast the Mean,"[11] is what Shun transmitted to Yü. Yao's one utterance is complete and perfect in itself, but Shun added three more in order to show that Yao's one utterance could only be carried out in this way. . . .

Subsequently sage upon sage succeeded one another: T'ang the Completer, Wen and Wu as rulers, Kao Yao, I Yin, Fu Yüeh, the Duke of Chou, and Duke Shao as ministers, received and passed on this tradition of the Way. As for our master Confucius, though he did not attain a position of authority, nevertheless his resuming the tradition of the past sages and imparting it to later scholars was a contribution even more worthy than that of Yao and Shun. Still, in his own time those who recognized him were only [his disciples] Yen Hui and Tseng Ts'an, who grasped and passed on his essential meaning. Then in the next generation after Tseng, with Confucius' grandson Tzu-ssu [reputed author of the *Mean*], it was far removed in time from the sages and heterodoxies had already arisen. . . .

Thereafter the transmission was resumed by Mencius, who was able to interpret and clarify the meaning of this text [the *Mean*] and succeed to the tradition of the early sages; but upon his demise the transmission was finally lost. . . . Fortunately, however, this text was not lost, and when the Masters Ch'eng, two brothers, appeared [in the Sung] they had something to study in order to pick up the threads of what had not been transmitted for a thousand years, and something to rely on in exposing the speciousness of the seeming truths of Buddhism and Taoism. Though the contribution of Tzu-ssu was great, had it not been for the Ch'engs we would not have grasped his meaning from his words alone. But alas, their explanations also became lost.[12]

Chu goes on to explain with what difficulty he pieced together and pondered for himself the essential message of the *Mean* from the fragmentary material available to him. He reiterates not only the theme of the precariousness of the Way as transmitted by human hands, but also the successive struggles of inspired individuals to recover its true meaning. Thus, *tao-t'ung* almost literally has the sense of "linking or stitching the Way together."

A few key points should be noted in this passage. One is that the *tao-t'ung* involves the transmission of a teaching which comes down from the sages but is discontinuous after the age of the sage-kings.[13] Then there is the tribute to individuals like Confucius, Mencius, and the Ch'eng brothers for reviving the Way after it had fallen into disuse. Another point is the importance to these individuals of the surviving fragmentary texts as a clue to the sage's teaching; in the case of the Ch'engs "they had something to study in order to pick up the threads of what had not been transmitted for a thousand years." Finally, there is the statement "had it not been for the Ch'engs, we would not have gotten the mind [of the sages] from the words of Tzu-ssu alone."[14]

Taken together these statements characterize a tradition which depends on both text and interpretation for its transmission. One cannot have a "wordless transmission" as in Ch'an Buddhism, nor on the other hand can one depend simply on the preservation of texts and their literal reading. Only a few inspired individuals are capable of grasping the inner meaning of the text, and their contribution is indispensable. Without it, texts like the *Mean* and *Great Learning* are as lifeless (according to this Neo-Confucian view) as they had been for over a millennium since the passing of Mencius. On the other hand, without the texts there is no objective, public record, only subjective imagination and private experience, incommunicable in words (as in Ch'an Buddhism)—which cannot serve to reestablish the Way of the sage-kings as the solid basis for a humane polity and community.

In *Neo-Confucian Orthodoxy and the Learning of the Mind-and-Heart*, I have distinguished two aspects of the *tao-t'ung*, as prophetic and scholastic, depending on whether one emphasizes the inner inspiration or solitary perception which Chu so highlights in this passage, or whether one appeals to received authority by continuous transmission either of texts or instruction from teacher to student.

This ambiguous legacy is the product of Chu's own intellectual situation as heir first to the Ch'eng brothers, and then to other Sung masters. He affirms at once the Ch'eng brothers' independent access to the essential meaning, or heart *(hsin)*, of the Way, along with the collective contributions which other Sung thinkers, starting with Chou Tun-i, made to his own philosophical synthesis. The constructing of this synthesis was itself a creative process, depending on both inner inspiration and Chu's unique "linking-up" of elements drawn from diverse sources. Chu's *Reflections on Things at Hand (Chin-ssu lu)* is a good example of the latter. In it, he pulled together, in a way not done before, disparate elements from predecessors not themselves linked by any master-disciple relation or Ch'an-like succession. Moreover, his own experience in trying to piece together the philosophy of the Ch'eng brothers from the discrepant and conflicting versions of their disciples and successors, is another example of the need actively to repossess the Way rather than just passively to receive it.[15] Yet it was equally important that this synthesis be grounded in classical texts, which is why Chu devoted so much of his time in later years to editing or commenting on the classics as the documentary foundation of his synthesis. Chu's commentary on and preface to the *Mean* was recognized as one of the most important statements of this mature scholarship. Every word of Chu's in it was chosen with extreme care.[16]

Both versions of the *tao-t'ung*, prophetic and scholastic, appear frequently in later Neo-Confucian writings. It is rare indeed that a scholar in the later tradition does not orient himself or his scholarly lineage, in one way or another, to the tradition of the Way as set forth in this preface to the *Mean*. Like Chu's preface to the *Great Learning*, it was among the first things read by students almost anywhere in East Asia as part of their basic education in the Four Books.

T'ung (here translated as "tradition" or "succession") conveys the senses both of a chain or link and of overall control or coordination. The term *cheng-t'ung*, in its Neo-Confucian guise, appeared at about the same time as *tao-t'ung* to express the idea of legitimate succession by virtue of reestablishing control over the empire (and not necessarily in direct succession to the previous dynasty).[17] For Chu Hsi *tao-t'ung* represented the active repossession or reconstituting of the Way in a manner akin to regaining or reconstituting the Empire as the basis for legitimate dynastic succession.

In 1172, some seventeen years before Chu wrote his preface to the *Mean,* a work entitled *Sheng-men shih-yeh t'u* (Diagrams of the Proper Business of the Sages' School) was produced by Li Yüan-kang, a follower of the Ch'eng brothers and Chang Tsai.[18] The first of Li's *Diagrams* is entitled "Ch'uan-tao cheng-t'ung" (The Legitimate Succession in the Transmission of the Way; see figure 1). Its account of this succession is similar to that in Chu's preface, showing the Ch'eng brothers to be the direct successors to Mencius, and including no mention of Chou Tun-i or Chang Tsai.[19] The great eighteenth-century scholar Ch'ien Ta-hsin (1728–1804) drew attention to this, saying, "The two characters *tao-t'ung* first appear in Li Yüan-kang's *Sheng-men shih-yeh t'u.* The first diagram speaks of 'The legitimate succession to the transmission of the Way' in explanation of the Ch'engs' inheriting it from Mencius. This work was completed in 1172, contemporaneous with Chu Hsi."[20]

In this very brief note Ch'ien Ta-hsin is quite precise in stating only what he knew—that Li's work represents the first appearance of these two characters in an extant text (though not abbreviated to the compound *tao-t'ung),* and that this appearance was contemporaneous with Chu Hsi. He does not say that it was the first *use* of the term *tao-t'ung,* or that Chu got the compound term from this source. He leaves open the possibility that it had been current in the Ch'eng brothers school and might have come to Chu by another route.

The only reason this minor point was worth noting at all by Ch'ien was that his readers would be familiar with Chu Hsi's reference to *tao-t'ung* in the preface to his commentary on the *Mean,* a reference repeatedly cited by generations of Neo-Confucian scholars, whereas hardly anyone would have seen or known about Li's charts. Ch'ien was reporting an out-of-the-way fact about the Succession to the Way everyone had come to know through Chu Hsi, as the dominant authority in the later tradition.

In Chu Hsi's preface the active agency of the individual mind in grasping the meaning of fragmentary texts and discerning the original intent of the sages was indicated. In Li Yüan-kang's charts the role of the mind is also greatly emphasized (see figures 2, 3, or original diagrams 4, 5, 8, 9, and 11). But, aside from this, it was the immediate juxtaposition of the Succession to the Way *(tao-t'ung)* with the Method of the Mind *(hsin-fa)* that led to the association of the two in the Learning of the Mind *(hsin-hsüeh)*.

2. *The Method of the Mind (hsin-fa).* At the beginning of Chu Hsi's commentary on the *Mean* and immediately following his preface in most early editions, he quoted some comments of Ch'eng I on the general nature of the Mean:

This work (the *Chung-yung*) represents the method of the mind-and-heart as transmitted in the Confucian school. Tzu-ssu feared that in time it would become misunderstood, and so he wrote it down in this work so as to pass it on to Mencius. This book was the first to explain that the unitary principle, from its position of centrality, is dispersed to become the myriad things and from its outer reaches returns to become one principle; release it and it fills the universe; roll it up and it is retracted into the most hidden recesses. Its savor is limitless. It is all solid learning. The careful reader, having searched its depths and savored its meaning until he has truly gotten it, can use it throughout his life without ever exhausting it.[21]

This quotation, which is a concatenation of several different phrases appearing in the extant writings of Ch'eng I[22] became the primary reference to the method of the mind among later Neo-Confucians. Here too, however, we have it prefigured by one of the diagrams by Li Yüan-kang, entitled "The Essential Method for the Preservation of the Mind" *(Tsun-hsin yao-fa)* (see figure 3). The contents of the diagram come largely from the *Mean*, as interpreted in the light of Mencius and Ch'eng I; they concern the preservation of the equilibrium of the mind in the unaroused and unexpressed state, and the attainment of harmony in one's expressed thoughts and desires through such disciplines as self-watchfulness, caution and apprehension, holding to reverence. Thus both Li and Chu Hsi associate the method of the mind with the *Mean* and with a transmission from the sages. Chu confirms this later in a subsequent preface to the *Mean* which also cites Ch'eng I and the method of the mind handed down from the sages.[23]

The message from Ch'eng I as quoted by Chu, however, is more metaphysical than Li's and has a more oracular tone. It speaks of the mysterious process by which principle manifests both its unity and diversity, and thus can serve as the ground for a practical learning based on solid principle. From this it is evident that *hsin-fa* could cover a range of meanings from the most abstruse to the very practical. Later writers took full advantage of this flexibility to make *hsin-fa* serve their own purposes.

One use to which it should not have been put, however, was the earlier Buddhist use of the term to represent a nonverbal communication of enlightenment from mind-to-mind, as from master to disciple, or patriarch to patriarch.[24] Earlier I have discussed preexisting Buddhist and Neo-Confucian use of *hsin-fa* and need not repeat that here.[25] Chu Hsi made plain in his preface that the transmission from the sages differed fundamentally from that of the Buddhas, and he did so further in his commentary on the important passage in the Analects (12:1) dealing with Confucius' disciple Yen Yüan and "subduing the self and restoring riteness." There Chu specifically identifies *hsin-fa* with this key concept of sustained moral discipline:

This chapter, with its questions and answers, represents a most cogent and important statement concerning the method of the mind-and-heart as handed down to us [from the sages]. If one is not altogether clear in his mind about this, he will not be able to discern its subtle points, and if one is not altogether firm about it, one cannot carry out one's decisions. Thus what Yen Yüan alone had been able to hear and understand [by virtue of his determined effort] no scholar should fail to apply himself to. Master Ch'eng's admonitions [cited in the commentary] too are most revealing. The scholar should savor and ponder them deeply.[26]

Elsewhere, in the *Classified Conversations*, Chu emphasized the point that the Buddhists might have a method of self-control but they do not have the method of "restoring riteness" *(fu-li)*, as a way of defining the norms of practical action. Here in his commentary Chu points out that rites are not to be equated simply with principle in the abstract; rites are the measured expression of Heaven's principle *(t'ien-li chih chieh-wen)* and thus are the "the means whereby the virtue of the mind-and-heart may be perfected."[27] Without the latter the Buddhists and Taoists have no means of determining what specific standards should guide one's actions in the conduct of daily life. Thus principle remains for them something vague, amorphous, and subject only to the rule of expedient adaptation.[28]

Further in the *Classified Conversations of Master Chu (Chu Tzu yü-lei)* there is a reference to Ch'eng I and the *hsin-fa* which clearly identifies the latter with the key elements in Chu Hsi's presentation of the *tao-t'ung* in his preface to the *Mean*: with the distinction between the human mind and the mind of the Way, with the method of refined discrimination and singleness of mind, with the transmission of the Way from Yao and Shun which lapsed after Mencius, and even with the essentials of mind-cultivation in the eightfold method of the *Great Learning*:

> Master Ch'eng says "The human mind is human desires; hence it is precarious. The mind of the Way is Heaven's principle; hence it is refined and subtle. 'Refined discrimination' is that whereby [the method] is carried out; singleness of mind is for preserving [the mind of the Way]. With this one is able to hold fast the Mean!" These words say it all! Refinement is to have refined discrimination and not let [the mind] become mixed and confused. Singleness is to concentrate on unity from beginning to end. Never since this was transmitted from Yao and Shun has there been any other theory. First of all there were these words, and ever since there has been no change in the sages' method of the mind-and-heart.
>
> In the classic [of the *Mean*] one finds many expressions of this idea. In what is referred to [in the Mean] as "choosing the good and firmly holding to it," "Choosing the good" is "having refined discrimination." "Firmly holding to it" is "singleness of mind." "Broad learning, judicious inquiry, careful thought, and clear differentiation" (in the *Mean* 20) are all "refined discrimination," and "earnest, resolute practice" is "singleness of mind." "Under-

standing the good" in the *Mean* (also ch. 20) is "refined discrimination" and [in the same chapter] "achieving personal integrity" is "singleness." In the *Great Learning* the extension of knowledge and investigation of things cannot be accomplished without "refined discrimination," and achieving integrity of intention *(ch'eng-i)* is singleness of mind. He who pursues learning only has this principle to learn. When the transmission was lost after Mencius' time, it is just this that was lost.[29]

This was not, however, the first time that the method of the mind had been identified with the ruler's method of self-cultivation as taught in the *Great Learning*. As I pointed out in *Neo-Confucian Orthodoxy and the Learning of the Mind-and-Heart*, Ch'en Ch'ang-fang (1108–1148), in his "Essay on the Learning of the Emperors *(Ti-hsüeh lun),"* spoke of it as the essential message passed down from Yao and Shun to Confucius and Mencius. "Its content is identified both as 'the learning of the sage emperors and kings' and as 'the ruler's method of the mind' *(jen-chu hsin-fa)*. No other knowledge, no other capability, is so important for the ruler as being able to examine his own motives and conduct to insure that he is not misled into making errors of catastrophic consequence for the people."[30] Thus the method of the mind was already understood as a political doctrine before Chu Hsi's time, and it was so understood by followers of Chu Hsi like Ts'ai Shen and Huang Chen, whose views will be discussed presently.

3. *Transmission of the Mind (ch'uan-hsin)*. We have already noted in discussing the "Succession to the Way" *(tao-t'ung)* how important it was for Chu Hsi that this succession should be achieved by grasping the mind of the sages, or their true intention, based on a correct reading of the classic texts. In fact, for Chu Hsi, the "transmission of the [sage's] mind" was something that evolved from the earlier concepts of the "transmission of the Way *(ch'uan-tao)."* Ch'ien Mu has already shown, at some length and in detail, how this development took place from Chu's earlier writings to his articulation of the concept in his later works.[31] Chu's personal development is reflected in the regrets he expressed in 1163–64 over his own failure to appreciate fully the instruction he had received earlier from Li T'ung, because he had not yet grasped the significance of the "transmission of the mind [of the sages]."[32] Also, in a postface for the *Written Legacy of the Ch'eng Brothers (Ch'eng shih i-shu)* Chu speaks of the errors of "scholars who have not

yet learned the essentials of the transmission of the [sages'] mind and get stuck in the literal meaning of words." From this paraphrase of Ch'eng I and much other evidence Ch'ien concludes that for Chu "the transmission of the Way lay in the transmission of the mind [of the sages]," and that Chu had discussed this long before Lu Hsiang-shan.[33]

> Later scholars who call Lu-Wang the learning of the mind and Ch'eng-Chu the learning of principle do not realize what [Chu] had said about the "transmission of the [sages'] mind." . . . Impressed by Hsiang-shan's fondness for talking about the mind, they fail to take note of all that Chu had said about the learning of the mind.[34]

Given this genetic connection between the "transmission of the Way" and "transmission of the mind," we can more readily understand why Chu closely associated the succession to the Way *(tao-t'ung)* with what Ch'eng I had said about the "method of the mind transmitted from the sages." We note however that there is a shift in the content of what is considered essential in these transmissions. Li Yüan-kang's version of the "Essential Method for Preserving the Mind" had featured the concepts appearing in the *Mean:* the unexpressed and expressed states of the mind, self-watchfulness, etc., but these are not found in the message Chu conveys in his preface to the *Mean.* In the latter the keys to the Way and the essentials of the transmission are identified in what became famous as the "Sixteen Words" concerning the "human mind being precarious, the mind of the Way being subtle," "having utmost refinement and singleness of mind," and "holding fast to the Mean." This view, centering on the distinction between the human mind and the mind of the Way, predominates in Chu's later thought and in his commentaries on the Four books. His preface to the *Mean* (1189) may be taken as a definitive statement of this central concept.[35]

If however we refer back to Li Yüan-kang's charts again, we find that this same cluster of ideas is represented in the eighth chart, entitled "Secret Purport of the Transmission of the Mind" *(Ch'uan-hsin mi-chih),* wherein the mind is seen to combine two aspects (the human mind and mind of the Way); where one is instructed to follow Heaven's Principle while overcoming human desires; where refinement and subtlety are counterposed to the danger and insecurity of the human mind; and wherein singleness of mind is spoken of as appropriate to the mind of the Way, while refined discrimination is proper to the human mind. Thus Li identifies with the Transmission of the Mind what Chu identifies with the Succession to the Way, while both associate the Method of the Mind (hsin-fa) with the Mean but in different ways. From this it would appear that these concepts were closely related in the thinking of late twelfth-century representatives of the Ch'eng brothers school, and that this cluster of associations clung to Chu Hsi's use of the terms when he incorporated them into his widely used prefaces and commentaries on the Four Books. Since each of them stood as an alternative to Buddhist understandings of the same term—of the Way and its transmission, of the mind and its cultivation—it was only natural for early followers of Chu Hsi to think of this ensemble as representing the Confucian alternative to the Buddhist Learning of the Mind, and for a much later scholar like Ch'ien Mu to think of them as the Ch'eng-Chu Learning of the Mind in contrast to that which became identified with "Lu-Wang." Neo-Confucians did not think of these Chinese expressions as having become the exclusive property of Buddhism, any more than did Han Yü, who, in his celebrated essay "On the Way (Yüan tao)," was unwilling to concede to Buddhists an exclusive right to interpret the Way in their own terms.[36]

There is one other concept concerning the mind which has an important place in Chu Hsi's teachings on the mind. This is hsin-shu, representing basic attitudes, dispositions, or habits of mind. It is a major category of self-cultivation in Chu Hsi's Elementary Learning, and because of the latter work's wide use as a Neo-Confucian textbook was a term much employed by thinkers who also discussed the learning of the mind-and-heart.[37] It is not, however, encountered frequently in discussions of hsin-hsüeh itself, and does not appear to have had such a direct connection with it as did the sixteen-word message concerning the human mind and mind of the Way, the tradition of the Way, or the transmission of the mind of the sages. While, therefore, it may be taken as evidence of the basic orientation of Neo-Confucian thought toward a discipline of mind, hsin-shu is not part of the cluster of terms—tao-t'ung, hsin-fa, and hsin-ch'uan—that constitute the essential core of the hsin-hsüeh in early Neo-Confucian discussions of the learning of the mind-and-heart.

The view of the orthodox tradition presented above is reiterated by Chu Hsi's premier disciple, Huang Kan (1152–1221),[38] in his "General Account of the Transmission of the Succession to the Way Among the

Sages and Worthies" (Sheng-hsien tao-t'ung ch'uan-shou tsung-hsü shuo), wherein he explains the content of the "sixteen-word" teaching concerning the human mind and mind of the Way as the essential message handed down from Yao and Shun in the Succession to the Way (tao-t'ung).[39] Elsewhere, commenting on the work of his colleague Huang Shih-i,[40] entitled "Two Diagrams on the Transmission of the [Sages'] Mind from Shun and Yü, and the views of Chou and Ch'eng on Human Nature" (Shun Yü ch'uan-hsin Chou Ch'eng yen hsing erh t'u), Huang Kan confirms that the teaching concerning the human mind and mind of the Way is the authentic "transmission of the mind" from Shun and Yü as interpreted by Chu Hsi in the preface to the Mean, but he criticizes the interpretations of Huang Shih-i which would blur the distinction between these two aspects of the mind.[41] From this we can see that Huang Kan equated the Transmission of the [Sages'] Mind (ch'uan-hsin) with the Succession to the Way (tao-t'ung) as imparted by the Sages, on the basis of their common content in the doctrine of the mind set forth in Chu Hsi's preface to the Mean.

From another major disciple of Chu Hsi, Ch'en Ch'un (1159–1223), often considered one of the most reliable interpreters of Chu Hsi, we get a similar picture.[42] In his important Yen-ling lectures Ch'en gave a concise summary of Chu's mature teachings, how they were to be studied and practiced, and how the Confucian Way has been transmitted through many vicissitudes. In the second lecture, entitled "The Source of Teachers and Friends (Shih-yu yüan-yüan)," Ch'en gives a fuller and more systematized account of the orthodox tradition than is found in Chu's preface to the Mean. Having described the lapse in the tradition after Mencius, he speaks of its resumption in the Sung by Chou Tun-i, who "did not receive it from any teacher but got it directly from heaven,"[43] and then passed it on to the Ch'engs and Chu. Of Chu himself Ch'en Ch'un says, "He got at the subtle words and ideas the Ch'engs had left to posterity, and refined and clarified them. Looking back he penetrated the mind of the sages; looking to the present he drew together the many schools and assembled them as one."[44] As a result of these efforts, says Ch'en, those who would seek to attain sagehood have a sure guide in Chu. "But should anyone refuse this guidance and seek to enter upon the path to sagehood by some other gate, there would be no reason to believe that he could attain the true transmission of the mind of the sages."[45]

Further, in the Fourth Lecture concerning the order in which the

Four Books should be read, Ch'en reaffirms the sequence Chu Hsi had recommended, starting with the *Great Learning*, going on to the *Analects* and *Mencius*, and ending with the *Mean*.[46] Of the latter he says:

> Coming to the Book of the Mean *(Chung yung)*, it represents the method of the mind handed down in the Sages' School.[47] Master Ch'eng I said: "Its savor is limitless. The careful reader, having searched its depths and savored its meaning until he has truly gotten it can use it throughout his life without ever exhausting it."[48] But what it speaks of refers mostly to the higher level and there is relatively little that refers to the lower level. This is not something the beginner can start talking about all at once. He must familiarize himself with the *Great Learning*, the *Analects*, and *Mencius* before he can expect to reach this level, for only so can he appreciate that it is all, without any doubt, solid, practical learning.[49]

Ch'en Ch'un, as an able student closely acquainted with Chu Hsi's thought in his later years, has long been recognized as an authoritative interpreter of Chu's teaching. In the preceding passages he confirms the following points relevant to our inquiry:

1. In the repossession of the Way after Mencius, the penetrating insights of the Sung masters and the great intellectual powers of Chu Hsi—both analytic and synthetic—play a key role in the reinterpretation of classic texts. Among the Sung masters Chou Tun-i, unmentioned in Chu Hsi's account in the preface to the *Mean*, assumes the path-breaking role Chu had previously assigned to the Ch'eng brothers, but this role is still a "prophetic" one in that Chou was said to have had no teacher and received his inspiration from Heaven.

2. If the mind of Chou Tun-i was directly illumined by Heaven, Chu Hsi's contribution was made through the depth and subtlety of his insight into the thought of the Ch'engs and his penetration of the mind of the sages. As a result Chu became the true heir and supreme authority on the "transmission of the Sage Mind."

3. Ch'en Ch'un sees the *Mean* as the culminating expression of this mind in the Four Books, but acknowledges that much of it is metaphysical. He repeats, however, Chu's quotation from Ch'eng I about the *Mean* representing the method of the mind transmitted from the sages,

and tries to explain, like Ch'eng, how this teaching, while seemingly abstruse, can serve as the solid basis for a truly practical learning.

Thus, in this succinct presentation of Chu's legacy, Ch'en Ch'un closely associated the sages' method of the mind (hsin-fa), the transmission of the mind of the sages, and the sixteen-word teaching concerning the human mind and mind of the Way, with the succession to the Way (tao-t'ung). If both Huang Kan and Ch'en Ch'un agree on these points in their summation of the essential teachings of Chu Hsi, it is not reasonable to suppose that these were inadvertent, ill-considered, or gratuitous appendages to the system.

In fact this conclusion is confirmed by prefaces to Ch'en's work written by scholars in the thirteenth, fifteenth, and eighteenth centuries successively: in a preface of 1247 the Pei-hsi tzu-i is described as containing the Message or Method of the Mind (hsin-fa); another preface of 1490 speaks of Ch'en Ch'un as the successor to Chou, the Ch'engs, Chang, and Chu as perpetuators of the Learning of the Mind-and-Heart; while still another of 1714 speaks of Ch'en's work as an integral synthesis of the Learning of the Mind;[50] thus over a span of five centuries the same characterization of Ch'en's (and Chu's) thought was acknowledged.

Another disciple of Chu Hsi was Ts'ai Shen (1167–1230), whose father Ts'ai Yüan-ting (1135–98),[51] also considered a student and colleague of Chu Hsi, had had a special interest in the Great Plan (Hung-fan) section of the Book of Documents (Shu-ching). After the elder Ts'ai's death, Chu, in failing health himself, sensed that he would be unable to fulfill his own ambition of compiling a commentary on the Documents and, in the winter of 1199, asked Ts'ai Shen to carry out this task. In his preface to the Collected Commentaries on the Book of Documents (Shu-ching chi-chuan), Ts'ai modestly disclaims any qualifications for the task but says he felt compelled to undertake it, not only out of filial obligation to parent and teacher, but also because of the great importance of the Book of Documents, which held the key to good government:

> The orderly rule of the Two Emperors and Three Kings was rooted in the Way, and the Way of the Two Emperors was rooted in the mind-and-heart. If one could grasp (lit. "get") this mind, then the Way and orderly rule could be expressed in words. What then were these words? "Be refined and single-minded. Hold fast

the Mean." This was the method of the mind handed down from Yao, Shun, and Yü. Establishing the Mean and setting up the Supreme Norm was the method of the mind as passed on by King T'ang of Shang and King Wu of Chou. Call it "virtue," call it "humaneness," call it "reverence," call it "sincerity"—the expressions may differ but the principle is one and the same. They are all without exception means of explaining the wondrousness of this mind. As expressed in terms of Heaven, it conveys the majesty whence this mind derives. As expressed in terms of the people, it conveys the care with which this mind is to be exercised. The rites, music, and transforming power of education issue from this mind. All institutions and cultures are products of this mind. The regulation of the family, ordering of the state, and bringing of peace to all-under-Heaven are extensions of this mind. Thus indeed does the virtuous power of this mind flourish abundantly. . . .

Preserve this mind and order prevails; lose it and there is disorder. The difference between order and disorder is determined by whether or not this mind is preserved. How so? Rulers in these later ages, if they aspire to the orderly rule of the Two Emperors and Three Kings, cannot but seek their Way; if they aspire to this Way, they cannot but seek this mind; and if they seek the essentials of this mind, how can it be done except through this book?[52]

Here the message of the mind transmitted from Yao and Shun is identified with the sixteen-(here abbreviated to four) word formula which Chu Hsi had spoken of in the preface to the *Mean* as the orthodox tradition *(tao-t'ung)*. Its central importance is further underscored by Ts'ai's description of it as embracing the central Confucian virtues that should constitute the basis of the ruler's self-cultivation.

The same point is reiterated by Ts'ai in commenting on the apocryphal text of the sixteen-word formula itself as it appeared in the "Counsels of the Great Yü" in the *Book of Shang (Shang-shu)*. After explaining the distinction between the human mind and the mind of the Way, and the need to be discriminating and single-minded, he concluded:

The ancient sages, at the point of handing over the empire to others, never failed to pass on with it the method for its orderly rule.[53] Seeing it like this in the classic, rulers today cannot but ponder it deeply and reverently take it to heart.[54]

Later in the next generation of Chu Hsi's school, the distinguished historian, classicist, and official, Huang Chen (1213–1280), a student of one of Chu Hsi's principal disciples, Fu Kuang (n.d.),[55] had occasion, when commenting on the "human mind/way mind" formula in the *Book of Shang*, to complain of how this had been misconstrued. He noted that in the original context of the passage, it had a hortatory and admonitory significance in the handing on of the mandate to rule. This is ignored, he says, by those who make much of the passage for purposes other than those originally intended:

> Nowadays those who delight in talking about the Learning of the Mind-and-Heart disregard the original context and concentrate only on the mind of man and the mind of the Way. The worst of them just seize upon the two words "Way mind" and proceed to speak of the mind as the Way. This is to fall into Ch'an Buddhism and not realize that one is departing far from the basic mandate transmitted by Yao, Shun, and Yü.
>
> Ts'ai Chiu-feng [Ts'ai Shen], when he wrote his commentary on the *Book of Documents*,[56] cited Master Chu's words as follows: "The ancient sage-kings, at the point of passing on the empire to others, never failed to pass on with it the method for governing it." We can say that this truly conveys the basic meaning of this passage. Although by this Chiu-feng meant to set forth clearly the "mind of the emperors and kings," for him it was the mind-and-heart for governing the state and pacifying the world. This view is solidly grounded in principle.
>
> Although Chiu-feng himself took this as setting forth the mind of the sage emperors and kings, in his explanation of this mind as the root and basis of ordering the state and bringing peace to the world, he certainly affirmed the correct principle. Later, those who presented his commentary at court spoke of it as the "transmission of the mind" of the three sages, whereupon scholars of the time pointed to the sixteen-word formula as the essence of the "transmission of the mind" and Ch'an Buddhists borrowed this as support for their own view [of the transmission].[57]
>
> In my humble opinion the mind does not need to be transmitted. What pervades heaven-and-earth, links past and present, and is common to all things, is principle. Principle inheres in the mind and is experienced in things and affairs. The mind is what coordi-

nates these principles [within and without] and makes distinctions of right and wrong. Worthiness or unworthiness among men, success or failure in human affairs, order and disorder in the world, are all determined in this way.[58]

In contrast to this, says Huang, Ch'an Buddhism sees the principles articulated by the sages as handicapping self-realization and impeding enlightenment, so they simply point directly to the mind and seek to transmit hints without the use of words. The mind of the sages, however, was common to all men and the principles which should govern affairs were clearly known to all without the need for any special transmission of mind. It was only necessary for men to act on these principles and for their minds to make the necessary judgments in dealing with human affairs.

If Huang Chen found the "transmission of the mind" an unfortunate choice of words susceptible of misappropriation by Ch'an Buddhists, he did not disagree with Ts'ai Shen's basic view of moral self-cultivation and its importance for the mind of the ruler, or with Ts'ai's view, as Huang put it, that "this mind is the root of ordering the state and bringing peace to the world." Such a view of the nature and nurture of the morally responsible, socially conscious mind, was what the true learning of the mind-and-heart was about, in contrast to the wordless transmission of the Ch'an Buddhists.

Huang made this still clearer in his discussion of the orthodox tradition in the Sung. Tracing the "correct teaching" as it came down from Chou Tun-i to Chu Hsi, and thence to Huang Kan, he acknowledges that in the course of its transmission two followers of the Ch'eng brothers, Yang Shih (1053–1135) and Hsieh Liang-tso (?–1120), became somewhat tainted by Ch'an. Nevertheless enough of the original teaching was conveyed to Lo Ts'ung-yen (1072–1135) and Li T'ung (1093–1163) so that the latter "could save Chu Hsi from falling into Ch'an," and Chu, with his brilliant powers of analysis could shed great light on the teachings of the Ch'engs and regain the main road of the orthodox way. This was possible only because Li T'ung, "through this clarifying of the learning of the mind, could, despite the proclivity to become diverted toward Ch'an, himself hold onto the correct learning of the mind *(hsin-hsüeh)*.[59]

From this one can say that despite his reservations concerning the use of the expression "transmission of the mind," Huang Chen saw the "learning of the mind" itself, not as a deviant form of Confucianism contaminated by Buddhism, but precisely as the authentic orthodoxy holding fast against such occasional lapses.

At about the same time Ch'en Ta-yü (c.s. 1259),[60] a Ch'eng-Chu scholar in the line of Huang Kan, in his commentary on the *Book of Shang* asserted that the passage on the human mind and mind of the Way "presented the tradition of the Way *(tao-t'ung)* as transmitted in the method of the mind *(hsin-fa),*" while the immediately following passage in the same text, having to do with the love and respect which the ruler should command, represented the succession to rulership *(chih-fa).*[61] Thus he makes the same connection as Ts'ai Shen between the tradition of the Way, the method of the mind, and the succession to rulership.

Ch'en Ta-yü's views on the point are reiterated by another commentator on the *Book of Shang,* Ch'en Li (1252–1334),[62] known for his devotion to Chu Hsi, who cites the latter's *Recorded Conversations (Yü-lu)* as confirmation of the view that the formula of "refinement and singleness of mind" was the method or practice *(kung-fu)* handed down from Shun to Yü as the Sages' method of the mind *(hsin-fa).*[63] Thereafter the practice *(tzu-ti)* in the Confucian school followed this formula. Though the methods of self-cultivation set forth in the *Mean* and *Great Learning* were expressed in different terms, the meaning was the same as the method of refinement and singleness. "What one needed to study was only this principle, and when, after Mencius, the transmission was lost, it was this that was lost."[64] In other words, the practice of "refinement and singleness" was the "method of the mind" and the latter was the heart of the "tradition of the Way" passed down from the sages but lost after Mencius.

This view is also found in other writings of Ch'en Li. In his preface to the Collected Commentaries, he says: "The *Book of Shang* records the orderly rule of the early emperors and kings. One seeks the Way through the cultivation of reverence in the mind-and-heart, and one seeks orderly rule through the practice of the Mean in government.[65] The teaching concerning the human mind and mind of the Way, he says, is the essence of the Tradition of the Way *(tao-t'ung),*[66] while the teachings of "refinement and singleness" and "holding fast to the Mean," as found in Chu Hsi's preface to the *Mean,* are indispensable ingredients of the Tradition of the Way *(tao-t'ung).* They represent as well the practice of the real principles and real learning spoken of in

Ch'eng I's characterization of the message of the mind placed by Chu Hsi at the beginning of his commentary on the *Mean*.[67] Moreover, since this message is concerned with "real principles," it is in no way incompatible with the "learning of the Way" *(tao-hsüeh)* and "learning of principle" *(li-hsüeh)* which comes down from Chou Tun-i, the Ch'engs, Chang Tsai, and Chu Hsi.[68] Finally, Ch'en sums it all up in his comment on the *Analects'* passage in which Confucius speaks of setting his heart on learning at age fifteen (a comment of Ch'en's preserved in the Ming *Great Compendium on the Analects (Lun-yü ta-ch'üan)*, though Ch'en's own commentary on the Four Books *(Ssu-shu fa-ming)* has been lost):

> The learning of the sage [Confucius] began with his heart set on learning [at the age of fifteen] and ended (at age seventy) with his being able to follow his heart's desire without transgressing the norm. From beginning to end it was all learning of the mind-and-heart *(hsin-hsüeh)*.[69]

For another view of the matter among the early followers of Chu Hsi, we may cite the testimony of Wei Liao-weng (1178–1237) and Lo Ta-ching (n.d.). Wei is often cited with Chen Te-hsiu as a principal leader of the learning of the Way in the early thirteenth century. Together Wei and Chen were responsible for the Sung courts' reversal of the ban on Chu Hsi. Lo Ta-ching, active in the mid-thirteenth century,[70] had a great admiration for Chu Hsi, Chen Te-hsiu, and Wei Liao-weng, and in a miscellany of reading notes included the following quotation from a letter by Wei to a friend concerning the role of the mind in studying the classics:

> "One should study the classics, reflecting on each word so as to get it oneself. One cannot just employ the method of simply following what has been said by former scholars." He also said, "In employing the method of fathoming principles through the investigation of things, one should always bear in mind and keep in one's heart the model of the Three Dynasties. If one just follows in the tracks of the Han and Chin scholars, one will not have done the job." Wei also said: "Just reading a great deal in the recent interpretations and reflections of former scholars is not as good as reading the sages' classics one by one for oneself. . . ."

These comments of Wei Ho-shan are something students should cherish and respect. I have compiled a work entitled *"Classics and Commentaries on the Learning of the Mind-and-Heart"*[71] in ten fascicles, and have said in the preface: "It will not do if one does not seek to learn from Chou [Tun-i], the Ch'engs, Chang [Tsai], and Chu [Hsi], but [on the other hand] only to learn from them and not base it all in the Classics would be like neglecting one's father's memory and venerating one's elder brother. One must certainly not fail to read the Six Classics, but only to study them and not reflect upon them in one's own mind would be like buying a jewel box and throwing away the pearl.[72]

If one considers this passage in the light of what was said earlier about Chu Hsi's insistence on the equal need for reading the original texts, studying the commentaries and reflecting oneself on the meaning of texts, as combined in Chu Hsi's conception of the "transmission of the mind [of the sages]" *(ch'uan-hsin]*, we can recognize another component of the learning of the mind-and-heart referred to earlier by Ch'ien Mu (see above, pp. 24–27). Since Wei Liao-weng and Lo Ta-ching were both from Kiangsi, one might suspect some lingering influence on them of Lu Hsiang-shan, but in fact the kind of classical textual study recommended here and practiced by Wei Liao-weng was quite in contrast to the teaching of Lu, as was the emphasis above on the fathoming of principles through the investigation of things. Moreover Wei Liao-weng was associated with Fu Kuang, a leading disciple of Chu Hsi, and though like Chen Te-hsiu, disposed to minimize the differences between Chu and Lu, had no comparable association with the latter's limited following in the early thirteenth century.[73]

It was at about this time that Chen Te-hsiu compiled his Classic of the Mind-and-Heart *(Hsin-ching,* abbreviated here as "Heart Classic"), based on passages in the Confucian classics and the interpretations of the Sung masters, which, as anthologized in concise form, became a "classic statement" of the Learning of the Mind-and-Heart. That this "Learning" was clearly identified with the well-known sixteen-word passage from the *Book of Documents,* as quoted by Chu Hsi in his preface to the *Chung-yung chang-chü,* is shown by Chen's choice of it as the opening passage of the *Heart Classic,* together with Chu's comment on it.[74] Moreover, that Ts'ai Shen had served as an intermediary in linking this "message of the mind" and "transmission of the mind" is suggested by a eulogy Chen had written for Ts'ai Shen in which he praised his commentary on the *Book of Documents* and cited it particularly for its account of the transmission of the Sages' and Kings' doctrine of the mind and its practice in rulership.[75] To his own "classic" Chen Te-hsiu appended a paean of praise for this "Learning," which begins with the lines:

> *Transmitted from Shun to Yü*
> *Were these sixteen words,*
> *The Learning of the Mind-and-Heart for all ages*
> *Had its inception here.*[76]

These words were quoted by the late Sung scholar Hsiung Chieh (c.s. 1199), a Chu schoolman who studied under Huang Kan, when he compiled his *Anthology on Human Nature and Principle,* showing that this use of the term *hsin-hsüeh* was in no way incompatible with the view of Chu Hsi's teaching as centrally concerned with human nature and principle *(hsing-li).*[77] In the anthology it is included in the matter prefatory to selections from Chu Hsi, as if to sound a keynote.

Elsewhere Chen made it clear that *hsin-fa* represented not only the essential message handed down from the sages, but also the essential method to be practiced and attitude to be cultivated by all those committed to the Way of the Sages:

> When one has committed himself to this Way, to what should he then devote his practice of it? If we look to remote antiquity, we can see that in the one word 'reverence,' as passed down through a hundred sages, is represented their real method of the mind-and-heart *(hsin-fa).*[78]

Chen's *Heart Classic* had an especially deep influence on the great champion of Ch'eng-Chu orthodoxy in Korea, Yi T'oegye (1501–1570), for whom Lu Hsiang-shan was completely anathema. Yi wrote his own summation of the essentials of the tradition in *Ten Diagrams of the Sages' Learning (Sŏng-hak sip-do),*[79] the seventh diagram of which was entitled "The Learning of the Mind-and-Heart" (see figure 7). Yi incorporated therein most of the concepts discussed above, and acknowledged that his chart was based on that of Ch'eng Min-cheng (c.s. 1466) (see figure 6), which was in turn devised from an earlier Yüan dynasty prototype by Ch'eng Fu-hsin (1257–1340)[80] appearing in the latter's *Diagrams and Explanations of the Four Books (Ssu-shu t'u-shuo)* of 1313[81] (see figures 4, 5).

Ch'eng Fu-hsin was from Chu Hsi's ancestral hometown of Hsin-an in An-hui. Early accounts speak of him as having studied the words of Huang Kan and Fu Kuang and having become thoroughly "devoted to Chu Hsi's teaching, through which he was able to grasp (lit. 'get') the mind of Confucius, Mencius, Tseng Tzu and Tzu-ssu (i.e., as revealed in the Four Books)."[82] He believed that the *Great Learning* particularly featured the doctrine of the mind, while the *Mean* featured the teaching concerning the nature *(hsing)*, which was equated with principle *(li)*. The two texts together thus expounded the combination of mind and principle so central to the tradition of the Way and to the early learning of the mind in the Ch'eng-Chu school, a combination emphasized in Ch'eng's diagrams.[83]

Besides citing Ch'eng's views on the Learning and Method of the Mind in the text accompanying his own diagram, T'oegye, in his *I-hak t'ong-nok* (Comprehensive Record of the Learning of Principle),[84] identified this source of his Learning of the Mind with the Learning of Principle (to which he said Ch'eng made signal contributions) and also with the orthodox succession.[85] This orthodox tradition of the Learning of the Mind-and-Heart T'oegye clearly identified with the message and method of the mind *(hsin-fa)* coming down from the sages to the Sung masters as is indicated in his commentary on Chu's "Precepts of the White Deer Grotto," summarized by Yi as "the essentials of the Method of the Mind."[86] Ch'eng presented his own *Diagrams and Explanations of the Four Books* to the Yüan court in 1313, at precisely the moment in Chinese history when the Four Books were first being adopted for use as the standard texts in the resumed civil service examinations. Prime among Ch'eng's sponsors in this presentation was Ch'eng Chü-fu (1249–1318), the chief architect of the system that would remain the official orthodoxy of China and Korea down into modern times.[87] (For illustration of above, see T'oegye's diagram in the Japanese edition of *Ri Taikei Zenshū*, 2:260.)

From the foregoing discussion of the Neo-Confucian Learning of the Mind-and-Heart in its initial phase, we may draw the following conclusions as to its essential characteristics:

1. Although the expression *hsin-hsüeh* was not used by either Chu Hsi or Lu Hsiang-shan, Chu had much to say about the nature and

nurture of the mind which warranted his immediate followers' use of the term to differentiate Chu Hsi's view of the mind from the Buddhists' or Taoists'.

2. Chu's early followers identified this Learning of the Mind with three concepts appearing in key writings of Chu—key in the sense that they dealt with central issues and also, having wide dissemination, played an important role in shaping the new Learning of the Way as it left the hands of Chu Hsi. These concepts were the "Tradition of the Way" *(tao-t'ung)*, the Method of the Mind *(hsin-fa)*, and the Transmission of the [Sages'] Mind *(ch'uan-hsin)*. Early writers of the Chu Hsi school spoke of these as inseparably related aspects of a core tradition handed down from the sages.

3. The passage most often cited as expressing the kernel of this teaching was the sixteen-word formula identified by Chu Hsi with the "tradition of the Way" *(tao-t'ung)* in his preface to the Mean. Elsewhere Chu, and others after him, also referred to it as the Message or Method of the Mind *(hsin-fa)*, thus establishing a close correlation between this method and the tradition of the Way.

4. Though the "sixteen words" were obscure in themselves and drawn from an apocryphal version of the *Book of Shang*, they were taken by Chu Hsi as scriptural authority for the distinction between the human mind and the Mind of the Way—a crucial distinction in Ch'eng-Chu philosophy between the fallible mind of the ordinary man and the Sages' mind of pure principle (the mind of the Way). As moral injunctions these dicta comprised a method of self-cultivation including constant self-examination; making fine moral and cognitive distinctions (corresponding to the manifold particularizations of the Way in practice); concentrating the mind on the oneness of principle as constituting the essential unity of the human order with the creative process in Heaven, Earth, and all things; and holding to the Mean in the conduct of human affairs. Thus principal Neo-Confucian doctrines, especially as based on the *Mean*, were seen as implicated in these sixteen words.

5. Further, this kind of correlation was extended to include the methodical steps of intellectual and moral cultivation found in the *Great Learning*. From this the sixteen-word formula came to be seen as a concise, though cryptic, encapsulation of the Confucian teachings found in the *Great Learning* and the *Mean*, now coordinated by Chu Hsi's commentary with the interpretation of the Four Books as a whole, and most particularly with the important passage in the *Analects* on the

discipline of "subduing the self and restoring riteness." Given the almost mystical language in which Ch'eng I, as quoted by Chu, spoke of the "method of the mind," it took on the aspect of an oracular message from the primordial age confirming not only the perennial truths of Confucian self-cultivation but also the fully articulated speculations of the Sung philosophers.

The cryptic character of this message is not to be confused with the kind of secret transmission spoken of in Ch'an (Zen) or Esoteric Buddhism. It involves no passing on of a truth which goes beyond all formulation in words, nor is there any implied distrust of language such as one finds in the Ch'an "nondependence" on words and phrases (pu-li wen-tzu). When Chu Hsi speaks of the "secret purport" of the sixteen-character message he means only that the words alone do not convey the full-meaning and significance of the sages' teaching. It is a teaching, however, written by Heaven, so to speak, on the mind-and-heart of everyman, by its endowment of the luminous rational and moral nature replete with all principles. All that is needed for the comprehension of this truth is clarity of perception—the kind of unobstructed vision possessed by the sages and the Sung masters, vouchsafed, in terms of their psycho-physical dispositions, by a specially clairvoyant ethereal endowment, brought to its full realization by a corresponding effort at self-cultivation of their individual natures.

Thus the Sages' teaching remains in the domain of rational discourse, and the orthodox tradition, far from claiming to be a private or exclusive transmission, is something open to all. Indeed it is this open and public character of the Way, so vital to its educational propagation in the late Sung and Yüan periods, to which appeal is made by later Neo-Confucians who protest the tendency to make of the orthodox tradition a private or exclusive possession in a single line of transmission.

6. Since this Tradition of the Way had come down from Sage-kings who had presided over a social order fully consonant with that Way, the injunctions discussed in no. 4 above were thought to have a special relevance to rulership. Here was the crucial link between the Neo-Confucian philosophy of mind and its political philosophy: the method of self-discipline and intellectual cultivation that was key to the governance of men (hsiu-chi chih-jen)—a point emphasized by early commentators on the sixteen-word passage in the Book of Shang.

7. The process by which this message was communicated—a combination of careful textual study and inspired interpretation by the Sung

masters—was expressed in the term "transmission of the mind [of the sages]" (ch'uan-hsin). For Chu Hsi the significance of this transmission lay in the balance of cognitive learning, critical reflection, deep insight, and lofty vision as the Way was reconstructed in the mind of the dedicated scholar seeking to realize the ideals of the sages. There was no established process, no automatic transmission by which the tradition of the Way (tao-t'ung) could be assured of perpetuation in a given age. In this view the routine scholarship of the Han and T'ang had failed to appreciate the inner dynamic of the classics that had come into their possession, a dynamic which could be perceived by reading between the lines, bridging the gaps in the texts, piecing together the fragments, and entering body and soul—indeed, heart and mind—into both the spacious halls and secret recesses of the sagely mind.

8. Each of these Neo-Confucian terms and concepts had parallels in Buddhism and Taoism for which they might be mistaken, but Chu Hsi and his followers saw this as no reason for surrendering the use of such terms as the method of the mind (hsin-fa) or transmission of the mind (ch'uan-hsin) to Buddhism. Instead they spoke of the former as a systematic moral and intellectual discipline in the service of the latter as an explicit, publicly transmitted and documented discourse, open to reexamination and rational discussion.

9. From the foregoing a further conclusion can be drawn of the greatest importance for the later development of Neo-Confucianism: this learning of the mind-and-heart was also understood to be a learning of principle. There could be no opposition between hsin-hsüeh and li-hsüeh for these Neo-Confucians because their whole view of the mind, in contrast to the Buddhist, was that this mind was fundamentally imbued with the rational, moral principles implanted in it by Heaven. There might be some—but few enough in the thirteenth century— who questioned the distinction between the human mind and the mind of the Way, but none among the Neo-Confucians who doubted that the whole point of this mind was to understand and express Heaven's principles.

The Learning of the Mind-and-Heart, as a term or concept in itself, was not a major focus of discussion in the early Ch'eng-Chu school, but it was a way of characterizing disciplines and doctrines considered essential to the learning of the Way. When Chen Te-hsiu promoted that learning in the early thirteenth century, acclaiming it as the Learning of the Mind-and-Heart, he was also recognized as the great champion of the Learning of the Way and the Learning of Principle in his time, not as someone propounding an idiosyncratic or deviant doctrine.

Nevertheless, as we have seen, it was a doctrine, for all its exoteric professions, not free of its own enigmatic and ambiguous formulations. As the sixteen-word formula had it, the mind of the Way was subtle and difficult to perceive, while the human mind was unstable and liable to err in its judgments. Whatever the Neo-Confucians might say about the palpability of the word or constancy of the Way, the endurance of the teaching—even on Chu Hsi's terms—was contingent upon its critical reexamination and creative reinterpretation. As the teaching spread, and became deeply rooted, one could expect to see new buds bursting from the old wood and new branches reaching out—which also means contending with each other—for a place in the sun.

*Diagrams Illustrating the Succession
to the Way and Learning
of the Mind-and-Heart*

Correct Succession in the Transmission of the Way

Successive Generations of Sages and Worthies Transmit the Way of the Great Mean and Perfect Correctness, carried out through myriad ages without defect

Isolated practice by sages and worthies, whose Way can help the world for a time but cannot be transmitted for myriad ages

Yao
Shun
Yü
T'ang
Wen
Wu
Duke of Chou
Confucius

Tseng Tzu   Yen Tzu
Tzu Ssu

Liu-hsia Hui   Po I

Mencius

Yang Hsiung   Hsün K'uang

I-Ch'uan   Ming-tao

Isolated practice by sages and worthies, whose Way can help the world for a time but cannot be transmitted for myriad ages

Lao Tan   Gau-tama

Mo Ti   Yang Chu

54

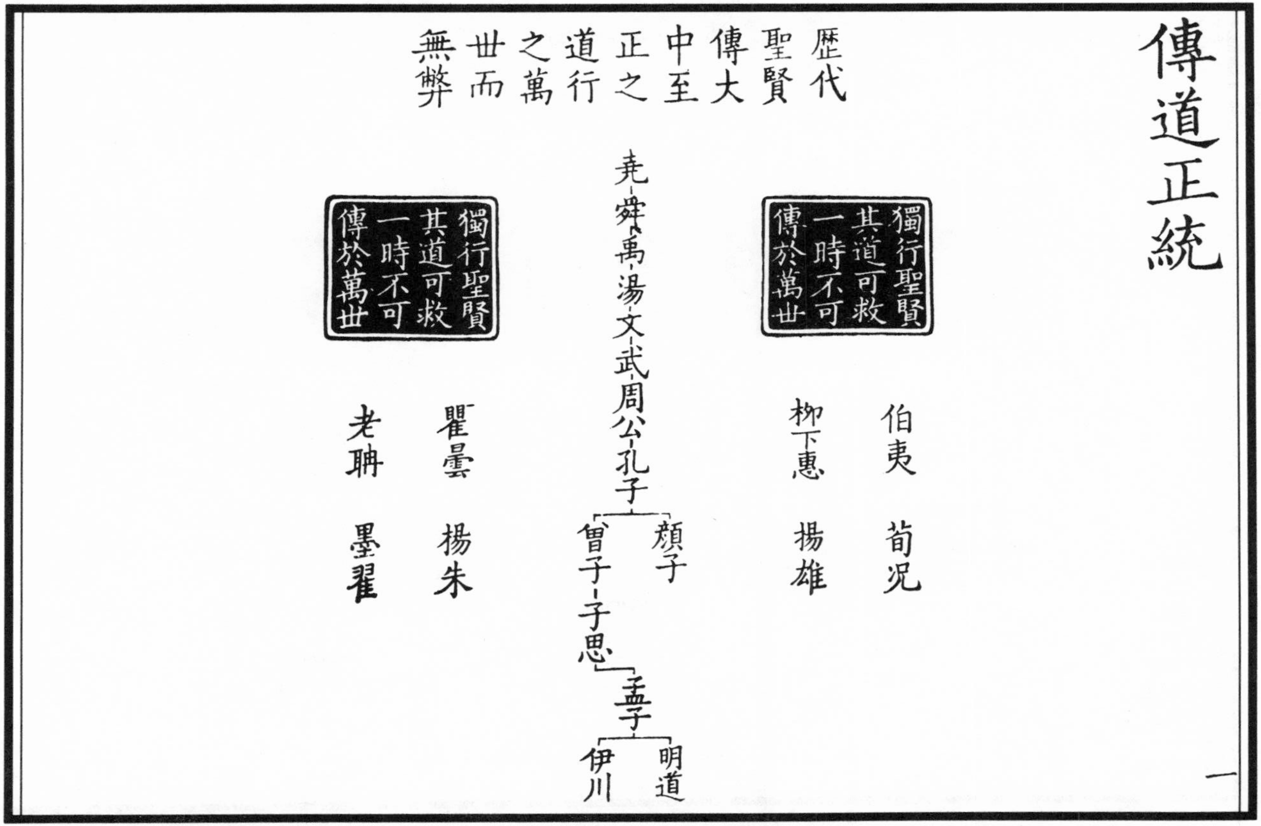

傳道正統

歷代聖賢傳道正統之大中至正之道
萬世而無弊

聖賢行道可救世
獨詣一世時於萬世而不可傳也

伯夷　柳下惠
荀況　揚雄

堯　舜　禹　湯　文　武　周公　孔子
顏子
曾子　子思
孟子
伊川　明道

瞿曇　揚朱
老聃　墨翟

聖賢行道可救世
獨詣一世時於萬世而不可傳也

1

Figure 1.　Diagram No. 1 by Li Yüan-kang (n.d.) in 1172: "The Legitimate Succession in the Transmission of the Way" (see p. 31).　For translation see facing page.

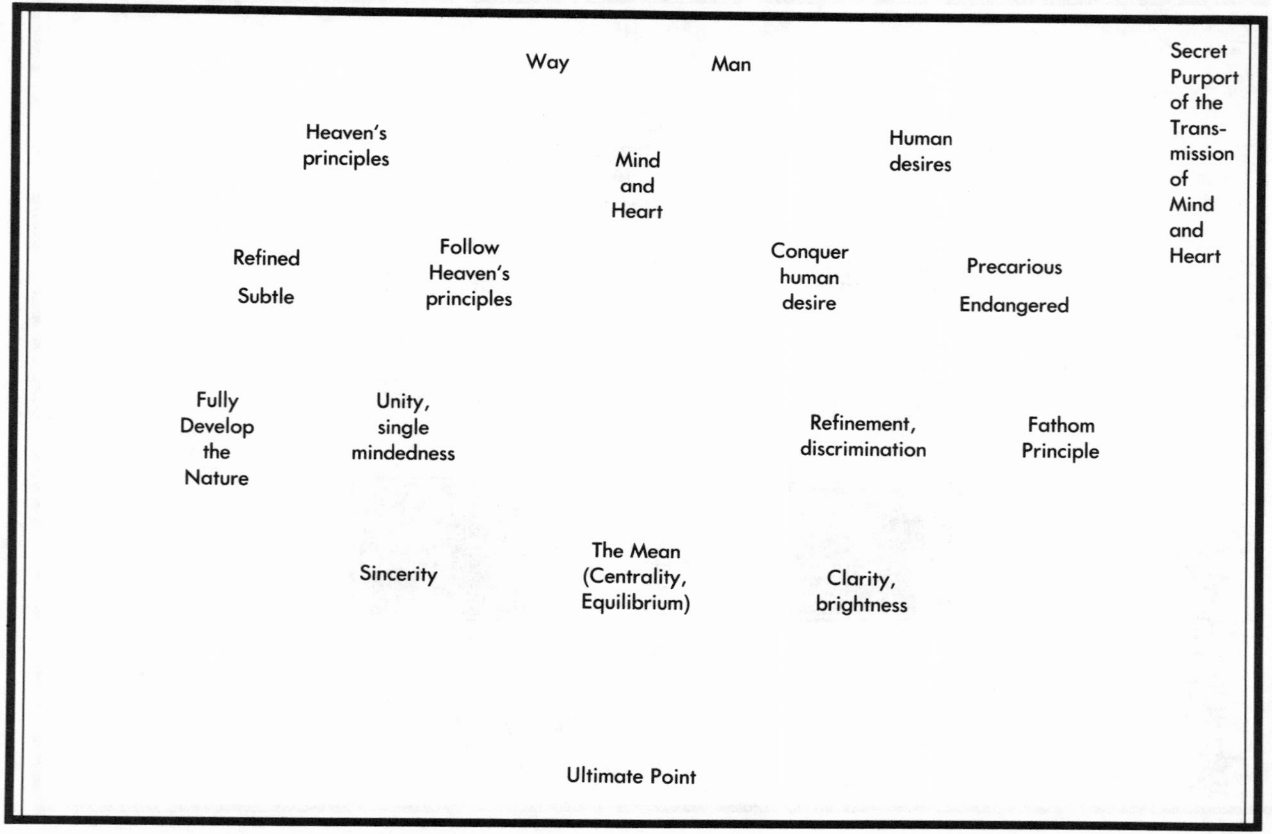

Secret Purport of the Transmission of Mind and Heart

Heaven's principles

Refined
Subtle

Follow Heaven's principles

Way

Man

Mind and Heart

Human desires

Precarious
Endangered

Fathom Principle

Conquer human desire

Refinement, discrimination

Clarity, brightness

Unity, single mindedness

Fully Develop the Nature

Sincerity

The Mean (Centrality, Equilibrium)

Ultimate Point

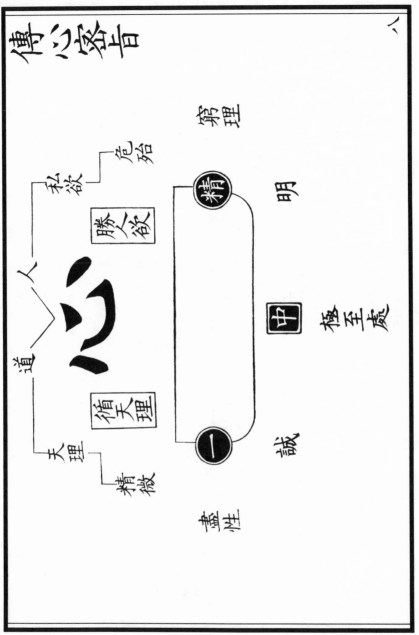

Figure 2. Diagram No. 8 by Li Yüan-kang: "Secret Purport of the Transmission of Mind" (see p. 32). For translation see facing page.

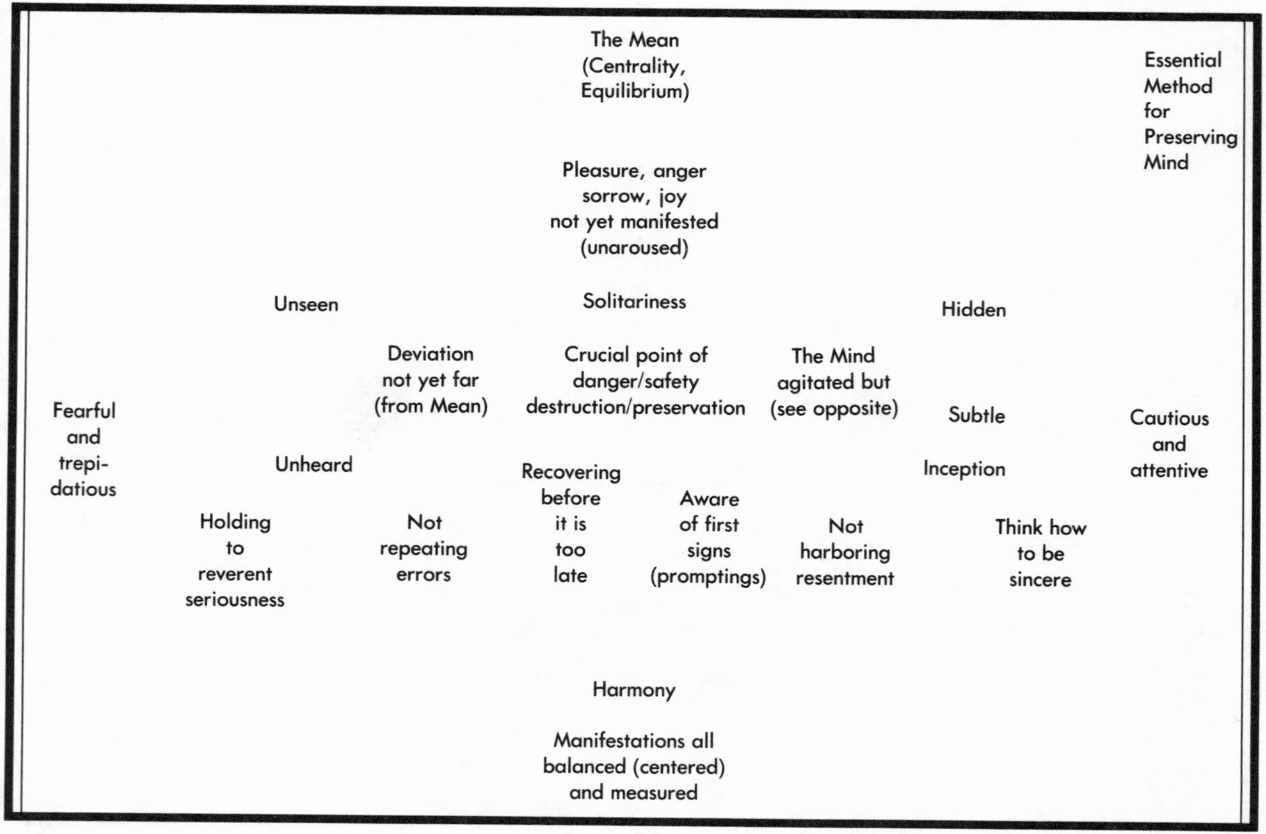

Essential Method for Preserving Mind

Cautious and attentive

Hidden

Subtle

Inception

Think how to be sincere

The Mind agitated but (see opposite)

Not harboring resentment

The Mean (Centrality, Equilibrium)

Pleasure, anger sorrow, joy not yet manifested (unaroused)

Solitariness

Crucial point of danger/safety destruction/preservation

Aware of first signs (promptings)

Recovering before it is too late

Harmony

Manifestations all balanced (centered) and measured

Deviation not yet far (from Mean)

Not repeating errors

Unseen

Unheard

Holding to reverent seriousness

Fearful and trepidatious

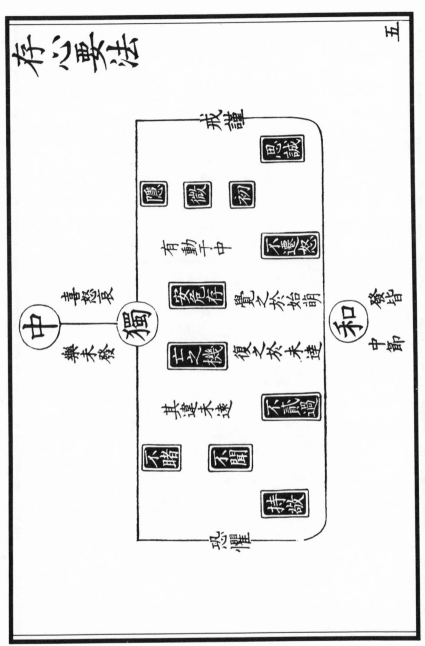

Figure 3. Diagram No. 5 by Li Yüan-kang: "The Essential Method for the Preservation of the Mind" (see p. 32). For translation see facing page.

Original Mind   Naturally Good Mind

Empty and Spiritual
Conscious

Mind of   Enlightened   Mind of
mature person   innocent child
                           Mind

Master of whole person

Mind   Human
of the Way   mind

Discriminating,
chooses the Good

Singleminded,
holds to unity

Cautious and   Watchful
apprehensive   when alone

Maintains   Subdues [selfishness]
control   and restores [riteness]

Thinking   Reverent   Presence of
mind   Seriousness   mind

Reflects upon   Master of the   Recovers
and nourishes mind   mind and heart   strayed mind

Fully develops   Rectifies
the mind   mind

[Like Confucius]   [Like Confucius]
At age seventy follows   At age forty
heart's desires   mind is unmoved

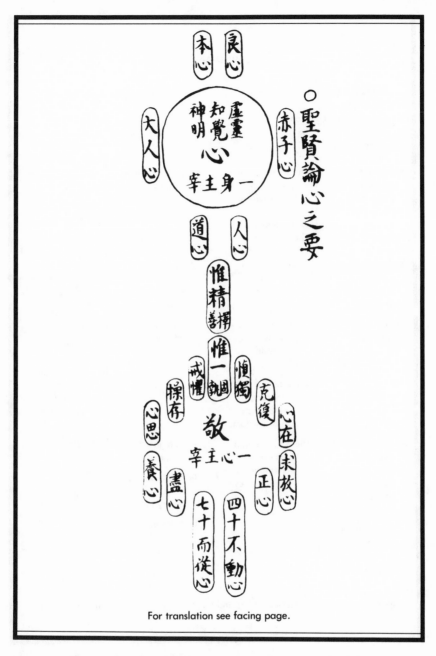

For translation see facing page.

Figure 4.   Diagram by Ch'eng Fu-hsin (1257–1340): "Essentials of the Sages' and Worthies' Exposition of the Mind-and-Heart" (see p. 48).

THE MIND-AND-HEART

Aroused it becomes the Emotions		Unaroused it is the Nature	
The Emotions		**The Nature**	
Material Force	Principle	Material Force	Principle
Aroused it becomes the Seven Emotions:	The sense of commiseration as the manifestation of humaneness.	Psycho-physical Nature	Original Nature
Pleasure	The sense of shame and dislike as the manifestation of rightness.	As purely clear, wholly good	Humaneness as the Principle of Love
Anger		As a mixture of the pure and turbid, mixed good and evil.	Rightness as the Principle of Propriety
Sorrow			
Joy	The sense of modesty and deference as the manifestation of riteness.	As purely turbid wholly evil.	Trustworthiness as the Principle of Genuineness
Love			
Hate			Riteness as the Principle of Reverence
Desire	The sense of right and wrong as the manifestation of wisdom.		Wisdom as the Principle of Differentiation
As balanced and measured, these are impartial and good.	These Four Beginnings are correct emotions without any evil	In its higher state —the wise	These Five Virtues altogether Heaven's principles, surely without any evil
As unbalanced these are selfish and evil.		In its intermediate state—the ordinary man	
		In its lower state —the stupid and foolish	

Exposition of the Mind Coordinating and Controlling the Nature and the Emotions

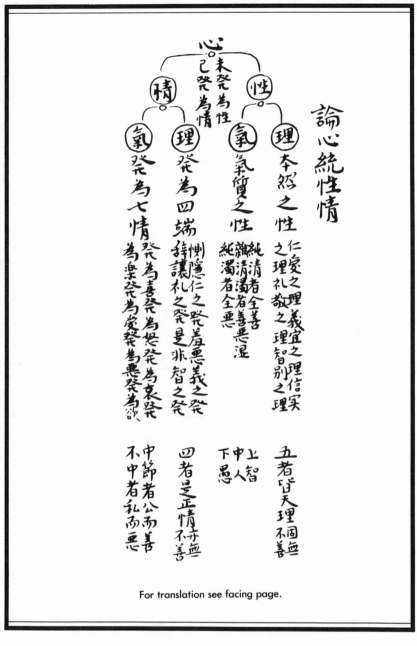

For translation see facing page.

Figure 5. Diagram by Ch'eng Fu-hsin: "Exposition of the Mind-and-Heart Coordinating the Nature and Emotions" (see p. 48).

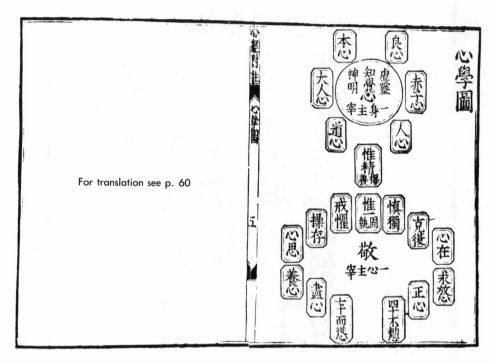

For translation see p. 60

心學圖

心經附註 心學圖

良心
本心
赤子心
大人心
虛靈知覺神明心宰主身一
人心
道心
惟精善擇
慎獨
惟一執固
戒懼
克復
操存
敬 宰主心一
心在求放
心思養心
正心
盡心
四十不動
卞而從

Figure 6. Diagram by Ch'eng Min-cheng (c.s. 1466): "Diagram of the Learning of the Mind-and-Heart" (see p. 47).

64

心經附註卷一　西山眞氏

帝曰人心惟危道心惟微惟精惟一允執厥中。

朱子曰　心之虛靈知覺一而已矣而以為有人心道心之異者以其或生於形氣之私或原於性命之正而所以為知覺者不同是以或危殆而不安或微妙而難見爾然人莫不有是形故雖上智不能無人心亦莫不有是性故雖下愚不能無道心二者雜於方寸之間而不知所以治之則危者愈危微者愈微而天理之公卒無以勝夫人欲之私矣精則察夫二者之間而不雜也一則守其本心之正而不離也從事於斯無少間斷必使道心常為一身之主而人心每聽命焉則危者安微者著而動靜云為自無過不及之差矣○附註朱子曰堯舜以來未有議論時先有此言聖人心法無以易此經中此意極多所謂擇善而固執即惟精惟精也固執即惟一也又如博學審問謹思明辨

Above is the first page of Ch'eng Min-cheng's edition of Chen Te-hsiu's *Heart Classic, with Supplementary Notes*. In bold-face type is the sixteen-word "Message of the Mind," followed by Chu Hsi's commentary on the Mind of the Way and Human Mind (as quoted by Chen) and Chu Hsi's explanation of the Method of the Mind (*hsin-fa*) as added by Ch'eng to Chen's version. (From Japanese ed. in Naikaku bunko.)

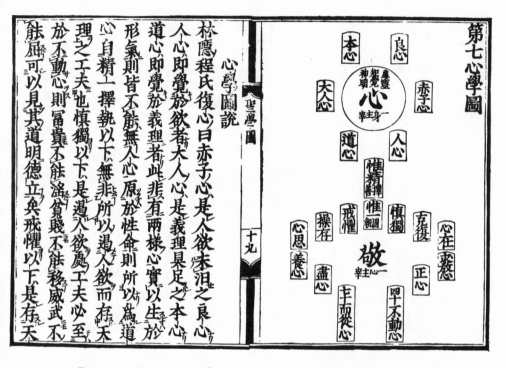

Figure 7. Diagram No. 7 by Yi T'oegye (1501–1570): "Diagram of the Learning of the Mind-and-Heart" (see p. 47). The text at left cites Ch'eng's interpretation of the Diagram and is followed by Yi's further comment. For translation of diagram see p. 60, facing figure 4.

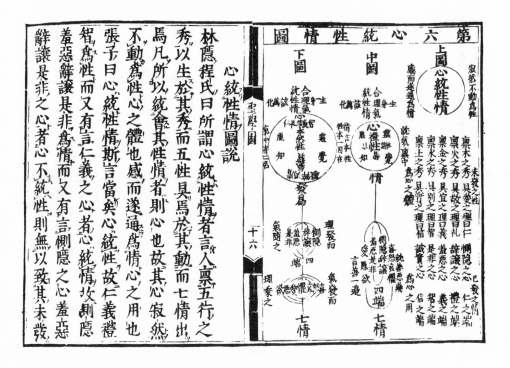

Figure 8. Diagram No. 6 by Yi T'oegye: "Diagram of the Mind Coordinating the Nature and Emotions." For translation see Michael Kalton, *To Become a Sage* (New York, Columbia University Press, 1988), pp. 120–124.

Diagram of Heaven, Earth and Sagehood

Extreme of
summer

Mean
equilibrium

Rightness

Beginning of summer

Beginning of autumn

Supreme
Mid spring   Motion   ultimate   Quiescence   Mid autumn

Return
(recovery)

Beginning of spring

Beginning of winter

Humanity

Correctness

Extreme of
winter

Outer circle: Sixty-four hexagrams of Book of Change

Mind-and-Heart

The accompanying text explains that this diagram represents the natural process of motion and quiescence in the mind of Heaven, which is the source of man's nature. The sage is connatural with the mind of Heaven, and the diagram illustrates how the Supreme Ultimate generates the process of motion and quiescence which manifests itself in the sixty-four hexagrams, the succession of the seasons, and the powers or virtues appropriate to each.

For explanation see facing page.

Figure 9. Diagram by Ch'en Chen-sheng (1410–1473): "Diagram of Heaven, Earth and Sagehood" (see p. 192).

69

Diagram of the Noble Man Modeling Himself on Heaven

Four essentials of Sagehood [through practice of reverent seriousness]:
Making unity the master, without any preconceptions
Strict and stern in ordering and regulating
Constantly alert and attentive
Heart and mind collected, allowing nothing [to preoccupy it].

(from Ch'eng I, Hsieh Liang-tso and Yin Tun,
as quoted by Chu Hsi in *Ta-hsüeh huo-wen* 2ab)

Heaven
(male)

Motion mastering Quiescence	Li (hexagram) Brightness	Reverence	Kan (hexagram) Sinking	Quiescence mastering motion
		Motion Quiescence		
		Return		

(female)
Earth

Heart-and-Mind

According to the accompanying text the noble man, understanding the natural process represented by the Diagram of Heaven, Earth, and Sagehood, is able to practice reverent seriousness in order to experience and realize the efficacious results of modeling himself on Heaven. The process begins with making reverent seriousness the master of the mind in its phases of motion and quiescence, as expressed in the extension of knowledge and making the intention sincere, and is completed in the realization of sagehood. This was the method of instruction handed down from the sages to Confucius and Mencius, but thereafter became lost until the Sung masters again brought it to light. After Chu Hsi's death, it became obscured again. "Though the Ch'eng-Chu texts were taught in the schools of the late Sung and Yüan, the method of official recruitment followed the examination system of the Sui and T'ang, and this Method of the Mind-and-Heart, being unused and little sought after, ceased to be truly transmitted."

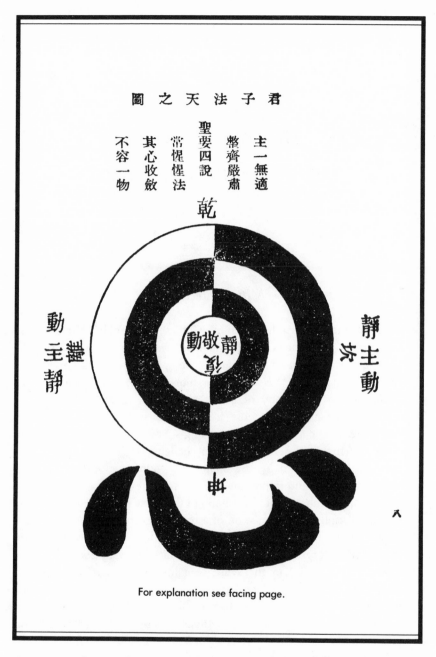

For explanation see facing page.

Figure 10. Diagram by Ch'en Chen-sheng: "Diagram of the Noble Man Modeling Himself on Heaven."

3

The New Learning
of the Mind-and-Heart

Ming Antecedents

When the modern historian of Chinese philosophy Fung Yu-lan wrote that "Lu Chiu-yüan (Hsiang-shan) was "the real founder of the rival idealistic *(Hsin-hsüeh)* school," he spoke more as a philosopher than as a historian. *"Hsüeh"* was more real to him as a form of "learning," a philosophy or set of ideas, than as a "school" in the institutional sense. Thus, most "real" to him was the fact that Lu had anticipated some of Wang Yang-ming's key doctrines, especially in being the first important thinker to challenge Chu Hsi's view of the mind as characterized by the duality of "human mind/mind of the Way." Less real and important to Fung was the fact that Lu had little use for the establishment of a school, in the sense of an academy for the formal, disciplined transmission of a body of doctrine, and would have been most unlikely to claim credit for founding such. Nor was Fung particularly concerned with the historical fact that very soon after Lu's death, his "school," in the sense of a line of teachers and students devoted to his teaching, soon lapsed. Even the academy most identified with his prime disciple Yang Chien (1141–1226), had converted within a few decades to the teaching methods and texts of his "rival" Chu Hsi.[1]

In the Yüan period, as I have related in *Neo-Confucian Orthodoxy*, Part II, Chu Hsi's dominance of the fast-growing school system and academy movement was almost complete. As Wing-tsit Chan has said, "There was simply no Lu School to speak of in the Yuan."[2] This indeed was true right down to the time of Wang Yang-ming in the sixteenth century. Looked at from this historical standpoint, the "real founder of the rival Idealistic School," here understood as the so-called "Lu-Wang School of the Mind" was Wang Yang-ming himself, for it was he who put forth the rival doctrine and inaugurated the new learning which would, retrospectively, recognize Lu as its forebear and come to be known as the "Lu-Wang School of the Mind" (hsin-hsüeh), eventually to be juxtaposed to the Ch'eng-Chu School of Principle (li-hsüeh). In this there is a basic asymmetry between the two "schools" since one can trace a line of teachers and disciples from Ch'eng I to Chu Hsi but not between Lu and Wang.

During the early Ming, as during the Yüan, the teachings and texts of Chu Hsi remained dominant both at court and in the schools. "By the beginning of the Ming," says Wing-tsit Chan, "all Neo-Confucianists were followers of the Ch'eng-Chu school."[3] This does not mean that in the academies all was compliance and conformity with official doctrine, but only that it was the Ch'eng-Chu curriculum—the Four Books with Chu Hsi's commentaries, the Five Classics with Neo-Confucian interpretations, along with other texts of Chu Hsi, like the Elementary Learning (Hsiao-hsüeh), the Family Ritual of Master Chu (Chu Tzu chia-li), Reflections on Things at Hand (Chin-ssu lu), to name only a few, that provided the basis for the intellectual and moral formation of educated Chinese during the Ming. It was from this source that the springs of new thought, as represented by Ch'en Hsien-chang (1428–1500) and Wang Yang-ming, gushed forth. There was nothing comparable from the hand of Lu Hsiang-shan which could serve the same educational function or, as Chan has put it, "which could form the basis for his followers to rally around" or "serve as a focal point for his philosophy."[4]

In the meantime the Ch'eng-Chu teaching was still referred to, even by some of its most committed followers, as a "Learning of the Mind," and the mind remained a principal focus, if not by far the most important subject, of study and discipline in the Learning of the Way (tao-hsüeh). Clearly this could not refer to any Lu School or Learning of the Mind. As Chan says further, "It would be wrong to suppose that the early Ming Neo-Confucianists were influenced by Lu. They did not get their inspiration from him."[5]

Ts'ao Tuan (1376–1434) and Hsüeh Hsüan (1389–1464) are often spoken of as two early leaders of the Ch'eng-Chu school in the Ming.

Ts'ao Tuan is frequently seen as a fierce defender of Neo-Confucian orthodoxy and relentless critic of all heterodox influences from Buddhism and Taoism.[6] Yet the last thing this implied for him was a mere external conformity to the prevailing orthodoxy. As a self-educated scholar, who had struggled hard to gain his own understanding of the Way, it was natural enough for Ts'ao to believe that the Way to sagehood, as an alternative to Buddhism or Taoism, was something essentially learned for oneself. He summed up his discussion of the Sage Learning (sheng-hsüeh) by saying that "sagehood is something that can be learned and the essential method for doing so does not lie outside the one mind."[7] And again: "The business of learning to be a sage stresses the one mind as the most important thing," and "The method (kung-fu) whereby one can enter upon the high road of the Confucian school is to apply oneself to the mind in all things and affairs."[8]

Like other Neo-Confucians before him, Ts'ao believed in the need to enter fully into the mind of the sages, and not just read the classics in a literal way. Yet perhaps no one before him expressed this thought in such shocking terms as he did: "The Six Classics and Four Books are only the dregs and leavings of the Sages' mind. One must depend on them initially in order to find the Way, but in the end one must set them aside in order to find the truth."[9] If this sounds like a Ch'an master on the point of tearing up the scriptures, or like Lu Hsiang-shan who regarded the classics as mere footnotes to himself, it should be quickly added, as Ts'ao Tuan did, that "the Four Books express the distilled essence of the Six Classics and make clear the method of the mind of the thousand sages."

Speaking of the essential points in each: in the Analects, it is humaneness (jen); in the Great Learning, reverent seriousness (ching); in the Mean, sincerity (ch'eng), and in Mencius, humaneness and rightness (jen, i). Put them together and you have the Sage Emperors and King's "refinement" and "singleness of mind," and "Hold fast the Mean."[10]

Elsewhere Ts'ao extends this thought to include the Sung masters, saying that after the Six Classics and Four Books were written, it was not until such great scholars as Chou Tun-i, the Ch'engs, Chang Tsai, and Chu Hsi appeared that anyone was "truly able to grasp the intentions of Confucius and Mencius and transmit the message of the mind coming down from the sage-emperors and kings."[11] Further he notes how Chu Hsi had linked Ch'eng's "message of the mind" with the injunction to Yen Yüan in *Analects* 12:1:

> [The maxim] "To subdue the self and restore riteness is humaneness" constitutes the message of the mind which Confucius conveyed to Yen Yüan. "In my way there is one thread running through it all" was the message of the mind as Confucius conveyed it to Tseng [Tsan], in *Analects* 4:15. The sages' message of the mind is one. How could what was transmitted not be one in essence?[12]

If Ts'ao Tuan was concerned about the mix of mind and text in the transmission of the Sages' Way, Hsüeh Hsüan was no less so. Already by his time there was a problem—not new by any means—that the inspirational message of the sages was not getting through, and that scholars paid only lip service to the established teaching, having learned how to recite Master Chu's words and use them as a means to gain official preferment, without reflecting upon either the classics or Chu's teachings in relation to their own lives or selves. Thus "the real intention of the teachings of the sages and worthies did not come to any substantial result."[13] Hsüeh thought of himself as a firm upholder of Chu's doctrines concerning the relationship of principle and material force, but as regards cultivation for sagehood, the mind was for him the crucial agency. Citing the doctrine of the *Mean (Chung-yung)*, he said, "The two words centrality and harmony embrace limitless principles but the essence of it lies simply in the mind."[14] In this vein Hsüeh identified the Ch'eng-Chu teaching as it came down to him not only as a learning of principle but also as a learning of the mind. "Since the demise of Master Chu the perpetuation of the Way has not gone beyond the literal meaning of words and phrases. There was only one person who was able, from his reading of these words and phrases, really to grasp (lit. "get") Master Chu's learning of the mind, and that was Hsü Lu-chai (Hsü Heng, 1209–81)."[15]

The Japanese scholar Takeuchi Hiroyuki has recognized Hsüeh Hsüan himself as an exponent of this learning of the mind but traces it down from Hsü's predecessor Chen Te-hsiu and Chen's *Heart Classic*, with its lines quoting the sixteen words from the *Book of Shang* as the "source of the learning of the mind-and-heart for all ages."[16] Takeuchi further sees this learning as having passed on down to Hu Chü-jen (1434–84) and Lo Ch'in-shun (1465–1547), both well known as scholars representing the Chu Hsi school, though in different ways.

About Lo Ch'in-shun, who was to become a vigorous opponent of Wang Yang-ming and his new learning, more will be said later. Hu Chü-jen's deep commitment to Chu Hsi's teaching was particularly expressed in a strong emphasis on the virtue of reverent seriousness *(ching)*, which he saw as a fundamental attitude of mind prerequisite to even the "investigation of things," the normal starting point for Chu Hsi's method.[17] In this vein Hu rejected any view of the mind and principle as being in opposition to one another. If the outward expression of principle in conceptual terms had been corrupted, and this led to immorality or heterodoxy, the source of this disorder lay in the mind-and-heart and in the desires. Hence one had to come to an understanding of the relation between outward expression and inner intentions and feelings. "The learning of the mind-and-heart cannot but discuss the desires, how the correcting of the mind requires the clarification of principles, and how mind and principle are not two separate things."[18] From this it is clear that for Hu the learning of principle *(li-hsüeh)* and the learning of the mind-and-heart *(hsin-hsüeh)* were inseparable.

Indeed, from the outset of Hu's main work, the *Chü yeh lu*, he rules out any understanding of the learning of the mind which is not premised on the unity of mind and principle. So central is this question to the true learning of the sages that Hu not only devotes his first chapter to the discussion of "The Mind and Nature" but he takes issue with those (probably with Ch'en Hsien-chang in mind) who speak of the Learning of the Mind in terms of practicing quiescence (i.e., quiet-sitting) in order to cultivate the state of "having no mind" *(wu-hsin)*. Could they really believe it possible to reach a state beyond "mind and principle"? No, whatever has life from Heaven also has the nature (principle) as an integral part of its endowment, and there can be no true cultivation of the mind in quiescence except through the nurturing of principle and directing of the mind in accordance with it. When Chou Tun-i spoke about nothingness and quiescence, by "nothing" *(wu)* he meant the formless state [of principle] and not nonexistence. As Chu Hsi had explained it, quiescence is not nothingness, and what Chou meant by "nothing" was only what had not yet taken shape or form in the mind.[19]

Thus, says Hu: "The mind and principle are essentially one. Although the mind is empty (i.e., open, receptive), principle is real (substantially present) . . . Principle is what the mind is for, mind is that in which principle inheres. . . . What former scholars said men should study is just mind and principle. . . . In the sages, mind and principle are one."[20]

Finally, in the *Daily Conversations by the Eastern Stream (Tung-hsi jih-t'an lu)* of the scholar Chou Ch'i *(chin-shih,* 1481)[21] who came out of the school of Hsüeh Hsüan, we have discussions of the Learning of the Mind by an orthodox Neo-Confucian who was praised by the editors of the Imperial Manuscript Library Catalogue for his fidelity to this line of Ch'eng-Chu tradition,[22] a line which he himself traced down from Chu Hsi to Huang Kan, Chen Te-hsiu, Wei Liao-weng, Hsü Heng, Wu Ch'eng, and Liu Yin to Hsüeh Hsüan.[23] In his characterizations of the Learning of the Mind Chou combined all the elements cited by his Neo-Confucian predecessors and strove to keep a proper balance among them. For him "the sages from Yao and Shun to Confucius were the great exemplars of the Learning of the Mind, while the Sung masters from Chou Tun-i to the Ch'engs and Chu Hsi served as the standard bearers of this Learning of the Mind in later times" (6:5b). By contrast Lu Hsiang-shan was seen by him as "one-sided" in comparison to Chu Hsi's balanced emphasis on honoring the moral nature and pursuing the path of scholarly inquiry (15:14b–15a).

For Chou Ch'i the injunction "Hold fast the Mean" was the essential message of the Learning of the Mind, while refinement and singleness of mind constituted the practical method ancillary to this learning. "The learning of the ancients regarded getting it with one's own mind-and-heart as the primary thing (8:8a). In saying this Chou was not expressing a distaste for book-learning but only for superficial learning that passed in and out of the sense organs without being properly evaluated and assimilated by oneself. "What we call the Learning of the Mind-and-Heart is something learned through the mind and not through the mouth. Only when one's learning is taken to heart [gotten in the mind] can it be given confirmation in one's conduct (9b).

At the same time it was important for Chou to keep a balance between the objective and subjective aspects of learning.

The nature lies in the mind-and-heart, and principles in books. If one does not pursue learning in the mind, then the nature in the mind becomes atrophied and learning is obscured by superficial impressions. If one pursues learning in the mind and does not pursue it in books, then the nature in the mind has nothing to substantiate it and becomes blinded by wild imaginings. (8:8b)

Like Chu Hsi and Hu Chü-jen, but unlike Lu Hsiang-shan and later Wang Yang-ming, Chou Ch'i regarded reverent seriousness as an attitude of mind fundamental to all learning.

The nature is the root and source of elementary learning. Reverent seriousness is the method for cultivating (kung-fu) the Learning of the Mind-and-Heart. In the Way of all-under-Heaven, is there aught that lies outside of reverent seriousness? If there is, it is not what we would call learning. . . . If one is reverent and serious, one's mind is preserved; otherwise it is not. . . . Just so, when Mencius spoke about preserving the lost mind, was it not the Learning of the Mind-and-Heart he was referring to? (8:9a)

Chou also identified this learning with what Confucius had said to Yen Yüan in *Analects* 12:1 about "subduing the self and returning to riteness," which Chu Hsi had described in terms of Ch'eng I's method of the mind (hsin-fa):

When Confucius instructed Yen Yüan about the Four Don'ts (i.e., do not look, listen, speak, or act contrary to rites), this was to control his lower self so as not to let it disturb his greater self. The merit of the Learning of the Mind derives from its being rooted in the nature and its practice lying in reverent seriousness. Its perversion comes from the selfishness of the sense organs. This is why Shun declared to Yü: "The human mind is precarious; the mind of the Way is subtle. Be discriminating and single-minded. Hold fast the Mean." (6:10a)

Here then, on the eve of Wang Yang-ming's reformulation of the Learning of the Mind, we have a succinct recapitulation of those elements which earlier representatives of the Ch'eng-Chu school had associated with the *hsin-hsüeh*. Chou noted especially that in this learning, based on the nature and principle, the method of the mind served as a moral discipline insuring one's adherence to principle. Whatever else may be said about the Ch'eng-Chu school in contradistinction to what followed it, it cannot be maintained that this "learning of principle" *(li-hsüeh)* favored principle over mind, for the orthodox teaching was also, as its leading exponents in the fifteenth and sixteenth centuries testified, a learning of the mind which stressed the cultivation of principle through the "method of the mind."

Wang Yang-ming's Reformulation of the Learning of the Mind-and-Heart

If Wang Yang-ming is the "real founder" of the "Lu-Wang School," as I hope to show, it means not only that the connection between Lu and Wang was first made by Wang, but also that Wang, in terms of his scholarly antecedents, had no genetic connection with Lu. Wang's early education was in the Four Books as explained by Chu Hsi, and his mentor Lou Liang (1422–91) had himself studied under a scholar deeply devoted to Chu Hsi, namely, Wu Yü-pi (1392–1469).[24] Moreover, Wang's earliest philosophical concerns—and doubts—arose naturally from an earnest commitment to the achievement of sagehood following Chu Hsi's method, i.e., the investigation of things as taught by Lou.[25]

For Wang to come to question this kind of investigation as he did, implies that something other than simply the concepts and method of Chu Hsi entered into the picture. Wang's was a restless temperament; he had a venturesome spirit and a mind that ranged widely in search of truth. Thus his experience of life was highly diverse. Yet there is significance in the fact that Wang shared this lively independence of mind with other Ming thinkers who, like Wang, had been schooled in Chu Hsi's teaching, and who, like him, best exemplified it by their determined effort to "get" the Way for themselves and make their own contribution to it. Examples are Ch'en Hsien-chang (1428–1500),[26] Hu Chü-jen (1434–1484)[27] and Chan Jo-shui (1466–1560),[28] among the diverse disciples of the Ch'eng-Chu scholar and teacher Wu Yü-pi.

Nor is the whole story to be told in terms of pedagogic lineages. Wang Ken (1483–1541), who was to become one of the most dynamic propagators of Wang Yang-ming's teachings, had been largely self-taught and only encountered Wang after his own views were well formed. He had studied Chu Hsi's version of the Four Books on his own, been inspired to the pursuit of sagehood, and developed his personal version of the "investigation of things," which was called the *"Huai-nan ko-wu"* after his native region. Then upon first hearing Wang Yang-ming, he recognized a close similarity in their two views and decided to join the latter.[29] Here we have what appears to be an independent convergence in the thinking of the two Wangs, and yet the similar lines of their thought must also be understood as having emerged from a common matrix of Ch'eng-Chu ideas and practices, particularly as found in the Four Books. Only so can we understand how large numbers of Ming scholars, deeply indoctrinated as they were in Ch'eng-Chu teaching, could show such a widespread common susceptibility to the new waves of thought that would sweep over China in the sixteenth century. There ensued such a conversion to the new movement that it came almost totally to dominate the intellectual scene in the late Ming. In effect Wang Yang-ming took over the existing Learning of the Mind-and-Heart from Ch'eng-Chu, almost indeed to the point where the new "Lu-Wang" learning replaced the "Ch'eng-Chu" teaching as the official orthodoxy in the late sixteenth century. Here I refer to the enshrinement in the Confucian temple of Lu Hsiang-shan in 1530 and of Wang Yang-ming in 1584, a turn of events which convinced observers in Korea that China had declined into a fatal decadence, leaving Korea as the last bastion of orthodoxy.[30]

If one takes Wang Yang-ming's *Instructions in Practical Living (Ch'uan-hsi lu)* as any indication, one could not say that Lu Hsiang-shan had loomed large in Wang's early thought. He is mentioned in this important work only a few times, and then not always with unqualified endorsement,[31] whereas Chu Hsi's doctrines remain a main preoccupation of Yang-ming. Even when he comes to disagree with Chu, as he feels he must, Wang does so as if in pain, protesting (even if perhaps too much) that he could hardly bring himself to differ with his revered master.[32] Yet in Yang-ming's mature thought he has clearly come to a position more sympathetic to Lu than to Chu on several key issues. One of these is the Learning of the Mind-and-Heart, which Wang too understands as the Sage Learning, but interprets differently from Chu. This is revealed in his preface to the *Collected Writings of Hsiang-shan* (1520) written for the first reprinting of Lu's neglected works since 1212:

The Sage Learning is the learning of the mind-and-heart. As it was handed on from one to another by Yao, Shun, and Yü, it was said:

"The human mind is precarious; the mind of the Way is subtle. Be discriminating and single-minded. Hold fast the Mean." This is the source of the learning of the mind. The "Mean" refers to the mind of the Way. When the mind of the Way, being refined [discriminating] and single, is referred to as "humaneness," it is what we call the "Mean." The learning of Confucius and Mencius, which urged the pursuit of humaneness, carried on the transmission of the sages' refinement and singleness. Nevertheless a prevalent evil at that time was found among those who insisted on seeking this outside the mind. Thus the question arose with Tzu-kung as to whether Confucius' learning consisted in acquiring much cognitive knowledge [*Analects* 15:2] and whether humaneness consisted in "extensively benefiting and assisting the people" [*Analects* 6:28]. So Confucius told him about the pervading unity [running through it all] and taught him how to take what is near at hand [in oneself] as a gauge of the feelings of others, which meant having them seek within their own minds. Then in Mencius' time Mo Tzu spoke of humaneness as going so far as to wear the hair off one's scalp and heels [on others' behalf] while the likes of Kao Tzu talked about "humaneness being within and righteousness being without [the mind]" which did grave harm to the learning of the mind-and-heart.[33]

Despite Mencius' efforts, Wang goes on to explain, the Way of the Sage-Kings declined and a utilitarian view came to prevail which identified principle with selfish gain and in effect disconnected it from the moral mind of Heaven's imperative. With this "the mind and principle became two separate things and the learning of refinement and singleness [unity] was lost." Scholars occupied themselves with the external pursuit of the principles in things without realizing that there is truly no difference between the principles in the mind and the principles in things. Likewise the Buddhist and Taoist teachings of emptiness dispensed with the moral constants which should govern human relations, again not realizing that the mind and principle are inseparable and that moral constants cannot be dispensed with.

Finally, in the Sung, Chou Tun-i and the Ch'eng brothers tried to rediscover the essential meaning of Confucius and Yen Yüan, and with such doctrines as the "Non-finite and yet Supreme Ultimate"; "stabilizing the mind with humaneness and rightness," "the mean and correctness"; "putting quiescence first"; "stability in both action and quiescence"; "neither external nor internal" and "neither following nor going forward to meet events" (referring to *Chuang Tzu* 6, 3:7b), they came close to the original idea of refinement and singleness. "After this," Wang says, "came Lu Hsiang-shan, who, though not the equal of the two Chengs for purity of character and equability of disposition, nevertheless was able, through his simplicity and directness of mind, to connect up with the transmission from Mencius." Indeed, "his insistence that learning must be sought in the mind was singleness of mind itself. It is for this reason that I have adjudged the learning of Hsiang-shan to be the learning of Mencius.[34]

Seeing Lu, and not Chu Hsi, as the true heir to Mencius and the Way, Wang goes on to defend Lu against the charge of lapsing into Ch'an Buddhism—an issue which, however, need not detain us here. It should suffice to note the parallel between Wang's account of the Learning of Mind and Chu's presentation of the Succession to the Way in his Preface to the *Mean*, consistent with earlier identification of this text with the Learning of the Mind-and-Heart. Where Wang differs in his account is his insistence on the unity, stability, and quiescence of the mind, in contrast to Chu's earlier emphasis on the fallibility of the human mind and the subtlety of the Mind of the Way. Reflecting this difference, according to Wang, Lu's method was direct and simple; Chu's was burdened (as Wang now saw it) by the need for caution and objective investigation. The basis for Wang's endorsement of Lu's approach is not only his acceptance of the idea that the mind and principle are inseparable—which Chu himself had said—but his view of them as indeed identical. Wang expressed this idea unequivocally in a memoir of 1524; when he said that the constant unvarying Way was "endowed in man as his nature and as the master of his person was called the mind. The mind is the nature, Heaven's Imperative, the One, pervading man and things, reaching out to the Four Seas, and filling Heaven-and-earth."[35]

To my knowledge this characterization of Lu Hsiang-shan in terms of the Learning of the Mind-and-Heart stands as the earliest attribution of that Learning to Lu Hsiang-shan. It is always possible, of course, that some earlier identification of Lu and *hsin-hsüeh* may turn up, but since none of the standard biographical accounts or prefaces to Lu's works, pre-Wang Yang-ming, refers to his teaching in this way, we may assume that *hsin-hsüeh* had not been identified with Lu before this. Wang Yang-ming's attribution of it in clear reference to the sixteen-word message from the sage-kings seems patently an effort to link Lu's teaching to what has all along been considered the orthodox Learning of the Mind-and-Heart.

In a later adversion to the same theme, when Wang wrote a memoir on the reconstruction of the Shan-yin prefectural school (1524), he took no issue with Chu's distinction between the human mind and the mind of the Way. The real problem lay elsewhere:

> The Sages' learning is the "Learning of the Mind and Heart." It is learning which seeks fully to employ the mind-and-heart. What Yao, Shun, and Yü passed on from one to the other was "The human mind is precarious; the mind of the Way is subtle. Be discriminating and singleminded. Hold fast the Mean." The "mind of the Way" refers to what [in the *Mean*] "follows the nature." It is unmixed with the human, has no sound or smell, and is manifested with the utmost subtlety. It is the source of sincerity. The mind of man is mixed with the human and thus becomes prone to err. It has the potential for unnaturalness and insincerity. When one sees an infant about to fall into a well and feels a compassionate impulse [to rescue it], that is [an instance of] the Way guiding human nature. If that impulse becomes confused by thought of gaining the approbation of parents or a reputation in the community, that is the human mind. . . .
>
> To be single-minded is to be one with the mind of the Way; to be discriminating is to be concerned lest the mind of the Way should lose that oneness and possibly become divided with the human mind. Always to be centered on the Mean and to be unceasingly one with the mind of the Way is to "hold fast the Mean." If it is one with the mind of the Way, the mind will always be kept on center, and in its expressed state there will be no disharmony. Thus, following the mind of the Way, its expression in a parent-child relationship is always affectionate; as expressed in the ruler-minister relationship it is always right; expressed in the relationship of husband-wife, senior-junior, friend and friend, it is always respectful of gender differences, always respectful of precedence, always respectful of fidelity to friends. . . .
>
> Shun had Hsieh as minister of education see to instruction in these moral relationships and teach people the Universal Way.[36]

At that time people were all noble men and could all be entrusted with the responsibilities of noble rank. There was no instruction but this instruction, and no learning but this learning. With the passing of the sages, however, the learning of the mind-and-heart became obscured, human conduct unnaturally strove for fame and profit; those who pursued the learning of textual exegesis, memorization and recitation, and literary embellishments arose together in confusion and profusion. Fragmentation and divisiveness flourished apace. Month by month and year by year, one scholar copied from another, each confirming the other's mistakes. Thus day by day the human mind became more swollen with self-importance and could no longer perceive the subtlety of the mind of the Way. . . . How then is the learning of the mind to be clarified? . . . The learning of the sage seeks fully to employ the mind-and-heart so as to form one body with Heaven-and-earth and all things . . . for in this learning there is no distinction between self and other, internal or external; the mind is one with Heaven and earth and all things. The Ch'an learning however arises from self-interest and expediency, and cannot avoid division into internal and external. This then is the reason for the difference between the two. Today those who pursue the learning of the mind and nature while treating human relations as external to one, and leaving out things and affairs, are truly followers of Ch'an learning. Those who would never treat human relations as external or leave out things and affairs, but rather would concentrate on preserving the mind and make it their business to nourish the nature, certainly represent the learning of refinement and singleness in the Sages' school.[37]

In this memoir Wang sees the method of "refinement and singleness" as a means of preserving the mind of the Way, originally and essentially one with Heaven, Earth, and all things. As something already complete within the mind, it requires nothing external to it but only unmixed, unobstructed expression of its humane feelings—its natural empathy for all things. There is no place then for principles to be studied as if these were objects of investigation, no room for the nature, as Heaven's principle in man, to be learned or assimilated from outside. All one needs in the learning of the mind is single-minded concentration on the unity of the mind and principle, the oneness of man with Heaven and earth and all things.

Wang's new interpretation of the Learning of the Mind-and-Heart, based on his revision of the Tradition of the Way, immediately preceded his enunciation of the doctrine of innate knowing *(liang-chih)* and was followed by his important "Inquiry on the Great Learning" *(Ta-hsüeh wen)* in 1527. Among Wang's disciples, such as Ch'ien Te-hung, the editor of his *Literary Records (Wen-lu)*, the "Inquiry on the Great Learning" was seen as conveying the essence of Wang's mature teaching.[38] Wing-tsit Chan has called it "Wang Yang-ming's most important writing, for it embodies his basic teachings and represents his final conclusions."[39]

As the title implies the *Inquiry* deals with central questions in the text of the *Great Learning*, but also as Ch'ien Te-hung points out in a prefatory note, it presents the starting point and basic premises of Wang's teaching as drawn from both the *Mean* and the *Great Learning*.[40] In other words, even though Wang is contesting Chu Hsi's philosophical position, he is doing so on Chu's chosen ground—the same issues that Chu had brought forward in his prefaces and commentaries to these two key texts, and most particularly the question of the relation between man's mind and his nature. Chu had explained the *Great Learning*'s "manifesting of bright virtue" in terms of the original endowment of Heaven's nature (principle) in the mind, to be nourished and cultivated by methodical practice of intellectual inquiry, the refining of value distinctions, and the exercise of moral restraints—lest the human mind, being prone to err, should stray from correct principles as represented by the mind of the Way. Wang's alternative view was that "bright virtue," instead of being a mind of the Way at odds with the human mind, consisted essentially in the cardinal virtue of humaneness, as expressed in a feeling of oneness with Heaven and earth and all things. Cultivation of this virtue, then, should consist essentially of encouraging the free and full expression of that empathetic feeling, without the intervention of any ratiocination or calculation involving self/other or subject/object distinctions. In this Wang placed a prime value on the feeling of love for, or oneness with, all creation and on the natural integrity of the mind, as opposed to a mind divided against itself by the counterposing of the human mind to the mind of the Way (i.e., the nature).

The original pure mind Wang identified with the "highest good" of the *Great Learning*, regarding it not as a perfection beyond one, to be reached or achieved, but as an inherent perfection within, to be expressed or extended to others. He says:

As the highest good emanates and reveals itself, we will consider right as right and wrong as wrong. Things of greater or less importance and situations of grave or light character will be responded to as they act upon us. In all our changes and movements, we will stick to no particular point, but possess in ourselves the mean that is perfectly natural. This is the ultimate of the normal nature of man and the principle of things. There can be no consideration of adding or subtracting anything to or from it. Such a suggestion reveals selfish ideas and shallow cunning, and cannot be said to be the highest good. Naturally, how can anyone who does not watch over himself carefully when alone, and who lacks refined discrimination and singleness of mind, attain to such a state of perfection? Later generations fail to realize that the highest good is inherent in their own minds, but exercise their selfish ideas and cunning and grope for it outside their minds, believing that every event and every object has its own peculiar definite principle.[41]

In this passage we see how Wang incorporates into his doctrine of the mind the language of the Ch'eng-Chu method of the mind—the method of refined discrimination and singleness and holding fast to the Mean—and focuses it on the unity of principle rather than on the diversity of principles in events and things. Thereby he sets a higher priority on primary intuition, or undifferentiated sensibility, than on acquired learning or secondary rational and moral judgments. In the same way, Wang places a prime emphasis on the substantial unity of innate knowing, rather than on the different steps in the *Great Learning*'s method of self-cultivation. He says:

While the specification of tasks can be expressed in terms of a graded sequence of priorities, in substance they constitute a single unity and in reality there is no distinction of a graded sequence to be made; yet, while there is no such distinction to be made, in respect to function and its refinements [discrimination] *(wei-wei)*, these cannot be left wanting in the slightest degree. This is why the [*Great Learning's*] doctrine of investigation, extension, being sincere, and rectifying can be taken as a correct exposition of the transmission from Yao and Shun and evinces the mind of Confucius.[42]

Here, in his conclusion to the *Inquiry*, Wang makes a point of casting his basic argument concerning the method of the *Great Learning* in the language of the sixteen-word formula from Chu's preface to the *Mean*, and of identifying it as the true transmission of the mind of the sages. Moreover Ch'ien Te-hung, in his comment following Wang's *Inquiry*, stresses the same point when he says: "The teaching of the *Great Learning* had, after Mencius, found no worthy transmitter for more than a thousand years, but with this exposition in terms of innate knowing *(liang-chih)*, it was restored to full clarity of understanding as if one day had encompassed all of time past."[43] Ch'ien thus completed the thought implicit in Wang's finale—that Wang's doctrine of innate knowing represented the new dispensation of the tradition of the Way and succession to the mind of the sages.

Wang's *Inquiry*, written in 1527 shortly before Wang's death, was seen by Ch'ien as the final revelation of his teacher's essential teaching. It followed shortly after Wang's own proclaiming of Lu Hsiang-shan as the authentic heir to Mencius and the Succession to the Way *(tao-t'ung)* in 1520, and the republication of Lu's collected writings under the aegis of Wang in 1521. Moreover, it was only three years later that Lu, with this great boost from Wang, rose from relative neglect or deprecation to become installed in the official Confucian temple. One may conclude that it was through the influence of Wang's new teaching and personal charisma that Lu's elevation and canonization was accomplished.

If, however, this was enough to establish a clear association of Lu with Wang, and both of them with a new version of the learning of the mind, it was only the beginning of the controversial process that would lead, much later, to the binding together of "Lu-Wang" with the "school of the mind," as opposed to the "Ch'eng-Chu school of principle."

The Response to Wang Yang-ming

In the early sixteenth century, there were still impediments to the acceptance of such a simple dichotomy. Wang Yang-ming himself, though he opposed the idea of studying principle as something apart from the mind, obviously did not see mind and principle as themselves opposed; indeed, the whole point of his teaching was to underscore their essential unity. Further, among his followers, whether on the so-called right or left wings of his school, one finds no disposition to repudiate the learning of principle. Wang Chi,[44] often classed among the most liberal of Yang-ming's disciples and the bête noire of "orthodox" Neo-Confucians, when discussing the development of Neo-Confucian thought in the Ming, did not hesitate to claim for his master a leadership role in the school of principle: "In my humble opinion," he wrote, "the learning of principle *(li-hsüeh)* [in the Ming] had its inception in [Ch'en] Pai-sha, and reached its greatest brilliance in my former teacher [Wang Yang-ming].[45]

This statement was made in response to the assertion of his correspondent that the correct transmission of the learning of principle had two fountainheads in the Ming, one Hsüeh Hsüan (acknowledged leader of the Ch'eng-Chu school) and the other Wang Yang-ming, recognized here as having coined his own brand of *li-hsüeh*. Wang Chi, however, by identifying Ch'en Hsien-chang (Pai-sha), along with Yang-ming, as one of the two main sources of the learning of principle in the Ming, was staking out an even larger claim for the new thought as the authentic heir to both the sages' transmission and the mantle of *li-hsüeh*. According to Wang Chi:

Innate knowing is the spirituality of the mind, the principle *(tse)* of Heaven. One extends this knowing by extending this principle in the mind to the things and affairs one finds oneself in the midst of, so that each follows its own principle. What we call the "investigation of things" is the learning by which unity is achieved in the school of the sages. If you say that principle *(li)* lies in the world and one must investigate the principles for bringing peace to the world, or that principle lies in the state, family, person, or mind and one must investigate the principles whereby these are [respectively] governed, regulated, cultivated, or rectified, then unavoidably there is a division between the two and principle still lies outside the mind."[46]

From the foregoing it is clear that while Wang Chi thought of Yang-ming as opposed to the investigation of things and affairs as if their principles were external to the mind, he did not see the doctrine of innate knowing or learning of the mind as other than the true learning of principle.

In contrast to Wang Chi, Nieh Pao (1487–1563)[47] is often considered to represent the more conservative wing of the Wang Yang-ming school, sometimes also called the "quietist" wing in contrast to the freer, more dynamic interpretation of innate knowing found in Wang Chi and Wang Ken. One index of the relative conservatism or liberalism of the two wings is the degree of their adherence to the practice of quiet-sitting, which had become a standard discipline in the Ch'eng-Chu school and was closely associated with the learning of the mind as an orthodox method of self-examination and moral restraint. Nieh Pao's "quietists" continued this practice, while Wang Chi and Wang Ken tended, like Yang-ming himself in his later years, to deemphasize it as a needless formalism, favoring instead the extension of innate knowing to any and all human activities.

Against this background, one can appreciate the importance for Nieh Pao of the "method of the mind" and its sixteen-word formula, which Nieh understood as enjoining the strict practice of single-minded concentration, moral self-scrutiny, and watchfulness over one's conduct. Thus, like Chen Te-hsiu and other Neo-Confucians, he regarded the [apocryphal] passage concerning Yao in the *Book of History* as the ultimate source of the sages' teaching: "These are the words by which Yao, Shun, and Yü handed down the mandate from one to another. They are the source of the Learning of the Mind-and-Heart for all ages." From this it is clear that Nieh Pao held to the view of this learning as based on the "method of the mind' and "tradition of the Way" which Chu Hsi had featured in the preface of the *Mean*. He saw Wang Yang-ming's teaching as fulfilling, not abrogating, this method and this learning. Thus, in this first generation of Wang Yang-ming's followers, across the spectrum of interpretive opinion, there is evidence that the new teaching was seen as repudiating neither the learning of principle *(li-hsüeh)* nor the established learning of the mind.

Evidence for this from a somewhat different angle is found in the case of Chan Jo-shui (1466–1560).[48] Chan's teacher, Ch'en Hsien-chang, shared with Yang-ming's teacher, Lou Liang, an intellectual lineage going back to Wu Yü-pi and the Ch'eng-Chu school, but Ch'en has often been seen as one of the major independent Ming thinkers, along with Yang-ming, and Chan's own thought reflected this mixed inheritance. Moreover Chan was a highly influential teacher and promoter of education through the thriving academy movement in late fifteenth- to early sixteenth-century China, as well as a scholar-official prominently engaged at court.

Like most of the other Neo-Confucians of his age, Chan gave much thought to the mind and to the learning process defined by Chu Hsi in terms of "the investigation of things and extension of knowledge (knowing)." At the same time he shared with Ch'en Hsien-chang and Wang Yang-ming a concern for the freedom and natural spontaneity of the mind, lest it become too burdened by the acquisition of knowledge or conformity to norms seen as external to it. To reconcile these opposing claims, Chan sought to overcome the opposition between the internal and external through a process of learning and acting which brought the active realization of principle (in the sense of both knowing and acting), through the conjunction of principle in the mind and things, amid all one's life experiences and in all human affairs.

One of Chan's key phrases was "to experience the principle of Heaven in all situations *(sui ch'u t'i-jen t'ien-li)."* By this he meant to affirm the engagement with principle in things and affairs as well as in the mind, and the need for the mind to learn and realize principle in active contact with externals (including book-learning). To this extent he upheld the objectivity of principle, the need for study, and the value of standards and scholarship so important to the Chu Hsi tradition.

At the same time, to a greater extent even than other Ming Neo-Confucians, Chan repeated Mencius' phrase "neither to forget nor to abet (the natural workings of the Way)," meaning that one should neither "forget" principles or value distinctions (in the way Chuang Tzu would) nor, on the other hand, should one overstrain one's moral effort, overdo things, or strive to live up to external standards as if the Way were beyond one rather than within one. He said,

"Neither to forget nor to abet" is expressed in the one word "reverence." The substance of the mind does not consist in either forgetting or abetting. This is the most subtle and refined point in the Learning of the Mind-and-Heart, which does not allow of even the slightest forcing [of things].[49]

If in this respect Chan might be seen as taking up a position midway between Chu Hsi and Wang Yang-ming, in respect to the "learning of the mind-and-heart" Chan's interpretation both reflects the established formulation of this learning in the Ch'eng-Chu school and moves strongly in the direction of Wang Yang-ming's conception as expressed in the latter's "Inquiry on the Great Learning."

In the many discussions of the mind in his writings Chan refers to the learning of the mind-and-heart *(hsin-hsüeh)* and the message or method of the mind-and-heart *(hsin-fa)* in the terms of the Ch'eng-Chu school, especially as set forth in Chu's preface to the *Mean*. "The Learning of the Sages is the "Learning of the Mind-and-Heart,"[50] he said, and again "From Yao and Shun down to Confucius and Yen Hui [this learning] is all the Learning of the Mind-and-Heart."[51] "The Learning of the Emperors and Kings is the Learning of the Mind-and-Heart."[52] The Learning of the Sages is clearly identified with the message and method of the mind in several of Chan's essays.[53]

Perhaps the fullest explanation of what this means to Chan is found in his "Essay on the Message of the Mind as Transmitted in the Confucian School" (using here the language of Ch'eng I as found at the beginning of Chu Hsi's commentary on the *Mean*). The basic text for this message is the familiar one in which a distinction is made between the human mind and the mind of the Way. Yet Chan, like Wang Yang-ming, minimizes this distinction and prefers to concentrate on the unity of the mind-and-heart.

The essence of the mind is one with things and affairs. . . . Humanity is the vital principle of Heaven, the mind is the vital principle of human beings, the nature is the vital principle of the mind, and the Way is the vital principle of the nature. Heaven cannot but give life to human beings. Human beings cannot but have minds; this mind cannot but have a nature; the nature cannot but have the Way. Thus the Way and Heaven-and-earth function together (cooperate); the nature and Heaven-and-earth have the same substance; the mind and Heaven-and-earth have the same spirit; and human beings are filled with the same stuff as Heaven-and-earth. The mind then is the master of Heaven and humanity, and the gate to the nature and the Way. Therefore the mind cannot but be preserved. . . .

The method of the mind is for preserving the mind. Now the mind is self-possessed and self-preserved. It is not something conferred by a teacher on the student, nor is it something received by the student from a teacher. Indeed, what is there to be transmitted or received? It is not the mind, but the method of the mind that is to be transmitted.

Neither to exceed nor fall short—this is the *Mean's* method of the mind. For the mind to embrace all external things, and things and affairs to be central to the mind, represents the joining of the internal and external. This is the method. Thus when there is neither internal nor external, neither excess nor deficiency, neither forgetting nor abetting, then the mind is one. . . .

This is the essential purport of the *Mean*, a principle Tzu-ssu got from Confucius, Confucius got from Kings Wen and Wu and the Duke of Chou, they in turn got from T'ang the Completer, T'ang from Yü the Great, Yü from Shun and Shun from Yao. "Hold fast the Mean" is what Shun said. It is the method of centering the mind [holding it to the Mean]. In transmitting it to Yü he said "Be refined and single-minded," which means to be discriminating in respect to excess and deficiency, to be single-minded in reaching [the proper limit]. Not to exceed or fall short is how one reconverges and reaches oneness. It is the method of holding to the Mean. . . . Thus, the method handed down by the sages and worthies comes down to just this, just this.[54]

For Chan this was not only a teaching handed down from the sage-kings, but a teaching for the reigning monarch which he incorporated in lectures on the classics and memorials to the throne. His first lecture from the Classics Mat was on the subject of the Counsels of Yü the Great and the sixteen-word method of the mind.[55] In the learning of the Sages, he says in another lecture, nothing is so important as knowing the essential, which for the ancient emperors and kings consisted in holding to the Mean, as Yao conveyed it to Shun, and being refined and single-minded, as Shun conveyed it to Yü.[56] In another memorial Chan put it, "There is nothing greater in the Learning of the Sages than to seek humaneness. Humaneness lies in forming one body with men and things."[57] The same doctrine is asserted as a fundamental premise of his "Explanation of the Diagram of Mind and the Nature" *(Hsin-hsing t'u-shuo).*[58] This then is a theme which runs throughout Chan's writings, as of course it does in Wang Yang-ming's important "Inquiry on the Great Learning," with a principal emphasis on the unity of the mind, achieved through discrimination and single-mindedness, and with less attention paid to the perils which beset the human mind or the imperceptibility of the mind of the Way.

At the same time Chan insisted that his conception of "oneness" differed from Wang Yang-ming's:

> The Sage Learning is the learning of the mind-and-heart. What we refer to as "heart" does not one-sidedly point to the square inch within the breast in contradistinction to [objective] things and affairs. Without things and affairs there is no mind-and-heart. When Yao and Shun speak of "holding fast to the Mean," they do not simply refer to things and affairs but to the unity of the mind with things and affairs. "Holding fast" means joining things to the mind-and-heart and their becoming one.[59] [Moreover] when we speak of Heaven's principle, it is to personally experience it in the mind-and-heart. This then is the Learning of the Mind-and-Heart.[60]
>
> Wang Yang-ming's and my way of viewing the mind-and-heart differ. What I refer to as the mind-and-heart embodies the myriad things and affairs and leaves nothing out. When Yang-ming refers to the mind-and-heart it indicates what is within the human breast. Consequently it appears that what I am talking about is external. [But] it is wrong to take "experiencing principle in all life situations" as seeking it in externals. The mind-and-heart responds to things and affairs and only then is Heaven's principle perceived. But Heaven's principle is not external to one. It is only that when things and affairs appear, the mind is stimulated and responds accordingly. Thus when things and affairs arise, what experiences them is the mind-and-heart, and when the mind achieves the Mean and correctness [in its response], that is Heaven's principle.[61]

Thus it is fair to say that Chan, as compared to Wang, still sought the unity of principle through the experiencing of principle in all life situations, i.e., through a balanced pursuit of the diverse particulars in things and methods in the handling of affairs, while upholding objective standards and scholarly study as appropriate means of achieving this end. In other words, he kept more of a balance between the "unity of principle and its diverse particularizations" *(li-i fen-shu)*.

More could be said, of course, about the similarities and differences between Chan and Wang. For our purposes here, however, the important points are that their teachings emerged from the Learning of the Mind as passed down from Chu Hsi, that both clearly identified this learning with the message and method of the mind *(hsin-fa)*, and, in developing new teachings out of this earlier formulation of the learning of the sages, both felt the need to explain themselves in the terms used earlier by Chu Hsi in his discussion of the sixteen-word formula cited in his preface to the *Mean*.

It only need be added that Chan gave no credit for any of this Learning of the Mind to Lu Hsiang-shan, whom he thought as unrealistic in his view of the mind as the Chan Buddhists and Taoists.[62] It might also be significant, in view of the increasing dispute over the orthopraxy of "quiet-sitting," that Chan and the Kan-ch'üan school were identified as moral conservatives by their practice of reverence *(ching)* and the apprehension of Heaven's principle through quiet-sitting.[63]

From another quarter—those who defended the Ch'eng-Chu teaching against Wang Yang-ming's criticisms—comes renewed testimony that, Wang Yang-ming notwithstanding, orthodoxy still identified itself with the learning of the mind and was not content to yield this ground to Wang. Lo Ch'in-shun (1465–1547),[64] though not himself uncritical of Chu Hsi on some points,[65] in his scholarly correspondence with Wang, and in his *Knowledge Painfully Acquired (K'un-chih chi)* vigorously rejected Wang's concept of the mind and nature, and affirmed that Chu Hsi's views on these issues remained the authentic learning of the mind. In the latter work he said that Chu Hsi "in his last letter to Chang Shih (1133–80)[66] discussing the 'equilibrium and harmony' [of the *Mean*], set forth the subtleties of the Learning of the Mind so that nothing was left unrevealed. From this one can see the depth of his self-cultivation *(ch'i so tsao chih shen*, using the language of Mencius' passage on 'getting it oneself' *(tzu-te)]*."[67]

Further, in a letter to Huang Yün-ch'i, Lo clearly identified the learning of the mind with the Ch'eng-Chu method of the mind, while resisting Wang Yang-ming's inclination to place greater weight on the unity of principle than on its manifold particularizations:

The mind of the Way is the nature, and the nature is the substance of the Way. The human mind is the emotions, and the emotions are the functioning of the Way. The substance is one only; when it functions there are a myriad differentiations, but they are all just one Way. This principle is very clear, and the expression of it in words has not been subject to alteration. . . . The four words "precarious," "subtle," "refined," and "single-minded" are the original source of the Learning of the Mind-and-Heart. This is where I apply my own effort.[68]

Here Lo takes issue with the view he attributes to Wang Yang-ming that practice, because it takes differentiated form in Chu Hsi's sequential method of cultivation, is somehow less real than the substance of the mind (innate knowing) as the unity of the Way. Whereas Wang had put primary emphasis on unity and single-mindedness, Lo believes that the distinctions made by Chu Hsi in regard to the method of the mind and the eight-fold method of the *Great Learning* are the substantial basis for the learning of the mind as a method of concrete practice *(kung-fu)*.

Ch'en Chien and His "General Critique"

Even more influential than Lo's refutation of Wang Yang-ming was the critique advanced somewhat later by Ch'en Chien (1497–1567),[69] whose *General Critique of Obscurations to Learning (Hsüeh-pu t'ung-pien)* came to be viewed as perhaps the most vigorous and thorough-going defense of Ch'eng-Chu orthodoxy. It is particularly noteworthy for its sharp response to Wang Yang-ming's espousal of Lu Hsiang-shan. In the process of indicting Lu and Wang together as collaborators in a vast conspiracy to betray Confucianism, Ch'en repeatedly stigmatized them as "outward Confucians and covert Buddhists." So virulent was this attack, and so effective in associating Lu with Wang as cocon-spirators against orthodoxy, that Chen could be said to have played a large part in setting up the Lu-Wang combination as thinkers of the same ilk.

Once the lines had become drawn in this way, it would seem only natural, looking back at Wang Yang-ming's special pleading on behalf of Lu, that it should have invited counterattack along the same lines. But in Ch'en's rejoinder there was far more bite and passion than in Lo Ch'in-shun's earlier replies to Wang. The latter, though no less pointed in rejecting Wang's claims, were restrained by the norms of civility and politeness that governed epistolary exchange among peers; in Lo too they bespoke the poise and self-assurance of a scholar-official of no less high-standing than Wang Yang-ming. Ch'en's case and his stance, however, were different.

From a family of scholar-officials in Kwangtung, Ch'en Chien had passed the provincial examinations but never succeeded at the metropol- itan level. After serving in relatively minor educational posts, he retired early, in 1544, to a life of study, teaching, and writing. This gave him the leisure in which to complete the documentation of his case against the enshrinement of Lu Hsiang-shan in 1524. (Ch'en himself claimed to have devoted ten years to this task of documentation, and took extraordinary pains in identifying his sources.)[70] Ch'en was in fact a prodigious scholar, whose contributions to the study of Ming history would eventually gain him considerable recognition, though in his own dynasty, as in the succeeding Ch'ing, there were attempts at official suppression of Ch'en's works on account of his outspoken opinions on politically sensitive matters. Thus Ch'en, at some remove from the center of power, was already distanced from goings-on at court and disposed to be critical of those in high places who failed to uphold Confucian norms which he, as an educational official and serious scholar, felt responsible for.

It is obvious from the timing and contents of the work, as well as from Ch'en's stated intentions, that it was originally provoked by the official canonization of Lu Hsiang-shan, as well as by Wang Yang- ming's writings concerning Chu Hsi's views in relation to Lu—espe- cially the claim that Chu, though differing with Lu earlier, had largely come to agreement with him later in life.

In those circumstances Lu himself, even more than Wang Yang- ming, became the prime focus of Ch'en's critique. Indeed, given the widespread popularity and official favor enjoyed by the Wang Yang- ming school at this time, it is understandable how Ch'en would feel— not only that he was resisting a surging tide, but also that a trend of such magnitude—for him so threatening to education—could only have come about in consequence of a much longer, and more deep-seated, process of subversion, reaching all the way back to the introduction of Buddhism.

If Ch'en's work thus took on a beleaguered and somewhat paranoid tone, Ch'en's scholarly capabilities were nevertheless up to the task of documenting a highly plausible case for his views. That case was structured in four parts along the following main lines:

1. Chu Hsi, instead of coming closer to the views of Lu Hsiang-shan late in life, had increasingly felt the need to take issue with Lu and to define their differences with greater precision.

2. The writings of Lu Hsiang-shan and his principal follower Yang Chien show unmistakable influences of Ch'an Buddhism. Disavowals of this by Lu only show his deviousness in outwardly professing to be a Confucian while inwardly sympathizing with Chan.

3. The views of Lu and other ostensible Confucians (especially Wu Ch'eng, Ch'en Hsien-chang, and Ch'eng Min-cheng) as shown in their writings, betray a basic affinity with doctrines of Buddhism (particularly Ch'an), as revealed in their own texts. The process of infiltration began when Chinese writers used Chinese terms to express (and thereby disguise) Buddhist ideas in ambiguous language, thus giving this foreign religion entree to Chinese minds.

4. The correct Ch'eng-Chu doctrines were often misinterpreted, and there is a need for clarification of them. There are also points on which Ch'eng-Chu schoolmen in the Ming, like Hu Chü-jen and Lo Ch'in-shun, though valiantly defending orthodoxy against Ch'an Buddhism, failed to grasp all the issues and adequately meet the challenge of heterodoxy among Neo-Confucians.

Our purpose being more limited than Ch'en Chien's we may extract from his presentation those points most consequential for the learning of the mind-and-heart. The first of these appears at the very outset of his personal preface, where Ch'en's opening lines state: "There is nothing under Heaven greater than scholarship, and no greater calamity for scholarship than obscuration [of the truth].[71] The failure to make clear distinctions leads to confusion of issues and to the blurring of Chu Hsi's teachings vis-à-vis those of Lu Hsiang-shan. Here a basic difference between the two which must be recognized is that Lu's self-cultivation aimed at a "nourishing of the spirit," emphasizing an emptiness and quiescence which derived from Taoism and Buddhism, whereas Chu Hsi aimed at scholarly study and discursive analysis, emphasizing concrete facts, things, and affairs. In contrast to Lu's "nourishing of the spirit," according to Ch'en, stands the true Confucian aim of "nourishing principle." He quotes Hu Chü-jen: "Confucians nourish the Way and principles; the Buddhists and Taoists nourish the spirit."[72]

In the end we shall see that Ch'en's counterposing of scholarship to spirituality will prove to be a crucial issue in the developing conflict over the "learning of the mind." Here, however, we should be careful to note that this does not mean, on Ch'en's part, that he is prepared to concede to Lu exclusive rights in the sphere of religious and moral cultivation, and content himself simply with the intellectual superiority of orthodox scholarship. Far from it. He insists rather that the cultivation of a reverent seriousness is, in Chu Hsi, a prerequisite to such scholarship, along with the nourishment of principle inherent in the mind.[73] In fact, to Ch'en, Chu's method represents the true cultivation of the mind as opposed to a cultivation of spirit which does not recognize the constancy of principle in the mind. As a corollary to this, in his critique of Lu in the second part of the work (hou-pien), he goes to great lengths to establish that the terms in which Lu's "cultivation of the spirit" are couched came from Taoist and Buddhist sources, while they are not found in the Confucian classics. In other words he challenges Lu, not on the ground that there was no "learning of the mind" in Confucius and Mencius, but rather that there was in them no "cultivation of the spirit" as Lu advocated it.[74]

In his exposé of Lu Hsiang-shan's errors and "obscurations," Ch'en makes a particular point that Lu employed the language of Confucian scholarship, as if to invoke its authority, while using this subtly to undercut book-learning. Citing the classics, Lu in effect argued the case for dispensing with the classics, and indeed for dispensing with any essential dependence on the written word. This, of course, in Ch'en's eyes, was only a thinly disguised version of Ch'an Buddhism's "non-dependence on words and phrases" (pu-li wen-tzu).[75] Moreover he sees a clear affinity between Lu's view and that of Ch'en Hsien-chang in the Ming, who likewise emphasized the practice of quiet-sitting at the expense of the scholarly study of books, and who claimed to have had some experience of "enlightenment" after having set aside book-learning and engaged in a prolonged period of intensive contemplation.[76]

Elsewhere in his Critique, Ch'en devotes considerable attention to the clarification of "quiescence" and "quiet-sitting" in Confucian cultivation. His position is essentially that while these attitudes and practices were admittedly accepted by early Sung masters, it was on the strict condition that they be used for the nourishment of principle and curbing of selfish desires, and not for a mindless, anesthetic quiescence. This strict qualification was canonized in Ch'eng I's assertion of the priority of reverent seriousness *(ching)* over quiescence *(ching)*. Only reverent seriousness, as a constant habit of mind, was compatible with the active social concerns of the Confucians; prolonged practice of quiet-sitting, involving disengagement from human needs and affairs, created a false dichotomy between action and quiescence, whereas Ch'eng I's reverent seriousness, as a constant attitude of mind, could bridge the two.[77]

In the course of this argument Ch'en opposes as unbalanced and one-sided what he calls a "preoccupation with, or leaning toward, quiescence" *(p'ien-ching)*, which leads in the direction of Ch'an Buddhism.[78] Here again, though he has been at some pains to discredit other terms and practices borrowed from Buddhism and Taoism, in this case Ch'en cannot go so far as to disallow quiet-sitting altogether, since it had undoubted sanction in Ch'eng-Chu practice *(kung-fu)*; yet he feels compelled to reaffirm Chu Hsi's reservations on this score. For others later this was to become the opening wedge in a move to disown quiet-sitting altogether, while for still others it remained, with Ch'en's qualifications, an acceptable practice within Ch'eng-Chu orthodoxy.

A final point worthy of notice in Ch'en's argument is his refutation of yet another view of mind closely parallel to the dichotomy of spirit/principle. This is the identification of the mind with consciousness *(shih)*, again at the expense of principle. According to Ch'en, Chu Hsi had identified the "empty, spiritual consciousness" with the "human mind," and "principle" *(li)* or man's nature *(hsing)* with the mind of the Way. Chu had insisted that the distinction between consciousness and what in Western terms approximates "conscience" should not become blurred, as it was essential for self-cultivation that principle ("conscience") should guide consciousness, and especially that it should prevail over the senses and selfish desires.[79]

This distinction had been a main issue in Chu Hsi's earlier dialogues and correspondence with Chang Shih (1133–80), who had tended, following Hsieh Liang-tso (1059–1120 or 1121), to equate consciousness with humaneness *(jen)*, i.e., with man's nature.[80] For Chu Hsi this amounted to identifying the nature more with sentience, sentiment, or emotion, i.e., equating humaneness with love, and not recognizing the indispensability of the norms that should guide the expression of these emotions, if they were to be cultivated and developed into the fullness of virtue. "It is all right to say that the mind of the humane man is conscious, but not that consciousness is humaneness."[81] Chu (and Ch'en) saw this as akin to the error of equating Buddhist compassion with Confucian humaneness; the former, to him, was no more than a vague and lofty sentiment, incapable (because devoid of the necessary value judgments) of being translated into effective or appropriate action.[82]

Further, Ch'en saw this same weakness in the teachings of Ch'en Hsien-chang, and especially in Wang Yang-ming's identification of mind (consciousness, sentience) with the nature (humaneness). Ch'en likened this to the teachings of the Sixth Patriarch of Ch'an, Hui-neng, who, in his *Platform Sutra*, collapsed the distinction between wisdom (enlightenment) and meditative practice, substance and function.[83] Further, Ch'en extended the comparison, saying that just as Ch'an Buddhism had no regard for scripture, Wang Yang-ming too tended to minimize book-learning and the importance of the Four Books, which had been so central to Chu Hsi.[84]

To say that Wang had no use for the classics, as did Ch'en, was no doubt going too far. Nor need one understand Wang's teaching as basically anti-intellectual or prejudicial to all scholarly learning (since many of his followers were themselves outstanding scholars, and even great bibliophiles!).[85] Nevertheless it is true that Wang regarded book-learning as not essential to the attainment of sagehood, and deplored the increasing preoccupation of Confucians with bookish pursuits. Thus there is a genuine difference in emphasis between Chu and Wang on this point, and one can appreciate how Ch'en Chien, who had said "Nothing in the world is greater than scholarship," would feel that Wang's teaching was a threat to his most cherished value.

Having exposed these "obscurations" and refuted the views of Lu Hsiang-shan, the Buddhists, and Wang Yang-ming, in conclusion Ch'en puts forward a positive alternative to them, i.e., a correct view of the mind-and-heart. This he identifies from the outset with Chu Hsi's distinction between the human mind and mind of the Way. In tabular form he defines and analyzes the two on several levels:

THE MIND

Humaneness, Rightness, Rites, and Wisdom (jen-i-li-chih)	Empty, spiritual consciousness
The moral nature *(te-hsing)*	Spirituality *(ching-shen)*
Moral principles *(i-li)*	Psycho-physical endowment *(ch'i-pin)*
The Mind of the Way *(tao-hsin)*	The human mind *(jen-hsin)*

In the Counsels of Yü it says: "The human mind is precarious; the mind of the Way is subtle."
Master Chang [Tsai] says: "Combining the nature and consciousness, there is what we call the mind."
In my own humble opinion: The nature is the mind of the Way.
The consciousness is the human mind. As an explanation of the mind, the above is right on target.

Further on, Ch'en quotes Chu Hsi:

What we Confucians cultivate is humaneness, rightness, rites, and wisdom. What Chan Buddhists cultivate is simply consciouness. They only recognize the human mind, not the Mind of the Way.[86]

The key to the distinction between Confucianism and Buddhism is just this. As I have already explained, the Learning of the Sages and Worthies is the Learning of the Mind-and-Heart. The Ch'an learning and Lu's learning also call themselves the "learning of the mind"; what they do not realize is that, although it is the same term "mind," there is a difference in what is meant by "mind." With the tabular presentation of the mind above, one can distinguish quite clearly the similarities and differences. Thus Confucius and Mencius both speak of mind in terms of humaneness and rightness. The Ch'an Buddhists speak of mind in terms of consciousness.[87]

So stating his basic position, Ch'en leaves no room for doubt about his main purpose: it is to set forth the correct view of the Learning of the Mind, and not to disassociate himself from it. The correct "Learning of the Mind," as he understands it, is as it was formulated by his predecessors in the Ch'eng-Chu school, based on the distinction between the human mind and the mind of the Way, using the terms Chu Hsi had identified with the "Tradition of the Way" (tao-t'ung)[88] and the language of Ch'eng I in speaking of it as the Method of the Mind (hsin-fa). Significantly, Ch'en also says that it is the true "learning for the sake of oneself."[89] And speaking of the basic texts which convey the correct message to followers of the Way, he quotes Hsüeh Hsüan:

The Collected Commentaries on the Four Books represent the distillation of Chu Hsi's study of all the learned commentaries, as well as his own analysis and evaluations in terms of moral principle. They are truly broad, great, fine, and subtle. One should read them carefully and reflectively, immerse oneself in them, experience them deeply and practice them energetically, so as to get something for oneself.[90]

Wang Yang-ming's Learning of the Mind is of another sort entirely. According to Ch'en, it is akin to the earlier views of Lu Hsiang-shan, who in the Sung had provided the major opening for Ch'an Buddhism's infiltration of Confucianism. The danger of such a subversion of Confucianism had existed ever since Buddhism was translated into Chinese terms. This is especially true of its sinicized Ch'an form, wherein the ambiguities of the language lent themselves to "obscuration" and verbal seduction. But in his own time Chu Hsi had stood forth heroically to refute the errors of Lu's ways, and now it is imperative for someone to make a similarly heroic stand against the insidious ideas of Wang Yang-ming. Yet precisely because Ch'en perceives the danger as one of an ever-present threat from Buddhism, he thinks of this not in terms of a tradition or school handed down from Lu to Wang (nowhere in his work, to my knowledge, does the expression "Lu-Wang School" appear), but rather in terms of how certain individuals, susceptible to the virulent contagion from Buddhism, have lent their talents to the great deception, the masking of this view of the mind behind the language of Confucianism, as did Ch'en Hsien-chang and Wang Yang-ming.[91]

About a century later Ku Yen-wu, in his Record of Daily Knowledge (Jih chih lu), commenting on Wang Yang-ming's thesis that Chu Hsi, late in life, had come to a position close to Lu Hsiang-shan, spoke highly of the efforts of Lo Ch'in-shun and Ch'en Chien in refuting

Wang's claim. He said Lo's *Knowledge Painfully Acquired (K'un-chih chi)* and Ch'en's *General Critique of Obscurations to Learning (Hsüeh-pu t'ung-pien)*, stood like "immovable rocks of integrity in the face of the on-rushing current of the day."[92] It was the overpowering influence of Wang Yang-ming's teaching in the late Ming to which Ku referred, and against which such a reaction eventually set in that Ku himself was prepared, as we shall see later, to disown the Learning of the Mind altogether and quarantine it as wholly un-Confucian. Yet in the time of Lo and Ch'en this divide had not yet been reached. As "immovable rocks" they still stood their ground on behalf of the correct Ch'eng-Chu learning of the mind. Yet, especially in Ch'en's *Critique*, the refutation of Wang had taken a direction that would significantly shape the later debate. Henceforward Wang's views would become inextricably tied to those of Lu Hsiang-shan, and it would be difficult to see the two except as inseparable ideological bedfellows or as fellow travelers of Ch'an Buddhism. Further, in that drawing of the line around Lu, Wang, and Chan, Ch'en Chien's stigmatizing of them as purveyors of a seductive spirituality, undermining the intellectual and moral foundations of Confucian scholarship, would contribute to a growing view that there could be no middle ground between Lu-Wang anti-intellectualism and Confucian classical learning. The debate was being shaped in such a way that sound scholarship alone could be seen as providing an adequate defense of Confucian principle. As Ch'en had said at the outset, "There is nothing greater under Heaven than scholarship . . ."

T'ang Po-yüan's Rejection of the New Learning

A contrasting response to the same issue came from T'ang Po-yüan (c.s. 1574),[93] another critic of the new Learning of the Mind, who rose to challenge the enshrinement of Wang Yang-ming in the Confucian temple, just as Ch'en had opposed such honors being done to Lu Hsiang-shan.

In 1584 it had been proposed that Wang be honored in the Confucian temple along with two other Ming scholars, Ch'en Hsien-chang and Hu Chü-jen. The following year T'ang, then an acting bureau director in the Board of Revenue in Nanking submitted a memorial protesting this. In the *Veritable Records* for the Ming Wan-li period, it is recorded that T'ang attacked Wang Yang-ming, opposed his enshrinement, and said,

" 'There is no talk of the Learning of the Mind in the Six Classics, and there was no teaching concerning the Learning of the Mind in the school of Confucius. The heterodox teachings of [Wang] Shou-jen mislead the people.' At the same time he recommended The Ancient Text of the *Great Learning* As Inscribed on Stone [for official use in the examinations]." The account concludes by saying that the Emperor denied both requests and punished T'ang by demotion to a post in the provinces.[94]

The fact that Wang's enshrinement was carried out, while critics like T'ang and Ch'en Chien found themselves unable to mount effective opposition may help to explain both the paranoid tone of Chu Hsi's defenders in those days, and why, after the fall of the Ming, there should have been such an intense reaction to the dominant role of the Wang Yang-ming school in the late Ming, which was held responsible for the dynasty's decline and fall.

In the early Ch'ing period both Huang Tsung-hsi, in his *Case Studies of Ming Confucians (Ming-ju hsüeh-an)*, and Ku Yen-wu, in his *Record of Daily Knowledge (Jih chih lu)*, took note of this event and recorded the views of T'ang Po-yüan. Ku quotes a letter of T'ang's as saying:

> Since the new learning arose and has been proclaimed by noted scholars, not a few people have accepted it blindly. Yet what it calls "learning" is nothing but the Learning of the Mind. I have heard that in the past there was "Learning of the Way" *(Tao-hsüeh)*, but I have never heard of "Learning of the Mind." I have heard of [Confucius'] "love of learning" but never of the "love of the mind." The two-word expression "mind learning" is not spoken of in the Six Classics or by Confucius and Mencius.
>
> Those who speak of this learning today say that the mind is the Way, but to me this is inexplicable. Why? The reason lies in [a proper understanding of] the meaning of "precarious" and "subtle".[95]

This passage quoted by Ku is not found in the extant writings of T'ang,[96] but from other letters, from excerpts included in Huang's *Case Studies*, and from a manuscript copy of T'ang's original memorial preserved in the Academia Sinica, Taiwan,[97] we get a fairly clear picture of T'ang views. Concerning this key passage quoted by Chu Hsi from the apocryphal text in the *Book of Documents,* and cited by T'ang above, he says further:

"The human mind is precarious" refers to the mind. When it says that it is subtle [and difficult to perceive], how could there be no evil? Therefore it is said that if you control it, it may be preserved, and if you let it go, it is lost.[98]

Elsewhere T'ang says concerning the same point:

The nature is like the formless [the metaphysical], which is good but subtle [and difficult to perceive]. The mind lies in the realm of form [the psycho-physical]; how could it be regarded as altogether good? The nature is lodged in the mind, but the mind cannot fully exhaust the nature. The nature attains Heaven, but cannot comprise Heaven in its entirety. It is only the sage who succeeds in fully joining Heaven and man, and in unifying the mind and nature.[99]

Here and in the passage quoted by Ku Yen-wu, T'ang refers to the prevalent view in the liberal wing of the Wang Yang-ming school that the "mind is the way" and that, as such, the substance of the mind is a transcendental perfection beyond good and evil. In opposition to this T'ang emphasizes Chu Hsi's distinction between the human mind and the mind of the Way, as well as the difficulty of man's holding to the mind of the Way (i.e., the normative nature). Where Wang Yang-ming had stressed the reality of sagehood in every man, T'ang emphasizes the active effort and self-control needed to realize the perfection of sagehood. Where Wang had taught the unity of the nature and the mind, of Heaven and man, T'ang insists on recognizing the difficulty of achieving this identity, which is something attained fully, and only rarely, by the sage.

Here, and in refuting Wang's view of the mind by invoking Chu Hsi's dichotomy of the human mind and mind of the Way, T'ang cites the very phrases from the apocryphal text of the *Book of Documents* which had earlier been identified with the Method of the Mind *(hsin-fa)* as the essence of the orthodox Learning of the Mind. T'ang himself had come out of the school of Chan Jo-shui (1466–1560)[100] who, though he differed with both Chu Hsi and Wang Yang-ming on certain points, referred to the Learning of the Mind as a valid concept, congruent with the learning of principle in Neo-Confucian discourse.[101] T'ang could hardly have been unaware of this. Consequently when he says "I have not heard of the Learning of the Mind," "I have not heard" should probably be taken to mean simply that this term as such did not appear in the classics.

Among T'ang's scholarly correspondents was Ku Hsien-ch'eng who had written a preface to Ch'en Chien's *General Critique,* endorsing its defense of Chu Hsi but at the same time defending some of Wang Yang-ming's views concerning the nature and practice of the Learning of the Mind.[102] T'ang took issue with this in a letter to Ku:

> Learning is nothing but self-cultivation. Nevertheless [you may argue] the mind dwells in the midst of the nature and the self (person), so why shouldn't it be studied? The answer is that one can follow and conform to the nature, but one cannot conform to the mind. Insofar as the mind is attached to the self, the self can be reflected upon, but the mind cannot return upon itself. . . . The Learning of the Mind takes the mind itself as what is to be learned. To take the mind as what is to be learned is to take the mind as the nature. The mind can contain the nature, but it cannot make the mind its nature.
>
> For this reason if one seeks the lost mind [of Mencius 6A:11] it is all right, but if one seeks the mind itself, it is wrong. If seeking the mind is wrong, however, it is not wrong to seek within the mind. What I fault in the Learning of the Mind is its seeking the mind itself. If one knows the difference between seeking the mind, seeking within the mind, and seeking the lost mind—then one understands the Learning of the Mind.
>
> When the School of the Mind takes the mind as what is to be learned, it is expressed as: "To learn is to learn this mind, and to seek is to seek this mind."[103] But if the substance of the mind is something that must be sought after, it can only be something different from myself, and if the mind is to be learned, then don't [Mencius'] controlling the mind through rites and preserving the mind through humaneness [4B:28] actually become impediments to the mind?
>
> This error originated with Lu [Hsiang-shan]'s mistaken interpre-

tation of [Mencius'] "Humaneness is the human mind-and-heart' [6A:11], and Lu's mistake derives from the Buddhists' erroneous conception of the original mind.[104]

Here T'ang sees Wang Yang-ming's errors as first having appeared in Lu Hsiang-shan, and, in Lu, as having been derived from misconceptions of the Buddhists. As we have seen, this tendency to associate Wang with Lu and Buddhism was already found in Ch'en Chien. Yet for T'ang, as for Ch'en, this does not represent a continuous line of transmission down to Wang; rather both he and Ch'en view these as individual lapses into heterodoxy, attributable to the bewitching power of Buddhism.

From T'ang's point of view, the true teaching, as expounded by Chu Hsi, was carried on in succession from the Sung masters by such Ming scholars as Hsüeh Hsüan, Hu Chü-jen, and Lo Ch'in-shun, who each contributed to the clarification of the Way.[105] Even Ch'en Hsien-chang, sometimes seen as a forerunner of Wang Yang-ming, did not, according to T'ang, depart from essential orthodoxy;[106] instead he represented a separate transmission of the Way through Chou Tun-i (as distinct from the Ch'eng brothers). It was only, says T'ang, when the "new teaching" (hsin-hsüeh) appeared with Wang that the true Way was thrown into utter confusion.

At several points in his discussion of the matter T'ang refers to the "learning of the mind" (hsin-hsüeh) as "the new learning" (hsin-hsüeh).[107] The account in the Veritable Records, we recall, also quotes T'ang as referring to Wang's doctrines as "new," and Huang Tsung-hsi's version of T'ang's protest against Wang's enshrinement, as found in his Case Studies of Ming Confucians, also emphasizes that, in T'ang's view, Wang's doctrine of innate knowing was a novel creation of his.[108] Ku Yen-wu's citation of T'ang has him speaking in the same vein of this "new learning,"[109] and Ku himself so refers to it when discussing "Chu Hsi's Definitive Views in Later Life."[110] Later the Ming History (Ming shih), though possibly not uninfluenced by Huang Tsung-hsi's views, has the Veritable Records as support for its description of T'ang as attacking Wang's "new interpretations."[111]

From this we may conclude that while T'ang clearly called into question Wang Yang-ming's fidelity to the original Confucian teaching, saw it as having no basis in the classics, and recognized it as having an affinity to similar heterodox ideas in Lu Hsiang-shan and Buddhism, he did not go so far as to identify this connection in terms of any succession to or continuity of a Lu school reaching down to Wang Yang-ming, but instead recognized the singular responsibility of the latter for bringing forth this novel doctrine, which so confounded the orthodox tradition in his day, and, because of its sudden rise to such enormous popularity and influence, created a threat to orthodoxy of unprecedented proportions.

As a postscript to this new development, we may note the manner in which Huang Tsung-hsi, having presented T'ang's views, sought to discredit them by pointing to the considerable discussion of the mind and learning in Confucius and Mencius, which for him constituted a "learning of the mind" in fact if not in name.[112] Huang was hardly impartial in the matter of Wang Yang-ming, and seemed to be looking for any stick with which to beat down T'ang's criticism of Wang. Noting the latter's insistence that there is evil, or the danger of evil mixed with good, in the human mind (as indeed Chu Hsi's characterization of the human mind/mind of the Way implied), Huang immediately links this to the classic issue between Mencius and Hsün Tzu, suggesting that T'ang has in effect adopted the view of human nature as evil, without openly acknowledging it, and has abandoned Mencius' view of the mind-and-heart which identified the goodness of human nature with the promptings of the Four Beginnings—the sense of empathy and commiseration, right and wrong, etc. In saying that there cannot but be evil tendencies in the human mind-and-heart, T'ang, in Huang's view, "was advocating the doctrine of the evil nature of man, and if he sees human nature as evil, it is hardly any surprise that he would speak ill of the Learning of the Mind-and-Heart."[113]

Notwithstanding his defense of Wang's Learning of the Mind, for Huang the matter had become so controverted, and the issues so confused, that Huang himself was unwilling to stand by the Learning of the Mind" as a basic category of classification in compiling his *Case Studies of Ming Confucians*. In his Explanatory Note he acclaims the achievements of Ming scholars in the "learning of principle" and includes under this broad heading many thinkers who, in subsequent accounts, might be identified with the School of the Mind.[114] Thus Huang's survey, rather than being drawn along lines of rival traditions representing the learning of principle and the learning of mind, presented Ming Confucian thought in terms of individual schools, each reflecting the distinctive personal or local characteristics of the leading teachers and their disciples.

Significant references to Wang Yang-ming's Learning of the Mind-and-Heart are found in the writings of two contemporaries of T'ang Po-yüan which help us to place the new teaching in relation to the earlier *hsin-hsüeh*. One of these is Teng Yüan-hsi (1529–1593),[115] a Kiangsi scholar who had studied under a leading disciple of Wang Yang-ming, namely, Tsou Shou-i (1491–1562).[116] Tsou had been a prominent figure in the more conservative wing of the Wang school that flourished in the Kiangsi area, a group which may be said to have emphasized intellectual and moral discipline as an essential corollary of Wang's "innate knowing," even while its individual members exhibited considerable diversity among themselves.

These characteristics are reflected in the work of Teng himself. Though generally identified with the Wang Yang-ming school, he became known primarily for his scholarly integrity and independent views as a historian. Among several important historical writings of his the most significant is probably the *Huang-Ming shu* ("History of the August Ming"), a kind of biographical history of the Ming period up until Teng's time, yet in a format original with him (i.e., departing from the categories of the usual dynastic history). Among the headings adopted by Teng were ones identifying scholars with the Learning of Principle and the Learning of Mind. Since this may well be the first instance of a historian's use of such labels, what Teng meant by them is worth our considering.

In a succession of types from emperors and empresses through eunuchs, ministers of state, and generals, Teng has three chapters *(chüan)* devoted to the "Learning of Principle" (ch. 35–37) and three more devoted to the "Learning of Mind" (ch. 42–44). One notes, however, that in the four intervening chapters are found such headings as "literature," "exemplary character," and "filial conduct," so that the "learning of principle" and "learning of mind" are not directly juxtaposed. Nor in the contents of the respective sections do we find a strict separation of philosophical tendencies. In the first grouping are such scholars as Hsüeh Hsüan, Wu Yü-pi, Hu Chü-jen, Ts'ao Tuan, and Lo Ch'in-shun, often enough regarded as in the Ch'eng-Chu line, but with them is the more controversial Ch'en Hsien-chang, frequently thought less "orthodox." In this respect, Teng's line-up is not too different from the succession to the Way according to T'ang Po-yüan (who likewise had accepted Ch'en as within the pale of orthodox learning) and Teng treats them as individual thinkers worthy of respect, not as misguided adherents of a sterile orthodoxy.[117]

True, in his introduction to the Learning of Principle, Teng as historian recounts the significant role of Ch'eng-Chu scholars at the founding of the Ming. Followers of Chu Hsi had indeed served as advisers of Ming T'ai-tsu, and this had resulted in the official recognition of Chu's works and teachings. Moreover in the Yung-lo reign this had been confirmed by the compiling of the Great Compendia on the Four Books, Five Classics, and Human Nature and Principle, as the standard for all to follow. Yet along with these essential historical facts, Teng points to the equally basic fact that this doctrine included a learning of the mind-and-heart directed mainly at the self-cultivation of the ruler.[118]

In the section on the Learning of the Mind itself, Teng accords one full chapter out of three to Wang Yang-ming, an honor done to no other single figure among Ming scholars. Clearly he sees Wang as making a major, original contribution which justifies treating this as a new and distinctive phase in Ming Confucian thought, centering on the teaching of innate knowing. The new learning of the mind, however, has for Teng strong links to the past. It is an extension and fuller exposition of the Learning of the Mind that has come down from the sages, especially in the form of the sixteen-word formula concerning the human mind and mind of the Way. The perilous condition of the human mind, its proneness to error, and the need for constant vigilance through self-scrutiny, are still much emphasized. Only for the sage, as for Confucius at seventy, does self-control come with natural ease and perfect freedom. For all others persistent moral effort is needed to assure that one's intentions are sincere. Without it there is a great danger of falling into the delusory freedom of Ch'an, which recognizes no moral imperatives and subordinates the moral nature to an indeterminate Buddha nature.[119]

Further, if making one's intention sincere is the heart of the method of the Great Learning, the starting point of the learning of the Mind, as allied to Mencius' "seeking the lost mind," "cleansing the mind," and "polishing the mirror of the mind," is still the point underscored by Chu Hsi himself—the "investigation of things" and the "extension of knowledge." No doubt Teng understood these in a sense congenial to Wang Yang-ming's interpretation of innate knowing, but was mindful also of the need for study and the acquisition of factual learning along with moral knowledge. As a scholar and the conserver of voluminous historical records, Teng could not be unmindful of the importance of book-learning.[120]

This point comes all the more into focus in Teng's treatment of Wang's successors. Instead of dilating simply on the liberating effect of Wang's teaching on so many of Teng's contemporaries and declaring them ready-made sages, he likens the outcome to that among the many disciples of Confucius, who varied greatly in their comprehension of and fidelity to his teaching. Moreover, if this were so of those who had the benefit of Confucius' personal instruction, how much more would it apply to Wang's followers.[121]

Part of the difficulty in Wang's case arose from the fact that his essential teaching was at once so simple and so subtle.

The Master has been concerned lest the world take cognitive learning as [true] action, so he put forward the doctrine of innate knowing as the secret of the sages, at once knowing and acting, at once broad learning and ritual restraint, so that all under Heaven would know that sagehood can be learned and thereby proceed, without let or hindrance, to rediscover their original minds.[122]

Unfortunately the heart of this message, which words could not fully express and could only be realized in silence at a given moment of timely action, had become largely divorced from the study of the classics, and with the neglect of book learning had come the attenuation and distortion of its true meaning. In consequence there arose such misleading interpretations as the notion of Wang Chi (1498–1583) that a kind of sudden, transcendant enlightenment was available to those of higher comprehension who had direct access to sagehood, in contrast to the slow, plodding method of moral effort appropriate for those on a lower level of attainment—a teaching which, according to Teng, was bound to undermine both scholarship and public morality.[123]

In keeping with this view of Teng's, his treatment of the later followers of the Learning of the Mind features Wang's more orthodox disciples Tsou Shou-i, Ou-yang Te (1496–1554), Nieh Pao (1487–1563), and Lo Hung-hsien (1504–64), while Wang Ken (1483–1541) is one of the few on the left wing of the school admitted to this company.[124]

From this we may see that Teng shared many of the views and

apprehensions of T'ang Po-yüan concerning the new Learning of the Mind, while still insisting that anti-intellectualism and libertarian conduct were neither necessary consequences nor were they based on correct interpretations of Wang's teaching. Further we may note from Teng's account of the historical development of Ming thought that he recognizes Wang's teaching as a new departure from the old Learning of Principle, and makes no attempt to portray it as a lineal descendant from Lu Hsiang-shan: There is no mention of a Lu school connecting up with Wang; instead, while Teng acknowledged Mencius as the ultimate source of Wang's inspiration, the proximate source of his Learning of the Mind is Chu Hsi's formula for the supposed sixteen-word transmission of the sages concerning the human mind and the mind of the Way.

Another conclusion we may draw from this is that the conservative wing of Wang's school itself manifests deep anxiety over anti-intellectual tendencies growing out of too liberal or radical an interpretation of this new Learning of the Mind. It is not only the Ch'eng-Chu scholar Ch'en Chien who sees this as a threat to Confucian scholarship, but also a serious scholar of the Wang Yang-ming school like Teng himself.

Confirmation of these points is found in later comments on Teng's work by another scholar of the same general lineage and intellectual tendency, Ch'en Lung-cheng (1585–1645).[125] Ch'en had been a student of the Tung-lin leader Kao P'an-lung (1562–1626), was passionately committed to political and social reform, and as such was an admirer of Wang Yang-ming for his heroic leadership qualities. Like his colleague Liu Tsung-chou (1578–1645), he eventually starved himself to death rather than acquiesce in the Manchu conquest. Ch'en's collected writings contain the following note on Teng's classification of Ming schools as it bears on prevalent distortions of Wang Yang-ming's concept of innate knowledge:

Recently the retired scholar Teng Yüan-hsi compiled the *Huang-Ming shu*, listing Hsüeh Wen-ch'ing (Hsüeh Hsüan) and his followers under the "Learning of the Way" *(Tao hsüeh)* and treating the Wang school separately as the "Learning of the Mind." This "Learning of the Mind" is Master Teng's own way of referring to it. In my view this "Learning of the Mind" is not [the learning of the Mind in] Ch'an Buddhism. Its being a learning of the mind lies in its doctrine of extending innate knowing. Its not being Ch'an lies in its not abandoning human relations and not rejecting things and affairs.

"Extending innate knowing" is not something set forth here for the first time: it is nothing more than another term for [the Great Learning's] "Manifesting the moral nature" (ming ming-te). . . . Mencius spoke of "innate knowing" as involving no premeditation, and said nothing about "extending," so Wang Yang-ming added the one word "innate" in the middle of the [Great Learning's] "extending knowledge" (chih chih) and to the "innate knowledge" [of Mencius] he added the one word "extend," combining the ideas of Confucius and Mencius in one expression. This was not starting something new, but just giving another name to "manifesting the moral nature. . . .

As to its not being Ch'an, this consists in sincerely realizing that human relations cannot be discarded and things and affairs cannot be rejected. Yet what is to be said about the claim that the mind being without good and evil, or things being without good and evil, are not to be understood on the ordinary level? Innate knowing refers to a mind concerned with right and wrong. If there is neither good nor evil, how can there by any right and wrong; if there be no right and wrong, how can one love the one and hate the other . . . or make oneself a genuine person?[126]

The remainder of the essay, which sees this learning of the mind as the key to Wang Yang-ming's great success as a statesman—a success, Ch'en says, unmatched by anyone since the founding of the Han—need not detain us here. The point for us is that Ch'en confirms the distinction made by Teng between the Ch'eng-Chu line and new/old learning of Wang Yang-ming; he celebrates Wang's genius while claiming no originality for him, but he also extends no credit at all to Lu Hsiang-shan.

Interestingly Ch'en refers to the alternative tradition as the "Learning of the Way" (Tao-hsüeh), rather than the "Learning of Principle" (li-hsüeh) as in Teng's work. This in itself is indicative of the extent to which the Learning of the Way was becoming identified with the Learning of Principle, while the Learning of the Mind, as formulated by Wang Yang-ming, was becoming separated from the Learning of the Way. The same form of reference is used in the account of Teng's Huang-Ming shu found in the Ch'ing dynasty Catalogue of the Impe-

rial Library, which likewise refers to *li-hsüeh* as *tao-hsüeh* (apparently following Ch'en's usage rather than Teng's).[127] The editors of the *Catalogue*, while noting Teng's admiration for Wang, credit him with great independence of judgment, and applaud his condemnation of the tendency to seek enlightenment at the expense of morality and scholarship. From their standpoint this seems to warrant treating the Learning of the Mind as a separate category, though for reasons different from Teng's. On the other hand, since they see Teng's work as to be judged in the genre of dynastic history, the editors question whether either *tao-hsüeh* or *hsin-hsüeh* are appropriate categories to be used in place of the more general and more normal "Confucian scholarship" *(ju-hsüeh)*.[128]

Further reactions to Wang Yang-ming and his critics, and additional testimony as to how the new Learning of the Mind was perceived in relation to the old, comes from a close contemporary of Teng Yüan-hsi and a scholar of impressive erudition, Chang Huang (1527–1608).[129] Chang was from the same area of Nanchang, Kiangsi, as Teng, and had a reputation for strict orthodoxy in his thought, scholarship, and conduct of life.[130] Thus he and Teng were later linked together among the so-called "Four Noble Men *(chün-tzu)* of Kiangsi," and Huang Tsung-hsi, in his *Case Studies of Ming Confucian Scholars*, placed Chang immediately after Teng in his account of the conservative "Right Bank" Wang school.

Huang characterized Chang's thought in the following terms:

In his discussion of "knowing where to rest" and "cultivating the self" [as in the *Great Learning*] Chang was close to Li Chien-lo (Li Ts'ai, ca. 1520–ca.1606);[131] in his discussion of "returning to solitude" he was similar to Nieh Shuang-chiang (Nieh Pao, 1487–1563).[132] What he emphasized most was making it clear that the psycho-physical component is not [as such] one's nature, yet neither can the nature be grasped apart from the psycho-physical constitution. In this his views tallied almost exactly with what was said by my late teacher Liu Chi-shan (Liu Tsung-chou, 1578–1645)."[133]

This characterization lines up Chang with followers of Wang Yang-ming known for their solitary self-cultivation, strict moral standards, and scholarly inquiry. Accordingly, in Chang's dicta on learning as quoted by Huang, there is strong criticism of the tendency in the left or liberal wing of the Wang Yang-ming school to proclaim the sagehood of the common man, as if the minds of the great mass of ordinary men were identical to the sage—a fact which they only needed to recognize for themselves, without any effort at self-cultivation or study. Confucius' example of the lifetime pursuit of learning, according to Chang, stood in obvious refutation of this misconception.[134] For him, then, the true view of learning was to be found in the "correct transmission of the learning of the mind as it had come down in the sages' doctrine concerning the human mind and mind of the Way, and in Confucius' teaching concerning the control and preservation of the mind."[135]

Chang is best known for an encyclopedic work entitled *T'u-shu pien (A Compilation of Charts and Writings)*[136] in 127 chapters, an illustrated and documented conspectus of all valid learning, embracing the classics, cosmology, and astronomy, as well as historical and physical geography and a vast range of practical knowledge concerning man and human institutions. Among the latter Chang included discussions of the Learning of the Mind-and-Heart and the Succession to the Way. For Chang indeed this "Learning" represented the key to an understanding of the Way of Man *(jen-tao)*. Elsewhere he refers to the Sung school as the Learning of Principle *(li-hsüeh)*, but this is presented as an extension of the original Tradition of the Way and Learning of the Mind, not as a rival school.[137]

From the encyclopedic nature of Chang's research in the written record of past knowledge one may readily discern that he, though a follower of Wang Yang-ming who also had significant associations with the school of Chan Jo-shui, rejected any idea that the Learning of the Mind or Wang's innate knowledge were antithetical to book-learning or opposed to tradition. Further, from the fact that Chang was acquainted with and criticized Ch'en Chien's *General Critique of Obscurations to Learning* (77:54a), one may well surmise that he had in mind not only to refute the latter's attack on Wang, but to show how Wang's teaching represented the culmination of the orthodox tradition of *hsin-hsüeh*. In the process he was equally at pains to disassociate this learning from libertarian interpretations which would lend some credence to Ch'en's *Critique*.

For Chang the Learning of the Mind-and-Heart consists of cognitive knowledge as well as moral insight. It seeks to understand principle in both its unity and diversity. The true mind achieves its full employment in a "getting" of principle that is both a reaching out and a meeting within. Yet, since this process is subject to partiality, deflection, and deviation, one's speech and conduct may be led astray from principle. Hence the need for constant vigilance and watchfulness so as to keep to the Mean (77:53a).

Originally there was, and essentially there is, no mind without principle and no principle external to the mind. In the days of the sage kings this was in fact the case, but thereafter divergent teachings arose, creating the need for Confucius to compile the classics in order to provide a simple and easy means by which to guide men's minds and bring them back to unity in a "single norm of correctness and centrality" (77:53a).

Unfortunately the further removed in time one got from the great Sage Confucius the greater the proliferation of heterodox views, and the more subtle and refined these were, the more misleading and divisive they became. Buddhism, a teaching of the barbarians, only made things worse, confusing things with its own learning of the mind to the point where a rupture occurred between the learning of the mind and the learning of principle (77:53b). What all minds have in common is principle, moral principle. If one sets this aside, there is nothing left of the unity of the mind except its undifferentiatedness. One would lose the original unity of the mind of Heaven by which the sages had tried to discriminate and refine the differentiated consciousness of the human mind so as to preserve singleness and hold fast to the Mean. The basis for moral effort, by which one achieves self-integration, would thus be lost (77:53b–54a).

As Chang said in his critique of methods of learning, "The learning of the sages is the Learning of the Mind-and-Heart. It is the learning which seeks the full employment of the mind." The mind of the Way, unmixed with the human, is the source of sincerity and genuineness. Mixed with the human it becomes exposed to danger and insecurity and is thus liable to err. To guard against this, says Chang, the sages stressed singleness of mind to preserve the unity of principle, while at the same time they taught adherence to moral principle as differentiated in the human moral relations. Everyone learned these moral relations and this was what constituted the Learning of the Mind-and-Heart for the sages. (77:46 a, b).

After the sages had passed away this true learning became obscured by philological exegesis of the classics and was subverted by utilitarian doctrines. Ch'an Buddhism appeared as a specious learning of the mind which dispensed with human moral relations, thus opening the way to the selfish pursuit of enlightenment beyond the sphere of human social concerns, and leaving the way open for utilitarian doctrines to corrupt human society. Chang insisted, however, that there should be no confusion of this kind of learning with the true learning of the mind, and the latter, which holds to human relations and nourishes principle, should never be called "Ch'an" (as Ch'en Chien had done) (77:47b–48a).

In the Way of the Great Learning, Chang says, "manifesting bright virtue (the moral nature) starts with self-cultivation and rectification of the mind, but these are preceded by making one's intention sincere and extending knowledge through the investigation of things" (74:22b). If this method is not followed, and instead one goes directly to the mind and its empty spiritual consciousness, mere subjective opinion may be taken for transcendental insight (77:54b). So it is with the doctrine that innate knowing and the substance of the mind are beyond good and evil, as Wang Chi had asserted. While it is true that the original state of the mind is perfectly good, when activated in the affairs of men, it cannot but be involved with evil, i.e., it cannot but respond to the good and evil in life. To respond properly requires learning and effort, and without these one cannot reach the point of "resting in the highest good" (74:22b–23a).

On this point then Chang's understanding of the *Great Learning* is close to Chu Hsi's but without this being seen as in any essential conflict with Wang Yang-ming. Similarly, according to Chang, with Lu Hsiang-shan: for him to be accused of error in this respect as Ch'en Chien did in his *General Critique* is quite unwarranted. Lu had emphasized the unity of principle in the human mind and was not at all guilty of abandoning the pursuit of principle (74:54a). Instead he had talked about the unity of the mind of the sages precisely on the common ground of the moral nature:

The universe is my mind and my mind is the universe. If a sage arises in the East he will have this mind and this principle. If he arises in the West, he will have this same mind and principle . . . (and similarly with North and South). Whether in thousands of ages past or thousands of ages to come, whenever a sage arises, his mind and this principle will be the same. (74:18b)

From statements such as these, concludes Chang, it is evident that Lu's teaching equally emphasized mind and principle. He would never have thought to propound a Learning of the mind at the expense of the learning of principle. Nevertheless to fulfill the unity of mind and principle, and thus fully employ and exhaust the mind's capacities, is a lifetime enterprise, as it had been for Confucius. In the latter's case it was only at the age of seventy that he could fulfill his heart's desire without transgressing the norm. This means, says Chang, that it took Confucius fifty-five years of dedicated effort and learning before he reached the stage of effortless and easy non-transgression. Only when he had fully employed his mind for a lifetime, did he reach the stage at which his mind and principle were wholly at one (74:18b–19a).

This same approach to the mind and principle applied to learning and the succession of the Way:

> The essence of the tradition of the Way (tao-t'ung) is the learning of the mind encapsulated in the formula of "holding fast to the Mean," as handed down from Yao to Shun, and in the "one thread running through all" as transmitted from Confucius to Tseng Tzu. There was no difference at all in the earlier sages and later sages in their wishing to find this one thread. (14:25a)

From the foregoing one can chart the route that Chang would take in his discussion of the succession to the Way. Even though a defender of Wang Yang-ming and Lu Hsiang-shan against Ch'en Chien, he was unlikely to invoke the prophetic or intuitive claim available in the concept of the Way as a broken or lapsed tradition, awaiting some brilliant and insightful mind to rediscover it in later ages. Rather he dwelt on the essential unity and continuity of the tradition, arguing that Wang and Lu fully conformed to all the essential criteria of the original message as it had been cited by Chu Hsi in his preface to the *Mean*. Contrary to what one might expect if one thought of this Learning of the Mind as simply pitting individual intuition against defined orthodoxies, Chang Huang devoted much attention to tracing the true succession to the Way, and did so in the manner that I have labeled "scholastic" rather than "prophetic."

It could not have been expected that Chang would derive this tradition and succession from any source other than the sage kings and the famous sixteen-word formula. The real question would come at the breaking point after Mencius. Here the "charts" of Chang's title *Tu-shu pien* (A Compilation of Charts and Writings) become highly significant, and one sees quite graphically how Chang stresses continuity and scholarly consensus, rather than highlighting the discontinuities out of which individual heroes of prophetic insight emerge to reclaim the Way.

Chang's first chart diagrams the Succession to the Way coming down from Fu-hsi to Confucius, and his second chart, "The Transmission of the Tradition of the Way in Confucius' school," shows a succession leading from Confucius through Tseng Tzu and Tzu-ssu to Mencius, with a separate transmission to Yen Hui that ends there. The third chart shows the filiation of scholars in the Sung Learning of Principle, with the transmission going from Chou Tun-i to the Ch'eng brothers and, among four lines of succession from the latter, one which brings the transmission down to Chu Hsi through Yang Shih, Lo Ts'ung-yen and Li T'ung. A final chart shows successive generations of Chu Hsi's followers in the late Sung, while a parallel diagram, placing Lu Hsiang-shan alongside Chu Hsi, indicates that Lu's teaching lapsed after the one generation of his own students (77:61b–66b).

Chang gives no chart to bring the process down into the Yüan and Ming, but in an accompanying explanatory text he indicates that Hsü Heng and Wu Ch'eng continued the transmission in the Yüan period. He also endorses, in the Ming, the four officially canonized Confucians: Hsüeh Hsüan, Hu Chü-jen, Ch'en Hsien-chang, and Wang Yang-ming, while arguing that Wu Yü-pi too deserves recognition for shouldering the responsibility of the perpetuation of Confucian teaching in his time (Wu having been the teacher of Hu and Ch'en and indirectly of Wang Yang-ming) (77:61–67).

Finally Chang cites with approval the view of Lü Nan (1479–1542), recognized as an orthodox critic of Wang in the school of Chan Jo-shui, that though Chu Hsi and Lu Hsiang-shan had different starting points, they were in broad agreement on all essential points. "Basically they were at one" (77:67a).

In this way Chang represents the Tradition of the Way in later times as broadly inclusive of both the Learning of Principle and Learning of Mind, but with the main line coming down through the Chu Hsi school (and not Lu Hsiang-shan) to Ch'en Hsien-chang and Wang Yang-ming.

There is no split between schools of Principle and Mind, no Lu-Wang school, and no departure of Wang Yang-ming from the Tradition of the Way. Buddhism alone—except for such deviationists as Wang Chi—stands apart as having abandoned adherence to principle.

Here then we have a significant updating of the earlier combination of the Learning of the Mind with the Succession to the Way. Reconstructed by centrists of the Wang Yang-ming school, who minimized their differences with Chu Hsi and sought the common denominator among Ming thinkers (i.e., reaching out to include Ch'en Hsien-chang, as we saw Ch'en Lung-cheng of the Chan Jo-shui line, do earlier), it presented a historically plausible account of the mainline Neo-Confucian tradition. This was a version sufficiently credible to appeal to others looking for a consensus in fundamental values on which to base a program of moral and political reform. It also had, in scholars like Teng Yüan-hsi and Chang Huang, exemplary figures who combined the traditional moral virtues with a notable erudition. Even among these scholars influenced by Wang Yang-ming, there are signs of a return to book-learning and scholarship as primary pursuits of the Confucian tradition, along with an urge to contain the damage—insulate the central tradition—from the allegedly anti-intellectual elements in Wang's school.

To appreciate the scholarly and traditional character of Chang's account of the Succession to the Way, we may contrast it to the more prophetic, and indeed almost ecstatic, version found in a nearly contemporary account of the more populist Wang Ken, as rendered by one of his followers, Wang Tung (1503–81):

In the Ch'in period the true-learning was destroyed and when the Han arose scholars of the classics appeared who would only memorize and recite texts handed down from the ancients. From one to another they passed on a learning which became the exclusive property of classicists and literati. Lost and untransmitted was the learning which the ancient sages had intended to be understood and shared by all men. Then Heaven gave birth to our teacher who sprang from the eastern shore. Large-spirited and uniquely enlightened, he directly succeeded to the legacy of Confucius and Mencius which went straight to the mind-and-heart of man. Then untutored common folk and unlettered persons all could know that their own nature and spiritual intelligence sufficed for their self-fulfillment and self-sufficiency, and that it did not depend on externals, whether by oral, aural, or visual instruction. With that the message untransmitted for two thousand years was restored to man's comprehension again as if in a single morning.[138]

It was in reaction to this more radical and prophetic tendency that the neo-orthodox Tung-lin movement arose in the late Ming. Since it has already been the subject of much scholarly discussion, we need not dwell at length on the Tung-lin here. For our purposes, it may suffice to cite the views of one of its principal leaders, Ku Hsien-ch'eng (1550–1612), on our theme of the Learning of the Mind-and-Heart. These are found in a preface Ku wrote for a work entitled "The Essence of the Learning of the Mind." In discussing this learning, Ku is first of all concerned to distinguish the Confucian understanding of it from the Buddhist. For this he insists on a distinction being made between the Buddhist view of the mind as originally or essentially "empty" and the meaning of "emptiness' in Confucianism. In Confucianism, he says, it refers to the intangible but nonetheless very real, moral and spiritual values which are described in the *Mean* as "without sound or smell." What the Buddhists mean by "empty" is being "without good and evil" (i.e., beyond the moral sphere). Between these two views there is only a fine shade of difference, says Ku, but a miss is as good as a thousand miles.[139]

> To apply the Buddhist sense of emptiness rather than the Confucian to the learning of the mind can only cause great confusion for all under Heaven. For goodness is the substance of the mind; in one's manner it is expressed as respect; in speech it is to be agreeable; in sight it is clarity of perception; in hearing, quickness of apprehension; in thought, penetration; in parents, loving concern; in rulers and ministers, rightness, etc. . . . Such being the case, how could one consider them absent or nonexistent? And even if one asserts that *wu* means, not nonexistence or extinction, but only non-attachment, how can one accept non-attachment to the good as being better than attachment to the good?[140]

Perceived as "having no sound or smell," goodness is seen as something so fine that one can only approximate it in words—that is emptiness in reality. From the standpoint of being "without good or evil" goodness appears so coarse that it is spoken of only as something to be discarded and destroyed; that is shadow emptiness. . . . To manifest goodness is to establish the substance of the mind, not to suffer its loss; To manifest its substance is to achieve emptiness in reality, not an emptiness apart from reality. Thus for this work to be entitled "The Essence of the Learning of the Mind" is as much as to say that the scholar may, in one reading, clearly perceive the mind of the sages.[141]

Ku's scholarly lineage is similar to Teng Yüan-hsi's and Chang Huang's inasmuch as it derives from Ou-yang Te on the more conservative side of the Wang Yang-ming school. Ku's teacher Hsieh Ying-ch'i (c.s. 1535), however, was drawn increasingly toward Chu Hsi, and Ku's thought moved in the same direction. Though he accepted Wang's practice of extending innate knowing (chih liang-chih) as a stimulus to moral action, Ku sharply criticized the doctrine of "without good or evil" as undercutting moral action.[142] In the preceding preface it is clear that Ku rejects the latter interpretation, sanctions the former as the true Learning of the Mind-and-Heart, and affirms it as the correct transmission of the mind of the sages.

Given the great diversity of late Ming thought it would not be possible here to cover the full spectrum of scholarly views on the Learning of the Mind. Nevertheless, from the cases cited above one may draw at least some conclusions concerning the more orthodox reactions in the late Ming to Wang Yang-ming's reinterpretation of this learning. First there was the total rejection of the latter by Ch'en Chien as a Buddhist subversion of the orthodox Learning of the Mind which had come down from Chu Hsi. Next there was the repudiation of Wang's views by T'ang Po-yüan as a new and unprecedented teaching for which one could find no basis in the classics. In contrast to both of these we have the effort to reconcile the teachings of Wang Yang-ming and Chu Hsi, while redefining the Succession to the Way as a mainline tradition broad enough to include both. Though moving in such different directions, however, these two tendencies were marked in common by strong resistance to the perceived danger of rampant anti-intellectualism, neglect of scholarship, and the weakening of traditional Confucian morality.

All three of these views carry over into the early Ch'ing and are powerfully reinforced by the shock effect of the Ming collapse in the mid seventeenth century. In none of them, however, do we find any support for the idea that the Learning of Principle and Learning of Mind were inherently antithetical, or that such an antithesis could be identified with rival lineages of Ch'eng-Chu and Lu-Wang schools.

4

The Learning of the Mind and Succession to the Way in the Early Ch'ing

It is almost a truism of modern intellectual history that early Ch'ing thought was born in the travail of dynastic upheaval and in reaction to the decadence of late Ming thought. Recent studies have questioned how much of this decadence is attributable to Wang Yang-ming,[1] but one can hardly doubt that among the leading thinkers of the early Ch'ing—themselves products of the late Ming—there was a widespread belief that the Ming had been mortally weakened by libertarianism and anti-intellectualism. In consequence of this, "back to basics" became the order of the day in both scholarship and morality.[2]

Even before the Ming demise this fundamentalist reaction had set in, and well after that cataclysmic event the sense of shock was still there, along with a deep desire for healing. This is shown in the efforts of Sun Ch'i-feng (1585–1675),[3] among many others in the first Ch'ing decades, to rally scholars around a main line, conservative consensus and avoid partisan recriminations.

Sun, a scholar active in North China, is usually considered to have emerged from the moderate wing of the Wang Yang-ming school and moved toward rapprochement with Chu Hsi, much as had the late Ming scholars just discussed, who were generally active in the South. In this sense Sun represents a further extension into the early Ch'ing of the neo-orthodox trend found in the Tung-lin school, a tendency indicated also by the especially high place Sun accords to Ku Hsien-ch'eng and Lo Hung-hsien, as well as by the esteem he holds for Chang Huang and Teng Yüan-hsi, among other predecessors aiming at Chu-Wang consensus.[4]

Sun's biographers point to his emphasis on three main points: strict personal rectitude through vigilant self-watchfulness *(shen-tu)*; "personally experiencing Heaven's principle: *(t'i-jen t'ien-li)*; and "carrying it out in the actual conduct of daily affairs and personal relations *(jih-yüeh lun-ch'ang wei shih-chi)*.[5] Here we have a fundamentalist morality in terms expressive of shared values among the teachings of Ch'eng-Chu, Wang Yang-ming, and Chan Jo-shui. Moreover Sun's personal character and conduct seem to have measured up to these ideals. Though a leader in local resistance to the Manchus, his reputation for moral and scholarly integrity later led to his receiving repeated invitations to serve the latter or accept their honors (all declined), and much later, in 1828, to his enshrinement in the Confucian temple as a paragon of Confucian virtue. A leading disciple of Sun's, T'ang Pin (1627–87), to be discussed later (in chapter 5), became a key adviser to the K'ang-hsi emperor and played an important role in the official revival of Chu Hsi orthodoxy. Thus Sun stands as an important bridge between the Wang Yang-ming school and Ch'ing Chu Hsi "orthodoxy."

Sun's best known work is his *Li-hsüeh tsung-ch'uan* (The Essential Legacy of the Learning of Principle), an account of Sung, Yüan, and Ming Neo-Confucianism which attempts to redefine the tradition on the basis of another synthesis of old and new. Although one can say that Sung's aim is similar to Chang Huang's, his account has its own distinctive features and cannot simply be dismissed as another routine exercise in a conventional genre. While making no pretense here at a full evaluation of its significance for intellectual history, we may note a few key points. They are in fact points to which Sun himself draws attention in his introduction to the work.

The first and perhaps too obvious point is that Sun speaks of the Neo-Confucian development, overall, as the Learning of Principle, and overrides any distinction between this Learning and the Learning of the Mind. In doing so he not only rejects the antithesis drawn between the two in some of the polemics against Wang Yang-ming, but also he ignores the simple distinction between them made by Teng Yüan-hsi, with whose work he was generally familiar (though possibly not with the *Huang Ming shu*).[6] That this is quite deliberate in Sun becomes clear from the opening lines of his introduction, where he identifies principle *(li)* as the most fundamental, integrating element in the pursuit of sagehood, and also equates it with the cosmic principle of origination *(yüan)* as well as with Heaven's Imperative *(t'ien-ming)* implanted in human nature. Chou Tun-i, seen earlier as the progenitor of the Learning of the Way *(tao-hsüeh)*, is quoted here for his saying that "the sage aspires to Heaven" (equating Heaven with principle), while Ch'eng Hao is cited for his assertion that "although in my learning there are things I have received from others, as regards Heaven's Principle it is something experienced for myself."[7] For Sun this means that anyone, sharing in the universal human endowment of Heaven's moral imperative, can experience the same for himself. Here then is the common ground in the Learning of Principle for Wang's innate knowledge, which makes it superfluous to speak of the latter as a separate Learning of the Mind. One only need experience this for himself as principle, the moral nature, in one's own mind.

If this universal accessibility of principle meant for Sun that it was unnecessary to have any special Learning of the Mind apart from the Learning of Principle, it bore the further implication that no need existed either, nor was there any special warrant for an exclusive Succession to the Way *(tao t'ung)* or Method of the Mind as the key to the Tradition of the Way. Here Sun drew attention to the *tsung-ch'uan* of his title.[8] It had two meanings, one to represent the figures who in their life and thought had most enlarged men's understanding of principle, and the other to represent the process of transmission *(ch'uan)* by which that understanding was conveyed through time. In this he did not limit the actors in the process to a few heroic, prophetic or sagely figures. Many scholars contributed, though not all to the same degree or extent; some were more comprehensive in their vision and others more partial, but there were none who did not share in the substance (principle) of sagehood, which was everywhere present and ever the Heavenly source of Confucian learning—meaning also the supreme value to be revered in the past *(tsung)*.[9]

Further, just as states (dynasties) have degrees of legitimacy and families revere greater or lesser figures in their genealogies, so there are degrees in learning, as Heaven's principle becomes incarnate over time in the human mind. Here Sun propounds a cyclical view of human history, by which major figures are seen to be endowed with a greater or lesser grasp of principle, in a fashion analogous to the rise or decline of dynasties, or who appear in preordained cycles similar to the natural succession of the cosmic force in the *Changes*. The upshot of Sun's complex, and sometimes arbitrary calculations, is that the appearance of great minds is somehow predictable in numerical and temporal sequences (rather than wondrously, by Heaven's unpredictable inspiration, as in the prophetic view of the succession). Yet there are many lesser minds too who help to carry the tradition down through the intervening ages.

Such is the cosmic/temporal framework in which Sun casts both his luminaries and lesser lights. The great luminaries in the Sun-Yüan-Ming period are eleven in number: Chou Tun-i, the Ch'eng brothers, Chang Tsai, Shao Yung, Chu Hsi, Lu Hsiang-shan, Hsüeh Hsüan, Wang Yang-ming, Lo Hung-hsien, and Ku Hsien-ch'eng—all dignified as Masters. The lesser lights in this same period, classed as "Confucian scholars" (ju), total one hundred twenty-seven. There are in addition six scholars, including Wang Chi, Lo Ju-fang (1515–1588), and Chou Ju-teng (1547–1629?), whom Sun removes to a supplementary chapter for those quarantined as heterodox because they have misinterpreted Wang Yang-ming in a Buddhist sense.[10]

Sun's scheme bears several implications. The category of "masters" includes most of the figures normally identified with the Succession to the Way (tao-t'ung) in the "orthodox" Ch'eng-Chu Learning of the Way (Tao-hsüeh), but it is stretched to include Lu, Wang, Lo, and Ku.[11] This has the effect of associating the latter with a synthetic orthodoxy, here labeled the Learning of Principle, broad enough to establish a new mainline tradition of Neo-Confucianism without resort to such terms as tao-t'ung, tao-hsüeh, or hsin-hsüeh. Yet Sun goes further to identify a subset of the eleven masters in which special status is accorded to Chou, the Ch'engs and Chang (together in time) and Chu Hsi—figures whom he wishes to set up in parallel with Confucius, Yen Hui and Tseng Tzu, Tzu-ssu and Mencius in the classical age.[12] But, having treated the Ch'engs and Chang together as one group in time, he asks rhetorically (and rather disingenuously, it would seem) who is to be regarded as the fourth luminary in this constellation, someone worthy to complete the cycle of latter-day saints? The answer, he says, must be Wang Yang-ming.[13] In this way Sun manages to elevate Wang into the ranks of tao-hsüeh philosophers, while relegating Shao, Lu, Hsieh, Lo, and Ku to somewhat less central positions. Moreover, by another set of interwoven linkages he identifies Chou Tun-i as the true heir to Confucius' teaching and Wang Yang-ming as the heir to Chou, thus again elevating Wang's stature and foreclosing any derivation of Wang's thought from Lu's, because Lu, having criticized Chou, could not be considered as in the same line of transmission or inheritance.[14]

Here we have a scheme by which the Learning of the Mind is quietly subsumed under the Learning of Principle, and something vaguely like the mantle of the Tradition of the Way is thrown over a company of scholars, now seen less as individual heroes and prophets than as senior members of a Confucian academy. Nevertheless Sun succeeded so well in endowing them with the old aura of the *tao-t'ung* that his nineteenth-century biographer Hsü Shih-ch'ang (1855–1939), for whom the concept of the "Succession to the Way" had become a fixture of the historian's mental furniture, readily spoke of Sun's lineup as representing the *tao-t'ung*, even though Sun himself had not identified it as such.[15]

Issues Sun had bypassed here, however, came up later in his explanatory notes concerning the principles of organization and classification adopted in his work. After he had completed his compilation, someone had questioned his relative emphasis on principle rather than mind in his introduction. "Was not the sages' doctrine of the 'human mind and mind of the Way' a doctrine of the mind? When Confucius spoke about 'following his heart's desire without transgressing the norm,' was he not speaking of the mind-and-heart? Why should one regard only Ch'an Buddhism as based on mind?"

Sun's answer (no doubt anticipating criticism that he was diverting attention from Neo-Confucian *hsin-hsüeh* or disguising it as *li-hsüeh*), insisted that the sixteen-word method of mind culminated in the injunction to "hold fast the Mean," and the Mean, says Sun, represents Heaven's principle. In Confucius' talk about "not transgressing the norm," the "norm" represented Heaven's principle. On this basis a true understanding of mind was grounded in principle, and it was a misconception even to think of Buddhism as a true learning of the mind since it had nothing to do with the Mean or a defined norm.[16]

Another anticipated objection had to do with Sun's placing Wang Yang-ming among the elect of the Learning of Principle even though Wang had endorsed the suggestion that the substance of the mind (i.e., principle) was without or beyond good and evil. This notion, the putative questioner suggested, was akin to Kao Tzu's conception of human nature as neither good nor evil, in contrast to Mencius' view of it as good, and it could also be equated with the Ch'an view of the nature as essentially beyond predication in moral terms. Sun's reply is that when Wang Yang-ming spoke of the substance of the mind as being beyond distinctions of relative good and evil he was actually affirming the perfection of the nature as the highest excellence. This is the same as the undifferentiated state of mind which is perfectly good, i.e., as the mind of the Way, before the mind is aroused by human desires and faces a conflict between good and evil. In no way, says Sun, is it a view incompatible with the doctrine of the goodness of human nature.[17]

With arguments such as these Sun anticipated objections to his scheme of classification from two main directions: first, those orthodox scholars who would be loathe to concede that Ch'an alone had a philosophy or method of the mind, and would be unhappy to see Sun placing such heavy emphasis on principle rather than on the sixteen-word "method of the mind" which had earlier been seen as the core of the Tradition of the Way; and second, those who refused to accept Wang Yang-ming's new doctrine of the mind as compatible with the Learning of Principle. Sun's replies suggest an underlying defensiveness on these issues, an awareness that his attempt to define a new consensus in the name of Principle ran counter to earlier understandings of what was central to orthodoxy. In meeting these, and especially in his attempt to place Wang Yang-ming at the heart of orthodoxy, he tried to extricate the latter from the increasingly unfavorable connotations which had become attached to the term *hsin-hsüeh*, and he therefore sought to associate Wang more with figures like Chou Tun-i and Chu Hsi than with Lu Hsiang-shan. It is not surprising then that in laying out his new interpretation, and in his discussion of the individual thinkers identified with the Learning of Principle, he nowhere alludes to any Lu-Wang School or Lu-Wang Learning of the Mind.

Sun's *Li-hsüeh tsung-ch'uan (The Essential Legacy of the Learning of Principle)* has often been seen as a forerunner of the *Ming-ju hsüeh-an (Case Studies of Ming Confucians)* by his younger contemporary Huang Tsung-hsi (1605–1685). I have already referred to two distinguishing features of Huang's approach to the writing of intellectual history—one that he referred to Sung Ming Neo-Confucianism in general as the Learning of Principle, including in its scope, as Sun Ch'i-feng had, Wang Yang-ming and many others who might have been associated with Wang's Learning of the Mind. Another feature of his *Case Studies* is that, aside from using the general rubric of *li-hsüeh* for Ming thought as a whole, Huang avoided labeling schools in terms of orthodoxy or heterodoxy, Learning of the Way, Learning of the Mind, etc. Instead he preferred to organize his presentation of scholars and schools on the basis of personal filiation or regional groupings. His own affinity for Wang Yang-ming was to be expressed in geographic terms through their common home region of Yao-chiang, the river running through Yü-yao in Eastern Chekiang, and not in their common allegiance to *hsin-hsüeh* (even though Wang Yang-ming had proclaimed more than once his belief that the Learning of the Sages was essentially the Learning of the Mind).

In Huang's view it was important to emphasize the overall unity and continuity of Confucian thought, even while recognizing individual and regional differences. It was, after all, a basic article of Neo-Confucian belief that principle was one and its particularizations diverse; one could thus affirm the positive value of the latter as long as the particularizations were only diverse and not divisive. Yet the divisive aspect was precisely what marked the Learning of the Way in Huang's view. Thus he deplored the tendency in the dynastic histories to divide and subdivide Confucian thought and scholarship into ever more specialized compartments.

In the early histories, according to Huang, Confucian scholarship (*ju-lin*, lit. "The Confucian grove") was the broad cover for the many cultural activities of the Confucians. Only later, in the T'ang, as nitpickers began to make finer and finer distinctions, did the "garden of literature" *(wen-yüan)* become separated from Confucian scholarship as a whole. Then in the Sung came the further differentiation of practical and political affairs from classical studies, followed in the Yüan dynasty compilation of the *Sung History* by a distinction between the Learning of the Way and the rest of Confucian scholarship. The cleverer people got at this business, observes Huang, the finer the distinctions they made and the more the original unity of the Confucian Way became fractured. Subsequently, notes Huang, in the *Huang-Ming shu* Teng made the distinction between the Learning of Principle and the Learning of Mind, which carried this analytic, chopping-and-slicing process to an absurd extreme. (No doubt it was these comments of Huang on Teng that the editors of the Imperial Catalogue had in mind when they registered similar objections to Teng's classifications, as seen earlier.)

Now so far has this practice gone that Confucian scholarship, in Huang's view, has been broken up into separate, mutually exclusive departments. "Those who talk about the Learning of the Mind will have nothing to do with the study of books or the fathoming of principle. Among those who talk about the Learning of Principle, the reading of books is confined to the study of scholarly commentaries on the classics, while the fathoming of principle does not go beyond lexical analysis."[18]

Then too there is the evil of exclusivity, narrowness, and preciosity found in those who profess the Learning of the Way but refuse to grapple with the urgent problems of human society and regard the purity of the sages, as honored in the Confucian temple, to be something so lofty and rarified as not to be compromised or sullied by the admission of practicing Confucian statesmen to the elite circle of the philosophers. Speaking of the exclusion of seven eminent statesmen of the T'ang, Sung, and Ming from enshrinement in the temple, Huang says:

These seven gentlemen had nothing beyond the teachings of Confucius to guide them in their actions. How could they have been privy to some other transmission, outside of that coming down from Confucius, or seek to maintain a school of their own? How could the school of Confucius be so pedantic and narrow that it would be concerned with nothing but self, have nothing to do with order and disorder in the world, and be ready to cast into the ditch all those heroes of past and present who have tried to shake the world into action? How incredible then that these seven gentlemen remain unenshrined [in the Confucian temple].

It may be argued that those enshrined are distinguished for their refinement in the discussion of mind and human nature, not for the mark they have left on the conduct of affairs. I reply: These gentlemen held fast to one teaching and did not turn back no matter how many reverses they suffered. Their courageous spirit filled Heaven-and-earth; no trace of selfish desire remained in them. If what you want are those who close up their eyes, dull their senses, and reduce the mind to a state of unimaginable purity —a never-never land of consciousness—that is the teaching of Buddha and your candidates for enshrinement would have to be found among those who transmit the lamp [of the Ch'an masters].[19]

In the preceding passage concerning the classifications of the dynastic histories, Huang would seem to have uttered an equal curse on both the Learning of Mind and Learning of Principle. Yet coming from a known admirer of Wang Yang-ming, this backing away from Wang's self-identification with the Learning of the Mind has special significance, as does Huang's inclination elsewhere to speak of Ming thought in general as the Learning of Principle, even though one would have thought it to have been preoccupied with mind. Since this is true also of Sun Ch'i-feng, who has similar roots in the Wang Yang-ming school, it may well reflect a changed climate of opinion by the 1660s in which the "Learning of the Mind" has come more and more into dispute and disrepute. That name is to be avoided, if possible, as bearing increasingly unfavorable connotations. At the same time, since partisanship itself has come into disfavor and there is such a powerful urge to work out a fundamentalist consensus, the condition for salvaging any of Wang's Learning of the Mind, as part of this process, might have seemed to be that its essential teachings be sheltered under some other name—the Learning of Principle.

Another name to be reckoned with in this period is Huang's contemporary Ku Yen-wu (1613–1682), often classed, along with Huang and Wang Fu-chih (1619–1692), as one of the three greatest scholars of the early Ch'ing. As Ming survivors both Ku and Huang were deeply influenced by the dynastic debacle and its aftermath, but also by the renewed emphasis on practical learning and broad scholarship which had emerged in the late Ming. An important difference between them however lay in Ku's sharp criticism of the Wang Yang-ming school in contrast to Huang's continuing respect for Wang. Among later scholars who regarded Ku as almost the supreme exemplar of sound learning, the section devoted to the Learning of the Mind in Ku's celebrated *Jih chih lu* (Record of Knowledge Gained Day-by-Day) no doubt had a substantial effect in stigmatizing the Learning of the Mind in the late seventeenth century.

Interestingly this effect depended less on what Ku himself actually said than on his selective quotation from earlier writers. First he led off with a long quotation from Huang Chen in the late Sung (who in turn had quoted Ts'ai Shen, as we have seen earlier). As quoted, Huang Chen's passage seems to emphasize the alleged Buddhist connotations of the method of the mind *(hsin-fa)*, which prejudice and distort Ts'ai's basic moral and political message. Ku's own brief comment on this expresses regret that Ch'eng I had resorted to questionable Buddhist terminology in this matter, but he does not go into the non-Buddhist usage of *hsin-fa* in the Sung, which would have been more relevant to Ch'eng I's case, nor does he mention the fact that Huang Chen, elsewhere in his *Huang shih jih-ch'ao*, uses the term "learning of the mind" *(hsin-hsüeh)* as a legitimate form of reference to the Tradition of the Way (as I have shown earlier.) We have no reason to doubt Ku's honesty here, but only to believe that he was unduly influenced by the prevailing tendency to discredit the learning of the mind as tainted by Buddhism.

The second set of quotations by Ku come from T'ang Po-yüan, whose views have been discussed above. The main impression left by these quotations is that Wang Yang-ming was purveying a new learning of the mind for which there was no basis in the classics. Ku does not cite any of the rebuttals to this charge by writers sympathetic to Wang, but he is within his rights, so to speak, insofar as they could only claim that the ancients had a philosophy of mind, and not that the term *hsin-hsüeh* itself was to be found in the classics.

Taken together with his own brief comments, Ku's material conveys two messages having a significant relation to trends of thought and scholarship in the early Ching. The first is that the Learning of the Mind is not just to be thought of as Wang's creation, but has clear antecedents in Sung Neo-Confucianism, and—even more telling—roots in orthodox Ch'eng-Chu doctrine. There is in this nothing which would lead one to project a Lu-Wang connection, but only a Ch'eng-Chu-Wang derivation. On this question Ku's evidence served as a reminder that there had indeed been a *hsin-hsüeh* before Wang Yang-ming, and —for those who connected up the different links in the chain—that Wang's new "Learning of the Mind" was only the latest version of a Neo-Confucian philosophy of mind which had arisen as a response to the challenge of Buddhism in the Sung.

The second point is much simpler: the contrast set up between this Neo-Confucian derivation (as Ku sees it) and the original simplicity and purity of the classical Confucian teaching. This too is of a piece with the prevailing fundamentalist trend, a large segment of which would shift scholarly attention back to Confucius and the original classics, and away from the philosophical issues addressed by Sung-Ming Neo-Confucians, or, as Benjamin Elman has put it, "from philosophy to philology."[20] On this major trend of Ch'ing scholarship, Ku's debunking of the Learning of the Mind could not but have an impact, encouraging Ch'ing scholars first to distance themselves from their immediate antecedents and then to produce a revisionist view which, greatly simplifying their Sung-Ming past, helped men to forget much of it.

At this point it might seem logical to extend the discussion to Wang

Fu-chih, the remaining member of the Three Great Scholars of the early Ch'ing, but Wang's impressive, independent studies were pursued at a considerable remove from the mainstream of Ch'ing scholarship and were little noticed by others until the late nineteenth century. Thus he did not, so far as I am aware, contribute significantly to shaping the outcome of the Learning of the Mind. On the other hand there is another contemporary of Huang and Ku, who may well have had as much of a hand in it as they. This is Lü Liu-liang (1629–1683).

Like Wang Fu-chih, Lü became famous in the late Ch'ing for his anti-Manchu, Chinese loyalism; unlike Wang, however, he had a distinct influence in his own time on the reassertion of Ch'eng-Chu orthodoxy. If we take Huang and Ku as representing two important strains of evidential learning in classical and historical studies, Lü may help to fill out the other end of the spectrum of Ch'ing thought by standing as a hardline exponent of Ch'eng-Chu doctrine. His achievements were not in the text criticism which would later have such an impact on redefining the classical legacy, but rather in shaping the educational orthodoxy that became established in the civil service examination system. This he did through his published lectures and discourses on the Four Books and through the model examination essays he edited which had a wide audience among the educated men of his day. Even though Lü's thought as a whole is deserving of more attention than we can give it here, we cannot leave out of our account his views on such key issues as the Learning of the Mind, the method of the mind, and the succession to the Way.[21]

It is hardly a surprise that Lü, contrary to the prevailing instinct for consensus and compromise among conservative Confucians, which often led them to seek a common denominator between Chu Hsi and Wang Yang-ming, was unyielding in his adherence to Chu Hsi and opposition to Wang Yang-ming. What may be surprising, since it runs contrary to the usual expectation with "orthodoxy," is that Lü has little use for tradition as it has come down to him, and his fundamentalism rests squarely on Chu Hsi and the Four Books. The final revelation came with Chu and thereafter, whatever one might say about a Ch'eng-Chu school in the centuries since 1200, it was almost all downhill.

Lü had a pretty good understanding of Chu Hsi's philosophy and his commentaries on the Four Books,[22] with little reason to think that tinkering could improve upon them and a strong conviction that subsequent tampering had only made things worse. His view of the Succession to the Way was a prophetic, not a scholastic, one. If there had been a lapse of over a thousand years after Mencius, it was not difficult to believe that Chu Hsi too had been largely misunderstood by his nominal successors, which really meant that a new prophetic voice was needed to set things right. Indeed Lü's fundamentalism was radical enough so that he took an extreme position politically, refusing not only to recognize the Manchus as rulers but even to accept imperial dynastic rule—and its whole panoply of centralized bureaucratic institutions—as legitimate.

This meant that Lü held to a narrow view of the *tao-t'ung* as an essential tradition, but not as a viable succession among generations of scholars. Rather his conception of the late Sung-Yüan and Ming periods was more like that of Ch'en Chien in his *Critique of Obscurations to Learning*, i.e., a long sorry record of betrayal by crypto-Buddhists in Confucian disguise.

As part of the essential tradition Lü did believe in the method of the mind *(hsin-fa)*. For him it was a method of strict self-examination and moral discipline, based on the Heavenly imperative (i.e., principle) implanted in every human mind as the mind of the Way. The "Learning of the Mind," however, was something else entirely, a seductive Buddhist concept surreptitiously infiltrated into Confucianism by Wang Yang-ming. Thus Lü referred to it as Wang Yang-ming's formulation when the issue first arose in his *Recorded Conversations*. In the question and answer format characteristic of the Neo-Confucian teaching situation, and recorded in the *Conversations*, the first question deals with the opening lines of the *Great Learning*, characterizing it as education for the adult or for the Great Man who would achieve the full development of his human capacities. It is clearly a leading question:

> It has been said "The learning of the Great Man consists simply in employing the mind-and-heart to its fullest. To clarify and manifest bright virtue is to preserve this mind; to renew the people is to extend this mind to others; and to abide in the highest good is fully to employ this mind so that nothing is left unfulfilled."[23]

The question is a leading one because the Three Guiding Principles are given an interpretation in terms of the Learning of the Mind-and-heart, which prompts Lü to dispel any possible ambiguity on this score:

The Master said: In the *Great Learning* if one does not emphasize that the moral principle in the mind is rooted in Heaven, that the employment of the mind is fulfilled only in knowing what is right, and that the preserving of the mind is only possible through its constant rectification, then it cannot be accepted as "clarifying" or "renewing." With regard to the mind, if it is not of the moral nature and the mind replete with bright virtue, but simply of the mind that one speaks, then it is the learning of the original mind [of Lu Hsiang-shan and the Buddhists] and not the sage learning of which one speaks.[24]

Others in Lü's time who professed fidelity to Ch'eng-Chu teaching might well have taken the initial statement of the question at face value and not made an issue of it.[25] For Lü, since the issue had already been raised by Wang Yang-ming's interpretation of the mind as identical with principle, it is imperative that one specify the exact relationship of the mind to principle. Otherwise it leaves open the dangerous possibility that the mind could be understood as simple, undifferentiated consciousness, naturally good, without the need for moral effort and constant self-rectification to achieve its fulfillment.

A few lines later on in the text of the *Great Learning*, the same question comes up. Someone proposes that the "stability, composure, repose, and deliberation" spoken of in the *Great Learning* text represent the wondrous interaction [of principle and ether] in the Learning of the Mind-and-Heart. Master Lü says:

One can speak of the Learning of Heaven, of the [moral] nature, of principle and of the Way, but not of the learning of the mind. The mind is that which learns and cannot be what one learns. It is only to the Original Mind of the Buddhists, which takes the mind as the ultimate reality, and in relation to which Heaven, the moral nature, principle, and the Way are all seen as derivative and subordinate, that one refers when one speaks of the Learning of the Mind *(hsin-hsüeh)*. Indeed whenever one speaks of the Learning of the Mind, it is the Buddhist view they refer to.[26]

Here Lü is less than exact when he states that there was no *hsin-hsüeh*, other than the Buddhist Learning of the Mind, with which to identify Lu Hsiang-shan and Wang Yang-ming, since, as we have seen, there had been a Neo-Confucian Learning of the Mind accepted by early followers of the Ch'eng-Chu school who considered it an orthodox Confucian alternative to the Buddhist view of the Mind.[27] One may take it that Lü is straining to make a point, to differentiate Wang Yang-ming's teaching on the mind from the Learning of the Confucian Sages, and to identify Wang's as originally and essentially Buddhist.

A relevant passage for this purpose is Lü's comment on Confucius' familiar statement in the *Analects* (2:4) that "at fifteen he had resolved to pursue learning." Lü seizes this opportunity to demonstrate that "learning" did not mean for Confucius something naturally and spontaneously known but rather something achieved through a lifetime of effort.

> The Learning of the Sage is the learning of the [moral] nature, the learning of Heaven. In ancient times there was no talk of studying the mind. Whenever there was the mind of the Way there was the mind of man [to be directed], so the mind [in and by itself] could not be the object of study or learning. Learning is that by which one corrects one's mind. "Directly pointing to the mind of man, seeing into one's own nature and achieving Buddhahood," is learning turned in upon itself, not learning to be a sage. So all talk in terms of just the "learning of the mind" betrays the confusions of heterodox teachings and leads to [Wang Yang-ming's] "beyond good and evil."
>
> "When the Sage [Confucius] spoke about "following his heart's desire without transgressing the norm," he emphasized the three words "without transgressing the norm." What then is the norm? It is the [moral] nature, it is Heaven, the highest good. When the mind-and-heart are one with the nature and Heaven, that is the highest good, that is the Learning of the Sage, something superior to the mind [as mere consciousness]. So if one speaks of the Learning of the Sage as applying one's effort to the mind-and-heart, that is acceptable, but if one speaks of the Learning of the Sage as the Learning of the Mind, it is not acceptable. . . .[28]

From what Confucius said about "not transgressing the norm" one can know that in the Sage's mind there was always this Heavenly Principle present. It is not that the mind itself is the Way. This is the difference between the "original mind" and one rooted in Heaven's principle, which is the basis of the Ch'eng-Chu teaching that one should make reverent seriousness the master [of the mind]."[29]

Here Lü insists that one cannot take the mind-and-heart simply as undifferentiated consciousness ["original mind"], but because the mind is always the human mind—a compound of Heaven's principles and psycho-physical drives—it is imperative [in the sense of the innate Heavenly Imperative, *t'ien-ming*) that the mind as moral agency see to it that man's emotional and appetitive drives are properly directed— that through the constant exercise of reverent seriousness, principle, as Heaven's imperative, will prevail.

In a comment on learning as discussed in *Analects* 1, Lü says:

> What Confucians are conscious of is principle; what heterodox teachings are conscious of is mind. One can only become conscious of principle through the investigation of things and the extension of knowledge; then with the understanding of human nature and of Heaven comes the fullest employment of the mind. If however one sets aside the principles of things and tries to look directly into the mind, it makes the investigation of things and extension of knowledge seem superfluous and diversionary. If one thinks of oneself as directly perceiving the substance of the mind, the principles of things amount in the final analysis to no more than useless appendages.
>
> Just so, in the theory of the outward Confucians/covert Buddhists the order of learning is reversed so as to seek first the substance of the mind and leave till later the fathoming of the principles of things. Thinking that they hold the secret within themselves, they do not realize that when one first restricts oneself [through the discipline of ritual] and later broadens oneself with culture, or first seeks unity and later engages in learning, the latter turns out to be superfluous and diversionary. This is not the teaching of those who follow the sages."[30]

Lü emphasizes here that the only way to understand principle is through investigation which develops principle in the mind as it explores principles in things and affairs, and thus enables one to fulfill the moral nature of Heavenly endowment. If one assumes that the nature is already perfect and complete, and only needs to be realized by direct self-awareness and self-expression, then even though one speaks of extending such "knowing" outward to others and to things, there is really no need to do so, assuming that the substance is already fully attained. The kind of continuing effort to learn which Confucius speaks of in the opening lines of the *Analects* would be redundant.

Lü rejects any notion that morality is extrinsic to the self, or that principle stands as an impediment to the natural vitality of the mind. In his explanation of Mencius' final chapters on the full employment of the mind, he cites Chang Tsai's doctrine of the mind as combining and coordinating the nature and the emotions, and refers to Chu Hsi's explanation of this as found in his commentary on "bright virtue" in the opening lines of the *Great Learning:*

> Chang Heng-ch'ü's dictum, "The mind coordinates the nature and emotions" refers to the full employment of the mind. What Chu Hsi calls "empty, spiritual and transparent" indicates the substance of the mind; "furnished with a multitude of principles" refers to the coordinating of the nature; "responding to all things" refers to the coordinating of the emotions.[31] The mind is an active, living thing. Being empty and spiritual, it can be furnished [filled with] the nature and emotions; being furnished with the virtuous powers of the nature and emotions, its empty spirituality can directly embody Heaven's substance.[32]

The trouble with those who speak about the "Learning of the Mind" under the influence of Buddhism—the so-called Outward Confucians/ Covert Buddhists—is that they deny the constancy of principle in the structure and direction of the mind and take the mind simply as a stream of consciousness. In other words, using the language of Chu Hsi, they see it as "empty, spiritual, and transparent," but not as structured or directed by principle and not as needing any coordination of the emotions. In fact they see any holding to fixed principle as an obstacle to the transcendant freedom of the mind and an obscuration of its empty transparency and receptivity. This leaves them without any control over the emotions, so that in practice the mind is not only driven by the emotions but dominated by them—human desire prevails over Heaven's principles. Taking the mind's empty spirituality alone as the substance, they speak of it as marvelously subtle, pure, empty, and still—in the same terms as Bodhidharma's description of the Buddha-nature.[33] So, says Lü,

> Lo Cheng-an [Ch'in-shun] said "the Buddhists have insight into the mind but not into the nature." In reality, however, they are wrong on both counts. Seeing only the activity of the mind and not its directional norm (chi), on the higher level they cannot match the Heavenly substance, and on the lower level the mind cannot be of any practical use. Hence it is necessary to understand the nature and Heaven, so as to see the ultimate directional norm. Then one can achieve full employment of the mind.[34]

Lü's view of the Learning of the Mind as essentially Buddhist is similar to Ku Yen-wu's, though the point is argued in philosophical terms, and is not accompanied here by the same kind of historical and textual evidence as Ku offers. We have, so far as is known, no indications that Lü and Ku were in contact, and Lü's Recorded Conversations appeared some years before the full publication of Ku's Jih chih lu.[35] The two works may well be independent articulations of a similar tendency of thought, but Lü's is in a way the more revealing. Ku had little stake in defining or defending Neo-Confucian orthodoxy, but Lü did, and the latter's repudiation of what for many generations had been so closely bound up with the Succession to the Way and Method of the Mind, is significant. Prior to this the Ch'eng-Chu critics of Wang's Learning, with the exception of T'ang Po-yüan, had insisted that it was only a deviation from the true Learning of the Mind-and-Heart, not that such learning had never existed in the Confucian school.

Accompanying this disavowal is a noticeable tendency also for Lü to distance himself from other ideas and practices that had been associated with the orthodox Learning of the Mind: e.g., quiet-sitting and Chu Hsi's idea of a "breakthrough to integral comprehension" (huo-jan kuan-t'ung), which had been understood by some as a kind of Neo-Confucian enlightenment. Lü did not by any means intend to upset Chu Hsi's delicate balance between the subjective and objective aspects of learning, but these examples suggest how, in order to preserve that balance, he was ready to shed some of the accretions to Chu Hsi's teaching which had importance for, e.g., the neo-orthodox Tung-lin school and would remain so for orthodox Neo-Confucian schools in

Korea and Japan.[36] Some of these in fact would still be of importance in that form of orthodoxy known as the "Sung Learning" of the Ch'ing period.[37]

Thus we have intimations here of a significant shift, and one might go so far as to say a split, in Neo-Confucian orthodoxy. Lü's emphasis on the intellectual and scholarly side of Ch'eng-Chu learning, evident in other aspects of his thought than those we deal with here, corresponds to a similar shift in Ch'ing thought generally. How much of the initiative for this comes from Lü, or how much additional momentum he gave to trends already in motion, is difficult to say. In any case this development created new problems for the long-standing tension within Neo-Confucianism between its more intellectual and scholarly pursuits and its religious or spiritual aspirations. This would become all the more significant for the successors of Lü Liu-liang who had a direct role, as he did not, in shaping the official orthodoxy and deciding the place in it of the Learning of the Mind and the Tradition of the Way.

In Lü's own time another scholar widely known for his adherence to Chu Hsi's teaching, as well as for his personal and scholarly integrity, was Chang Lü-hsiang (1611-1674).[38] Early in life Chang had been exposed to Tung-lin teachings, and then to those of Liu Tsung-chou, but he became completely converted to Chu Hsi's doctrines through reading Chu's *Reflections on Things at Hand (Chin-ssu lu)* and Chen Te-hsiu's *Extended Meaning of the Great Learning (Ta-hsüeh yen-i).*[39] Declining to pursue an official career he led a relatively frugal but independent life as a scholar and tutor, and supported himself in part by working the land (incidentally, contributing to the literature on agriculture and arboriculture). Thus he represents a link between the Chu Hsi school and the practical learning *(shih-hsüeh)* of his day, but with no involvement in politics or the state. During his later years he gave special attention to education and assigned a priority to such writings of Chu Hsi as his "Articles of the White Deer Grotto Academy" and Chu's "Amended Version of the Lü Family Compact."[40]

Like Lü, a native of Chekiang, Chang was known and highly respected by Lü, who invited him to serve as a tutor to Lü's children. Chang and Lü shared many views in common, and it is not unlikely that Lü only gave sharper and more forceful expressions to many ideas originating with Chang. A distinct difference in temperament may enter in here, for we get a somewhat more modulated treatment of the same issues when they are addressed by the more reserved and scholarly Chang than when vented by the more radical, prophetic voice of Lü.

In Chang's case when he speaks about the Learning of the Mind it means for him primarily the Wang Yang-ming version, the overwhelming popularity of which is clearly reflected in Chang's comments (as indeed it has been in Lü's). Chang's main concern is with the way in which the mind is conceived as an inner essence divorced from principle, and especially far removed from principle in things and practical affairs.

> The method among scholars today is to "seek the mind," but they regard all personal manners, outward discourse, or conduct of affairs as something other than the mind (as says Chang, so does Ch'an Buddhism). . . . (Actually) one's manner or bearing is a mark of inner virtue; speech is the sound of the heart, conduct is a manifestation of the mind. . . . To seek the mind apart from these is to fall into emptiness and extinction. . . . When Confucius was asked by Yen Hui about the practice of humaneness, he expressed it in terms of applying oneself to what one hears, sees, says, and does. What else could it mean but that the sage was averse to a method which simply turned inward?[41]

Elsewhere Chang presses his challenge to the idea, which he sees as central to both Wang Yang-ming and Ch'an Buddhism, that the true mind or self is not to be found in the realm of human discourse or action:

> Words are the sound of the mind and heart; actions are manifestations of the mind-and-heart. There is no such thing as words or actions that are not rooted in the mind-and-heart. . . . Today's talk about the learning of the mind-and-heart is quite cursory in regard to words and actions. Although it is insisted that this is not unorthodox, I don't believe it. Also, the question is raised about Shao Yung's saying that it is easy to avoid errors in personal conduct but difficult to keep the mind-and-heart from erring. I believe the body (person) and mind are one. If one can avoid errors of personal conduct, then I can believe the mind is free from error. But if the mind is in error, it is impossible that this would not be manifested in one's personal conduct.[42]

And again, commenting on the view of Ch'en Ch'üeh (1604–77),[43] a late Ming follower of Wang Yang-ming, he says:

> Those who follow the Buddha do not resort to words but emphasize going directly to the mind-and-heart. Those who follow Confucian teaching believe that conduct should have priority over knowledge. In the learning of the mind as (Ch'en) Ch'ien-ch'u advocates it, every matter or affair requires that one should first put his faith in the mind and that knowing should have priority over conduct. . . . Even though he does not devote himself to Ch'an study, without realizing it he has himself fallen into Ch'an. Ch'ien-chu dresses himself up in the language of the Learning of the Mind, but the teaching of Yao-chiang (Wang Yang-ming) is truly the worst kind of Ch'an learning.[44]

Ming Neo-Confucianism had put much emphasis on naturalness and sincerity, in revolt against a false conformity or mere lip service to established values. Cant and hypocrisy were much execrated, especially in the Wang Yang-ming school. For Chang, however, it was another thing entirely to belittle conventional morality altogether, and go so far as to avoid even the appearance of proper conduct. Hence he felt a need to defend ordinary virtue:

> Being loyal and trustworthy, modest and pure, is the basis for one's self-cultivation and proper conduct. Today scholars wish to avoid any suspicion of being goody-goodies, and instead devote themselves to learning how to be wild (and unconventional, k'uang). . . . But I think that if a man's only thought is to avoid suspicion of being a "goody-goody," there is no way he can do any good. (2:16ab)

Confucius had said he would prefer, as companions along the road to virtue, those who were madly ardent (k'uang) instead of those who were merely conformists. To Chang, however, the former description did not fit those who actually scorned virtue and were simply willful egoists (2:33b–34a):

> Scholars today never stop talking about the mind, but what they call mind is only their own [private or selfish] mind. . . . The mind

of the sages is the mind of Heaven-and-Earth, the ultimate of humaneness, . . . which cannot be found apart from the Four Books, Six Classics, and the doings and sayings of the sages. (2:35b)

Like Lü Liu-liang, whenever Chang speaks about the Learning of the Mind it is the Wang Yang-ming school he is thinking of, and he links it to Ch'an. Usually such negative references are prefaced and qualified by an expression like "those who talk about *hsin-hsüeh* today . . ." or "in the recent talk about *hsin-hsüeh* . . ." Unlike Ku Yen-wu Chang does not go so far as to say that there can be no Confucian learning of the mind, and that all talk of it is but Ch'an in disguise. Chang has read Ch'en Chien's *General Critique of Obscurations to Learning* (2:14b), and been much impressed by it. In so doing he must also have noted Ch'en's insistence that the views of Lu Hsiang-shan and Wang Yang-ming were not to be mistaken for the true Neo-Confucian Learning of the Mind, which Ch'en was at some pains to diagram and explain. Moreover, as one who had read and admired Chen Te-hsiu he would no doubt have been familiar with Chen's Learning of the Mind as formulated in terms of the Method of the Mind. This method, for Chang too represents the correct teaching—"the method of Yao and Shun (4:31b):

"The human mind is precarious, the Mind of the Way is subtle." How then can the human mind be rectified except by making the mind of the Way the master of the whole person and having the human mind follow its commands? Only by the extension of knowledge and making one's intention sincere can this be accomplished. Those who are fond of talking about the Learning of the Mind, if they first discard the method of investigation of things, can only have minds like those Mencius (2B:2) spoke of as "clouded," "depraved," "way off" and "far gone" (4:12b)

Chang also says that there are many who talk about "the method of the mind and of the emperors and kings" but few who give serious attention to the pursuit of principle in concrete things and affairs.[45] Here, and in the preceding quotations, we note his repeated emphasis on a method which starts with the investigation of things or the pursuit of principle in specific instances. This is in keeping with another recurrent theme in Chang's writings: principle is one and its particularizations diverse. The great error of the current Learning of the Mind is its preoccupation with the oneness of principle (seen earlier in the discussion of Wang Yang-ming), to the neglect of knowledge gained through study and practice related to concrete things and affairs. There is, he says, no method *(kung-fu)* applicable to the unity of principle as an undifferentiated inner essence; there is only a method applicable to the diverse particularizations of principle.[46] For this reason too he, like Lü, avoids the subject of a "breakthrough to integral understanding," which Chu Hsi had spoken of in his special note on "investigating things and extending knowledge," no doubt because it was too often understood as referring to some sudden enlightenment.[47]

On this score Chang criticizes Lu Hsiang-shan for a simple and easy method of quiet-sitting which focuses only on the unity of principle and neglects its application to differentiated affairs. It is true that Chou Tun-i had stressed the practice of quiescence, but he did so to eliminate selfish desires; thus Chou's method was a preparation for moral practice which avoided the twin extremes of Mo Tzu's undifferentiated love (as a counterfeit of humaneness) and Yang Chu's egoism (as a deviation from moral propriety or rightness, *i*).[48]

Chang extends this critique also to the Tung-lin thinkers who had regarded quiet-sitting as a method of orthodox spiritual and moral praxis but aimed at a kind of quietistic enlightenment.[49] In this they were following the mistaken view of Wang Yang-ming, whose method likewise had concentrated on an undifferentiated consciousness, with emphasis on the psycho-physical aspect of mind rather than on principle in the mind.[50]

As a corrective to this, Chang advocates a method based on the study of books and the acquisition of knowledge embodying specific principles. This method is orthodox enough. It starts with abiding in reverence to preserve the mind, along with fathoming principle in order to extend one's knowledge. In studying the classics one should read carefully and reflectively, so as really to steep the mind in principle and then carry it out in practice, rather than just rush through to memorize and accumulate more facts.[51] To do this one must employ the "art of the Mind" *(hsin-shu)*,[52] which means first rectifying the mind and then proceeding to fathom principles one by one, an "art" which Chang also sees as the true application of the method of the mind *(hsin-fa)*.[53] Nevertheless, if this seems to put too much emphasis on the learning of principle through the study of books, Chang is no less insistent on the need to put one's learning to the test of practice in the conduct of life and

especially in open discussion with others, to see if one's own understanding is confirmed by theirs. Indeed this is in keeping with the
essential "method of the mind," for discussion is the way to arrive
at a true sense of the Mean in action, that is, of "holding fast the
Mean."[54]

On most of these points there is agreement between Chang and Lü.
We do find some difference in approach as regards their views of the
Confucian tradition in the recent past, because Chang, more conservative or moderate than Lü, is less ready to throw out all thought and
scholarship subsequent to Chu Hsi as corrupt or misleading, and his
judgments on earlier Sung-Yüan and Ming scholars are more apprecia-
tive, nuanced, and less sweeping than Lü's.[55]

Yet, for all his emphasis on the Method of the Mind as the essence of
the tradition of the Sages, Chang has little to say about the *tao-t'ung* as
the Succession to the Way, and it may well be that he shares Lü's
suspicion that this idea too is influenced by the Buddhist concept of a
patriarchal succession, and thus not to be relied upon.[56]

It is significant, moreover, that Chang nowhere refers to the Learning
of the Mind, his bête noire no less than Lü's, by the term "Lu-Wang."
More than Lü, he is apt to think of historical connections along with
philosophical affinities. Thus he speaks of "Ch'en/Wang," linking Ch'en
Hsien-chang and Wang Yang-ming (both out of the Chu Hsi school as
transmitted by Wu Yü-pi).[57] And when he does link the thought or
"learning" of Wang with Lu Hsiang-shan's, he in several instances
refers to it as "Wang-Lu,"[58] as if to acknowledge that the new prominence of Lu's ideas derives from Wang, rather than Wang's thought
deriving from Lu's.

There is one other seventeenth-century figure prominent in the return to Ch'eng-Chu orthodoxy in the early Ch'ing who must be mentioned here, even though our brief treatment of him will be out of
proportion to his importance as a scholar. This is Lu Shih-i (1611–72),
known for his catholicity of mind and breadth of learning, who drew
upon several strains of Neo-Confucian thought to produce an impressive practical learning *(shih-hsüeh)*.[59] Most especially, Lu followed up
that line of Ming thought which emphasized the psycho-physical reality
of ether or material force *(ch'i)*, as represented by Hsüeh Hsüan, Lo
Ch'in-shun, Chan Jo-shui, Ku Hsien-ch'eng, and Kao P'an-lung.[60]

In doing so Lu took as a central concept the unity of principle and the diversity of its particularizations *(li-i fen-shu)* in concrete forms and actual human affairs. In other words, he affirmed the equal importance of principle and material force, implying the need to study the former in direct relation to the latter. This would not in itself distinguish Lu from Lü Liu-liang or Chang Lü-hsiang, who clearly accepted the same premise, but Lu did contribute significantly to studies in both classics and history (with special attention to institutional history), neither of which were much developed by Lü. Moreover Lu viewed the legacy of Confucian thought itself more in historical terms, recognizing the individual contributions of diverse thinkers and seeing these too as varied expressions of underlying common principles. In finding a common denominator among them, he avoided either an uncritical eclecticism on the one hand or a narrow exclusivism on the other.

Lu's basic approach was orthodox in the sense that it combined, on the most fundamental level, Chu Hsi's "abiding in reverence and fathoming principle *(chü-ching, ch'iung-li)*, or, as he put it in other terms, "reverence for Heaven" as an underlying habit of mind, together with the practical application of "moral principles" in concrete cases. That he described this method as the "Sages' and Worthies' Method of the Mind" *(Sheng-hsien hsin-fa)* in contrast to Wang Yang-ming's learning of the mind, which he saw as only a momentary enthusiasm rather than a consistent effort, indicates how his practical learning grew out of the earlier Neo-Confucian tradition.[61]

Indicative of this was Lu's view of the Succession to the Way and the Learning of the Mind. Lu recognized that there were two tendencies at work in the Succession to the Way, both of which were vital to it. One was the special inspiration vouchsafed to a few whose spiritual perception of the Way (what I have called the prophetic element) was somehow elevated above the ordinary.[62] The other was transmission through scholarly learning. Neither of these is to be equated simply with transmission from a teacher, for, says Lu, the succession to the Confucian Way was not dependent on direct reception from a sage teacher, or on some master (as in Ch'an) setting his personal seal on one (30:1b, 3a). The former type of perception is seen especially in Chou Tun-i, whom Lu sees as the key to the rediscovery of the true Way in the Sung. That Way, in Chou's case, is to be identified with the Way to Sagehood as exemplified by Confucius and his disciple Yen Hui. In colloquy with his students, Lu is reminded that Ch'eng I had called his older brother

Ch'eng Hao the direct successor to Mencius after a lapse in transmission of almost fifteen hundred years, and also that Ch'eng I had said nothing about Chou Tun-i as an intermediary. Lu explains that the lapse of time from Mencius is one thing but the content of the learning involved is another. One can see from Chou's *Penetrating the Changes (I-t'ung shu)* that his most profound insight was into the Way to Sagehood as Yen Hui had pursued it, while Chou's perception of the Supreme Ultimate as the integrating principle of sagehood came from the classic of *Changes* as edited by Confucius (30:1ab, 3ab).

Lu argues further that despite Ch'eng's I failure, in his memorial tribute to his elder brother, to acknowledge any debt Ch'eng Hao owed to Chou, there was other evidence to indicate that the Ch'eng brothers had studied under Chou but had been reticent concerning certain matters like the Supreme Ultimate, which it was left to Chu Hsi to discern for himself (30:3ab).

In his discussion of the Succession to the Way after Chu Hsi, Lu does not single out any sages but he does praise a number of heroes like Chen Te-hsiu, Hsüeh Hsüan, Lo Ch'in-shun, et al., while he avoids sweeping statements like Lü Liu-liang's decrying the virtually complete decline of the Way in the Yüan and Ming. Rather he pays tribute to the individual contributions of many scholars, thus emphasizing the scholastic side of the tradition (30:17b-19a; 31:1a-21b).

Lu is similarly alert to the problems besetting the Learning of the Mind-and-Heart in his day. He is not about to evade these as too sticky and embarrassing, or to wash his hands of the *hsin-hsüeh* as all a Buddhist deception. Nor does he, like Ku Yen-wu, treat the "method of the Mind" *(hsin-fa)* as just a careless lapse on the part of Ch'eng I and Chu Hsi:

> In the "method of the mind" the character *fa* means the same as the "measuring norm" in the Sage's [i.e., Confucius'] saying about "not transgressing the measuring norm," which has reference to the Sage's following his heart's desire at the age of seventy. From the fact that he did not overstep the norm by the age of seventy, one can see that all his life until then he had simply toed the line [kept to the norm]. How could any one believe [as the Wang Yang-ming school does] that what the Sage had kept to all his life is something we could sweep aside all at once, as if we could hope to top the Sage!(31:17a)

The latter day School of the Mind, according to Lu, deprecates the written word and devalues the classics. Their reason for acclaiming Yen Hui (as distinct from his own reasons) is that Yen Hui left nothing in writing to communicate his teaching, as did Confucius, Tseng Tzu, Tzu-ssu, and Mencius in the Four Books, but rather symbolized a kind of Confucian wordless transmission similar to Ch'an. On this he comments:

Those in later times who delight in talking about the Learning of the Mind-and-Heart make Yen Hui the very patriarch of that learning, dwelling on the fact that he made no use of writings [to communicate the Way]. But does this mean that the teaching of Confucius [who did communicate in writing], was not the Learning of the Mind-and-Heart?(29:4b-5a)

The answer for Lu is obvious. Confucius did have a Learning of the Mind-and-Heart.

After the time of Mencius, however, the Confucian school in the Han and T'ang, for all its voluminous writings, had forgotten the learning of the mind. The great failing of Han scholarship lay precisely in the fact that it was not based on the mind-and-heart (29:11a). In consequence of this, says Lu, the mind and learning went separate ways, and Buddhism moved in with its own teaching concerning the mind. More recently what Wang Yang-ming and his school have advocated as the "Learning of the Mind" is actually the Buddhist variety, and should be so identified. Thus he calls it the Mind School (hsin-tsung), comparable to the Ch'an School (Ch'an-tsung), which teaches wordless transmission outside the scriptures from mind-to-mind. Of the School of the Mind in this sense Lu Hsiang-shan may indeed be thought its spiritual ancestor, though not the progenitor of a scholarly lineage (31:14a-15b).

In the rise of this school what has been lost sight of is the distinction between the human mind and the mind of the Way, which emphasized the need for caution and trepidation, lest one fall into error. Says Lu "In today's School of the Mind, when they speak about mind they really mean 'having no scruples' " (31:16b). Lu follows this up by identifying the true Learning of the Mind in these terms:

Chen Hsi-shan (Chen Te-hsiu) wrote the Classic of the Mind-and-Heart (Hsin-ching) and the Classic on Governance (Cheng-ching).[63]

His *Heart Classic* consists entirely of what was said about the mind-and-heart in the Four Books, Five Classics, and the recorded conversations of Confucian scholars. This then is the true Learning of the Mind-and-Heart. Today's School of the Mind *(hsin-tsung)* is about this essence *(tsung)* and not really about mind. (31:16b)

Lu Shih-i could be as critical as Lü Liu-liang of Wang Yang-ming and his Ch'an-like interpretation of innate knowledge, but he did not withhold full endorsement, as Lü and Chang Lü-hsiang did, of Chu Hsi's "breakthrough to integral comprehension" *(huo-jan kuan-t'ung)*, an enlightenment which emerged from the continual fathoming of principle. This integral comprehension was the fruit of a natural process, in which Lu saw learning itself as a kind of enlightenment, constantly deepened by further increments of knowledge and experience. But it was the product of a self-cultivation which put practice *(kung-fu)* ahead of substance and was therefore real or practical *(shih)*, rather than seeking the substance of the mind in itself, which was vain and impractical *(k'ung)* (3:13b-14b, 17b).

In this respect Lu was less obsessed by the danger of falling into Ch'an enlightenment than was Lü Liu-liang, who shied away from Chu Hsi's "breakthrough to integral comprehension." Yet on the subject of quiet-sitting he tended to hold the same strong reservations as Lü. Lu believed that quietude or composure came from holding to reverence, rather than reverence coming from quiet-sitting. Like Lü, he could defend Chou Tun-i's recommendation of quiescence as upholding principle versus selfish desires, while seeing the practice as a positive danger in the Wang Yang-ming school, wherein it was often used as a means to the direct apprehension of the essence of the mind.[64]

This was an issue on which Lü Liu-liang attacked the neo-orthodox Tung-lin thinkers for their continuing susceptibility to Wang school influences, including their emphasis on the physical aspect of the mind. What Tung-lin thinkers affirmed as the dynamic consciousness of the mind, Lü Liu-liang regarded as leaning dangerously toward the empty spiritual consciousness of Ch'an. Lu Shih-i, however, while cautioning against the Ch'an type of enlightenment, shared with the Tung-lin their sense of the mind as a dynamic fusion of principle and material force, to be brought into play in dealing with the diverse manifestations of principle in scholarly inquiry and the everyday conduct of life.

Here then we have a reminder that even among "orthodox" thinkers, sharing many of the same assumptions in regard to the constant values of the Neo-Confucian tradition, different possibilities existed with respect to key variables. Within the heart of orthodoxy Lu Shih-i's particular synthesis attempted to bridge the gap between divergent views of principle and material force, the mind and its cultivation, quiet-sitting and enlightenment.

Before proceeding to a discussion of orthodoxy in official circles, I should like to cite one more case of an independent scholar, representing an alternative "orthodoxy," who had significant opinions about the message and method of the mind. If we think of "orthodox Neo-Confucianism" primarily as a strict adherence to Chu Hsi, and call such movements as the Tung-lin school "neo-orthodox," the distinction made is between an insistence on exclusive fidelity to Chu's teaching as final and definitive, and a view of received tradition which leaves it open to new contributions—not so much for innovation's sake as from a feeling of the need to reaffirm perennial values in new settings and redefine the mainline tradition as a Mean among new interpretations. In the case of the Tung-lin, we had a "neo-orthodoxy" combining Chu Hsi with a revisionist view of Wang Yang-ming, the latter seen as complimenting the former rather than opposing him.

Li Yung (1627–1705) [65] is among the neo-orthodox, so defined, but merits special attention as a scholar recognized in the early Ch'ing as one of its most influential teachers. The eighteenth-century historian Ch'üan Tsu-wang is often quoted for his characterization of "three great scholars" of the early Ch'ing: Huang Tsung-hsi in the south, Sun Ch'i-feng in the north, and Li Yung in the West (i.e., the northwest). [66] The historian Chiang Fan includes Li Yung in his accounts of the Sung school in the Ch'ing, i.e., as an "orthodox" Neo-Confucian, but obviously according to the liberal interpretation I have labeled "neo-orthodox." [67]

Li was virtually a self-made man, orphaned early and educated mostly by his mother (whence he had a singular sensitivity to the importance of education for women, as well as to the kind of learning that would serve both men and women). Poor and struggling as a youth, he experienced enough hardship and overcame enough odds to give him a lasting sense of identification with ordinary people, whose everyday needs became for him the prime practical criterion of value. Whether for this reason or not he held himself aloof from official involvements and emoluments, carrying out his life mission as teacher to all classes of society. Since he had not served the Ming, it is probably more this sense of identification with the common man and woman than any fastidiousness of dynastic loyalty, which kept him from joining the official ranks or accepting any honors from the Ch'ing. Thus he defies categorization in the usual terms. A scholar for the common people, he was neither "intellectual" nor "anti-intellectual," but had a keen sense of the value of hard-won learning and little liking for literary embellishment or high-flown theory.

Emerging in Shensi province from no established school, Li is said, in the familiar language of Neo-Confucianism, to have taken upon himself the responsibility for carrying on the Way in the form of the native tradition of his region, the so-called "Kuan learning," [68] centered on the former capital of Ch'ang-an. This had been represented in the Sung by Chang Tsai and the Lü family but more proximately for Li by the Ming scholar Lü Nan (1479–1542).[69] Lü, also from Shensi, was admired as a scholar-official of the highest personal integrity, devoted to the Ch'eng-Chu teaching but also at some pains to try to understand Wang Yang-ming and find the common ground between Chu and Wang. This, of course, was to be true of Li Yung as well, but Li went further to try to find the good in even such "unorthodox" figures as Wang Ken and his T'ai-chou school, no doubt because they too stressed learning for the common man.[70] Hence Li's "neo-orthodoxy" is of the consensus variety: basic values for the common man, rather than high scholarly tradition or official ideology. He has little to say about the "orthodox tradition" (tao-t'ung), but sees earlier teachings as following two parallel lines, one from Confucius, represented in the Sung and Ming by the Ch'eng-Chu school and the Tung-lin, and the other from Mencius represented by Lu Hsiang-shan, Wang Yang-ming, and the T'ai-chou school.[71] The two tendencies spanned a remarkable range of thought, and one can easily imagine the tension that could exist between the more liberal (even if in some ways still fundamentalist) "neo-orthodoxy" of Li Yung and the stricter philosophical orthodoxy of a Lü Liu-liang.

Although Li draws equally on Chu and Wang, he does not simply split the difference between them, but strikes his own balance. The compiler of Case Studies of Ch'ing Confucians (Ch'ing-ju hsüeh-an), Hsü Shih-ch'ang (1858–1939), says that Li gave a certain priority to the study of Lu, Wang, and Ch'en Hsien-chang, to be followed by the Ch'engs, Chu, and their Ming followers, Wu Yü-pi, Hsüeh Hsüan, Hu

Chü-jen, Lo Ch'in-shun, et al.[72] This is certainly true of Li's discussion of the substance and function of the Way, wherein he identifies Lu and Wang with a more basic and integral approach to "learning for the sake of oneself" that has the widest applicability to human life experience, and not just on the rational or verbal level. On the other hand Li balances this by insisting on the superiority of the Ch'eng-Chu method of self-discipline, gradual cultivation, and methodical study. To him these are as complementary as substance and function. "The extension of innate knowing is the substance, and the practice of reverence, fathoming of principle, preservation of mind, and self-examination are the method of disciplined effort *(kung-fu)*."[73] Both aspects must be kept in mind and availed of by the individual depending upon his circumstances and the stage of his self-development.[74]

In effect Chu Hsi's method of practice is the way to "extend innate knowing," and "innate knowing" is the key to the constant renewal of the moral life. Without recourse to innate knowing one would lack a fulcrum for self-criticism, the moral and spiritual leverage necessary to self-renewal. "Innate knowing is the same as 'conscience' *(liang-hsin)*," he says. "To deny innate knowing is to deny conscience."[75] In this vein Li's favorite slogan "Repent one's errors and renew oneself" could be more freely translated as "Self-renewal through self-criticism."[76]

A somewhat contrasting impression may be gotten from Li's suggested reading curriculum which offers the familiar fare and follows the standard order of the Chu Hsi school, starting with a reading of the *Elementary Learning* (though, Li acknowledges, much of this text is too difficult for beginners); *Reflections on Things at Hand (Chin-ssu lu)*; the Four Books, Five Classics, Chu Hsi's *Family Ritual (Wen-kung chia-li)*, etc.[77] In the home regular reading of such orthodox texts as Ssu-ma Kuang's *Family Ritual (Chia-hsün)* and Ts'ao Tuan's "Family Rules *(Chia-kuei)*" are recommended.[78] Yet when one reads his interpretations of key texts, like the *Great Learning* and the *Mean*, they essentially follow Wang Yang-ming, even when the ideas are clothed in Ch'eng-Chu terms.[79]

Consider his interpretation of the "manifesting of bright virtue" in the *Great Learning:*

Bright virtue is the mind-and-heart. The mind is essentially limpid spirit *(ling)*. If the spirit is not obscured, bright virtue is clearly manifested. The mind is essentially one with all things. Not to separate oneself from others is to be kin to [love] the people. The mind-and-heart is in essence perfectly good. Not to appropriate this good to oneself alone is to rest in the highest good. (1:1b)

Here "bright virtue" *(ming-te)*, taken by both Chu Hsi and Wang Yang-ming to represent the moral nature *(te-hsing)* and as such Heaven's principle, is identified directly with the mind, and the mind is spoken of as "essentially limpid spirit." In this Li quite explicitly follows Wang Yang-ming and ignores Ch'en Chien's repeated, pointed attacks on Wang's equation of principle, mind, and spirit. Further, Li, for all his talk elsewhere about self-renewal, follows Wang's "loving the people" rather than the Ch'eng-Chu version of the second Guiding Principle as "renewing the people." Moreover he interprets the third Guiding Principle as the fullest possible manifestation of this virtue so as to form one body with Heaven-and-earth and all things. This too conforms to Wang's construction of things in his "Inquiry on the Great Learning," by which he implicitly installs the extension of innate knowing *(liang chih)* to form one body with all things as the alpha and omega of that text.

Similarly with Li's reading of the "investigation of things" *(ko-wu)*:

Ko-wu is the No. 1 principle by which one enters the gate of learning to be a sage. . . . *Wu* (things, matters, affairs) refers to the matters of self (person), mind, intention, knowing, family, state, and world [as in the eight items of the *Great Learning*]. *Ko* (investigating, rectifying) refers to the rules which rule one's making sincere, rectifying, regulating, ordering, and bringing peace [as respectively applied to the foregoing]. (1:4a)

The significance of this is further explained by Li through his interpretation of the *Great Learning's* assertion that things have their trunks and branches, as well as their beginnings and ends—referring to their order of practice. According to Li this originally meant that manifesting bright virtue throughout the world was all of one piece with things having their trunks and branches. But later scholars have not understood this. They have misapplied it to the "things" of *ko wu* so as to break everything down into separate, discrete sequences. Thus we end up with endless discussion and dispute over the successive steps in investigation, as partisan and petty as if one were engaged in a lawsuit over it. What is needed now is simply to accept "things" as the matters originally set forth in the *Ta-hsüeh* text and rectify *(ko)* each of them (1:4ab).

From this Li proceeds to equate *ko* (understood as "rectification") with choosing and manifesting goodness as it is spoken of in the *Mean* and with resting in the highest good as it is spoken of in the *Great Learning;* in the process he identifies this goodness with the goodness of human nature bestowed by Heaven. In other words, the investigation of things becomes the rectification of human affairs; this rectification becomes the manifesting of innate goodness; the latter is equated with "manifesting bright virtue" (the moral nature), and this in turn is seen as the essential basis of all the forms of effort and activity found among the eight items of the *Great Learning.* In the process Li reduces the Three Mainstays or Guiding Principles and Eight Items of the *Great Learning* essentially to this one principle, the manifesting of bright virtue, which is also the essence of the message and method of the mind transmitted from the sage-kings. Here the injunctions to be refined and single-minded and to hold fast to the Mean, are now implicitly understood as the extension of innate knowing. In short, innate knowing is the key to the method of the mind and attainment of the Way.

While Li makes no direct mention of Wang Yang-ming's innate knowing *(liang-chih),* elsewhere he clearly identifies it with this innate "bright virtue," and his argument is again strongly reminiscent of Wang's in the "Inquiry on the *Great Learning.*" Yet he sees it as a truth already clearly set forth in the Five Classics and Four Books, so that there is no need to look for it elsewhere. Even so, should one want corroboration it is to be found in a reading of Chu Hsi's *Reflections on Things at Hand (Chin-su lu),* Hsüeh Hsüan's *Reading Notes (Tu-shu lu),* Hu Chü-jen's *"Chü-yeh lu,"* Kao P'an-lung's *Essentials (Chieh-yao),* Chou Ju-teng's *Core Tradition of the Wang Yang-ming School (Wang-men tsung-chih),* and the *Essential Sayings of Lo Ju-fang (Chin-hsi yü-yao).* Moreover, without making direct reference to Chan Jo-shui, Li speaks of this teaching as essentially one with Chan's "personally experiencing Heaven's principle" in each and every life situation (1:5a).

Since Li often reaffirmed Chu Hsi's overarching aim of achieving "the whole substance and great functioning" of the Way, it is noteworthy that he does not limit the discussion to self-cultivation but goes on to show how this same principle is applicable to the kinds of studies which are concerned with bringing order to the state and peace to the world, specifically citing Chen Te-hsiu's *Extended Meaning of the Great Learning (Ta-hsüeh yen-i)* and Ch'iu Chün's *Supplement* to it, as well as the *General Study of Literary Remains (Wen-hsien t'ung-k'ao)* of Ma Tuan-lin in the Chu Hsi line of scholarship. Underlying these forms of encyclopedic learning is the one principle of the investigation of things as Li has interpreted it to mean the manifesting of one's innate bright virtue, i.e., in a sense similar to Wang Yang-ming's extension of innate knowing. This is Confucius' one thread running through all. If one grasps this he will not make the mistake of interpreting the "investigation of things" in terms of "broadening or enlarging one's learning" but will rather see that the pursuit of "broad learning" should be integrated by this one principle of the thread running through all (1:5ab).

In the foregoing passage, when Li speaks of *ko-wu* as the "Number One Principle by which one enters the gate of learning," he uses his preferred term *sheng-hsüeh*, as Chu Hsi had, for the learning of the sages or the learning of sagehood. Like Huang Tsung-hsi, he feels that the terms "learning of principle" *(li-hsüeh)* and "learning of the mind-and-heart" have become too polemical.[80] Yet like Sun Ch'i-feng he constantly reiterates the basic idea that "principle is inherent in the minds and hearts of all men." Heaven's principle is simply the goodness found in all ordinary men and women. It is the way of ordinary, everyday life."[81] And he deplores the tendency of those who prate about the learning of principle or the learning of mind, while forsaking what is ordinary and everyday for the more remote reaches of metaphysical speculation. Since such scholars stray from the ordinary speech of the Four Books, their doctrines amount to a "heterodoxy within the learning of principle."[82]

Nevertheless Li is not about to discard the message, method, or measure of the mind *(hsin-fa)*. He refers frequently to the sixteen word formula handed down from the sage-kings, and has no difficulty interpreting it in the sense either of Chu Hsi or Wang Yang-ming. In the former case the method of the mind is reverent seriousness *(ching)*, which Li insists upon as the starting point of all practice and praxis. "Reverent seriousness is the method of the mind *(hsin-fa)*. If one is capable of reverent seriousness, the mind is constantly alert and one has never-failing presence of mind."[83]

When asked, however, whether in quiet-sitting one should concentrate one's attention on the difference between principle and human desires, Li says one should neither fail to attend to it nor be obsessive about it. Just follow innate knowing and deal with each matter in a direct, natural, and appropriate way.[84] Similarly he interprets the injunctions "to be refined (discriminating) and single-minded" as referring to the operations of innate knowing, and views "holding fast to the Mean" as the application of innate knowing to ordinary life situations. Moreover he understands the one principle in term of Confucius' "measuring square":

What all minds have in common is principle and [the sense of] rightness. In all the world, in all ages, what is everywhere and always the same is principle and rightness. To speak of a mind dispensing with principle and rightness can only mean a mind without a measuring square. . . . The difference between the sage and someone who goes to extremes, between Confucian scholarship and heterodoxy, simply lies in this.

Principle and rightness are inherently possessed by the mind; they are not gotten through oral or written discourse. They are there in the ordinary mind to be applied in everyday use, in meeting all situations. In the investigation of things, it is this that is investigated. In broadening one's learning, it is this that is broadened [extended]. In restraining oneself with rites, this is the restraint. In being refined and discriminating, it is this that discriminates. In being single-minded it is this that one minds. Being single-minded without fail, this is holding fast to the Mean!"[85]

Given Li Yung's repeated insistence that learning must be closely attuned to the needs of ordinary life, it is all the more striking that he places so much emphasis on the practice of quiet-sitting. Chu Hsi, as we know, had his own reservations about the practice as perhaps tending toward quietism, and Wang Yang-ming, after recommending it earlier in his teaching career, had doubts similar to Chu's, though these were on different theoretical grounds, namely his doctrine of the unity of knowing and acting, by which he meant the involvement of innate knowing in all life situations, quiescent or active, rather than the use of a practice like quiet-sitting as a discipline preparatory to action.

Hsü Shih-chang sums up Li's teaching by saying that doctrinally it was expressed in the formula "repentance for one's errors and self-renewal," while in terms of practice it stressed quiet-sitting and contemplation of mind.[86] This is a characterization that finds ample corroboration in Li's collected works. Indeed Li himself takes note of the fact that Wang Yang-ming's view of quiet-sitting differed from his own, but concedes nothing to it. Though Wang turned away from quiet-sitting in favor of a unified approach to the problem of action and quiescence, Li says this was understandable in someone who, besides possessing exceptional abilities, had the advantage of retrospecting the matter from the high ground of his subsequent self-realization achieved by a lifetime of determined effort and struggle. For those just starting out on the path of self-cultivation, taking time for self-reflection and renewal through the regular practice of quiet-sitting, is still a good method. Even Wang Yang-ming, says Li, benefited from having practiced it early in life.[87]

Directing his teaching as always to the level of the common people, Li is unwilling to grant that there should be any difference in the approach to learning between ordinary folk and those supposedly of higher capability or superior discernment, as someone like Wang Chi had suggested in his interpretation of Wang's Four Dicta. Even the sages had to reflect upon and correct their own errors, he says. They too engaged in constant self-renewal. This indeed is the very hallmark of sagehood.[88] And even though Chu Hsi had questioned whether his teacher Li T'ung's practice of quiet-sitting was a practicable method for busy scholar-officials, actively engaged in the conduct of affairs, Li Yung for his own part repeatedly endorses Li T'ung's method of "silent sitting in order to experience it [the substance of the Way] oneself," a method he equates with the Mean's "self-watchfulness" or "solitary watchfulness."[89]

Moreover, while advocating this method always as a prelude to and preparation for action, rather than as an end in itself, Li Yung is explicit that quiet-sitting should focus on the quiescent, un-manifest (wei-fa) state of the mind before the emotions have been aroused, wherein the nature exists in its undifferentiated wholeness and integrity, i.e., the state of the Supreme Ultimate. The intention however should not be to achieve some sudden enlightenment. This may happen in certain cases, but ordinarily the regular sustained practice of quiet-sitting serves as a cumulative method for the development and fulfillment of one's own nature.[90]

Obviously, since Li follows neither Chu nor Wang in his heavy emphasis on quiet-sitting, one cannot treat it as simply a sectarian issue; nor, since Li remained a life-long commoner, can one consider quiet-sitting mostly as an outlet for the pressures and frustrations of official life. Rather, on the level of received teachings, one can see it as a product of that neo-orthodoxy which tried to safeguard Wang Yang-ming's "innate knowing" against the abuse of its new freedom by its more libertarian interpreters. On the conservative side of the Wang school, as we have seen, stood a Quietist wing which emphasized the need for moral rigor and for quiet-sitting as an aid to systematic self-examination. The Tung-lin followed this tendency, and Li admired Tung-lin scholars like Kao P'an-lung who exemplified it. Thus we can understand Li's strong support for quiet-sitting as at least in part a legacy of the late Ming, born first of conflict and contention and then of reform and renewal. Yet, recognizing Li's concern for popular education and individual self-cultivation, one cannot be wholly satisfied with a disposition of the matter on scholastic terms alone, which leave out of account Li's populism and especially his conviction that quiet-sitting could be beneficial for all, in any situation or status.

Parenthetically, Li's strong position on this matter may shed light on the earlier, equally firm, stance of Lü Liu-liang against quiet-sitting. Given Chu Hsi's ambivalence on the subject, and Wang Yang-ming's gradual distancing of himself from it, there would seem to be little warrant for Lü's making such an issue of quiet-sitting. Considering, however, that Li had come down from the northwest to lecture at the Tung-lin Academy and in the surrounding area, during the same years that Lü Liu-liang was mounting a hard-line defense of Chu Hsi ortho-doxy in the Kiangnan region and attacking the Tunglin for its alleged lapses, one may surmise that the polemics of Lü's recorded lectures on the Four Books (Ssu-shu chiang-i) are actually directed more at Li's views than those of Wang Yang-ming. Indeed at some points Lü's commentaries on the Great Learning and Mean read like direct rebut-tals of points Li makes in his Record of Self-Reflection on the Four Books (Ssu-shu fan-shen lu).[91]

One reason behind Li's strong support for quiet-sitting may be his wholehearted acceptance of Chu Hsi's basic formula for the moralization of politics, self-discipline as the key to the governance of men (hsiu-chi chih-jen).[92] This is a principle Li often invokes, and he speaks of quiet-sitting itself as contributing to the same end. It serves, he says, a crucial function in the moral transformation of self and society, "silently aiding in the political transformation of the Court (mo-tso ch'ao-t'ing chih *hua)." "By* it selfish human desires may be transformed into Heaven's principles, and petty men converted into noble men." [93]

Underlying this view of Li's is another fundamental Neo-Confucian principle, common to both Chu and Wang schools: that learning and education are ultimately and irreducibly personal matters, or to put it in the terms of Confucius so often quoted by Chu Hsi, "learning for the sake of oneself" *(wei-chi chih hsüeh)* through finding the Way in oneself *(tzu-te),* as Mencius had expressed it. [94] This was not said in any derogation of schools, the indispensability of which Li also recognized, but as a necessary corollary to education in schools. As he put it:

> The Hall for Clarifying Human Relations *(Ming-lun t'ang)* is the place in which to establish instruction; the moral transformation of human society must begin in the school. There can be no such thing as moral transformation which is not carried out through the school. Moral transformation however does not consist in talking airily about moral principles, but only in clarifying the mind and personally embodying principle. Everyone, possessing this mind and heart, by that very fact possesses principle. From the sages and worthies down to the most ordinary man or woman, everyone possesses this same mind-and-heart, this same principle. . . . In the past as in the present it is one and the same for all alike. But learning in the past was mostly for one's own sake, whereas learning in the present is mostly to please others.
>
> When Confucius instructed Tzu-hsia the reason he made a distinction among scholars *(ju)* between noble men and petty men was just to differentiate these two types of minds [intentions]. Learning for one's own sake means personally experiencing everything for oneself in one's own heart, mind, and body, without putting anything on for the sake of others. Learning for the sake of others not only aims at fame and profit, but in its pursuit of what is unwise and unworthy it renders any talent or intelligence totally unreliable. [95]

Quiet-sitting was an integral part of the learning process and the part most intimately connected with "getting it oneself" *(tzu-te).* Much reading, without the self-reflection and self-renewal that came from quiet-sitting, would become a meaningless routine. Significantly, however, Li also believed that discussion with others, in school or out, was important as a means of confirming in others' experience what other-wise might be mere subjective opinion.[96]

Indeed, so strongly did he believe in this combination of self-reflection and oral discourse as a very personal approach to learning that he put a relatively low value on reading and writing. As a result his so-called collected works consist mostly of recorded dialogues or personal letters, and even the writing down of his oral instructions was some-thing Li discouraged as tending to stand in the way of the student's "getting it himself."[97]

*   *   *   *   *   *   *   *

By now we have considered the views of seven major thinkers of the early Ch'ing, including four important in the Chu Hsi revival, and it is time to take stock of our situation—to assess how things stand with respect to the concepts, attitudes, and practices that relate to the Learning of the Mind-and-Heart.

In general it can be said that there is a strong trend toward the learning of principle, and especially the study of principle in things as well as the application of principle to things and affairs. Accompanying this is a movement away from the learning of the mind, particularly the Wang Yang-ming form of it but also to some extent a deemphasis even on the Ch'eng-Chu form (including quiet-sitting and Chu Hsi's conception of a "breakthrough to integral comprehension"). These develop-ments correspond to a more general trend in the early Ch'ing toward practical learning and evidential inquiry. They might even be taken to mean that the reaction from Wang Yang-ming to Chu Hsi contributed significantly to the larger Ch'ing trend toward critical scholarship and to a fundamentalism that emphasizes basic moral and intellectual values instead of philosophical speculation or religious aspirations.

Yet there are contrary indications and complications too. Some of these same trends are furthered by scholars much influenced by the moderate or conservative wing of the Wang Yang-ming School (Sun Ch'i-feng, Huang Tsung-hsi, Chang Lü-hsiang, and Li Yung). Lu Shih-i, a champion of Chu Hsi, resists the scuttling of the earlier Ch'eng-Chu *hsin-hsüeh* and several scholars reaffirm the method of the mind *(hsin-fa)* as fundamental to orthodoxy even while Ku Yen-wu casts strong doubt on it. The Succession to the Way *(tao-t'ung)* is deemphas-ized by some and reasserted in modified form by others, so that it becomes a problematical issue even among advocates of a return to Chu Hsi.

Worth noting, too, in the midst of the general trends observed above, is the significant variation among individual thinkers. On the issues we have been considering there is little evidence that the return to ortho- doxy brings with it an unthinking conformity. This is all the more significant when one considers that none of the seven scholars so far treated—all of them recognized as important in the shaping of early Ch'ing thought—served in the new government or could be viewed as exponents of an official ideology. Yet several did indeed have an influ- ence upon scholars who were to assume a large role in articulating the new official orthodoxy.

5

Orthodoxy Among the Mandarins

In an earlier study I made a distinction between Neo-Confucian orthodoxy in late imperial China and in Tokugawa Japan, calling the former Mandarin orthodoxy and the latter Bakufu orthodoxy.[1] By this I meant to identify the more clearly defined official teaching in Imperial China, where centralized bureaucratic institutions—and most notably the civil service examination system, with its supporting educational structure, officially promulgated texts and official shrines—provided more uniform standards of orthodoxy than could be found in Tokugawa Japan, where the comparatively decentralized "feudal" military government gave only loose direction at best to a far more autonomous pattern of Confucian education and scholarship.

Allowing for this general difference, there still remains a question as to how far the official orthodoxy in China actually went in defining or enforcing the allowable limits of interpretation. It is not my purpose to reexamine the whole question here, but it should already be apparent that among major scholars *not* serving the Ch'ing dynasty, there were indeed significant differences of interpretation in regard to the concepts and practices we have been discussing, some of them often thought to be matters quite central to the definition of orthodoxy. Thus the question naturally arises as to whether, among those other scholar-officials more closely associated with the ruling regime, a greater uniformity of thought is to be found on these same issues.

The facts do not lend themselves to simple answers, as our first case, Lu Lung-chi (1630–1693) demonstrates.[2] Lu's early ambition was not to be an official but rather to devote himself to a quiet life of scholar-

163

ship. Poverty and the exigencies of his family situation, it is said, compelled him to follow the examination route,[3] from which he eventually emerged with the advanced *chin-shih* degree in 1670. Twice Lu served as a magistrate and once as a censor, but his outspokenness kept getting him into trouble with higher authorities, even as his honesty and courage impressed others. Thus he did not hold office for long; altogether his official service lasted less than ten years, and the greater part of his life was spent with books and students, much of it as a private tutor. Hence his experience of life would seem to have been mostly in scholarly pursuits and his self-identification, one would suppose, was more with the cultural mission of the politically unsuccessful Confucius and Chu Hsi than with any great statesmen. Yet Lu came to be greatly admired for his character and scholarship by others highly placed. He was recommended for the special *po-hsüeh hung-tz'u* examination honoring distinguished scholars for their "wide learning and literary gifts" (though he did not actually participate). The influential guardian of Chu Hsi orthodoxy and President of the Board of Rites in 1724, Chang Po-hsing, held Lu in the highest esteem, and was probably responsible for Lu's elevation to the Confucian temple that year as the first Ch'ing scholar so honored. In this way Lu, held aloft for public admiration and emulation, became a fixture of the official cult.

To confuse this mixed picture of his role further, Lu took as his own great hero the forementioned Lü Liu-liang, whom he regarded as both the most faithful interpreter and redoubtable champion of Chu Hsi's teaching in times of great peril for the Way. Lu appreciated even Lü's radical political views, as well as his interpretations of the Four Books. Lu's own commentaries, *Discourses on the Four Books*, followed Lü's closely, and his collected writings, the *San-yü-t'ang wen-chi (Collected Writings of the Three Fishes' Hall)*, contained numerous references to Lü's ideas. Ironically, when Lü came under attack for his anti-Manchu, and more generally anti-dynastic, views, in the official campaign to suppress Lü's works, Lu's writings, too, with their frequent reference to Lü, came to be severely expurgated.[4] In consequence of his official suppression and censorship, it became extremely difficult to obtain access to the full record of these two most formidable exponents of "orthodox" Chu Hsi teaching!

What seems to have appealed to Lu in Lü Liu-liang was his unqualified adherence to Chu Hsi. Lü's stance contrasts sharply with the instinct for consensus and compromise one finds in others whose "orthodoxy" looks more for a common denominator than for clear statements of unambiguous positions. Lu's own writings reflect the latter approach. They scorn fuzzy-minded, mealy-mouthed compromise. Though not quite as dismissive of other Neo-Confucians as was Lü, Lu inveighed heavily against any but those most pure and correct in their interpretations of Chu Hsi. Of this attitude, Lu's three-part essay entitled *Critique of Scholarship (Hsüeh-shu pien)* is a good example.

It was common for Neo-Confucian scholars to make known where they stood in respect to tradition and recent views of it, and often enough this involved their interpretation of the Succession to, or Tradition of, the Way. In Lu's case we note several striking features almost from the beginning. In keeping with the trend in his times but contrary to the prevailing view in the Sung and Ming, Lu is relatively complimentary to Han and T'ang scholarship for its "correct learning" of Confucius. Then, in line with Ch'en Chien's earlier critique, he portrays the great threat to the Way as coming from the Buddhist inundation of China—at full tide "from the Sung on." For a time this flood was checked by the firm opposition of the Ch'engs and Chu, but later the Confucian ranks were penetrated by Buddhist ideas subtly disguised in Ch'eng-Chu terms. So well accepted had Ch'eng-Chu teaching by then become that everyone paid lip-service to it, which meant that the terms everyone accepted—Heaven's principle, reverence, quiescence—could be used to purvey something quite different. (Note that this trouble derived from the universal acceptance of the Ch'eng-Chu philosophy, not from any challenge to it on the part of Lu Hsiang-shan or a "Lu school.")

Lu then proceeds to expose the casuistic arguments by which Buddhist conceptions were masked in Ch'eng-Chu language, and says: "These evils had already appeared in the Sung and Yüan, but it was never so bad as in the mid-Ming, when Wang Yang-ming began his talk about innate knowing, fobbing off what was really Ch'an in the name of Confucianism." [5]

Lu goes on to relate how Wang's ideas "spread throughout the world" until the Tung-lin thinkers, Ku Hsien-ch'eng and Kao P'an-lung, led a counterattack, bringing people back to the study of Ch'eng-Chu. Nevertheless Ku and Kao themselves did not properly diagnose the root of the disease, but only treated its outward symptoms. Hence the subterranean decay continued to undermine public morality and the Ming body politic, until the dynasty itself was brought to ruin. Its downfall, insists

Lu, "was not owing to brigandage or conquest, or to factionalism [as so often charged], but to the failure of scholarship," which led the way to these other disasters.[6]

Lu then cites specious arguments offered against his own view: 1) that Wang Yang-ming honored Confucius and Mencius just as much as the Ch'engs and Chu, so one should emphasize what they all held in common, not attack Wang for slight differences; and 2) that the weaknesses of the Wang school are really more attributable to his followers than to Wang himself, and one should not lay at the door of Yang-ming such misinterpretations as Wang Chi's theory of the mind being without good and evil. Lu's reply is essentially that the sins of his followers can be traced back to errors in Wang, and that these are both so fundamental and so subtle that they must be exposed and refuted (2:2a-3a).

Another possible objection to his own position, which Lu cites later, is that no special significance should be attached to the fall of the Ming dynasty after the spread of the Wang Yang-ming school, any more than to the fall of Sung after Chu Hsi or of the Chou after Confucius and Mencius. Lu's counter to this is that the views of Confucius, Mencius, and Ch'eng-Chu were never accepted in their own time and could not have had any influence on the course of historical events, whereas the Wang Yang-ming school completely dominated the late Ming scene. They had usurped the place of orthodoxy and must bear responsibility for what befell the Ming (2:6a-7a).

In the second section of Lu's essay he details those key concepts in Ch'eng-Chu teaching which had been misappropriated by Yang-ming and given a Buddhist meaning, particularly the mind and nature. For the most part these are familiar arguments, but it is worth noting that Lu particularly emphasizes the errors into which the Tung-lin fell, for all of their good intentions and undoubted talents. These errors are the overemphasis on quiet-sitting as a method, especially Kao P'an-lung's "clearing the spirit by sitting in silence" (Ch'eng-shen mo-tso), which smacked of the undifferentiated spiritual consciousness of Ch'an meditation, and the neglect of the investigation of things through a preoccupation with apprehending the unitary essence within (i-kuan), while effectively ostracizing constant, determinate principles from the mind (2:3b-6a).

Unmistakable here is the fixing on Ch'an Buddhism, Wang Yang-ming, and the Tung-lin as prime targets of Lu's attack. Equally evident is the influence on Lu of Lü Liu-liang in his dissection of Ming thought and his unqualified rejection of any compromises with the syncretic solutions of the half-hearted defenders of Chu Hsi who are overgenerous to Wang Yang-ming. One may notice too that in this critique of Neo-Confucian learning, which would normally deal with the Succession to the Way, there is no mention at all of the *tao-t'ung*. Rather the spotlight is on Chu Hsi as the zenith of all true learning and then on Wang Yang-ming as its nadir. Lu Hsiang-shan does not enter into the picture at all, and there is no mention whatever of any "Lu-Wang School of the Mind." It is with the terms and concepts of Chu, not Hsiang-shan, that Wang is playing fast and loose, and it is in the middle and late Ming, not the late Sung, that the great catastrophe has occurred.

Lu concludes by citing the great errors which anyone truly devoted to the Way will renounce: "talking about innate knowing"; "uttering the words 'neither good nor evil' "; pointing to the mind-and-heart as principle"; "relying too much on quiet-sitting" [as the method of practice]; "taking the unitary principle as the key to the employment of the mind"; and "taking the subjective rectification of things and affairs as the fundamental thing in knowledge" (2:15ab).

These are mostly points which had already been made by Lü Liu-liang and Chang Lü-hsiang—points which negatively define a new line of Neo-Confucian fundamentalism centered on Chu Hsi and averse to all subsequent adaptations or redefinitions of his thought. One reason Lu makes such a repeated issue of quiet-sitting in Tung-lin thought and practice is that Chu Hsi himself had expressed reservations about its practice by his teacher Li T'ung and Li's predecessors, the Ch'eng brothers. Another obvious reason is its resemblance to Ch'an sitting, which tends to build a bridge between Buddhism and Confucianism rather than maintain the wall of separation Lu sees as so necessary to protect the true identity of the latter. On the other hand, where Lü Liu-liang and Chang Lü-hsiang had seen Chu's "breakthrough to integral comprehension" as susceptible of confusion with Chan enlightenment, Lu is outspoken in its defense. For him Chu Hsi's explanation of it is both convincing and compelling—truly it represents the fulfillment of Chu's method of the sustained investigation of things and fathoming of principle, and is not at all to be confused with Chan enlightenment or Yang-ming's pursuit of the unitary principle.[7]

Two other key points on which Lu stays close to Lü and Chang are the method of the mind and learning of the mind. The latter for him has only the pejorative connotation assigned it by Lü. It has come to represent the Wang Yang-ming school and its Buddhist philosophy of mind masked in the language of Chu Hsi. This, according to Lu, is the type of spirituality common to Lu Hsiang-shan, Wang Yang-ming, Kao P'an-lung, and Liu Tsung-chou, which places prime emphasis on inwardness of spirit and natural spontaneity in action—all of which, says Lu, marks the Learning of the Mind-and-Heart.[8] He also describes those who pursue the *hsin-hsüeh* as given to excesses of the spirit, seeking a learning that is too lofty and highflown, far from Chu Hsi's down-to-earth method for the investigation of things.[9]

All the same Lu strongly defends the "method of the mind" *(hsin-fa)* as the core of the message of the *Mean*,[10] drawing attention to Ch'eng I's formulation of the doctrine which Chu Hsi had placed prominently at the beginning of the text. Lu is aware that much doubt has been cast on the putative source of the sixteen-word formula concerning the human mind and mind of the Way. But so central and crucial is it to Chu's system of moral and intellectual discipline, as compared to the permissiveness of Wang Yang-ming's Learning of the Mind, that something of the sort would have had to be invented if no unimpeachable source existed. Thus he dismisses all questions of its scriptural authority as inconsequential. Chu Hsi himself had been aware of those questions, yet believed in the essential reliability of the tradition. For Lu that was enough.[11]

As Hellmut Wilhelm has truly said:

> Lu's unquestioning reliance on Chu Hsi is expressed in the following quotation: "He who now-a-days discusses the doctrine has no other resort than reverence for Chu Hsi. Holding Chu Hsi in reverence is the correct doctrine; not holding him in reverence is not the correct doctrine." Lu's fierce battle against Wang Yang-ming and his influences was dictated by this attitude.[12]

Wilhelm is also correct when he goes on to say that "Lu made a rather narrow selection from the comprehensive system of Chu Hsi."[13] This truly reflects the process then underway of stripping tradition down to its bare essentials, as shown in the fundamentalist tendency so characteristic of Lü Liu-liang and Lu Lung-chi. Yet when Wilhelm discusses quiet-sitting as a general practice of the Chu Hsi school in the early Ch'ing,[14] he fails to mention that this was another accretion to tradition which Lu was ready to cut out and which indeed he attacked directly and most sharply as subversive of sound scholarship. Lu's fundamentalism, then, while having its own fierce loyalties, was two-edged: by its attack on late Ming subjectivism (as Lu thought it to be), it also reinforced the trend toward objective scholarship and evidential learning. Moreover, in the matter of quiet-sitting it had its own evidence in Chu Hsi's writings that he had long ago cautioned against the practice. In this sense all fundamentalism was not necessarily blind, and the reemergence of Chu Hsi in the late seventeenth century was, against the background of the Ming experience and the results of its experiments with truth-in-action, a feeling of belated recognition that Chu Hsi had been right all along.

As we move further into the ranks of scholars who were active officials, it seems that the more clearly established a man's official identity became and the closer he got to the inner workings of officially defined Ch'ing orthodoxy, the looser became the definition of orthodoxy itself. T'ang Pin (1627–1687)[15] is a case in point. From a family in Honan holding hereditary military rank under the Ming, he rose early through the examination ranks, under the new Manchu regime, to a succession of posts, both local and at the capital, in which he distinguished himself as an effective administrator. T'ang also studied for a time under Sun Ch'i-feng in his native Honan region, and acquired a substantial reputation as a scholar. This led to his successful participation in the special *po-hsüeh hung-tz'u* examination at the capital, in which Lu Lung-chi did not take part because of his father's death. Thereafter T'ang moved on up to scholarly and administrative assignments of increasing responsibility to become chief supervisor of instruction at court, in charge of the education of the heir apparent. Not entirely immune to the vicissitudes of court politics, he had his own ups and downs in later years, but managed to contribute importantly to the compilation of the *Ming History*, to the compilation of the *Complete Writings of Chu Hsi (Chu Tzu ch'üan-shu)*, a major event in the revival of Chu Hsi studies, and to the compiling of the *Hsing-li ching-i* (Essential Ideas of [the Ch'eng-Chu Learning of] Nature and Principle), the official Ch'ing abridgement of the Ming's *Hsing-li ta-ch'üan (Compendium on Nature and Principle)*. In the latter two projects T'ang worked closely with Li Kuang-ti (1642–1718) [of whom more later], and historians have often mentioned the two together as major promoters at court of Chu Hsi "orthodoxy."[16] Successive posthumous honors culminated in T'ang's being named to the Confucian Temple in 1823.

It would be hard to find anyone more closely or formally identified with the establishment of the official orthodoxy than T'ang. Indeed he has been identified by Wing-tsit Chan as one of a group of scholars so exclusively loyal to Chu Hsi and so "close to the government" as to remove him from consideration as an independent scholar.[17] Yet he differed significantly in his views from Lu Lung-chi, who was given a place of honor in the Confucian temple well before T'ang. From this it is evident that orthodoxy, even on the official level, ran in more than one mainstream.

As the most distinguished student of Sun Ch'i-feng, it was natural for T'ang to write a preface for Sun's *Li-hsüeh tsung-ch'uan,* and in so doing, to comment on Sun's account of the tradition. When compared to Lu Lung-chi's "Critique of Scholarship," the differing approaches of the two scholars stand in clear contrast.

T'ang's account invokes the sixteen-word message passed down from Yao, Shun, and Yü, a prescription given concrete application in the Five Moral constants of human relations. These, he says, are the original sources of both the Sage Learning and the Way of the Kings, which were transmitted through the early kings and the Duke of Chou down to Confucius and his followers in the Chou. Thereafter comes the familiar long break in the transmission after Mencius, and its resumption by Chou Tun-i, the Ch'eng brothers, Chang Tsai, Shao Yung, Chu Hsi, and Wang Yang-ming—the latter's name being quietly affixed to the succession as if it had never been in question. These scholars all had their individual strengths and limitations, says T'ang (in the language of Ch'eng I), but in that they had personally experienced and realized the mind of the sages, it was the same mind with which they all communed. Just as Heaven and the Way do not change, so this essential mind has not changed over ages past nor will it in ages to come.

At this point in his exposition T'ang feels obliged to disassociate his mind of the sages from anything akin to the Buddhist mind, or from the kind of syncretic conception in which others saw Confucianism and Buddhism as essentially one. The Buddhist mind is not inherently bound up with human relations, and considers self-enlightenment to take priority over the moral imperatives which Confucians view as intrinsic to their conception of mutual self-fulfillment between oneself and others.

Those who talk about Confucianism and Buddhism being one do not realize that when the Buddhists speak of the mind and nature, it only sounds similar to the Confucian concepts of the moral mind and nature, but actually sets aside human relations and neglects human affairs. Theirs is a mind which springs from selfishness and their way is not one that can bring order to the world and the state. In our Confucian Way, it is investigating things, extending knowledge, making the intentions sincere, and rectifying the mind that constitute self-cultivation, and it is harmonizing the family, state, and world which constitute the Way of Learning. As the Way of restoring one's nature it is the Way of Learning to be a sage; as the way of restoring the natures of all under Heaven, it is the Way of the King. Herein substance and function have the same source; there is no separation of the perceptible and imperceptible [i.e., no two levels of truth]. How could Buddhism be compared to this?"[18]

If this recitation of the standard Neo-Confucian objections to Buddhism seems to belabor the point, it is no doubt because T'ang anticipates the objections that will be raised against his acceptance, which immediately follows, of Sun Ch'i-feng's expanded version of the Succession to the Way in the Sung and Ming. He hopes to disarm the criticism that, in raising Wang Yang-ming to a par with Chu Hsi, and admitting Lu Hsiang-shan, Lo Hung-hsien, and Ku Hsien-ch'eng to the elect company of the eleven masters, he has brought crypto-Buddhists into the Confucian pantheon. If T'ang, like Sun, considers these eleven masters all worthy of honor it is not because he fails to perceive the difference between Buddhism and Confucianism, but because he sees all eleven, whatever their relative stature or individual capacities, as equally models of the transmission of the sage mind and all qualified by their vigorous opposition to Buddhism.

Finally, he says that Sun's work contains the distilled essence of his lifetime's efforts and experience as a scholar, which should assist like-minded scholars to recover their own original nature as Heaven has implanted it in their minds. The completion of the process, however, depends on the efforts each makes to "get it" for himself.[19] In this T'ang highlights the same aspects of the Ch'eng-Chu system that Wang Yang-ming had drawn upon for his new learning.

In this preface T'ang nowhere uses the terms Learning of the Mind (hsin-hsüeh) or the Method of the Mind (hsin-fa), though he refers to their content as essential to the Tradition of [or Succession to] the Way, to the Sage Learning, the Way of the Kings, etc. In other words, aware of the opposition from Lü Liu-liang and Lu Lung-chi, he eschews controversial language, hoping thus to gain ratification, smoothly and without setting off any alarms, of Sun's instatement into the true succession of major thinkers identified with the latter-day Learning of the Mind. At the same time he attempts to reclaim the common ground between Chu Hsi and Wang Yang-ming, which has already been staked out by the line of neo-orthodox thinkers coming down to him through the right wing of the Wang school, the Tung-lin, and Sun Ch'i-feng. Yet, as he attempts thus to consolidate an official Neo-Confucian consensus, in order to disarm hard-line critics and maintain his own credentials as a hard-nosed defender of orthodoxy, he insists that there can be no compromise between Confucianism and Buddhism.

In a preface written for Sun Ch'i-feng, all this might seem no more than conventional deference to his teacher, but T'ang reiterates the same view on more than one occasion, while adumbrating the theme in other significant ways. In a discussion at court with the K'ang-hsi emperor, known to be well disposed towards Chu Hsi's teachings,[20] T'ang gives substantially the same account of the tradition, while arguing especially for Wang Yang-ming:

> From Master Chou down to Master Chu this learning was most pure, correct, precise, and fine, and it could serve as a standard for all scholars. But later scholars, sunk down into mere textual exegesis, lost the essential ideas of the Ch'engs and Chu. Wang Shoujen (Yang-ming)'s doctrine of "extending innate knowledge" sought to correct things and rescue this learning from its latter-day decadence, but his words did not always hit the mark exactly, and the later members of his school often incorporated their own empty views into what was received from him, thereby losing his essential meaning and putting forth instead the ideas of later scholars.[21]

Obviously there is no way that T'ang can define a new orthodoxy without identifying those responsible for the misinterpretation of his (and Sun's) chosen "masters." In the case of Lu Hsiang-shan, it is Yang Chien (1140–1225), who has distorted Lu's teachings, and in the case of Wang Yang-ming, it is Wang Chi who is principally to blame for the confusion of Yang-ming's teachings with Ch'an Buddhism.[22] At the same time, however, T'ang rises openly and strongly to the defense of major figures who had been attacked by Lü Liu-liang and Lu Lung-chi. One of these is Liu Tsung-chou, a teacher of Sun, for whom T'ang has the utmost praise: "his learning was consummate, and after the Ch'engs and Chu there was no one greater than he in embodying the essential spirit of the Way."[23] In a preface to Liu's *Recorded Writings (Wen-lu)*, he responds directly to the challenge hurled at Liu (and Tung-lin scholars) for their practice of quiet-sitting, citing the precedents in orthodox teaching for Liu's position: Chou Tun-i's doctrines of the stabilizing of the mind and "making quiescence the main thing" *(chu-ching)*; Ch'eng Hao's claim that in the matter of Heaven's principle it was something he had gotten by experiencing it himself, and by his instruction to students to take as their basis "reverence to straighten oneself within"; as well as Chu Hsi's statement that in "quiescence lay the reality of the nature," etc. Chu Hsi had received the practice of quiet-sitting from his teacher Li T'ung, who in turn had gotten it from Lo Ts'ung-yen (1072–1135) of Ch'eng I's school, but after Chu Hsi the lapse of his followers into exegetical studies and mere taxonomic scholarship led again to the fragmentation and disintegration of learning.

At this point T'ang proceeds with a discussion of Wang Yang-ming, Wang Chi, and the Four Dicta of "neither good nor evil" which closely follows what we have already seen. The argument leads naturally into the efforts of Kao P'an-lung, Ku Hsien-ch'eng, and finally Liu Tsung-chou to rescue the Way from its misguided interpreters and hostile detractors. After all, says T'ang, in his advocacy of "self-watchfulness" and practice of quiet-sitting, Liu was only reaffirming the original doctrines of the *Mean* and restoring the links that led back from Wang Yang-ming, through Chu Hsi and the Sung masters, to the integral teachings of Confucius and Mencius.[24]

In his "Dicta on Learning *(Hsüeh-yen)*, as found in his Recorded Conversations,[25] T'ang again makes a main issue of quiet-sitting. It is the basic means by which one establishes control of the mind and sets up the norm of perfection, or Supreme Ultimate, in each individual. Again the arguments are similar to those found in the discussion of Liu Tsung-chou, and the same orthodox pedigree is recited, but T'ang's reiteration of these points only underscores the importance of the question for him. He may hope to reconcile differences between two main streams of Neo-Confucian thought, but not at the cost of giving up quiet-sitting. On the contrary, he insists on honoring in the company of Neo-Confucian masters those who had most upheld this practice. Interestingly, Lu Hsiang-shan, though much given to quiet-sitting,[26] is not particularly emphasized in this connection, and certainly not in any connection with Wang Yang-ming. Thus, from this exponent of official "orthodoxy" one could not expect any formulation suggestive of a "Lu-Wang School of the Mind."

It may already have been noticed that T'ang prefers to describe the Tradition of the Way in terms of the "Sages and Worthies' Transmission of the Mind," *(ch'uan-hsin)* or "transmission of the sage mind," using an expression Chu Hsi himself had preferred to Learning of the Mind (see above, pp. 27–37). T'ang's conception of this "transmission of the Mind" includes Chu Hsi's idea of reading classic texts so as to gain a deeply personal experience of the principles they contain, and it embraces too the essential content of the "method of the mind" *(hsin-fa)*. The following passage illustrates both aspects:

> In the learning of the sages and worthies the most essential thing is simply preserving the mind-and-heart, and this simply means preserving Heaven's principle [in the mind]. Subtle and refined, principle can be neither seen nor heard, yet it is clearly manifested in human relations and everyday affairs. In the tradition as passed down from Yao and Shun it was recognized as imperative that one discern and differentiate the precariousness of the human mind and the subtlety of the mind of the Way. So doing, Confucius, who committed himself to learning at the age of fifteen, was finally able by the age of seventy to follow his heart's desire without transgressing the measuring norm.[27]

This is the tradition "that has been passed down, based on the mind, and the same from past to present." Nevertheless it lapsed after Mencius and was not resumed until the Sung. Later, says T'ang, the compilers of the *Sung History (Sung shih)* gave a special place to the Sung masters, identifying them with a School or Learning of the Way because they did not wish simply to equate them with the ordinary run of scholars. Unfortunately this resulted in a split between the Learning of the Way and the study of the Classics.

Actually the Learning of the Way constitutes the gist of the Six Classics and Four Books, to be experienced in one's own mind-and-heart and embodied in one's own conduct of life. It is not that there is something called the Learning of the Way that is transmitted separately from the Classics and Books. If one speaks of the Way as separate from the Classics and Books, it is a heterodox Way, and to speak of the classics apart from one's person and mind is to speak of the classics in the Way vulgar scholars do.[28]

This characterizes the Transmission of the [Sages'] Mind in much the same terms Chu Hsi had used earlier (see above, pp. 35–37). but it is typical of T'ang that he often puts special emphasis on the importance of "getting it oneself" *(tzu-te)* by "personally experiencing Heaven's principle" [in the mind] *(t'i tien-li)*. In this manner he was careful to leave room for Wang Yang-ming's "innate knowing" within the orthodox conception of the Transmission of the [Sages'] Mind.[29]

In concluding this discussion of T'ang's views, so much at odds with those of Lü Liu-liang and Lu Lung-chi at many points, it should be noted that T'ang did not conceal his differences with Lu but expressed them forthrightly in a letter to Lu himself. In this he reaffirmed the great contribution of Chu Hsi in expounding the Way of Confucius and Mencius, and even acknowledged that Wang Yang-ming had failed to match the clarity and precision with which Chu had expressed things. Nevertheless the criticism of Wang has gone too far, he says, and many charges are leveled against him which are not justified by a careful reading of his works. It is time, therefore, to restrain partisan zeal, avoid exaggerated charges and claims, and recognize that on essential points Chu and Wang stood together in defense of Confucian orthodoxy.[30]

For someone to speak thus who has been identified as totally devoted to Chu Hsi and as a major proponent of the official Ch'ing orthodoxy, shows that the establishment view was still far from being defined in terms of a Ch'eng-Chu Learning of Principle versus a Lu-Wang School of Mind.

At this point we reach the most important figure in the formulation of the official orthodoxy of the Ch'ing, Li Kuang-ti (1642–1718).[31] That orthodoxy was nowhere better defined than in the aforementioned *Hsing-li ching i (Essential Ideas of Nature and Principle)*; no work was compiled and promulgated with more close attention and supervision by the reigning emperor, and no scholar was more deeply involved either with the emperor or the work of compilation than Li. What the *Great*

Compendia, compiled at the direction of the Yung-lo emperor in 1415, had represented as a statement of official Ming orthodoxy, the *Hsing-li ching-i* represented for the Ch'ing dynasty.

This major work has already been the subject of an important study by Wing-tsit Chan, and one could have no better brief introduction to Li Kuang-ti than is given herein by Professor Chan:

> Li obtained the *chin-shih* degree in 1670, was selected a bachelor of the Hanlin Academy, and two years later was made a compiler at the capital. When he was home in 1674, he refused to join the rebel Keng Ching-chung (d. 1682). In 1675 he secretly submitted a memorial giving intelligence about rebels in his own province. For his loyalty he was rewarded in 1677 with a readership in the Hanlin Academy. In the following year he sent relatives to guide the Manchu armies to pacify his native region. As an additional reward, he was called to the capital in 1680 and appointed a sub-chancellor of the Grand Secretariat. From then on, he was greatly favored by the emperor. On his recommendation, Taiwan was retaken in 1681. In 1686, as a scholar under the director of the Hanlin Academy, he lectured daily on the Confucian Classics before the emperor and also served as official recorder of the emperor's daily life. In 1703, he was promoted to minister of civil personnel. From 1705 on he saw the emperor almost daily. The relationship between the two was so close that the emperor later said that "I knew Li the best and none knew me better than he." It was inevitable that Li exerted a profound influence on the emperor.[32]

If this conveys a strong impression of Li's influence on the emperor, two equally important—though to some eyes seemingly antithetical—facts should be noted. The first is that Li appears indeed to have been as totally loyal and obedient to the emperor as any minister could be—to the point that some later writers have thought him obsequious and almost slavish. The second is that, as Professor Chan brings out, Li had a mind of his own and stood out among scholars of the day. As Professor Chan has said: " 'Of all the men of prominence in the K'ang-hsi era,' it has been said, 'Li was the one who developed others' talents the most.' "[33]

On the matters that concern us here, Professor Chan has also provided a keen analysis of Li's handling of one: the Tradition of the Way *(tao-t'ung)* in the *Hsing-li ching-i*. Against the background of the Succession to the Way as presented in the earlier *Hsing-li ta-ch'üan*, Professor Chan notes that Li's account of Neo-Confucian thinkers follows much the same order, yet he also observes that Li does not include any Ming Neo-Confucians in the Succession. He concludes: "One is inclined to say that not only was the *Tao-t'ung* reaffirmed, but it was reaffirmed without even such modification as would bring it up-to-date." [34]

In view of the earlier discussion of the *tao-t'ung* by Lü Liu-liang and Lu Lung-chi, who had taken such a negative view of Ming thought and treated the Succession to the Way as virtually having lapsed after Chu Hsi, Li's handling of the matter is not so surprising—that is, if one accepts, as I do, the strong influence on Li of Lu Lung-chi and, either directly or through him, of Lü. [35] What actually seems to be happening here is that Li, while maintaining a rather strict definition of orthodoxy, backs off somewhat from use of the by-now conflicted definition of the Succession to the Way as represented by the term *tao-t'ung*.

One indication of this is the striking omission of any section on the *tao-t'ung* in the *Hsing-li ching-i* corresponding to that in the *Great Compendium* of the Ming *(Hsing-li ta-ch'üan)*. The omission is even more striking since the *Complete Works of Master Chu*, in the compilation of which Li also played a major role, had appeared just a year earlier (1714), with a section containing Chu Hsi's views on the *Tao-t'ung*. [36] Professor Chan says of the omission in the *Hsing-li ching-i*:

> If the *tao-t'ung* loomed so large in the Hsing-li ching-i, why was the section on it omitted? The *Explanatory Statement* is quite explicit on this point, namely, to avoid controversy. We have repeatedly, directly or indirectly, referred to factional controversy. Scholars were tired of partisanship. This was why Ku Yen-wu, Wang Fu-chih, Yen Yüan, and others developed in their own directions. On the part of the government, consensus was desired. What was wanted in the *Hsing-li ching-i* was the established tradition without discussion. [37]

My own view is similar to Professor Chan's on three points: that Li wanted to avoid controversy, was seeking consensus, and was trying to establish tradition without discussion. But I would go further to identify the nature of the controversy itself as one arising from the strongly conflicting versions of "tradition" among the two main lines of orthodox Neo-Confucianism in this period, namely the narrow one represented by Lü Liu-liang, Chang Lü-hsiang, and Lu Lung-chi, as opposed to the broader more liberal interpretation of Sun Ch'i-feng and T'ang Pin (among others). Both T'ang and Li had served as advisers to the K'ang-hsi emperor, and the latter could not have been unaware of the potential for hot dispute here. Li, a skilled politician as well as a scholar of some sophistication, found ways to establish his own preferred version of the tradition without stirring up the fires of controversy surrounding the *tao-t'ung*. Simply to record faithfully Chu's views in the *Complete Writings* was one thing. To present an ostensibly definitive view, with Imperial sanction, after the matter had been disputed so often since Chu Hsi's time, was another.

Confirmation of this comes from the works of Li Kuang-ti himself. Time and again he treats the tradition, and defines it in his own way, without directly invoking the concept of the *tao-t'ung*. In his discussion of Chu Hsi's preface to the *Mean*, wherein Chu originally set forth the concept of *tao-t'ung*, Li manages by skillful footwork to link the Ch'engs and Chu to Tzu-ssu, reputed author of the *Mean*, thus bridging the gap in the "learning broken off" (*chüeh-hsüeh*) after Mencius, without once mentioning the controversial terms Succession to the Way (*tao-t'ung*) or Method of the Mind (*hsin-fa*) (Li, familiar with Ku Yen-wu's writings, no doubt knew about the latter's impugning of the *hsin-fa*). Then too Li says that the succession was lost between the Sung and Yüan, thereby leaving the Ming in limbo.[38]

Moreover in his *Recorded Conversations (Yü-lu)* there is again no section for the discussion of the *tao-t'ung* itself, but special honor is paid to the Six Sung Masters, identified as Chou Tun-i, the Ch'eng brothers, Chang Tsai, Shao Yung, and Chu Hsi. These are of course incontestable choices, and one could even see them as representing the common ground between the Sun-T'ang version and that of Chang-LüLu. But Li's pantheon of six figures is much more exclusive than Sun Ch'i-feng's Eleven Masters, and it conspicuously leaves out Lu Hsiangshan.[39] This is true also of the selection made in the *Complete Writings of Master Chu (Chu Tzu ch'üan-shu)*, which emphasizes the prophetic aspect pre-Sung and thereafter scholarly continuity from the Ch'engs to Chu, but then omits Lu Hsiang-shan in favor of a lengthy discussion of study and teaching methods for understanding and passing on the

Way.[40] Still, Li is tactful enough to say a few good words for Hsiang-shan, rather than extrude him altogether from the fold: he says that Lu and Chu Hsi agreed on the fundamentals and only differed on details.[41] By this he meant that no one could disagree on the need first to establish [the moral nature, as] the primary thing," which Lu emphasized, even though one might differ on how this was to be done.[42]

If this showed a feeling for consensus, Li was also ready to concede that Lu possessed "great talent." [43] He went on to show, however, what an act of condescension this was on his own part by explaining how, without proper guidance, great talent can go wrong. The Ch'eng brothers and Chu Hsi had good teachers in Chou Tun-i and Li T'ung respectively, and this saved their talents from the folly of youthful excursions into Buddhism and Taoism, while it also enabled Chu Hsi, with his feet set firmly on the ground, to develop his talents and fulfill his high ambitions. With Lu, however, who prided himself on being self-taught and "getting the Way for himself," it was his own overweening self-confidence, says Li, that led him down the wrong road (18: 4a-5a).

Relevant to the key role of teachers is a striking parallel Li draws between Buddhism and Confucianism. In the former, he says, there are three types of teachers: scripture masters (fa-shih) entrusted with the disciplinary precepts; and meditation masters (ch'an-shih), who assist individuals to attain direct enlightenment without depending on verbal formulations. In Confucianism, Li says, Lu Hsiang-shan and Wang Yang-ming correspond to the Ch'an masters. Instead, however, of simply dismissing them as purveyors of a false teaching, he treats this enlightening function as merely a limited one in comparison to the Ch'engs and Chu, who, he says, combined all three methods in one way of cultivation (18:1b-2b).

In Li's *Recorded Conversations* (of which many items were written by himself), he devotes the first seventeen chapters to the Classics, the eighteenth to the six Sung Masters, the nineteenth to an assortment of Confucian scholars, and the twentieth to various "philosophers" or "masters" whose Confucian credentials are lacking or in doubt. The Confucians include such scholars as Tung Chung-shu and Han Yü (showing that the Way was not wholly lost during the Han and T'ang, even though Tung and Han did not measure up to the Sung masters) as well as Chen Te-hsiu (praised as pure and upright), and Hsü Heng (cited for being very real and genuine). The latter's *Recorded Conversations*, he says, excel all others after Chu Hsi's. Moreover Hsü was a great teacher, who, as libationer of the Imperial University, trained many men of outstanding ability (19:33b-34a).

Chapter twenty includes Lu Hsiang-shan and Wang Yang-ming, along with such types as Kuan Tzu, Wen-chung Tzu, and Buddhists and Taoists. Although the nineteenth chapter on Confucian scholars does not include Ming scholars as such, the twentieth includes, with obvious approval, Lo Ch'in-shun's critique of Wang Yang-ming (20:6b-7a), whom Li holds responsible for corrupting a whole generation of educated men *(tu-shu jen)* (20:7a). One also finds an extensive critique of Lu Hsiang-shan in chapter seventeen of Li's *Complete Works*.[44] Thus no doubt is left in the reader's mind about Li's refusal to compromise with Sun and T'ang on their effort to establish a *Tao-t'ung* consensus which would include Lu, Wang, and such followers of Wang as Ku Hsien-ch'eng, Kao P'an-lung, and Liu Tsung-chou.

If Li makes clear where his loyalties lie—mainly with his "Six Sung Masters," he more especially favors "Ch'eng-Chu," and above all Chu Hsi.[45] His unreserved admiration for Chu as the towering figure among the other Sung masters is expressed in his declaration that "the mind of Chu Hsi is the mind of Confucius" and in his rejection of Hsiang-shan's criticism of Chu Hsi, which he regards as tantamount to an attack on Confucius himself. Indeed the major role performed by Chu in the Sung is comparable to that of Confucius in Chou.[46] From what we have already seen of other "orthodox" thinkers in the early Ch'ing there can be no doubt that Chu Hsi had by this time emerged as the preeminent figure in Neo-Confucianism. Not that he had ever, since the Late Sung, stood any lower, but that in retrospect, and in fuller awareness of both the depth and breadth of his thought in comparison to others, his stature and his dominance stood out now in even higher relief. As Professor Chan has said, Chu Hsi himself was the "central focus of the *Hsing-li ching-i*" and this represented the culmination of "Chu Hsi's rise as the towering figure in seventeenth-century Neo-Confucianism."[47]

It is significant, however, that Li does not treat Chu as a prophetic hero, whose singularity derives from some special insight into the Way. It is true, as we have just seen, that he saw Chu Hsi as sharing in the mind of Confucius, and likewise true that Li conceives of the Way as "the transmission of the mind" *(ch'uan-hsin)* or "the transmission of the mind of the sages and worthies."[48] But Chu's brilliance is not described in the terms earlier used for Ch'eng Hao's or Chou Tun-i's direct grasping of the Way lost since Mencius, as if by Heaven's marvelous inspiration. Rather Li celebrates Chu as a great learner, a true scholar, and a powerful synthesizer—one who could draw from many sources and embrace the wisdom of the ages.

Chu was not unaware of the difficulties attaching to the prophetic roles of Ch'eng Hao and Chou Tun-i; nor was he indeed oblivious to the problems of finding a place for Confucius' disciple Yen Hui, the paradigm of the aspiration to sagehood in Neo-Confucianism, in any scheme of authoritative transmission (since Yen left no revelatory text).[49] In an age of critical rationalism, which stressed solid, practical learning (shih-hsüeh), as Li himself did,[50] he viewed Chu Hsi as the personification of patient learning and sound judgment, whose lofty vision was grounded in the hard reality of evidential and experiential fact. Li would no doubt have seen the revival of Chu Hsi in the early Ch'ing itself as contributing to the new spirit of critical scholarship.

If this places Li's view in the line of "scholastic," rather than "prophetic" interpretations of the Succession to the Way, there is a reason for it beyond his admiration for Chu's scholarship. We have already seen how greatly Li values both teaching and learning, and especially how he exempted Hsü Heng from the general execration of Yüan-Ming scholarship because Hsü had excelled as a teacher. This reminds us that Li's own relationship to the K'ang-hsi emperor was strikingly similar to that of Hsü Heng and Khubilai—both Hsü and Li himself served able rulers of conquest dynasties at the height of their power. One need not impute any special opportunism or cynicism to Li if one recognizes the enormous magnetism exerted by that power or the attractiveness to Li of the thought that his sovereign, so serious a student of Confucianism, represented an extraordinary opportunity and apt subject for conversion into a sage-king. Although Li's respect for the emperor may have carried him to the limits of enthusiastic cooptation, if not flattery, one cannot be unaware that he himself is all the while bidding for the role of sage mentor.

Such considerations cannot be overlooked in assessing Li's diffidence in handling the "Succession to the Way." Gingerly as he was about this, Li could not be unaffected by the association of it in his own mind with the concept of Legitimate Succession (cheng-t'ung). Understandably he adverted frequently to the question of how, before Confucius' time, the Way of Kingly Governance and the Succession to the Sages'

Way had become separated and how neither the ancient sage nor Chu Hsi had been in a position to see their ideas implemented, not having served as mentors to the throne. The hope of relinking the two Ways led Li into some wishful speculations, along with ingenious calculations as to the cyclical patterns in the affairs of men which might make the present moment particularly auspicious for the emperor to reunite in his own person the Way of Governance and the Way of the Sage (with, of course, some modest assistance from his humble mentor strongly implied).[51]

If such cosmic forces were indeed at work, they would naturally override purely scholarly considerations. Indeed, in that expectation, one could easily overlook the supposed long wasteland after Chu Hsi as no more than a fallow period awaiting the reinstitution of sagely rule and revival of the Way.[52] It is quite possible in fact that Li, predisposed to ignore or belittle whatever had occurred since Chu Hsi's time, was ignorant of how Neo-Confucians in Khubilai's era had entertained similar hopes of his reuniting the two Ways, only to see them come to nothing.[53] Of course, another explanation is also possible: that he knew of it, and yet in spite of that earlier disappointment this particular hope sprang eternal in the Confucian breast.

As to the content of that Way—the essential formula for sagely rule —it remained the same as Chu Hsi had expounded it in his preface to the *Mean*, namely: the message of the mind concerning the fallibility of the human mind, the difficulty of perceiving the mind of the Way, and the consequent need for the ruler to rely on the *Four Books*, and especially the *Great Learning*, for guidance.[54] The learning of the sages, says Li, took the ground of the mind as the basis for their learning. Recognizing that "the one mind contained the myriad principles, they believed that one should preserve this mind as the basis for the fathoming of principles."[55] In this sense, the method of learning proceeded from the one to the many, but such "learning" is not to be confused with heterodox enlightenment as is so often done by "those who speak for the learning of the mind."[56] Rather true learning must proceed from the fathoming of principle through the study of things and affairs, based on a proper cultivation of mind. One cannot have singleness of mind, as in the *hsin-fa*, or in Confucius' "one thread running through all" without that oneness or that mind being based on principle (4:20b-21a).

Thus Li summed up his view of Confucian teaching as consisting of three mainstays *(kang):*

Preserve the real mind *(ts'un shih-hsin)*
Manifest real principle *(ming shih-li)*
Perform real tasks *(hsing shih-shih)*. (23:3b)

With regard to "preserving the mind" Li had this to say:

The expressions "preserving" and "nourishing" come from Mencius [7A:1]. Mencius said [of the mind]: "If nourished, there is nothing that will not grow." And "if controlled, it will be preserved; if let go, it will be lost" [6A:8]. Also he spoke of "preserving the mind and nourishing the nature" [7A:1]. Now "the human mind being precarious and insecure," to preserve it means to keep it secure. "The mind of the Way being subtle and barely perceptible," to nourish it means to make it manifest. This is the basic idea of Mencius. . . . (23:17b, Hsüeh i)

The mind and nature are one and also two. One cannot preserve the mind without nourishing the nature [principle], nor can one nourish the nature without preserving the mind. . . . Essentially the method is the same for both mind and nature. But if one speaks about the learning of the mind and only brings out the preserving of mind [while not nourishing principle], isn't that very close to the emptiness of Buddhism and Taoism?" (23:18a)

In the preceding passages Li refers to the "learning of the mind" as something misrepresented in terms similar to Buddhist/Taoist emptiness and enlightenment. But in a closely related passage he implies that there was a true learning of the mind taught by Confucius and Mencius. Confucius, it is true, did not speak directly of the mind itself, but did discuss many aspects of the moral mind such as filial piety, loyalty, reverence, conscientious conduct, etc. "After the time of Confucius and Mencius, however, there has been no real discussion of the mind-and-heart. In the Han and T'ang periods, scholars only talked about literary composition, political economy, and psychic dispositions, while neglecting discussion of the nature of Heaven's imperative *(t'ien-ming chih hsing)* and the method of mind discipline (23:15b-16a).

On most of these questions Li's views are quite close to those of Lü Liu-liang, Chang Lü-hsiang, and Lu Lung-chi. The same is true with regard to the matter of quiet-sitting. He approves of it as sanctioned by Chou Tun-i's "quiescence" for the nourishing of principle and reduction of desires, but disapproves of it if practiced in a manner resembling Ch'an meditation:

> Chu Hsi once said that beginning students should practice quiet-sitting. At the same time he said that one should not overdo the pursuit of quiescence. One should combine the meaning of these two quotations and reflect on them deeply. With that the full import [of what Chu Hsi meant] will become apparent. (23:5a)

These few lines, in their balanced view of the matter, are typical of the more extended discussion of quiet-sitting in the *Complete Writings of Master Chu (Chu Tzu ch'üan-shu)*, which constitute a significant portion of the initial presentation of methods of learning and self-cultivation.[57]

Similarly, Li speaks more circumspectly than Lü and Lu about Kao P'an-lung and Liu Tsung-chou, who were much given to quiet-sitting. He says that they could not be called either Confucian or Buddhist, but their thinking was dangerously close to the latter. In most such matters Li tries to present a balanced view of things, and this is also true in his discussion of book-learning, which for him is obviously preferable to quiet-sitting as a method of pursuing principle. Yet factual investigation itself must be guided by principles, norms, and standards, lest even the most exhaustive and painstaking study come to nothing. "In reading, the mind is the most fundamental thing. If it is not all there, then no matter how much one applies one's efforts, it will be of no use. . . . The mind is the basis of all things, and yet the various matters and affairs each have their own root . . . and in the Learning of Principle, if one does not honor Chou, the Ch'engs, Chang, and Chu, then no matter how much one concentrates one's efforts, even for a whole lifetime, it is in vain."[58]

On this basis we can certainly agree with Professor Chan that Li Kuang-ti helped to move Neo-Confucian orthodoxy in the direction of evidential inquiry and practicality.[59] We can also recognize how he helped to move the official orthodoxy away from Wang Yang-ming (in distinct contrast to T'ang Pin), and to identify it, as well as the Learning of Principle, almost exclusively with Chu Hsi. Yet the true learning and method of the mind still remained for him an essential, and indispensable, component of the Transmission of the Mind of the Sages and Worthies, which was inseparable from the Tradition of the Way.

Given the very close working relationship between Li and the K'ang-hsi emperor, it is not surprising that the views officially ascribed to the latter, expressed in his preface to an Imperial edition of the *Great Compendium of Human Nature and Principle (Hsing-li ta-ch'uan)* and reprinted in the "Imperially Promulgated Writings of the K'ang-hsi Reign" *(K'ang-hsi yü-chih wen-chi),* echo these same views with regard to the key concepts in the Neo-Confucian learning of the mind-and-heart as found in the Learning of the Emperors and Kings *(ti-wang chih hsüeh),* the message and method of the mind *(hsin-fa),* the method of governance *(chih-fa),* and learning (method) of the Way *(tao-fa).*[60] While the K'ang-hsi emperor's view of these matters may have been somewhat broader than Li's, and more accomodative in allowing for a liberal understanding of them in the manner of T'ang Pin, there can be no more authoritative confirmation than one finds in the officially promulgated works of K'ang-hsi, that the Neo-Confucian learning of the mind-and-heart remained central to state orthodoxy at the time of its most definitive formulation.

Among the outstanding protegés of Li Kuang-ti was Chang Po-hsing (1652–1725),[61] a major figure in the process of defining both the official Ch'ing orthodoxy and the scholarly legacy of Neo-Confucianism. It was Chang, we recall, who nominated Lu Lung-chi for installation in the Confucian temple as the first Ch'ing scholar to be so honored. Thus Chang was instrumental in linking up the unofficial spokesmen for Chu Hsi—Lü Liu-liang and Chang Lü-hsiang—with Lu Lung-chi and Li Kuang-ti to complete the process by which this particular line of Chu Hsi orthodoxy gained official ratification.

Like Li, Chang was a scholar and statesman of broad experience, great attainments, and strong convictions—not just another ideological hack in the routine service of the state. His practical abilities were demonstrated early in life in the fields of flood control, famine relief, granary administration, justice, and education. From such activities and service in important provincial posts he rose to major responsibilities at court, not without the setbacks and struggles that afflicted almost any official career in Imperial China, but with increasing recognition and support from the Emperor. After his death Chang received the title of Grand

Guardian of the Heir Apparent, and in 1878 came his enshrinement among the worthies in the Confucian temple.

A true representative of the establishment, Chang combined scholarly work with public service and brought the same zeal to both, as if no distinction were to be made between them. From 1707–1713 he edited and published the monumental series of sixty-three works by orthodox Neo-Confucians known as the *Collectanea of the Hall for Rectifying Moral Principles (Cheng-i t'ang ch'üan-shu)*, a name taken from Chang's study. Subsequently he prepared a forty-volume work, *The Correct Tradition of Human Nature and Principle (Hsing-li cheng-tsung)* of which only his preface seems to have survived.[62] In both of these titles the word *cheng*, "correct," appears, and in his writings Chang showed a marked preference for the term "correct learning" *(cheng-hsüeh)*, instead of "learning of the Way" *(tao-hsüeh)* or "learning of principle" *(li-hsüeh)*, as a designation for Neo-Confucianism. In this he represents a strong trend toward the defense and reassertion of Chu Hsi's teaching as the sole correct one, to be clearly distinguished from rival claimants for the mantle of orthodoxy. In other words, Chang's is a defensive and exclusive concept of orthodoxy, not an expansive and inclusive one such as one finds in Sun Ch'i-feng, Li Yung, and T'ang Pin (such too as was more typical of Imperial patronage, which usually professed benign impartiality in anything bordering on the sectarian).[63] All this, by the way, was in addition to Chang's active antagonism toward Buddhism and Christianity and to the vigorous official measures he took against them.

Chang's strict view of the orthodox tradition draws much upon earlier formulations, but has its own significant features. Like Li Kuang-ti, he is sparing in his references to the term *tao-t'ung*, as no doubt still too controversial.[64] Nevertheless he cannot refrain from defining either the essential content or authoritative transmission of the "correct learning." Simply put, while placing Chu Hsi in a central position, he traced the inception of the tradition from the sages' teaching of "refinement," "singleness," and "holding to the Mean." Confucius, Tseng Tzu, Tzu-ssu, and Mencius make up, as usual, the classical quartet who succeeded to this teaching. After Mencius, the Way virtually disappeared, as we all know. Even Han Yü did not quite get it, and it was only with the Sung masters, Chou, the Ch'engs, Chang, and Chu, that it attained its full brilliance. Chu Hsi achieved the supreme synthesis, both most comprehensive and most pure, and so impressively did it carry the day that even Lu Hsiang-shan, with his "outward Confucianism, inward Buddhism" could have no sustained influence. Indeed, not until Wang Yang-ming's time did heterodoxy dare to rear its head again, this time in the form of Wang's attempt to mask Lu's ideas under the cover of Chu Hsi's, as Wang attempted to do in his revisionist interpretation of the views Chu arrived at late in life.

This should not have succeeded, according to Chang, since Chu's true views were clearly stated and altogether straightforward. Anyone who cared to study them could easily understand the basics: that Chu had given first priority to the attitude of reverence, had regarded the investigation of things and fathoming of principle as essential, and had recommended the practice of "preserving the mind and nurturing principle." Yet, according to Chang, scholars, seeing the impressive volume and variety of Chu's writings, shied away from reading them, or if they did so, were sufficiently confused that they failed to grasp these simple truths.

For some time, acknowledges Chang, Wang's views enjoyed enormous popularity, but the effects were disastrous. Not until Lu Lung-chi appeared did the tide begin to turn. As Chang described it in a preface to Lu Lung-chi's *Notes on Reading Chu (Tu Chu sui-pi hsü):*

> Lu Chia-shu (Lung-chi) was born in the same home region as Wang Yang-ming but remained untainted by him. In disciplined conduct he was most pure, and he emerged as the outstanding scholar of his day. Benefitting from his assiduous study of Chu Hsi's writings, he made notes on what he read and got from them.[65]

With these notes to guide him, the reader, Chang hopes, will be able to trace the Way back from Lu to Chu Hsi and from Chu Hsi back to Confucius, so that the "correct learning will be made clearly known and true Confucian culture *(ssu-wen)* rise to new heights day by day."[66]

In a preface such as this, it is natural enough for the writer to pay special tribute to the author (here Chu Hsi), but other accounts by Chang of the transmission of the "correct teaching" confirm the essential picture given here. Elsewhere, after describing how Wang Yang-ming had seduced the scholars of the late Ming, Chang again points to the heroic role of Lu Lung-chi as, "all by himself, he bravely resisted and refuted Wang."[67] Nor was this threat to orthodoxy all safely in the past. Even in his own time the twin dangers of Ch'an antinomianism and Yen Yüan's utilitarianism still threaten.[68]

When Chang is writing in this particular vein, he of course draws heavily on earlier renditions of the heroic and prophetic role played by the great figures in the transmission of the Way who rescue and restore it in difficult times. It is a view we recognize as much indebted, for its proximate sources, to Lü Liu-liang and Lu Lung-chi, who had dwelt on the long lapses in the transmission of the Way and on the singular contributions of a few individuals. At other times, however, Chang offers a more scholastic version, including in the tradition worthy scholars who should not be overlooked even if they do not quite measure up to the masters. Knowing what pains he took to preserve the writings of earlier Neo-Confucians in the aforementioned *Collectanea*, we can hardly be surprised by this more conservative view of the tradition as a great legacy being handed down from scholars past, a view which coexists in Chang's mind with the greater sense of urgency and more prophetic view of the Way received from Lü and Lu.

Typical of this balanced approach is Chang's preface to the *Correct Tradition of Human Nature and Principle*. Here he repeats basically the same account of the Sages' Way coming down to Chu Hsi, but gives credit in the Yüan and early Ming to the contributions of Hsü Heng, Hsüeh Hsüan, Hu Chü-jen, and Lo Ch'in-shun.[69] In his *Collectanea*, of course, the number of Neo-Confucians worthy to be recorded for posterity is much longer.[70] Also among the recommended works in a more selective, basic reading curriculum, Chang includes the principal works of Hsüeh, Hu,and Lo, as well as Ch'en Chien's *Critique of Obscurations to Learning (Hsüeh-pu t'ung pien)*—all identified as "correct learning" *(cheng-hsüeh)*.[71]

If this represents a less narrow view of tradition than Lü Liu-liang's, it is still less expansive by far than Sun Ch'i-feng's and T'ang Pin's. Not only are Lu Hsiang-shan and Wang Yang-ming totally excluded, but even the neo-orthodox Tung-lin thinkers are pointedly denied the status of masters accorded them by Sun, and even the works of Hsüeh Hsüan and Lo Ch'in-shun are expurgated. Chang is quite explicit on the point:

> When Sun Pei-hai treats Chou Tun-i, the Ch'engs, Chang Tsai, and Chu Hsi as the Five Masters [of the Sung], on a par with one another, it is quite right, but to place Hsüeh Hsüan, Hu Chü-jen,

Lo Ch'in-shun, and Kao P'an-lung on a par with the Five Masters, is certainly in error. And how could Kao even be put on the same level as Hsüeh, Hu, and Lo?

Lu Lung-chi criticized Kao thoroughly and in detail. He said, "In Master Kao's discussion of learning, when he speaks of the 'one thread [running through it all],' he thinks of it as the gateway to learning." When he speaks of "fully employing the mind," he means that one must exhaust the mind before one can apprehend principle. When he speaks of the investigation of things, he refers to "knowing the root" as the thing to be investigated. These ideas are often at variance with what the Ch'engs and Chu said about them.

If one wishes to make quiet-sitting the most important thing, it necessarily alters the method of the former masters in regard to extending knowledge, fathoming principles, preserving the mind, and nourishing the nature. It is true that the Ch'engs and Chu also spoke about quiet-sitting, but it was only to have quiet-sitting and moral concern reinforce each other, not to have one be separate from the other for even an instant. This is not the way Master Kao has it in his *K'un-hsüeh chi* [wherein it is said], that one should [first] clear one's spirit, sit in silence, and achieve a blank state of mind before one can reach the ground on which to respond appropriately to things and affairs. (8:13b)

What Chang refers to here as Lu's criticism of Kao P'an-lung were criticisms Lü Liu-liang had already made of Kao and other Tung-lin thinkers who gave a higher priority to quiet-sitting than to the investigation of things. Although Kao had thought of this practice as a discipline preparatory to action or study, Chang sees this practice of quiet-sitting as tending to become an end in itself, something which actually gets in the way of the investigation of things and the fathoming of principle. Whatever the merits of this charge (which is arguable even if this is not the place to do it), we can perhaps recognize it as springing from two marked changes in the intellectual situation from the days of the Tung-lin scholars. Scholarly inquiry, textual study, and evidential learning had come much to the fore in Chang's time, and received a higher priority than the spiritual cultivation which had still loomed large in the late Ming, when political pressures and national crises were a more compelling concern. Likewise, with the defeat of the Ming long since an accomplished fact, there was a natural tendency to put the painful past behind one, to distance oneself from the Ming failure, and to disassociate Neo-Confucianism from the reputed causes of that failure.

Nevertheless it was not possible to divest oneself entirely of practices which had become so closely identified with orthodoxy, and Chang himself is reluctant to go that far with quiet-sitting. Instead he is at some pains to distinguish between its authentic practice and perverted uses:

> To engage in quiet-sitting in order to apprehend the Way and principle is of course quite all right but just to pursue quiet-sitting for its own sake is not all right. If one clearly and thoroughly apprehends principle, one is naturally quiet and calm, but one can see that there is a great difference between sitting quietly to apprehend principle and the Buddhist's quiet-sitting which makes the mind like dried wood and dead ashes. In Buddhist quiet-sitting there is not supposed to be any active employment of the mind; in Confucian quiet-sitting the mind is meant to be active. Yet there must be quiet-sitting before one can perceive principle. If one does not practice quiet-sitting, the mind will be agitated and unsettled. How then could one perceive principle? But just to know about quiet-sitting and not know about the study of books, still leaves one unable to perceive principle. This is why Master Chu spoke about abiding in reverent seriousness and fathoming principle, so that the two legs would support each other. (1:8)

One reason for Chang's ambivalence about quiet-sitting is that the Sung masters themselves had not been of one mind about it. Chou Tun-i and the Ch'eng brothers had seemed to recommend it, and Chu Hsi's *Reflections on Things at Hand (Chin-ssu lu,* 4:63) included favorable comment on it by Ch'eng I (*I-shu,* 4:8b). On the other hand, Ch'eng I also thought reverent seriousness *(ching)* was preferable to quiescence *(ching)* as a basic mental orientation, and Chu Hsi too thought it less liable to be confused with Ch'an meditation. Thus we can appreciate Chang's reservations on the subject:

> Whenever I-ch'uan (Ch'eng I) saw people practice quiet-sitting, he exclaimed over their excellence in learning. In my own view

quiet-sitting with one's thoughts indistinct is like Chuang Tzu's sitting in forgetfulness, while quiet-sitting with one's thoughts agitated and overwrought is like sitting on a galloping horse. Neither can be called "excellence in learning." When practicing quiet-sitting one should make an effort at preserving sincerity and keeping reverent seriousness in charge; then it will be all right.

As the *Mean (Chung yung)* says: "Be watchful and attentive over what is unseen by others, and be cautious and apprehensive about what is not heard by others." Preserving and nourishing is the essence of it! (2:26)

Further to the same point Chang says elsewhere:

When earlier scholars taught people to practice quiet-sitting, it was because principles could not be perceived when the mind was all stirred up. Thus they urged quiet-sitting as a means to nourish the mind, clear it, and open it up, whereupon one could respond well in contact with things and not make mistakes. But if one sits blankly gazing at a wall, cutting off all thoughts, it amounts to stilling and extinguishing the mind. How could this be considered the "preserving and nourishing" of the sages and worthies? (7:12)

Implicit in the increasing ascendancy of Chu Hsi's own formulations over those of other Neo-Confucians was a preference, shown by Chang, for the kind of mind-cultivation he had recommended and for the terms he had used to describe it. Starting with a firm commitment to the Way, one could gradually enter into the mind of the sages from generation to generation. Says Chang:

If one is committed to the learning of the sages and worthies, one should try to experience it personally and carry it out vigorously, rather than just take it as something to be recited and talked about. The works of the Five Sung masters—Chou, the Ch'engs, Chang, and Chu Hsi—are all there to be studied—replete and resplendent with all the principles needed by rulers and ministers to govern the land, and with whatever scholars and teachers need to learn. . . .

All one need do is have a firm, sincere, and immediate resolve to learn why these principles are so right and necessary; coming thus to agreement with them in one's own mind, one should test them in one's daily conduct of affairs, and then extend them to the larger affairs of the family, state, and all-under-Heaven. Thus one would come close to fulfilling the "transmission of the mind" from Confucius, Tseng Tzu, Tzu-ssu, Mencius, as well as the great task undertaken by the sage-kings.[72]

Although Chang does not often speak of this Neo-Confucian learning as a "learning of the mind-and-heart," he does so in a preface to the *Collected Writings of Ch'en Pu-i.*

This is an abridged collection, included in Chang's collectanea, the *Cheng-i t'ang ch'üan-shu*, of writings by the fifteenth-century Ch'eng-Chu thinker, Ch'en Chen-sheng (1410–1473),[73] also known as "commoner Ch'en" (Ch'en Pu-i). He was self-taught and never took the official examinations or served in government. As an independent scholar, however, he became known for his deep knowledge of Ch'eng-Chu thought, especially in education and methods of self-cultivation. Among the latter he particularly emphasized the learning of the mind in terms of reverent seriousness *(ching)*; giving primacy to oneness (or singleness of mind) *(chu-i)*; and the practice of quiet-sitting. Chang's *Collectanea* includes two charts, to which attention is also drawn in the accounts of Ch'en in the official *Ming History (Ming shih)* and Huang Tsung-hsi's *Case Studies of Ming Confucians (Ming-ju hsüeh-an)*, since they were considered to represent the Learning of the Mind-and-Heart in concise, diagrammatic form (see figures 9, 10).

Thus Ch'en was well known for his independence as a scholar, his Ch'eng-Chu orthodoxy and his Learning of the Mind. Hence in writing a preface for Ch'en's works, it was natural for Chang to address the question which would arise in the minds of his contemporaries: how, given the prevailing association of the Learning of the Mind with the heterodox doctrines of the Wang Yang-ming school, does one account for its appearance in the earlier writings of this orthodox thinker? Chang explains that indeed there had been a correct Learning of the Mind earlier and one should not let use of the term by Wang Yang-ming discredit the correct teaching.

Chang explains, in answer to the following question, why this is mistaken: "Recently whenever reference is made to the Learning of the Mind, it is applied to heterodox learning. Is this so of Ch'en's learning?" Chang responds by quoting Chang Tsai to the effect that whenever one reads a book one should make an effort to grasp the overall meaning of what the author is trying to say. If, lacking a grasp of the real meaning, people just become accustomed to mouthing certain expressions, these can easily be misappropriated by heterodox teachings and misrepresented:

Confucius talked about the Way and virtue, and so also did Lao Tzu. The words "Way and virtue" were the same, but what was meant by them differed. We Confucians speak of the mind-and-heart and so also do the Buddhists. Confucius said (at seventy) he could follow his heart's desire without transgressing the norm (measuring square) (*Analects* 2:4). Mencius also said "The path of inquiry and learning is nothing more than seeking the lost mind!" (6A:11). The Buddhists say (however): "The mind itself is Buddha (enlightenment)." In thus working on the mind alone, though they associate themselves with learning they really have not learned. The effort and practice of us Confucians is different: it starts with the fathoming of principle and accepts the need for vigorous practice, for embodying it in one's own person and actually carrying it out in the affairs of the family, state and world-at-large, so that everything is given proper attention.

Speaking of the ground and source from which it springs, we can say no more than that it is just the reverent seriousness of this mind. From Yao and Shun to the Duke of Chou and Confucius, from Confucius to Chou Tun-i, the Ch'engs, Chang, and Chu, it has never been the case that one could pursue learning in disregard of this. What Hsieh Shang-ts'ai (Liang-tso) spoke of as "The method of constant awareness," [74] we Confucians call reverent seriousness. Among the Buddhists it is called "awakening" (*chüeh*). When Ch'en Pu-i spoke thus of the mind-and-heart, he was referring to its constant activity and ceaseless motion, which could not be sustained and controlled without putting reverent seriousness first. Can this be spoken of in the same breath as the emptiness, nothingness, stillness, and extinction of heterodox teachings?

Today when people speak ill of the learning of the mind-and-heart, they mean to criticize heterodox teachings. But if in criticizing heterodoxy they associate Mr. Ch'en with this, it is as if one associated Confucius' Way and virtue with Lao Tzu's Way and virtue, and criticized him for the latter, or as if in criticizing Lu

Hsiang-shan's view of honoring the moral nature one associated with it what the *Mean* says about the moral nature and proceeded to criticize the latter as well. Can one really believe that the *Mean's* method of the mind as transmitted in the Confucian school could be identified with the learning of the original mind [as taught by Lu Hsiang-shan]?[75]

From the foregoing passages it is evident that Chang Po-hsing believes there is a Confucian learning of the mind-and-heart which is identifiable in essence with the message of the mind transmitted from the sage-kings, and which was passed on down from Confucius to the Sung masters as a method of mind cultivation directly applicable to the problems of human society and its governance. This learning is also referred to by Chang as the "transmission of the mind" of the sages, a concept which has special relevance to the reading of texts in the larger context of the tradition and with the enlarged vision of the sage. Since intellectual inquiry, and particularly the study of the written record, are, in Chang's eyes, so vital an accompaniment to moral cultivation for the educated man, preservation of the written legacy has a high priority for him—as exemplified by the two major scholarly projects undertaken by him to define the Neo-Confucian canon.

The canon is thus meant to embody for Chang both the largeness of mind characteristic of the sage and the fine balance he is able to achieve among the competing claims made upon the individual's self-cultivation. One must be strict in defining the "correct learning," and decisively reject incompatible elements like Wang Yang-ming and Lu Hsiang-shan. In this respect, Chang adheres to a narrower definition of the orthodox tradition than Sun Ch'i-feng and T'ang Pin (and apparently even less generous than the K'ang-hsi emperor himself). Yet he finds more worth conserving in Yüan and Ming thought than Lü Liu-liang had allowed, and he insists that one should not disown the learning of the mind, as Lü and Ku Yen-wu did, just because it had been distorted by deviationists. On quiet-sitting he is generally more negative, but even so he will not surrender it to the claim—or charge—that the practice is essentially Ch'an Buddhist.

If for present purposes we take Chang Po-hsing as representative of Neo-Confucian orthodoxy in the so-called "high Ch'ing" period, we can say that he has established a conservative balance between the radical right on the one hand, and liberals who would define tradition broadly enough to embrace Wang Yang-ming and Lu Hsiang-shan on the other. Yet still within the central core so defined, the learning of the mind-and-heart *(hsin-hsüeh)*, the method of the mind *(hsin-fa)*, and the "transmission of the mind" *(ch'uan-hsin)*, all have a place. Less certain, and more controversial, is the place of quiet-sitting. Most unexpected of all is the dubious status of the concept of *tao-t'ung*. As representing Neo-Confucian tradition its content and central core remain largely intact, but as the "succession to the Way," which was, in a sense, "broken off" from the very beginning, it has become, at the very height of Chu Hsi orthodoxy's success, too controversial and in danger itself of becoming a lapsed tradition.

In another surprising reversal, Lü Liu-liang, the man who had precipitated so much of this controversy by his intransigent defense of strict Chu Hsi orthodoxy and his denigration of all Neo-Confucians who seemed less than pure by his own standards, himself fell victim to the new guardians of ideological orthodoxy. This came about in consequence of the abortive Tseng Ching plot of 1728–29,[76] in which Lü was implicated, through his writings, for having inspired a rebellion against the Manchu dynasty. One by-product of the incident was an attack on Lü's influential *Discourses* under the title of *Refutation of Lü Liu-liang's Discourses on the Four Books (Po Lü Liu-liang Ssu-shu chiang-i)*. Its author was Chu Shih (1665–1736),[77] a scholar and high official whose service at court overlapped that of Chang Po-hsing in the K'ang-hsi reign but extended further into the succeeding Yung-cheng period (1723–36). The combination of scholarly and administrative services rendered by him was no less important than Chang Po-Hsing's, and as Grand Tutor to the Heir Apparent he came to have a strong influence over the future Yung-cheng emperor. Hence, Chu had impressive qualifications as a spokesman for the official orthodoxy in the decade after Chang's death.

Chu's philosophical ties were with Li Yung and the Western school of thought centered in the Kuan-chung (Shensi) area, which Chang had labeled "Ch'an" because it included Lu Hsiang-shan and Wang Yang-ming within the bounds of orthodoxy (as had Sun Ch'i-feng and T'ang Pin). Whether as a result of Chu's influence or not, the Yung-cheng emperor himself showed little concern for strict orthodoxy—indeed he leaned strongly toward Ch'an.[78] Thus the extreme measures taken by the Emperor to disgrace Lü posthumously and punish his family, if they were not primarily political in motivation, probably arose from the ruler's resentment against strict Chu Hsi orthodoxy rather than from any desire to enforce it. No matter—it was still in the name of orthodoxy that Chu Shih mounted his ideological attack on Lü.

Whatever the personal and political ramifications of the case, Chu Shih had strong enough reasons of his own for challenging, in the name of orthodoxy, Lü Liu-liang's spurious learning *(wei-hsüeh)*,[79] and though his attack was highly polemical—even vindictive—in spirit, Chu was not without plausible arguments to adduce against his philosophical adversary. Here we cannot go into any but those issues having to do with the Learning of the Mind-and-Heart and the related one of quiet-sitting.

Chu Shih's *Refutation* follows a format of first paraphrasing a passage in Lü's commentary on the Four Books and then presenting his refutation of it. One need go no further than the first passage cited, however, to see that Chu is ready to do battle on Lü's challenge to the Learning of the Mind, which Lü himself has made a major issue from the start of his commentary on the *Great Learning*. Lü, according to Chu, had argued that the *Great Learning* does not emphasize the mind but rather Heaven's principle, and that to speak of the mind all by itself, without speaking of the extension of knowledge or the rectification of the mind, is the same as the Buddhistic "learning of the original mind" and not the Sage Learning.[80]

In refutation, Chu Shih cites passages in Chu Hsi's commentary which draw upon Chang Tsai and Mencius to confirm the doctrine that the mind coordinates human nature (principle) and the emotions, as well as the view that principle is inherent in the mind. Chu next proceeds to show that for the Buddhists the mind is the source of all illusory existence, while for Confucians both principles and things are real and arise from the creative power of Heaven's imperative *(T'ien ming)*. These are fundamentally different conceptions, Chu says:

> What we call "Heaven" is simply principle, and the mind's being replete with principle is simply what has been ordained by Heaven. It is the message of the mind as transmitted from Yao to Shun: "the human mind is precarious; the mind of the Way is subtle." . . . The mind of the Way is the "bright virtue" [moral nature] of the *Great Learning*. The precariousness of the human mind and subtlety of the mind of the Way are the reason why bright virtue needs to be clarified and made manifest. Refined discrimination

refers to the [*Great Learning's*] investigation of things and extension of knowledge and "singleness" refers to make the intention sincere and rectifying the mind. Chen Hsi-shan [Te-hsiu] said that "the sixteen words of the Great Shun constitute the source of the Learning of the Mind-and-Heart for all ages. As passed down from one sage to another, it was all Learning of the Mind-and-Heart." How then can one assert that to speak of the Mind-and-Heart is not the Sage Learning? . . .

When Liu-liang fails to point out the error in the Buddhists' conception of mind, and instead indiscriminately bans all talk of the mind, even to the extent of not allowing the mind to be considered moral or to be spoken of as a subject of learning, the harm he does to the learning and direction of the mind is not inconsiderable.[81]

Lü had argued that the mind was not itself a subject of learning but only the means by which one learned about Heaven, the nature, principle, and the Way. Only in Buddhism was the mind turned in upon itself as something to be "learned." To this Chu responds:

Shun's distinction between the human mind and the mind of the Way is the secret of the Learning of the Mind and Heart. T'ang the Completer "disciplined the mind-and-heart through ritual."[82] King Wen was "concerned at heart and very reverent."[83] Confucius "could follow his heart's desire without transgressing."[84] Master Yen's "heart did not violate humaneness."[85] Mencius spoke of "preserving the mind" and "nourishing the mind"; he spoke of enlarging the mind of humaneness and rightness.[86] How could the sages and worthies not have spoken about the mind-and-heart? Still this is not what the Buddhists take to be the learning of the mind, with their "not mattering about the mind" *(wu shih yü hsin)*. Consequently to tabu all discussion of the "learning of the mind" is like abandoning the eating of food for fear one might choke on it.[87]

Similar arguments are found elsewhere in Chu's *Refutation* of Lü Liu-liang's view that the Learning of the Mind is Buddhistic.[88] The foregoing may suffice however to show how Chu draws for his refutation upon the tradition concerning the method of the mind prior to

Wang Yang-ming, and also on the arguments offered by post-Wang Yang-ming writers who insist that there is a Confucian learning of the mind, even though they disagree on how liberally it is to be interpreted. One point at issue in that interpretation is the acceptability of their concept and practice of quiet-sitting. Lü Liu-liang has attacked the latter as heterodox; Chu Shih's attempt to defend it runs much along the lines already seen in Sun Ch'i-feng and T'ang Pin.

Concerning Lü's commentary on the *Mean*, Chu quotes Lü at length on the subject of quiet-sitting, Wang Chi and Ku Hsien-ch'eng. Lü's view is that Wang and Ku both overemphasize the psycho-physical aspect of mind, dealing with the mind as raw consciousness (the way Buddhism does) rather than with moral conscience. Chu, in rebuttal, concedes that Wang Chi's views are so one-sided as to be indefensible, but on behalf of Ku's position he argues that principle and the physical nature are inseparable and one must have a way of calming the physical nature and clearing the consciousness in order for principle to become clearly and fully manifest. The method of Chou Tun-i had been meant to make quiescence the basis for action and for the application of one's moral effort. Control over conduct must be established in quiescence. This was how Chu Hsi had explained putting quiescence first *(chu-ching)*, and it was also the idea underlying Chou Tun-i's "being without desires and therefore quiescent" *(wu-yü ku ching)*.[89]

Desires arise in response to the stimulus of things and affairs. If there is no active stimulus, there can be no desire. But if there is no deep effort at daily cultivation and nourishing, the mind cannot maintain control over itself and has no way of keeping out wayward thoughts. Thus, before one becomes involved with things, if one already has predispositions and attachments, then how, when one must respond to things, can one's actions be only good and without any evil? This is why the sages, in trying to integrate all action, insisted on quiescence as the basis. Quiescence is the substance of the "Non-finite Supreme Ultimate." Stressing the practice of quiescence is the way to establish the ultimate principle [within the mind]. . . .

When I-ch'uan (Ch'eng I) saw people practicing quiet-sitting he exclaimed over the excellence of their learning. This teaching of the Ch'eng school is found more than once in their writings. How then can it be rejected? Liu-liang says that Master Ch'eng's delight in their quiet-sitting was delight over their not chasing after externals. But isn't "not chasing after externals" precisely what quiet-sitting is all about? And so how can Lü say that quiescence is not something he taught?

Generally speaking, Chu Hsi's learning is based on the *Mean's* [combination of] honoring the moral nature and following the path of inquiry and learning. "As Master Ch'eng I put it, self-cultivation should rely on the practice of reverent seriousness, and advancement in learning on the extension of knowledge. Expressed in normal, everyday terms, this means that the approach to learning should involve the alternate and reciprocal practice of preserving the mind and extending knowledge. But from what Liu-liang says in attacking Yang-ming's innate knowledge it amounts to dispensing with mind-preservation altogether. When he speaks of principle it is thought of as outside the mind; when he speaks of learning, it is to ban all talk of putting quiescence first. With this one opens the way to division and fragmentation. It does away with the effort to establish the basis [of self-cultivation]. This is truly the worst sort of what Master Chu disparaged as pedantic, trivial, and vulgar learning. One cannot help but expose it to criticism.[90]

Whatever one thinks of this as a rebuttal to Lü Liu-liang (and one can easily see it as more polemical than logically compelling), we do not have to settle the score between him and Chu Shih. Taken just as competing claims to orthodoxy, each speaking for positions held at once by independent scholars and highly placed officials, Lü and Chu represent significant differences within what is often spoken of as orthodox Neo-Confucianism. In the passage just quoted Chu faults Lü for his repudiation of quiet-sitting, abandonment of the essentials of mind cultivation, and one-sided emphasis on scholarly inquiry. Without accepting the charge as stated, we can see it as perhaps a plausible reading of the shift in Lü toward objective scholarly inquiry and fixed moral standards along with a total rejection of Wang Yang-ming and more and more exclusive admiration for Chu Hsi. Ranged on the other side is a more inclusive view of orthodoxy—one indeed still ready to find room for Wang Yang-ming, Ku Hsien-ch'eng, and quiet-sitting.

Allowing for Lü's more radical, uncompromising stance as an independent scholar who has cut his ties to officialdom, we must allow too that those who stand in his line of orthodox lineage do not always adhere to such extreme positions as he on quiet-sitting and the Learning of the Mind. Thus despite clear cleavages between the two views of the orthodox succession, on the issue of the Learning of the Mind-and-Heart there is almost a consensus—not on what that learning consists in, but—on the fact that there had indeed been such a tradition in the Ch'eng-Chu school coming down from the Sung, and that this learning was not viewed as the exclusive domain of Wang Yang-ming.

6

Orthodoxy
on the Eve of
the Western Encounter

Thus far we have considered the views of more than thirty Neo-Confucians from the twelfth to eighteenth centuries, for the most part identified with Ch'eng-Chu orthodoxy or neo-orthodoxy, who carried on the debate over the Learning-of-the-Mind and Heart, generally reaffirming but sometimes reinterpreting its basic concepts. Much of the reaffirmation came in response to the mercurial challenge of Wang Yang-ming, whose success, on both the popular and elite levels, was demonstrated in the sixteenth century by the Ming court's canonization, first of Lu Hsiang-shan, and then of Wang himself. Thereafter the next major challenge to the orthodox view, exerting considerable influence on the Ch'ing scholarly elite, came with the rise of "evidential research" (k'ao-cheng) or School of Han Learning, which increasingly dominated the intellectual scene in the eighteenth and early nineteenth centuries.

While benefiting to some extent from the conservative reaction against liberal tendencies in the school of Wang Yang-ming, and in particular from the reemphasis on book-learning and sound scholarship, the new movement was also heir to advances in critical scholarship made in the very same liberal atmosphere of the late Ming. It showed the capability, while criticizing the Wang Yang-ming school, of extending this criticism to Sung-Ming thought as a whole, including the Ch'eng-Chu philosophy of mind along with Wang Yang-ming's version of it. Ku Yen-wu, though as much an exemplar of Neo-Confucian scholarship as a questioner of Neo-Confucian philosophy in the late seventeenth century, came to hold a commanding authority among scholars of the Han

Learning, and was much admired as an almost impeccable model of the kind of critical inquiry into the classics given special honor by Sung-Ming Neo-Confucians.

Thus the new trend, while riding the same conservative wave as Chu Hsi orthodoxy in the early Ch'ing, came increasingly to assert its own independence. Yet, as it stood more and more on its own feet, the new scholarship still found itself standing side by side, and uneasily, with the old orthodoxy. The latter remained well established in education and the examination system, while the influence of the new criticism was exerted mainly in the field of advanced scholarly research. In both of these spheres the developing contest between them cut across official and nonofficial lines.

Intellectually speaking, the influence of the Han Learning school (or School of Evidential Research claiming to base itself on Han dynasty scholarship) had, by the eighteenth century, become so dominant that Liang Ch'i-ch'ao, in his *Intellectual Trends in the Ch'ing Period (Ch'ing-tai hsüeh-shu kai-lun)*, would later refer to it as "the Orthodox School," which he says "carried on empirical research for the sake of empirical research and studied classics for the sake of classics."[1] Whether or not one accepts this perhaps too simple characterization of the Evidential School, Liang's reference to it as the Orthodox School is symptomatic. If there could be such a new intellectual "orthodoxy" coexisting with an older Ch'eng-Chu orthodoxy in education, as if in some symbiotic relationship, it tells us that even the mature Confucian tradition was far from simple and fixed but generated contending forces on more than one level at a time.

By the nineteenth century, however, the Han Learning had long prevailed in scholarly circles, as well as among their patrons in high Ch'ing officialdom, when a significant challenge was presented to it from the rear guard of Ch'eng-Chu orthodoxy in the writings of Fang Tung-shu (1772–1851). A sharp controversialist himself, Fang has also been seen as a highly controversial figure by intellectual historians, recognized as perhaps the most articulate spokesman for the Ch'eng-Chu school in his time. Liang Ch'i-ch'ao said of Fang's *Reckoning with the Han School (Han-hsüeh shang-tui* 1824) that "its courage in opposing [the Orthodox School] made it a kind of revolutionary work,"[2] whereas others like Hu Shih have seen Fang, by contrast, as leading a last reactionary outburst against the Han School on behalf of the decadent remnants of Neo-Confucianism, defending their sacred textual ground against the higher criticism.[3]

Fang came from a family of scholars identified with the T'ung-ch'eng school, which had attempted to revive the prose style and thought of the neo-classical movement in the Sung, represented in literature by Ou-yang Hsiu (1007–1072) and in philosophy by Chu Hsi. Fang had little success in rising through the examination system, and spent most of his life as an impecunious tutor in private homes, lecturer in local academies, or scholarly aide to high officials. If this suggests an insecure, marginal existence on the edge of the literocratic elite, such a dependent condition, economically speaking, in no way inhibited Fang's independence as a scholar and thinker. His outspoken views commanded attention, if not always assent. Fearless in challenging eminent scholars and high officials alike, he faulted the former for their scholarly errors and philosophical bankruptcy, the latter for the inadequacies of China's foreign policy and national defense. One of the most frequent targets of his criticism, Juan Yüan (1764–1849), was a highly respected scholar of the Han Learning, senior official, and governor general of Kwangtung and Kwangsi, whose policies Fang openly censured even while his livelihood as a scholar depended on Juan's patronage of a major scholarly project in 1821–22. That Fang could do this despite his low status, is an indication of the high regard in which his scholarship and opinions were held. Indeed the breadth and depth of his scholarship were most impressive. Contrary to the view of earlier twentieth-century scholars that the T'ung-ch'eng school was characterized by a "bigotry . . . which limited [the school] to the study of Chu Hsi's commentaries and to the prose-writing of a few men, branding other types of literature as harmful to the mind,"[4] Fang's learning actually stands as testimony to the Chu Hsi school's pursuit of "broad learning." It extended to the in-depth study of all the major schools of Chinese thought, including Buddhism, Taoism, and—even more rare—some ventures into Japanese *kangaku* scholarship. While the same might equally be said of an eclectic scholar-dilettante, Fang's seriousness as a scholar is attested by the notably analytic and penetrating critiques he made of other thinkers and schools.[5]

Fang is best known, however, for his *Reckoning with the Han Learning*,[6] which features a detailed list of charges against scholars of the evidential research movement, giving point by point rebuttals. Thus we are not surprised to find it often fiercely argumentative and polemical in tone. Like other champions of orthodoxy before him, Fang speaks with the voice of the Neo-Confucian prophet condemning a wayward generation of scholars and officials for their failure to keep to the true Way. No doubt this combative manner reflects the psychological burden borne by anyone who challenges the establishment, whether scholarly or official, as Fang himself seems to have realized.[7] Yet a more careful reading of Fang's work reveals a more complex picture, balancing the prophetic and scholarly roles in the tradition.

Like Lü Liu-liang in the early Ch'ing, Fang has his Neo-Confucian heroes: Chang Lü-hsiang and Lu Lung-chi[8]—proponents of the Ch'eng-Chu school in the early Ch'ing whom he regards as its only authentic transmitters.[9] (By this time the official condemnation of Lü Liu-liang and proscription of his works would have made it difficult for Fang to incur or acknowledge any direct debt to Lü.) Fang, too, has his villains —most of the leading figures in the Han learning movement from Ku Yen-wu on down. The Han learning is thus Fang's bête noire, as the Wang Yang-ming school had been Lü's earlier. Nevertheless there is much significance in their different choices of heroes (or ancestors) to be venerated and in their treatment of the villains who have betrayed the Ch'eng-Chu legacy.

Fang, like Lü, intimates that he feels it incumbent on himself to take up the prophetic mantle last worn by Chang and Lu,[10] but he is not so dismissive of other Neo-Confucians and is much less inclined than Lü to write off long centuries of history as mere wasteland stretching between the early prophets Confucius and Mencius, and the later Ch'eng brothers and Chu Hsi. This may be seen in part from his handling of the Han Learning itself. What Fang excoriates in this latter-day movement is its misappropriation of Han dynasty scholarship for its own dubious purposes. On the whole he sees Han dynasty scholars like Tung Chung-shu, Yang Hsiung, and Cheng Hsüan as having rendered an important service to the preservation of the Confucian tradition. After the repressions of the Ch'in dynasty and burning of the books, it was an indispensable contribution of these early scholars to have pre-served the classic texts, even in fragmentary and confused form, so as to pass them on to later generations.[11] And even though the T'ang commentators, like K'ung Ying-ta, could do no more than simply con-serve and codify the surviving texts, they too performed a necessary task of preservation and transmission.[12]

For all this, however, the Han and T'ang dynasties were far from

propitious ages for the reestablishment of sagely rule or the repossession of the sages' teaching. This left to the Sung the task of philosophical reconstruction, which the Ch'engs and Chu did brilliantly, grasping
the "whole substance and great functioning" of the Way by "following
the texts and discerning the mind of the sages."[13] Yet, successful
though this effort was in producing a long line of scholars devoted to
broad-learning and critical study of the classics (contrary to *Han hsüeh*
assertions),[14] the synthesis achieved by the Ch'eng brothers and Chu
Hsi could not but suffer at the hands of idiosyncratic interpreters.[15] Lu
Hsiang-shan diverged from it, Wang Yang-ming distorted it, and finally
the latter-day school of evidential research which claimed to speak for
Han learning virtually discarded Sung philosophy in favor of philological studies—mere displays of technical virtuosity and recondite anti-
quarianism that distracted scholars' attention from the central human
concerns of the Confucian tradition. Thus the so-called Han Learning
of the Ch'ing did not measure up to the responsibility bequeathed to it.
Scholars of the "evidential learning" failed to preserve and uphold the
legacy of the Sung even to the extent that Han scholars had conserved
the Confucian learning of the Chou dynasty.[16] Instead they openly
repudiated Sung learning. Hence their claim to fulfill the mission of
Han learning was itself false, and, having defaulted on this basic obligation to carry on the succession, they could stake no claim to speak for
the tradition as a whole.

From this rough account, which omits much of the historical and
documentary detail given in support of Fang's argument, one nevertheless gets Fang's sense of the continuity and cumulative character of the
tradition, so much in contrast to the prophetic version which had down-
played and downgraded Han and T'ang scholarship in order to highlight
the extraordinary insights of the Sung masters into the true depths of
the Sages' mind. Indeed one of the "Han Learning" scholars' most
telling criticisms of the Sung school had been its neglect of Han scholarship in favor of bold, new speculative interpretations of the classics.
Contrarily one of Fang's most revealing rebuttals cites how much actual
use had been made in the Sung, especially by Chu Hsi, of Han and
T'ang commentaries,[17] and how at each stage in the passing on of the
tradition there had been incremental contributions by dedicated scholars. All of this suggests that Fang could see the tradition in far more of
a scholastic than a prophetic light.

Even so, however—or perhaps one should say for that very reason

—Fang, who has much to say about the passing on of the Way, has little to say in his *Reckoning* about the *tao-t'ung* as a term or concept. From his discussion of the matter elsewhere, we know that he was highly conscious of the problem of continuity/discontinuity in the Succession to the Way, and even compared the post-Chu Hsi era to the long lapse in effective articulation of the Way after Mencius.[18] Whether uneasy over the conflicted nature of this concept after Chu Hsi and especially in the early Ch'ing,[19] which made it too sticky an issue for those who stressed continuity and consensus, Fang makes no great issue of the *tao-t'ung* as such. Nevertheless, as both scholar and prophet himself, he can invoke either side of the tradition depending on the nature of the occasion or the purpose to be served. Thus in a long essay on the nature of the Way, in a collection of his prose writings wherein Fang takes the offensive against Buddhism and the Han Learning, he dwells on their deceptive and misleading character, while glorifying the heroic role of such prophetic figures as Mencius, Han Yü, Ou-yang Hsiu, the Ch'eng brothers, and Chu Hsi.[20]

In one of his prefaces Fang offers an almost classic definition of the Confucian sage as prophet: " 'The great source of the Way is Heaven.' Heaven does not speak, but it gives birth to the sages, who speak for it. The words of the sages are all for explicating the Way in order to awaken the world and proclaim its principles . . ."[21] Thus the words of the sages are like signs from Heaven. Other prefaces, by contrast, celebrate the cumulative achievement of scholars in literature and learning who give even greater brilliance and clarity to Confucian culture, or honor heroes and martyrs like the Tung-lin scholars in the late Ming, who sacrificed their lives in resisting corruption and oppression and thereby kept the flame of the Way continuously burning.[22]

In his *Reckoning with the Han Learning*, however, Fang avoids arguing his case simply by an appeal either to authority or prophetic inspiration alone. His points are well-documented; his evidence—most often historical—is carefully martialed, and his judgments, though characteristically unreserved, are precisely defined—arrived at by a careful assessment of what may be accepted as valid in the claims of the Han Learning and what must be rejected as unsupported by the factual record. Often he prefaces his conclusions by saying, "Looking at this in a calm and balanced way, the fact is that . . ." (*p'ing-hsin erh lun, shih wei . . .)*[23] exhibiting, or at least professing, a judiciousness in the weighing of evidence that is a particular mark of his age. Fang can indeed make his own mistakes, but one is impressed by his detailed knowledge of the relevant literature, and, as with the Han Learning scholars themselves, by his keen sensitivity to the historical uses of key terms. Fang himself would no doubt contend that such scholarly finesse is no more than could be expected from anyone who had read and sought to emulate Chu Hsi, but we have reason to suspect that this arch critic of the Han Learning has learned much from it of the arts of criticism and evidential proof.

This then brings us to the crux of Fang's position and its relevance to our main theme. A central target of Fang's critique of the Han school is its charge that the Sung learning, in its speculative improvisations, departed from the original spirit of Confucian teaching and incorporated elements from Buddhism inherently alien to the tradition. One such issue pertains to the Neo-Confucians' use of the term *tao-hsüeh*, "learning of the Way," which Han School critics had alleged was a neologism of the Ch'eng-Chu school coined in support of its claim to a hold on absolute truth—a pretension to exclusive authority which only promoted partisanship and an intolerant sectarianism.[24] Fang, for his part, though prepared to dispute in detail the historical record as presented by such critics, does not rest his case on any evidence that such terms had a classical provenance. Rather he argues from the fact that the classics did indeed contain teachings which discussed and defined the true Way, even though it was left for the Ch'engs and Chu to furnish this doctrine with the new designation, Learning of the Way *(tao-hsüeh)*. This use of terms was legitimate as a means of showing that Confucians from the start had their own view of the Way and were not dependent for this on anything borrowed from Taoism or Buddhism. Nevertheless things had indeed become confused during the Six Dynasties and T'ang periods when the interpretation of the Classics and translation of Buddhist scriptures had both drawn on the language of Lao Tzu and Chuang Tzu, creating the impression of a close resemblance between Buddhist and classical Chinese teachings. One can only solve the problem, however, by studying the actual, original meanings of the terms, not by avoiding their use simply because of an adventitious, and actually specious, similarity to Buddhism.[25] It was not the fault of the Confucians that Buddhists had borrowed Chinese terms to dress up their foreign doctrines, nor should Confucians be accused now of "borrowing the language of Buddhism" as if the Buddhist's own borrowing had preempted forever all use of such terms by others.

Conscious, however, that such terms had indeed become contested issues, Fang himself tends to avoid their use in favor of others less open to dispute. Thus he most often refers to Neo-Confucian teachings as the Learning of the Sages, or Way of the Sages, as Chu Hsi had done, or simply as the Ch'eng-Chu learning. Yet when it comes to the expression "Learning of the Mind-and-Heart" (hsin-hsüeh) or "Transmission of the Mind" (ch'uan-hsin), Fang goes to extraordinary lengths to rebut the by-now celebrated challenge of Ku Yen-wu to the legitimacy of these Neo-Confucian concepts. Indeed he devotes a main portion of his Reckoning to taking issue here with Ku, and in the "Preface with Explanatory Notes" preceding this work he identifies them as major topics to be addressed.[26]

Fang launches the discussion by citing Ku Yen-wu's quotation of Huang Chen on the sixteen-word transmission of the Message of the Mind (presented above, pages 132–133).[27] Instead, however, of taking up Ku's final brief comment on Chu's quotation of Ch'eng I (to wit, "This work [the Chung-yung] represents the message of the mind as transmitted in the Confucian school, which is expressed in terms borrowed from Buddhism"), Fang avoids direct discussion of the term "message of the mind" (hsin-fa)[28] and focuses rather on Huang Chen's (originally Ts'ai Shen's) expression "transmission of the mind." Perhaps this choice of targets reflects Fang's reluctance to contaminate the debate with highly charged but ambiguous terms like tao-t'ung and hsin-fa, yet he cannot evade the question raised by Huang of the "transmission of the mind" as a borrowing from Buddhism. Undeniably the essence of the problem lies in one's view of the mind and how the sages and worthies conveyed their thinking (i.e., their mind) to later generations.

Fang's method of responding passage by passage to specific charges by different Han school thinkers does not lend itself to the logical presentation of a single line of argument, but for brevity's sake we may summarize the main points as follows:

Regardless of such use as the Buddhists may have made of the expression "transmission of the mind," the Confucian concept of mind was different, and required its own form of transmission. Chu Hsi in his preface to the Mean, and Ts'ai Shen in his commentary on the Book of Shang, invoked the sixteen-word formula as a way of expressing the ancient sage-king's concern for the ordering of human society. Their "mind" was an active social conscience in which the moral mind guided the minds of men as they gave defined form to human life in keeping with the Way. This, in effect, is what the sage-kings had a "mind" to do.

In the early canons of the *Book of Documents* one finds the specific measures instituted by the sage-kings to give definite shape to the world order, and in the other classic texts are found expressions of those same concerns on the part of Confucius, Tzu-ssu, Mencius, et al., as well as discussions of the nature and proper cultivation of the mind.[29] Revealed therein were a method of rulership and measures of government one in essence with the method of individual cultivation, both using the fulcrum of the moral mind to gain leverage on the world through the active agency of the human mind.

All of this was summarized in convenient form, says Fang, by Chen Te-hsiu in his *Heart Classic (Hsin ching)*, which cites over thirty passages from the Six Classics and utterances of Confucius dealing with the mind-and-heart (another indication, by the way, of Fang's sense that continuing scholarly contributions were important to the advancement of the Way, which did not simply lapse after Chu Hsi.[30]

The fact that Hsün Tzu was probably first to refer to the human mind as precarious and the mind of the Way as subtle, or that the sixteen words attributed to the sages in the apocryphal *Book of Shang* were put together in the fourth century A.D., did not invalidate the timeless truth of this teaching as it was later more fully clarified by Chu Hsi. Hsün Tzu's use of the terms was only further testimony to their currency and importance in the early Confucian school, which Ch'eng-Chu simply reaffirmed. Thus nothing in either Hsün Tzu or the "old text" of the *Documents* would warrant equating this Confucian view of the mind with the later Ch'an Buddhist view, which bypassed the moral and social conscience and led the mind to a blank wall.[31]

The instrumentalities by which the Sages ruled, as described in the *Book of Shang*, were all manifestations of the Sagely mind, based on specific judgments or determinations arrived at through the exercise of refined discrimination and singleness of mind. Without discrimination, indeed, one would have no way of finding the Mean, which is a mean in action, hitting exactly what is appropriate at a given place and time.[32]

As for "singleness of mind," Fang rejects any imputation that it could be mistaken for Buddhist concentration or oneness. The latter might be equated with the Mind of the Way, but if one identifies the mind solely with the Mind of the Way, through some direct intuition, one fails to take into account human fallibility and simply assumes that all men are sages, as did Wang Yang-ming with his saying "The streets are full of sages." This view is one-sidedly based on the Mind of the Way and does not address the mind of man.[33]

On the other hand, if one identifies the mind solely with the "human mind" and sees in it only a liability to err, then one would be inclined to view all men as deviants from the Way, incapable of self-improvement. Nor can the dilemma be avoided by resort to the sort of facile compromise which views the mind as simply conscious activity, morally indifferent. That is the view of Kao Tzu, which reduces human consciousness to animal consciousness, or of Ch'an Buddhism, which says "As is the mind so is the Way"—an abdication of moral responsibility. Only a teaching which recognizes both of these realities and avoids either extreme—seeing oneness rather as an integration to be achieved through refined discrimination and active self-mastery, thus putting the Mind of the Way in control of man's natural inclinations—is reasonable and in accord with the actual facts of human nature.[34]

Others will claim that when Mencius spoke of humaneness as the human mind (jen, jen-hsin yeh), it was as much as to say that the human mind cannot be identified with selfish desires. Yet Mencius also spoke about the possibility of losing one's mind, in which case the mind would become identified with selfish desires. Moreover, if one took the view that the human mind was all humaneness, without any selfish desires, what need would there have been for the sages to concern themselves with learning and teaching? Thus the human mind is essentially humane, but also liable to fall into dangerous desires. Wherefore the example of the sages engaged in refined discrimination, choosing to preserve the Mind of the Way and holding fast to the Mean, is an edifying one for all ages and peoples (2A:4a).

Granted, when all is said and done, that the essential teaching is simple: to be humane, still this is not the same as believing that it can be realized simply by self-enlightenment. One must get the message and actively practice the method of refined discrimination. This is why, according to Fang, the Sages outdid each other in their efforts to preserve and pass on the teaching, not daring to let it fall to the ground. Such then is what is meant by the sages' "transmission of the Mind" (2A:4b).

Those who confuse the Sages' Transmission of Mind with the Buddhists', or with Wang Yang-ming's, fail to realize that the latter lacks the sages' method of refined discrimination and singleness of mind, which provides the value judgments needed for dealing with human problems. Therein lies the essential difference between the Way of the Sages and Wang's or Chan's one-sided pursuit of the Mind of the Way (2A:5a).

Compared to this very real and basic difference, it is of little consequence whether the precise language of the sixteen-word formula may be of somewhat later provenance than once was supposed or by Sung times may even have acquired a Buddhist ring to it. If one were to confine oneself solely to the language of the earliest texts and allow nothing to be believed that does not exactly correspond to what is said in the original Six Classics, one would indeed have trouble reconciling the *Analects* with either the New or Old Text versions of the *Book of Documents*, since the *Analects* says things contained in neither (2A:5ab).

> Therefore, if Ku in his *Record of Daily Knowledge (Jih chih lu)* cites *Huang Chen's Daily Notes (Jih-ch'ao)* and the utterances of T'ang Jen-ch'ing (Po-yüan) to refute the Lu-Wang School of the Mind, there is nothing wrong with that; but if this be taken to mean that nothing was said in the Six Classics, or by Confucius and Mencius, about the Learning of the Mind-and-Heart, it is unacceptable! If it is taken to mean that the Six Classics, Confucius, and Mencius say nothing like Lu and Wang, that too is acceptable, but if it means that nothing is said in the Six Classics, Confucius, or Mencius about the mind-and-heart, then it is unacceptable. (2A:5b)

Fang next takes up a passage in Ku's *Record* in which the latter had quoted Huang Chen (see pages 132–133 above), but which Fang mistakenly takes to be Ku's own comment.[35] Huang had argued that since principle was immanent in the minds of all men, there was no need for any special transmission of the sages' mind in order to practice refined discrimination, singleness of mind, or holding to the Mean. Hence, when Ch'eng I, and later Chu Hsi, spoke of such a transmission of the Mind, they risked its becoming confused with the Buddhist transmission of mind, which was actually quite different, since it regarded holding to fixed principles as obstructing the mind and instead of relying on verbal or written communication simply aimed at transmitting the unspoken "seal of the mind."[36]

Of this Fang says that in any case one can discount Ku Yen-wu's arguments because he is predisposed against Chu Hsi and only uses these quotations from Huang as a convenient stick with which to beat Chu (2A:6b). Yet even so Fang cannot forego the opportunity it presents to sort out the different issues involved. He can agree with the characterization given here of the wordless Ch'an transmission of mind, while also pointing out inconsistencies in the Huang/Ku denial of the need for any transmission at all. Even on Ku's (actually Huang's) own account of the pervasion of principle in the minds of men, a necessary role had to be played by the mind as an active agent in the making of principled judgments. Not to recognize and affirm this role risked a separation of mind and principle, which was precisely the error of Ch'an Buddhists. One could not have even the "transmission of principle" assumed here without the active agency of the mind also being involved in the process (2A:7b).

Moreover, even the transmission of the Way depends on the mind, and not to transmit the mind of the sages would simply mean passing on one's own subjective opinion, i.e., a private experience of principle, rather than a way confirmed by both public testimony and historical experience. Hence to suggest that there is no need to transmit what all men already share in common (principle in the mind) implies that principle could, by its mere inherence in the mind simply pervade Heaven-and-earth without the mind's having to exercise any active control or direction in accordance with the Way. This comes perilously close to the view of Wang Yang-ming that "the streets are full of sages" who have no need of instruction (2A:8b-9b).

Huang and Ku, according to Fang, do of course recognize the harm done by Ch'an Buddhism and Wang's Learning of the Mind, but being unable to explain wherein the error of Ch'an and Wang lies, they want to put a stop to all discussion of the mind, even to the extent of doing away entirely with what has been said in the classics and the commentaries about the mind, including Confucius' saying that [at seventy] he was able to follow his heart's desire without transgressing the norm (measuring square) (2A:9b–10a). Moreover, extending the same approach to Ch'eng-Chu teaching, critics allege that in talking about mind and principle the latter too have fallen into Ch'an, not realizing, says Fang, that Ch'eng and Chu, being profoundly aware of the damage done by Ch'an in not extending knowledge and fathoming principle, criticized Ch'an precisely for this and strove to rectify any such deviant tendencies in Confucianism.

It is the Learning of the Sages that has been concerned with the proper use of the mind and Ch'an that has avoided it, the former that has always sought to fathom principle and Ch'an that has avoided it. Thus the facts are exactly the reverse [of what Han School critics allege]. The Han Learning proclaims its devotion to philology and lexicography, but, finding in these no sound basis for challenging the correct Ch'eng-Chu teaching or principle, it misrepresents the latter as using language borrowed from Buddhism. It fails thus to recognize that the Ch'eng-Chu teaching concerning the human mind, the mind of the Way, refinement, and singleness, holding fast the Mean, the extension of knowledge and fathoming of principle were all precisely meant to expose the errors of Ch'an. Nor do these critics realize that their own interdiction of all talk concerning the mind and principle falls into those same errors as Ch'an. (2A:12ab)

In the foregoing Fang concedes that the Han Learning is correct in finding a resemblance between Wang Yang-ming and Ch'an, yet it has nothing but circumstantial linguistic evidence for its claim that Ch'eng and Chu too have succumbed to Ch'an. Unless its critics are prepared to contest the issue on philosophical grounds, for which no amount of philological research can substitute (1:17a, 3:14b–15a), the Ch'eng-Chu record will show in what ways it has upheld a learning based on both mind and principle, with both of these addressed, as neither Chan nor the Han Learning have been, to the practical needs of human society. There is all the difference in the world between a learning of the mind that seeks to introspect the mind in a Ch'an-like *samadhi* or is noncommittal with respect to basic human values, and one which affirms Mencius' "mind of right and wrong" *(shih-fei chih hsin)* (3:18b–19a).

It is no doubt an exaggeration on Fang's part to say that the Han Learning ruled out all discussion of mind and principle, but he is not wrong in asserting that the Han school turned away from such questions and, in its preoccupation with empirical research, was inclined to be noncommittal in matters of moral principle. It is this silence of the Han Learning on value issues that Fang sees as common to it and Chan, while what distinguishes Ch'eng-Chu teaching from either of them is its commitment to the moral life and practical social action through a proper use of the mind on clearly defined principles. Only Ch'eng-Chu has squarely faced this need for definition, employing the learning and method of the mind along with the *Great Learning*'s investigation of things and pursuit of principle (2:12b).

The close link between the moral mind and scholarly inquiry is also seen in Fang's discussion of "singleness" and the unity of mind and principle in connection with the special note Chu Hsi had written on the investigation of things and the extension of knowledge in the *Great Learning*. This concerns his celebrated doctrine that one would experience "a breakthrough to integral comprehension" *(huo-jan kuan-t'ung)* as the culminating point in one's pursuit of scholarly inquiry and fathoming of principles. We have seen how problematic this matter had become, how suspect Chu's "breakthrough" was of being a Ch'an sudden enlightenment in Confucian disguise. It is not an issue Fang avoids. Rather he devotes much attention to it in his *Reckoning with the Han Learning* and his *Essay on Discriminating the Way (Pien-tao lun)*, since it is one of the grounds on which Han hsüeh scholars like Juan Yüan criticize Chu Hsi (2A:40b).

Juan Yüan had expressed a typical Ch'ing attitude in questioning whether the idea of such a breakthrough did not give undue weight to the enlightenment of the mind, at the expense of the action, conduct, or practice *(hsing)* with which Confucius had been so much concerned (2A:40b). Fang agrees that such doubts might well attach to the views of Lu Hsiang-shan and Wang Yang-ming, but not to Chu Hsi, who followed Confucius in discussing outward conduct always in close relation to the mind-and-heart within, and, by the same token, knowledge as indissolubly linked to action (2A:41c). Although Lu and Wang had stressed honoring the moral nature, Chu had insisted on balancing this with pursuit of the way of learning and inquiry, thus combining intellectual and moral cultivation, knowledge and action. Moreover, Chu had kept this same balance in recommending the *Mean's* five-step program of cultivation through broad learning, critical inquiry, careful reflection, discriminating judgment, and earnest conduct—all of which consciously avoided any one-sidedness in keeping with the aim of the sages to teach the Way as a Mean for all under Heaven to follow (2A:41ab).

As regards "sudden enlightenment," Chu had been quite emphatic in saying that the "breakthrough" he envisioned was not a kind of sudden illumination or gnosis, but rather something that could only come as the result of a prolonged effort at the investigation of things and fathoming of principles—a gradual and cumulative learning process

(2A:43b). Indeed, Chu's insistence on pursuing the investigation of things and fathoming of principles in direct relation to things and affairs was, Fang said, not essentially different from the Evidential Research school's often quoted aim of "seeking truth through facts" *(shih-shih ch'iu-shih)* (2A:38b–39a).[37] As a lifetime learning process it had a model in Confucius' own account of his life, starting with his commitment to learning at age fifteen and climaxed only at the ripe age of seventy by his feeling free to follow his hearts's desire without transgressing the norm.[38]

Finally, it should be noted that in his "Discriminating the Way" *(Pien-tao lun)*, written in his later age (undated, but after 1841),[39] Fang recapitulated his views on this subject and reaffirmed the important distinction between the mind of the Way and the human mind. This was the key to the gradual cultivation of Confucius and Chu Hsi, in contrast to the sudden enlightenment he attributed to Lu and Wang. The latter's direct approach went straight to the Mind of the Way, whereas Chu Hsi always kept the human mind in view and the need for human desires to be kept under the constant direction of the Mind of the Way by active, individual effort.[40]

In this regard it is probably significant that Fang, in the mid-nineteenth century, still sees this distinction as crucial to the Neo-Confucian doctrine and method, almost 700 years after Chu Hsi had enunciated it, while (except when he is directly quoting Ch'eng I or Chu Hsi) he avoids referring to it by the controversial term *hsin-fa*, and sees this method as fully compatible with the Han Learning aim of "seeking truth through facts."

Fang's linking of the method of the mind and the Great Learning's investigation of things is of more than routine significance. Much of the *Reckoning* is devoted to a defense of the Sung learning from the *Han hsüeh* charge that it had focused on the mind and neglected empirical investigation. Fang's counterattack charges Han hsüeh with neglecting both. Thus he attempts to establish factually, on the basis of the historical record, that it was actually the Ch'eng-Chu pursuit of the investigation of things, broad learning, and fathoming of principle that stimulated the later development of classical studies, including the Han Learning itself. Indeed the latter's ignorance of these facts, or effacing of them, betrays the speciousness of its claim to superiority in Evidential Inquiry.[41]

Fang takes up many specific textual and historical questions which, if we attempted to do them justice here, would draw us away from our main theme. Two points, however, may be relevant. Fang demonstrates in particular a detailed acquaintance with Neo-Confucian developments in the late Sung, Yüan, and early Ming (i.e., the early period from just after Chu Hsi up to Wang Yang-ming), showing how the broad and solid scholarship carried on in the Ch'eng-Chu school stood in contrast to *Han hsüeh* accusations that it had been totally absorbed in empty speculation (3:20a). He is aware of the exact historical steps by which the Neo-Confucian canon came to be codified and officially established, post-Chu Hsi (adding details left out of the account in the annotated Catalog of the Imperial Manuscript Library *(Ssu-k'u ch'üan-shu tsung'mu t'i-yao)*. This includes Chen Te-hsiu's part in presenting the Four Books at court for the first time—"The Inception of the Four Books" (3:9a)[42] —he says, as well as the major scholarly contributions of Hsü Heng and other Yüan scholars, etc. (which modern accounts too have largely overlooked) (3:34b).

All of this and more underscores Fang's conviction that the Han learning is simplistic and prejudiced in its account of the Neo-Confucian development. Narrowly specialized as it had become in studies of classical antiquity, the Han Learning was often less attentive to subsequent historical developments and scholarly contributions. If however Fang claims superior knowledge of the Neo-Confucian scholarship so defamed by the Han Learning, his broad scholastic view of the Neo-Confucian tradition, with its incremental contributions from successive generations of orthodox scholars, stands in even greater contrast to the earlier prophetic view of Lü Liu-liang, whose hard-line, fundamentalist, Ch'eng-Chu orthodoxy in the seventeenth century had tended to be as dismissive of Yüan and Ming Neo-Confucianism as the Han Learning was.

A major theme of the *Reckoning* is the continuing debate over the Han learning's primary concern with evidential research in historical linguistics and text criticism, on the one hand, and the primacy of moral principles among orthodox Neo-Confucianism, on the other.[43] Fang's objection to the former is on grounds of priority, not principle. Philology and phonology, no matter how sophisticated in technique, have for him a genuine instrumental value but no more than that. They are among the language skills which, according to the classical definition, had been classed as "elementary" learning *(hsiao hsüeh)*" preparatory to the higher studies discussed in the *Great Learning.* Indeed, by Fang's time *hsiao-hsüeh* had come to have the secondary meaning of "philology." Yet from his point of view the top priority given to philology by the Han learning has stood things on their head. Scholarly specialization has given priority to the solving of philological puzzles and antiquarian conundrums rather than to dealing with the larger human issues of self-cultivation, order in the family, disorder in the state, and peace in the world—all involving moral principles and thus, for Fang, the moral mind.[44] Fang pays special tribute to his forebear Fang Pao (1668–1749), an early leader of the T'ung-ch'eng school, who had evoked the reformist spirit of the Northern Sung scholars with their primary concern for the larger meaning or general sense of the classics.[45]

Philology, says Fang, must ever be guided by moral principles; it cannot be the reverse. Education and the higher learning should aim at dealing with the nature of humanity and needs of the larger world. These are what one should be committed to and have it in mind to do. And compared to these large human goals the Han Learning's debunking mentality, its petty preoccupation with philological niceties, simply confirms the prescient warning of Ch'eng Hao about the ease with which one can lose one's sense of direction and commitment when distracted by trivializing pursuits and diverted by learned baubles.[46]

Fang, however, does not wish to be caught in the position of juxtaposing moral principles (or proper principles *i-li*) and philology *(hsün-ku)* as if they were inherently antithetical values. Like the founding father of the T'ung-ch'eng school, Yao Nai (1732–1815), Fang believes that the Confucian Way should combine moral philosophy, philology, and literary composition, and keep a balance among them.[47] This is reminiscent of the early Sung formulation attributed to Hu Yüan: substance, function, and literary expression or cultural activity *(wen)*, wherein substance referred to basic principles in the classics, function to their practical application in one's own time, and literary expression to the need for serious writing to communicate principles and deal with intellectual, moral, and social questions of the day. The Sung "Learning of the Way" *(Tao-hsüeh)* had tended to emphasize the philosophical categories of substance and function, without placing as much stress on the literary aspect. Fang's and Yao Nai's reversion to this tripartite formula is natural enough in those who see Ch'an Buddhism as their great rival and threat, and who wish to disassociate their own conception of the transmission of the mind in words from the Ch'an "wordless transmission."

If, however, we consider this a basic trinitarian conception of the Way, when we compare the earlier and later versions, it would seem that the slogan "unity of moral principles *(i-li)*, evidential inquiry *(k'ao cheng)* or philology *(hsün-ku)*, and literary composition *(wen-chang)*," though it reaffirms the primacy of moral principles, has a more histori- cal and scholastic ring to it than the earlier philosophical language of substance, function, and expression. Perhaps it is not reading too much into a few words if we see this as reflecting the increasing role of disciplined historical scholarship, and a diminishing one for speculative philosophy, in a more secular Neo-Confucianism.

Moreover the synthetic balance struck here also fits Fang's sense of the continuity and inclusive character of the tradition, as compared to the discontinuities in transmission so much emphasized by Ch'eng I and Lü Liu-liang, with their prophetic version of the *tao-t'ung* as sagely learning long since cut off *(chüeh-hsüeh)* and nearly lost. The Sung learning of nineteenth-century Ch'ing China is not, as Fang serves it up, just the original Sung philosophy warmed over, but a recipe sea- soned by a long Neo-Confucian line of expert scholar-chefs.

If this leaves one with an impression of Fang as speaking for an essentially conservative tradition, comfortably eclectic but too burdened with history to meet the real challenges of the times, it would be misleading. Fang has his own prophetic warning and message to con- vey. This involves an aspect of his thought much discussed in the final chapter of his *Reckoning*, but rarely noted if at all by modern writers: the importance to him of human discourse and open discussion *(chiang- hsüeh)* as means of advancing the Way.

Chiang-hsüeh has often been translated as "lecturing," and it may be that in later times *chiang-hsüeh* had become so routine as to approx- imate mere lecturing. But there is another term *chiang-i (kōgi* in Japanese) more often used for formal lectures in both Chu Hsi's time and Fang's, and Chu himself made some distinction between the two. As it was understood among Neo-Confucians and by early historians of Neo-Confucianism, *chiang-hsüeh* had the clear implication of dialogue, group discussion, and even something approximating our "public dis- cussion."[48] "Public" might be misleading if it conjured up a picture of modern publicists at work, a substantial Fourth Estate or the availability of media for wide communication, which would contribute to the formation of "public opinion" in the current idiom. Such agencies did not exist in Sung and Ming China. The implicit original context is one of discussion among scholars, or in any case among a comparatively limited, literate social stratum, as well as one of debates largely carried on in schools and academies. In thus qualifying the use of the term *chiang-hsüeh*, however, we should overlook neither the significant enlargement and quickening of discussion that came with the spread of printing in Sung and Ming China, nor the close historical relationship of this technological advance to the spread of the Neo-Confucian movement, the rise of scholarly activity in local academies *(shu-yüan)* and the "discussion of learning" which flourished in this phase of China's development. For our purposes, while avoiding "public discussion" as perhaps too broad, and "scholarly discussion" or "lecturing" as possibly too narrow and elitist, the rendering of *chiang-hsüeh* simply as the "discussion of learning," "dialogue," or "debate" may be flexible enough to cover political discussions at court, scholarly exchanges in academies, and village meetings as part of community compact organization.[49]

The high-water mark for this kind of discussion came in the mid and late Ming, when Wang Yang-ming's liberal, and, in some branches of his "school," populist, version of Neo-Confucianism stimulated political discussion and popular education even among the illiterate or quasi-literate segments of society. After the Ch'ing conquest many writers, across a broad spectrum of philosophical allegiances, attributed the fall of the Ming to the divisiveness aroused in the sixteenth century by this kind of open discussion, free thinking, and partisan controversy. Ku Yen-wu was only the most prominent of the writers who considered the Ming to have been divided and weakened for foreign conquest by such controversy.

Given the complexity of the political forces at work in late eighteenth-century Ch'ing China, it is not surprising that conflicting interpretations would be heard. The Ch'ing court, as a conquest dynasty bent on maintaining its hereditary privileges over a largely Han Chinese bureaucratic elite, had its own expedient reasons for decrying factionalism and partisan controversy, while literati with divergent interests— literary, aesthetic, antiquarian, and political—usually found a bland eclecticism preferable to any strong moral advocacy bound to produce conflict.[50]

Yet another view of the matter, prejudicial to *chiang-hsüeh*, was that such discussions were most often vapid, tending too much toward airy speculation and not toward the addressing of practical needs—a view which seems to have gained wide currency in the late seventeenth and early eighteenth centuries. In this vein Ku Yen-wu saw the free and open discussion of the late Ming as a recrudescence of the "pure discussion" associated with Neo-Taoist and Buddhist speculations in the third and fourth centuries, which had been considered subversive of the traditional values identified with the "teaching of defined norms" (*ming chiao*). As Benjamin Elman has reported it:

> Ku Yen-wu linked the Sung-Ming penchant for a public lecturing style of teaching to the impact Buddhism had on *Tao hsüeh* scholars. He contended: "Classical studies are what studies of principle were called in antiquity." Ku equated emphasis on oral ratiocination of the type associated with fourth century A.D. Taoists and Buddhists with speculative discussion that would lead nowhere. Ku contended that the Sung-Ming adoption of the pure discussion approach was not only evidence of the influence of Ch'an Buddhism on Confucian discourse but was also of phony *li-hsüeh*.[51]

Fang's quotations from Ku and others in his *Reckoning* fully document this view; and what Elman describes here is precisely what Fang felt compelled to rebut in his *Reckoning with the Han Learning*. Elman's intriguing expression "oral ratiocination" to describe this phenomenon, incongruous though it may seem at first sight, accurately and appropriately combines two of the elements—reasoning and verbal articulation—that Fang would see as characteristic of Ch'eng-Chu learning. To him they were also what most differentiated it from Taoism and Ch'an Buddhism, both of which discouraged reliance on the word and taught an enlightenment going beyond rational and conceptual discourse.

As Fang lays out his rebuttal he challenges first the assertion that the Sung learning had neglected serious study of the classics in favor of free speculation. He offers a string of quotations from Chu Hsi in which the latter had urged students not to neglect the Han and T'ang commentarial literature on the classics, while at the same time he regretted that Han and T'ang scholars, preoccupied with philological and exegetical matters, had lost sight of the "larger meaning" (*ta-i*) of the classics, including both the ultimate questions of the Way, virtue, nature, and destiny, and the major proximate questions of self-cultivation and the urgent needs of human society.[52] Such being the case anyone seriously committed to "learning for the sake of oneself" was left to conclude that, inasmuch as Han and T'ang scholars offered no rational answers to such questions, one could only resort to intuitive means, introspecting the mind while neglecting things outside or beyond oneself. This, Fang says, was truly to "fall into the emptiness of Buddhism and Taoism"[53] (a charge which Ku and Han learning scholars had laid against Ch'eng-Chu and which Fang was now turning back upon the Han and Tang). This meant, too, that the latter had no grasp of the precise ways in which moral principles should be given defined form in correct systems and institutions.[54]

Fang goes on to address the further charge (not altogether consistent with the above) that open discussion encouraged partisanship and sectarianism, which do violence to the family and state. This too is a residue of controversies at the end of the Ming which many early Ch'ing scholars had deplored as partisan. If one bears in mind that even the orthodox Ch'eng-Chu scholar Lü Liu-liang criticized late Ming *chiang-hsüeh* for falling, like Wang Yang-ming, under the spell of Ch'an Buddhism, one can see how the accusation might have had some plausibility in the eyes of even some who would not necessarily have disagreed with Fang about the value of discussion as such. Indeed the free-wheeling "discussion of learning" in the late Ming drew unfavorable comment from many quarters in the early Ch'ing, including such a liberal thinker as Huang Tsung-hsi, on the ground that it ignored textual study and scholarly authority.[55]

This does not, however, deter Fang from vigorously rejecting the charge itself, as part of a pattern which would repress virtually all criticism and dissent. In Fang's view anyone who expresses alarm over dangers to state and society can expect to be labeled a partisan *(tang)*, or an adherent of the "Learning of the Way" *(tao-hsüeh)*, or "a disciple of the discussion of learning" *(chiang-hsüeh men-hu)*. Critics of the Sung school have alleged that it was the partisan divisions between the Loyang and Szechwan schools that sowed the seeds of the Northern Sung's destruction, while they place none of the blame where it belongs —on Ts'ai Ching, supposedly the responsible head of government at that time. Similar accusations have been made concerning the School of the Way *(tao-hsüeh)* and the fall of the Southern Sung, without mentioning the repressive role of Han T'o-chou, then prime minister, in proscribing that school. Finally, the fall of the Ming is all blamed on the partisanship of the Tung-lin group, who were out of power, while such powerful personages as Yen Sung and the eunuch Wei Chung-hsien are held in no way responsible.[56]

How can one fault the Confucians for what has happened when their advice has gone unheeded? Who can blame Confucius for the weakness of the state of Lu or Mencius for the disorders of the Warring States Period? Similarly with the fall of the Ming: How can this be attributed to the partisan spirit engendered by the Tung-lin's open advocacy of Neo-Confucian principles? Rather it was to the credit of the Tung-lin leaders that, being concerned lest the larger meaning and basic principles of the classics be lost, they assembled scholars to discuss them. This was necessary because scholars at court, even those in high office, dared not speak out against the evils of the day (3:22a–23a).

Here Fang's views are no doubt colored by the sense of powerlessness that attaches to his nonofficial status on the margin of the literocratic elite. Whether or not one identifies him, in that condition, as an independent scholar (i.e., one free of the responsibility that goes with holding office), or as one still dependent for his marginal existence on the patronage of officials, Fang chose to identify himself with those literati who felt a Confucian obligation to speak out. Whatever the limiting circumstances, he assumed the special role and burden of the prophet—the warner and protester against a soft and self-indulgent generation.

The whole original reason for the sage-kings' instituting of government, says Fang, was to provide the means for nipping evil in the bud, and the sixteen-word message of the sages concerning the human mind and mind of the Way had been the key to checking corrupt tendencies before they could get very far. These sixteen words were indeed "the discussion of learning" (chiang-hsüeh), says Fang (3:24ab). For that matter, many of the most celebrated teachings of the classics could be called "the discussion of learning," including the moral instructions in the Book of Documents and Rites of Chou; Confucius' teachings in answer to questions about humaneness (jen), government, the noble man, etc., in the Analects; Mencius' "Learning extensively and discussing minutely" (IVB: 15); the Great Learning's steps of rectifying the mind, making the intention sincere, regulating the family, etc.—in any of these matters "from the self to the state and nation, from a single item to the myriad kinds of affairs, what is there not subject to discussion? Therefore Confucius said (in the *Analects* 3:7): 'Not to discuss thoroughly what is learned . . . is something I would be concerned about' '' (3:25a).

Those responsible for maintaining the water courses will spare no effort to keep them open to traffic and communication. But compared to the blocking of water courses, the shutting up of the mouths of the people is far worse. When Confucius (*Mean* 19) discussed the steps for achieving personal integrity, he spoke first of extensive study, judicious inquiry, careful reflection, discriminating judgment, and only after that of following these up with earnest practice of the course of action so considered. "Hence if learning is not discussed, the Way will not be made clear, and if the Way is not made clear, how can one be sure of properly carrying it out in one's personal conduct?" (3:25ab).

In the transmission of the Way only when one discusses it can others hear about it, receive it, and carry it on. Accordingly Mencius talks about those who first learn of the Way apprising those who come after (5A:7). The *Book of Changes* speaks of the noble man discussing with his friends the practice of virtue (Hexagram 58), while the opening passage of the *Analects*[57] speaks of practicing what one has learned in the company of friends who have come from afar, and of "making friends through letters and enhancing one's humanity [through such intercourse] with friends" (12:24) (3:26a).

From these passages emphasizing the need for discussion of one's practice of virtue in the company of others, Fang goes on to a lengthy recital of other examples in the classics of the ruler consulting with his ministers in the making of decisions and fostering discussion among the people in order to ascertain their views on correct policies. Numerous cases in history are also cited of the beneficial results of such consultation with the people and the unfortunate consequences of rulers or their ministers failing so to consult. Moreover Fang also notes that Chu Hsi in formulating his Articles of the White Deer Grotto Academy specifically enjoins on its students the need to discuss the guiding principles of the school as a basis for their voluntary observance of its stated aims —much to be preferred over the imposition of any coercive or punitive regulations (3:26a–27b).[58]

From the foregoing much abbreviated synopsis of Fang's argument, one may perhaps glimpse some of the importance Fang attaches, not just to debating the issues raised by the Han Learning itself, but to arguing the need for scholarly debate on fundamental issues other than the purely scholarly, and above all for open discussion of questions involving the Confucians' traditional concern for "world-ordering" as an ever-present responsibility. These are matters he could easily have avoided had his motive been only the defense of scholarly turf. Instead, impelled by a sense that the very heart of the tradition was at stake, he went to extraordinary lengths to establish the ground in tradition from which he spoke—the classical examples of Confucius and Mencius engaged in dialogue and debate; the Sung revival of this Confucian advocacy and activism, along with its deeper philosophical probing of the principles which differentiate this reformism from Buddhism and Taoism; and later the heroic efforts of the Tung-lin movement to reassert this activism.

But if it is a tradition of outspoken reformism he speaks for, his protest is also offered from a new perspective, challenging the view received from the high Ch'ing—the view which had been dominant since the early years of the period, that controversy itself had become discredited by Neo-Confucian excesses in the Sung and Ming. Lü Liu-liang, founding father of Ch'ing orthodoxy (notwithstanding his later repudiation by the Ch'ing court) had shared Ku Yen-wu's view of late Ming neo-orthodoxy as perverted by Ch'an Buddhism. Now Fang, though heir to the Ch'eng-Chu line of Lü, Chang Lü-hsiang, and Lu Lung-chi in its criticism of the neo-orthodox Kao P'an-lung's philosophy and practice of quiet-sitting, finds great redeeming value, as most Ch'ing scholars had not, in the Tung-lin's courageous protest against the evils of that day.

Especially significant in the Ch'ing context, and against the background of the Ch'ing scholarly establishment, is Fang's insistence on the role of schools and academies as centers of discussion and debate. Earlier Huang Tsung-hsi, in his *Plan for the Prince (Ming-i tai-fang lu)* had made the same point, only to have it largely ignored through the long Ch'ing dominance—and also, we may be reminded, the dominance of the Ch'ing "orthodoxy" which Liang Ch'i-ch'ao had identified with the school of Evidential Research.

Fang, however, had his own experience of this kind of academic research as a scholar attached to major scholarly projects at leading academies in the Canton area, including the Hsüeh-hai t'ang Academy, center for the production of the monumental compendium of Ch'ing commentaries and treatises on the classics, the *Huang-Ch'ing ching-chieh* in 1400 *chüan* and 366 volumes, under the patronage and direction of the governor-general Juan Yüan. Whether Fang was aware of it or not, support for this academy and its projects more than likely came in part from profits of the opium trade and official collusion in it.[59] Nor was this something Fang needed to know in order to feel keenly, as he did, that the kind of classical scholarship conducted there, though respectable enough in its own way, fell far short of meeting the academies' responsibility for speaking out against dire evils like the opium trade and the threat of encroaching foreign military power.[60] To do this they would have to concern themselves with principles, not just facts. Earlier, a frequent complaint of Neo-Confucian reformers against schools and academies was that they put studying for the civil service examinations ahead of genuine "learning for the sake of oneself." Now a new scholarly disinterestedness had proven an even greater threat to such genuine learning and cultivation.[61]

Thus Fang's extraordinary emphasis on Confucian moral advocacy had immediate contemporary relevance as well as significance for the revival of tradition. Present dangers required decisive action, not more study of the past—unless it would be a study of the kind that had inspired reformers in the Sung and late Ming. Needed now was the large vision of a Chu Hsi combined with definite courses of action in keeping with basic human principles—in effect, Chu's teaching of the "whole substance and great functioning." What was missing, and most urgently needed in the present situation, was a new attitude of mind capturing the old message of the mind. Hence his extended discussion of that message as 1) the "transmission of the mind," contra Ku Yenwu; as 2) the measure or norm in the conscientious mind making the necessary value judgments; and as 3) the method of the mind, involving discussion and debate so that action can be guided by the collective judgment and experience of educated minds.

It is not for us to enter here into the historical application of that substance-function formula to Fang's contemporary situation or its outcome in the hands of others after him. That is another question deserving of further consideration. For our purposes it may suffice here to note a few main points relevant to the present inquiry:

1. Fang's renewed emphasis on the Ch'eng-Chu philosophy of mind and human nature, as well as the practical application of this to the conduct of contemporary affairs, arises from his sense of the moral bankruptcy of the Han Learning, shown in the inability of the value-free, facts-for-facts sake approach of the reigning scholarship to meet

the demands of the Confucian social conscience in responding to current crises.

2. As a remedy Fang reaches back to the Ch'eng-Chu sixteen-word formula concerning the human mind and mind of the Way, believing it to represent the essential thinking of Confucius and Mencius, re-articulated in new terms by Ch'eng-Chu in order to counter the Ch'an view of the mind. For Fang this message and method remains the very heart of the Confucian/Ch'eng-Chu teaching. Though he does not refer to it often as either *hsin-fa* or *hsin-hsüeh*, the distinction between the human mind and mind of the Way is central to all of his discussions, not only in this best known of Fang's tracts, *Reckoning with the Han Learning*, but in numerous essays in his collected writings dealing with the Way, Heaven, Human Nature, Principle, Quiescence, etc.[62]

3. This formula Fang connects with Chu Hsi's interpretation of the "investigation of things and extension of knowledge" (including his conception of a cumulative learning process leading to a "breakthrough to integral understanding")—thus blending the moral and affective with the rational and cognitive aspects of the mind. For him this is the true Learning of the Mind-and-Heart, echoing what Chu Hsi himself had originally said about the message of the mind. Nothing had been forgotten.

4. Fang's view of the Way is cumulative and collective, not in the evolutionary or progressive sense, but in recognizing the contributions of many scholars at different stages of history. He sees it not as a static tradition but a growing one, for which his preferred analogy is a typically organic one: the successive efforts of sowers, cultivators, and reapers in the growing of grain.[63] In the process there is some loss caused by the errors and failings of those who stray from the Way, but this may be balanced by the heroic achievements of scholars like the Ch'eng's and especially Chu Hsi.

Another way of putting this is to say that Fang, though orthodox in balancing the prophetic and scholastic view of the tradition, avoided a narrow fundamentalism. The assumption of the Evidential Research scholars was that one could get at the original, literal meaning of the classics, and peel away all subsequent accretions to get at the pure teaching of the ancients. Fang reminded them that there were important truths in the *Analects* not found in the earlier classics, and further advances made by Chu Hsi in meeting the challenge of Buddhism, which had been unknown in Confucius' time. Simply returning to the original source was not enough.

5. While reaffirming the essential elements of the Ch'eng-Chu Learning of the Mind-and-Heart, and firmly rejecting the idea that such a learning was contaminated by foreign intrusion into Confucianism, Fang tacitly accepts its altered status in the nineteenth century. He does not characteristically use the expressions "Learning of the Mind (hsin hsüeh) or method of the mind (hsin-fa), except when quoting higher Neo-Confucian authority. Normally he refers to the true teaching as the Way of the Sages, Learning of the Way, or "Ch'eng-Chu." And if he uses "hsin-hsüeh" without some clear qualification pointing to its authentic Ch'eng-Chu form, he does so most often in reference to Wang Yang-ming's Learning of the Mind.[64] The content of that Learning he deplores, but by his time the term has long since been relegated to Wang, or to the Lu-Wang teaching. Few recall, as does Fang, its earlier history or significance, or are aware that the first application of "hsin-hsüeh" to Wang Yang-ming by a historian, in Teng Yüan-hsi's Huang-Ming shu (1606), only gave a new and special thrust to what had already been an essential aspect of earlier Ch'eng-Chu teaching.[65] Even though Fang disputes Ku Yen-wu's interpretation of this development, it is as if he could not now hope to reverse the conventional equating of it with Wang Yang-ming or dispel the impression created by Ku that "hsin-hsüeh" was a contaminated term. This conclusion would confirm the picture given by James Polachek of Ku as so powerful an authority figure in the late Ch'ing that no scholarly movement could hope to succeed without doing homage to him and deferring to his opinions.[66]

6. Similarly, if Fang's synthetic sense of the traditions leads him, like his predecessor Yao Nai, to sum it up in the contemporary context as embracing "moral principles, philological research, and literary composition," we detect here too a shift in emphasis, noticeable in the lack of direct reference to the mind, which for the orthodox is increasingly subordinated to the primacy of principle. Fang has argued forcefully the basic Ch'eng-Chu position that mind and principle are inseparable, but in speaking to his contemporary audience, he sums things up in the current scholarly idiom, which reflects the change, even within the Ch'eng-Chu school, to a greater emphasis on principle as the most distinctive and crucial element in Neo-Confucianism—indisputably its own property—while the mind remains contested ground among the

several teachings. At the same time there is renewed emphasis on speech and literature as the means of expressing both principle and mind.

7. Finally, even while defending the essential content of the Ch'eng-Chu message and method of the mind, and the basic conception of the "transmission of the [sages'] mind, Fang has become conscious of the increasingly controversial nature of the Succession to the Way *(tao-t'ung)*. Through whom the succession ran, after Chu Hsi and his immediate disciples, or upon whom the authentic inspiration alighted in the six hundred years since Chu's death, had become a divisive issue rather than a unifying conception. Since the Ch'eng-Chu learning of the mind had been so closely linked to the *tao-t'ung* originally, the inherent difficulties and ever more problematic nature of this concept could not but undermine the plausibility and viability of "the transmission of the mind" as an effective medium for the passing on of the tradition.

Here then we have an emerging pattern: the renewal of orthodoxy in ways reflective of Neo-Confucianism's later historical development. Holding to tradition in both its breadth and balance, Fang, even while attacking the Han learning, lays claim to the accomplishments of Evidential Research as fruits of the Neo-Confucian "investigation of things and fathoming of principle." Nor is this a far-fetched claim, since Fang's contemporary T'ang Chien, an orthodox Ch'eng-Chu historian, classified Ku Yen-wu himself among the "supporters" of the Neo-Confucian Way *(i-tao)*, rather than with Huang Tsung-hsi as an exemplar of classical scholarship *(ching-hsüeh)*.[67]

Thus, Fang acknowledges, such inquiry can lead to new learning. This is not to say that such new learning would, left to itself, have produced something like the new learning of the West, nor on the other hand, that such possibilities were altogether precluded as inherently antithetical to the Neo-Confucian Way. It is only that for the Neo-Confucian, whatever the field of inquiry he probed or the facts he encountered, their value and significance could only be judged in reference to some defined view of human nature and the mind.

In a recent review Jerome Grieder has summed up the state of the question vis-à-vis Evidential Research in the following terms:

There is obviously a difference between asking, with Ku Yen-wu, Yen Jo-chü, Tai Chen, and their kindred spirits, "Which parts of the Classics may we accept as true because they are verifiably 'classical' in origin?" and asking—as these thinkers never did— "Are the Classics, properly understood, the repository of what is ultimately true?" The *k'ao-cheng* passion for "seeking truth from facts" did indeed lead to an increasingly sophisticated, discriminating, and—from the perspectives of orthodoxy—subversive understanding of the implications of factual evidence; but it did not eventuate in a reappraisal of the meaning of truth, as the subject of reflective speculation rather than evidential proof. Evidential scholarship was thus methodologically innovative, but in the final analysis it remained epistemologically sterile. "Why no Newton in China?" has become almost a dismissive cliché; should we not, perhaps, be asking instead (or as well), "Why no Kant?"[68]

Putting the question this way goes well beyond the challenge to *k'ao-cheng* laid down by Fang Tung-shu concerning the limits of factual evidence. Indeed one could equally ask of Fang whether his "reflective speculation" eventuates in a "reappraisal of the meaning of truth" as radical, say, as Kant's in the West. Yet two things might usefully be said about Fang in reply to this question: he at least kept the importance of reflective speculation alive, and by recognizing the distinctive contributions of later thinkers in the Neo-Confucian tradition, as they responded to new challenges in altered historical circumstances, held the door open to further reappraisals of the meaning of truth similar to Chu Hsi's own reinterpretation of Confucianism. This not only goes beyond the penchant of *k'ao-cheng* scholars to isolate the pure, uncontaminated truth in the past—an inherently sterile procedure—but it goes beyond the much acclaimed "pragmatism" of more recent advocates of "seeking truth through facts" in contemporary China. Fang stands as a reminder that fundamental questions concerning the mind and human nature still remain to be dealt with.[69] They are there today waiting to be addressed in the new context and the new idiom. And what becomes of the new "pragmatism" in China, for all its undoubted advantages over a doctrinaire Stalinism or Maoism, will depend in significant measure on how a new generation recognizes and responds to this need.

Conclusion

We have now completed a survey of major Neo-Confucian thinkers, as well as others less well known, who had something to say about the Learning of the Mind-and-Heart from the time of Chu Hsi in the late twelfth century to the mid-nineteenth century, when Chu's teaching reached the height of its preeminence in the official Ch'ing orthodoxy. This is a long span of time, and since the coverage is necessarily selective, our conclusions must be correspondingly tentative. Nonetheless, with that qualification in mind, I believe the following points may be made:

1. The Learning of the Mind-and-Heart was a vital element, along with the Learning of Principle, in the Ch'eng-Chu teaching of the late Sung, Yüan, and Ming periods down to the time of Wang Yang-ming. Its core teaching centered on three closely related concepts: the succession to, or tradition of, the Way (tao-t'ung); the message and method of the mind (hsin-fa); and the transmission of the Sages' Mind (ch'uan-hsin). Most of its early exponents sharply distinguished this doctrine from the Buddhist "learning of the mind."

2. Wang Yang-ming's new Learning of the Mind substantially reinterpreted its meaning, but claimed to follow through on the natural and logical development of Chu Hsi's thought in a way that also brought it close to that of Lu Hsiang-shan.

3. Up to this time there had been no school of Lu Hsiang-shan to speak of, but the enormous influence of Wang Yang-ming stimulated new interest in Lu and associated Lu with Wang as the two leading thinkers in the new Learning of the Mind. In the process, especially in

the popular mind, Wang's teaching seems to have occupied the domain and captured the flag of the earlier Learning of the Mind.

4. A strong reaction to the new Learning came from defenders of Chu Hsi's teaching who challenged Wang's claim to speak for the Learning of the Mind, focusing their attack on Wang's identification of Mind and Principle, which for them meant (among other things) the loss of the distinction between the human mind and the mind of the Way, so important to the "method of the mind" (e.g., Ch'en Chien, T'ang Po-yüan).

5. In the neo-orthodox reaction to Wang's great popularity there was a strong tendency, beginning in the late sixteenth century, to reaffirm Chu Hsi while also seeking a consensus on basic values shared by Chu and Wang, inasmuch as Wang himself had professed fidelity to Chu Hsi's essential ideas (e.g., the Tung-lin school and Liu Tsung-chou).

6. Amidst the intense controversy that preceded and followed the fall of the Ming dynasty, the consensus view was carried forward by certain thinkers, (e.g., Sun Ch'i-feng, Li Yung, T'ang Pin, Chu Shih), who had a significant influence on the formulation of the official orthodoxy in the late seventeenth and early eighteenth centuries.

7. Another brand of orthodoxy took a much narrower view, rejecting Wang and Lu altogether and repudiating even most of the neo-orthodox thinkers of the late Ming as having made unacceptable compromises with Wang Yang-ming and Buddhism. At the same time this tendency moved away from the subjectivism which, allegedly, had opened the door to Buddhist influence, and placed renewed emphasis on objective inquiry and the evidential learning which became so powerful a trend in early Ch'ing scholarship.

8. Both the "orthodox" and "neo-orthodox," as I have distinguished them, had proponents in and out of office. We cannot identify the "state" or officialdom clearly with one line or the other. The prevailing view varied from reign to reign and with shifting leadership among high officials.

9. Nevertheless, two contrasting elements emerge in this mixed picture. One is that some of the most intransigent exponents of strict Ch'eng-Chu orthodoxy, like Ch'en Chien in the sixteenth century, Lü Liu-liang in the seventeenth, and Fang Tung-shu in the nineteenth are either independent scholars or active only on the margins of officialdom, protesting from below heterodox deviations on high.

10. Meanwhile, despite the variability among leading scholars and

officials, the examination system continued to rely on the Four Books and Five Classics with their Ch'eng-Chu school commentaries, as the standard texts. Whatever the differences among scholars, there was no serious effort to replace Chu Hsi's texts in the basic curriculum. Thus even during the heyday of "evidential research and critical study of the Classics," the educational formation of Chinese literati (as of Korean or Japanese, for that matter) was still conditioned by these basic texts.

11. With the exception of Lü Liu-liang, who disowned the learning of the mind altogether because of its association with Wang Yang-ming and Lu Hsiang-shan, the other important spokesmen of Ch'eng-Chu orthodoxy still upheld the position that a correct learning of the Mind and especially the "method of the mind" and "transmission of the mind," remain key elements in orthodox teaching. Chu Hsi's Preface to the commentaries on the *Mean* continued to keep these ideas before educated minds.

12. The continuing dispute over which of the Ming thinkers, if any, should be accepted as orthodox, led to distinct cleavages over the true "succession to the Way" *(tao-t'ung)*. This became an issue so delicate that it was often avoided or finessed in official formulations. The practice of quiet-sitting was another point of continuing controversy, since it had been seen as an acceptable practice in the orthodox tradition of the Learning of the Mind but had come under increasing suspicion as too Buddhistic. In some cases this sensitivity even extended to Chu Hsi's concept of a "breakthrough to integral comprehension" *(huo-jan kuan-t'ung)*, the culmination of the learning process, as too close to Buiddhist enlightenment.

13. Although the exact nature and content of the official orthodoxy, or what has sometimes been called "Imperial Confucianism," requires further study, the evidence presented herein strongly suggests that it was far from monolithic, and that there were at least two main versions of orthodoxy (as referred to in nos. 6 and 7 above) contending for the favor of Ch'ing rulers up to the Yung-cheng period (1723–36), if not later.

14. Meanwhile in this contention and continuing controversy between the so-called Ch'eng-Chu and Lu-Wang schools, there had developed no clear separating out of "Ch'eng-Chu Learning of Principle" versus "Lu-Wang Learning or School of Mind." The participants in these controversies, on both sides, had reasons of their own for arguing that all along there had been an orthodox Neo-Confucian Learning of

the Mind, which affirmed both mind and principle as fundamental values. And for those who looked back at the earlier record, there was plenty of evidence to support this view. Even Ku Yen-wu, who deplored this "learning" as Buddhistic, testified to it as a historical reality in the Ch'eng-Chu school.

The conclusions reached above will leave some readers still wondering when the dichotomy of Ch'eng-Chu Learning of Principle versus Lu-Wang School of Mind first arose, if it had not done so in the long period of Neo-Confucian dominance. To this I have no precise and conclusive answer. It is only to be expected that the two terms would come into use as designations for the two schools, once polarization had occurred and each had been assigned, however simplistically, one predominant value or the other. However, none of the early histories of Ch'ing thought makes use of these labels as basic categories of analysis or organization, and there is no reason to believe that such a dichotomy marked the lines of scholarly filiation before formal classical education yielded to Western style learning in the early twentieth century. The two most recent dictionaries of Chinese philosophy both give Fung Yu-lan's *History of Chinese Philosophy* (first published 1934) as their authority (and they cite no earlier one) for the assertion that the antithesis of Ch'eng-Chu *li-hsüeh* versus Lu-Wang *hsin-hsüeh* represented a fundamental distinction in Neo-Confucian thought. Thus, while the idea of a "Lu-Wang School of the Mind" first arose in the seventeenth century, and is essentially attributable to Wang Yang-ming's influence or the reaction to it, the exclusive assignment of the Learning of the Mind to "Lu-Wang," and the retrospective juxtaposition of this to the Ch'eng-Chu Learning of Principle is more than likely attributable to Fung. Hence the explanation for this plausible but quite definite oversimplification of the historical facts takes us back to the very quotation from Fung's *History* which served as the starting point of this inquiry.

Notes

The following standard sinological abbreviations are used:

CKTHMCCC   Chung-kuo tzu hsüeh ming-chu chi-ch'eng
MJHA   Ming-ju hsüeh-an
SKCSCP   Ssu-k'u ch'üan-shu chen-pen
SPPY   Ssu-pu pei-yao
SPTK   Ssu-pu ts'ung-k'an
SSGTK   Shushigaku taikei
SYHA   Sung-Yüan hsüeh-an
TSCC   Ts'ung-shu chi-ch'eng

Preface

1. E.g., *Tz'u-yüan mao 3; Tz'u-hai, mao-chi,* 3b; *Tz'u-hai,* revised edition, p. 1096; Morohashi Tetsuji, *Dai kanwa jiten,* No. 10295–45; Shimonaka Kunihiko, *Ajia rekishi jiten,* 8:422b; Hihara Toshikuni, ed., *Chūgoku shisō jiten,* p. 225; W. T. de Bary, Wing-tsit Chan, and Burton Watson, eds., *Sources of Chinese Tradition,* ch. 21, espec. p. 564.

2. For a fuller discussion of this matter, see my introduction to *The Rise of Neo-Confucianism in Korea,* pp. 17–36.

3. *Ibid.,* pp. 8–14.

1. General Introduction

1. *Hui-an hsien-sheng Chu Wen-kung wen-chi, Wen-chi,* 47:33a (p. 3288), Ta lü Tzu-yüeh; *Chu Tzu ch'üan-shu* (1714 ed.), 1:30 ab; translation adapted from Wing-tsit Chan, *A Source Book in Chinese Philosophy,* p. 605.

2. Li Ching-te, ed., *Chu Tzu yü-lei* (hereafter abbr. *Yü-lei*, with consecutive pagination of this edition given after chuan, page, and item numbers), 126:48ab #129, 132 (pp. 4871–72), also 126:8a #34 (p. 4381).

3. Chu Hsi, *Ta-hsüeh chang-chu*, 6ab (pp. 17–18).

4. This point is more fully discussed in my essay "Neo-Confucian Individualism and Holism," in Donald Munro, ed., *Individualism and Holism: Studies in Confucian and Taoist Values*, pp. 351–58.

5. *Neo-Confucian Orthodoxy*, pp. 128–30.

6. *Neo-Confucian Orthodoxy*, pp. 30, 129.

7. Chu Hsi, *Chung-yung chang-chü*, Preface 1b (p. 38); *Chu Tzu ta-ch'üan*, 72:16a–46a, Tsa hsüeh pien. This includes a critique of the views of Lü Pen-chung, currently the subject of a study by Mr. Ari Borrell at Columbia.

8. Ch'eng I, *Erh Ch'eng ch'üan-shu*, 12:12b (p. 104).

9. Chu, *Yü-lei*, 78:17a #17 (p. 3193).

10. *Yü-lei*, 78:27a #16 (p. 3193).

11. *Yü-lei*, 62:9a #41 (2362).

12. *Wen-chi*, 67:20a–21b (pp. 4957–60).

13. *Shu ching*, "Counsels of Great Yü." Cf. translation by James Legge, *Shoo King*, p. 62.

14. *Mencius*, 6A:8.

15. *Shu ching*, "Counsels of Great Yü." Cf. Legge, *Shoo King*, p. 62.

16. *Ibid.*

17. Paraphrasing *Mencius*, 6A:8.

18. *Changes*, commentary on hexagram no. 2, *k'un* (Earth). Cf. Legge, *Yi King*, p. 420.

19. *Mencius*, 7A:1.

20. *Ibid.*

21. Translation adapted from Wing-tsit, Chan, *Source Book*, pp. 603–4.

22. *Yü-lei*, 62:8b #41 (2362).

23. Often expressed as "tso-yung shih hsing" *Taishō shinshū daizōkyō*, 51:No. 2076. *Ching-te ch'uan-teng lu*, 3:218b, Bodhidharma.

24. *Yü-lei*, 126:13a #59 (p. 4841), SSGTK, 6:379.

25. *Dai Nihon zoku zokyō*, 2.25.1 shang chüan, 28a, P'ang chü-shih yü-lu.

26. *Yü-lei*, 126:13a–15a, #59, 60, 61 (pp. 4841–45), SSGTK, 6:381–82.

27. *Yü-lei*, 62:8b #41 (p. 2362).

28. *Yü-lei*, 62:7a #39 (p. 2359).

29. *Yü-lei*, 62:8b #41 (2362).

30. Yanagida Seizan, "The *Li-tai fa-pao chi* and the Ch'an Doctrine of Sudden Awakening," p. 41.

31. Philip Yampolsky, *The Platform Sutra of the Sixth Patriarch*, pp. 130–32.

32. *Taishō daizōkyō*, 37:373; W. T. de Bary, ed., *The Buddhist Tradition*, p. 206.

33. *Taishō daizōkyō*, 47:8–11; *The Buddhist Tradition*, p. 203.

34. W. T. de Bary, ed., *Self and Society in Ming Thought*, pp. 176–77; *The Unfolding of Neo-Confucianism*, pp. 48–51.

35. See my *Neo-Confucian Orthodoxy and the Learning of the Mind-and-Heart*, pp. 79–83.

2. The Learning of the Mind-and-Heart in the Early Chu Hsi School

1. *Neo-Confucian Orthodoxy*, Parts I, II.

2. Typical examples are *Tz'u-hai*, 3b; *Tz'u-yüan*, p. 1096; Wei Cheng-t'ung, *Chung-kuo che-hsüeh tz'u-tien ta-ch'üan*, pp. 112–15. Morohashi Testsuji, *Dai kanwa jiten*, 1960 No. 10295–45; Hihara Toshikuni, ed., *Chūgoku tetsugaku jiten*, p. 225. Fung Yu-lan, *History of Chinese Philosophy*, Derk Bodde, tr., 2:500, 572, 586, 623; de Bary, Chan, and Watson, eds., *Sources of Chinese Tradition*, pp. 510, 559; Wing-tsit Chan, *Source Book in Chinese Philosophy*, p. 573. Chan's comments in this earlier work should be viewed in light of his later article in Wei Cheng-t'ung above.

3. Fung, *History*, Bodde, tr., 2:572, 586, see also pp. 500, 623. The corresponding passages in the original Chinese edition of 1934 remain unaltered in the latest edition, *Chung-kuo che-hsüeh shih*, 2:928–29, 938–39.

4. Ch'ien Mu, *Chu Tzu hsin hsüeh-an*, 2:1.

5. See reference to Ch'en Li (T'ing-yu)'s commentary on *Analects* 2; Shih yu wu chang.

6. Araki Kengo, citing the *Hsin hsüeh-an* 1:418, differs with Ch'ien on this. Although I do not find the language Araki cites on 1:418, similar statements are made here and on 2:106. Araki's view is presented in the aforementioned preface to his *Minmatsu shūkyō shisō kenkyū*, 27, 48.

7. *Hsin hsüeh-an*, 1:55.

8. Yang Wan-li, "Hsin Hsüeh lun," in *Ch'eng-chai chi*, SPTK, ch. 84–86, esp. 85:10b–12b. On Yang Wan-li see *Sung-shih* 433:12863–66; MJHA 44:74–81; *Sung-jen so-yin* 3186–88; Hervouet, *Sung Bibliography*, pp. 417–18. See also Wing-tsit Chan, "Hsin-hsüeh," in Wei Cheng-tung, ed., *Chung-kuo che-hsüeh tz'u-tien ta-ch'üan*, p. 113.

9. de Bary, *Neo-Confucian Orthodoxy and Learning of the Mind-and-Heart*, pp. 5–6.

10. As recounted in *Analects* 20:1.

11. *Book of History*, "Counsels of Great Yü," in James Legge, *The Chinese Classics*, 3:61.

12. Chu Hsi, Preface to *Chung-yung chang-chü*, in *Ssu-shu chi chu*, also in *Shushigaku taikei* (Tokyo: Meitoku Shuppansha, 1974), 8:451–52 (11–14). In references to this edition the Chinese text is cited first, the Japanese second. My translation has benefited from consulting, in addition to the Japanese translation of Tanaka Masaru and notes of Kurihara Keisuke, the draft translation by Wing-tsit Chan prepared for the *Sources of Neo-Confucianism* project.

13. An idea advanced by Han Yü and reiterated by Ch'eng I. See *Neo-Confucian Orthodoxy*, pp. 3–5.

14. Chu Hsi, *Chung-yung chang-chü hsü*, p. 3 (42).

15. Ch'ien, *Hsin hsüeh-an*, 1:186–96; 4:184.

16. *Ibid.*, 1:28–35, 143, 160–61, 169–70; 4:184–87, 197; and, 2:113, 4:218.

17. See de Bary, Chan, and Watson, eds., *Sources of Chinese Tradition*, pp. 503–9; Richard L. Davis, "Historiography as Politics in Yang Wei-chen's 'Polemic on Legitimate Succession' "; and Hok-lam Chan, *Legitimation in Imperial China*, pp. 38–40.

18. Li Yüan-kang, *Sheng-men shih-yeh t'u*, in *Pai-ch'uan hsüeh-hai*, 1927 photolithographic ed. of original Sung ed. of T'ao Hsiang as supplemented by the Ming Hung-chih (1488–1505) ed. of Hua Ch'eng; prefaces of Li dated 1170, 1173. See Hervouet, *Sung Bibliography*, p. 490.

The extant edition of the Diagrams also carries a post-preface dated 1172 by one Wang Chieh of San-shan. In paying tribute to Li, Wang expresses views common to Ch'eng I and Chu Hsi. Given Chu's great reputation and the wide influence of his writings, as well as mutual scholarly associations such as this, it is as possible that Li was familiar with some of Chu's ideas as vice versa. However, given the date of this preface, the Wang Chieh here could hardly be the Wang Chieh (1158–1213) identified as a follower of Chu Hsi from Chin-hua. See Ch'ang Pi-te *Sung-jen chuan-chi tzu-liao so-yin*, p. 106; Chan Wing-tsit, *Chu Tzu men-jen*, pp. 60–61; *Sung shih*, 400:12152–55; SYHA, 73:30–31; Pu-i, 73:6b.

Li Yüan-kang (n.d.); T. Kuo-chi, H. Pai-lien chen-yin. A reclusive scholar of Ch'ien-t'ang, Chekiang, known for his devotion to learning. He is linked by the *Sung-yüan hsüeh-an pu-i* with the school of Chang Tsai, but his diagram identifies the Ch'engs as the successors to the Way and makes no mention of Chang. *Sung-jen so-yin*, p. 951; SYHA, Pu-i, 17:18b.

19. Both Davis (p. 48) and H. L. Chan (p. 41) include Chou Tun-i in the transmission, but Li's chart is quite clear in representing the Ch'eng brothers as direct successors to Mencius, and has no mention of Chou Tun-i. Both Li and Chu Hsi bespeak a view apparently prevalent in the Ch'eng brothers' school. The other view, including Chou Tun-i, is found in Chu Hsi's "Memoir for the Altar to the Three Masters at the Yüan-chou Prefectural School," *Yüan-chou chou-hsüeh san hsien-sheng tz'u-chi*, in Chu, *Wen-chi*, 78:76a–77b (pp. 5709–12), which also describes Chou's reception of it in terms of a direct unmediated inspiration from Heaven, rather than a teaching acquired by some lineal transmission. So far as I know Chu never completely reconciled the two accounts, and later Neo-Confucians invoked both.

20. Ch'ien Ta-hsin, *Shih-chia chai yang-hsin lu*, 18:10a.

21. *Ssu-shu chi-chu, Chung-yung chang-chü*, 1:1 (p. 45).

22. *Neo-Confucian Orthodoxy*, p. 129 and n. 157.

23. Chu, *Wen-chi*, 81:10a; Shu *Chung-yung hou*, p. 5845.

24. Ch'ien, *Hsin hsüeh-an*, 1:112.

25. *Neo-Confucian Orthodoxy*, pp. 128–30. See also Wing-tsit Chan's article on *hsin-fa* in *Chung-kuo che-hsüeh tz'u-tien ta-ch'üan* (Taipei: Shui-niu ch'u-pan-she, 1983), pp. 111–12.

26. *Ssu-shu chi-chu, Lun-yü*, 6:12; Comm. on *Lun yü*, 12:1 (p. 307).

27. *Ssu-shu chi-chu, Lun yü*, 6:10b–11a; Comm. on *Lun yü*, 12:1 (p. 304).

28. Ch'ien Mu, *Hsin hsüeh-an*, pp. 121–22.

29. *Chu Tzu yü-lei*, 78:30ab No. 212 (Ta Yü Mo Item 37) (pp. 3199–3200). Here and in subsequent reference to the *Yü-lei* the first citation will be to the *chüan* and page number of the original edition, and the "p" number will refer to the overall pagination of the Cheng-chung reprint.

30. *Neo-Confucian Orthodoxy and the Learning of the Mind-and-Heart*, pp. 30–31.

31. *Hsin hsüeh-an*, pp. 104–105.

32. Chu, *Wen-chi*, 2:26a. Wan Yen-p'ing Li hsien-sheng san-shou (p. 349); 87:3a, Chi Yen-p'ing Li hsien-sheng wen (p. 6175).

33. *Hsin hsüeh-an*, pp. 104–5. See also Julia Ching, *To Acquire Wisdom: The Way of Wang Yang-ming*, pp. 18–19.

34. *Ch'eng shih i-shu*, 19:7a; Chu, *Wen-chi*, 75:16–17a (p. 5521); Cheng-shih i-shu hou hsü; *Hsin hsüeh-an*, 2:105–6.

35. *Hsin hsüeh-an*, 2:113.

36. *Ch'ang-li hsien-sheng wen-chi*, SPTK 11:1a–3b; de Bary, Chan, and Watson, eds., *Sources of Chinese Tradition*, p. 431 (Pb I, 376).

37. See Chu Hsi, *Hsiao-hsüeh chi-chu*, 3:1a–2b; 5:16a; 6:19b; Uno Seiichi, *Shōgaku*, pp. 139–49, 320, 469.

38. Huang Kan; T. Chih-ch'ing, H. Mien-chai. *Sung-jen so-yin*, p. 2865; Chan, *Men-jen*, pp. 261–62; *Sung-shih*, 430:1; SYHA, 63:5.

39. Huang Kan, *Mien-chai hsien-sheng Huang Wen-shu kung wen-chi*, 26:18a–20a.

40. Huang Shih-i (fl. c. 1170); T. Tzu-hung. A student of Chu Hsi from Fukien. See *Sung-jen so-yin*, p. 2884; Chan, *Men-jen*, p. 254; SYHA, 69:514–15.

41. Huang Kan, *Mien-chai hsien-sheng wen-chi*, 26:26b–28a. Shun Yü ch'uan-hsin . . . Huang Tzu-hung.

42. Ch'en Ch'un; T. An-ch'ing, H. Pei-hsi. *Sung-jen so-yin*, p. 2471; Chan, *Men-jen*, pp. 220–21; *Sung shih*, 430:12789; SYHA, 68:1.

Ssu-k'u ch'üan-shu tsung-mu t'i-yao, 91:1916–17 (see also Ch'en Ch'un, *Pei-hsi tzu-i*, pp. 95–96); Chan, *Men-jen*, pp. 220–21; also his introduction to translation of *Pei-hsi tzu-i*, published as *Neo-Confucian Terms Explained: The Pei-hsi tzu-i*, pp. 1–32.

43. Ch'en Ch'un, *Pei-hsi tzu-i* (The Meaning of Terms [in the Four Books] according to Ch'en Ch'un), p. 76.

44. *Ibid.*, p. 77. Shih-yu yüan-yüan.

45. *Ibid.*, p. 7.

46. Chu, *Wen-chi*, 82:26ab (5939–40); Shu Min-ch'ang so kan ssu-tzu hou.

47. Ch'en uses the same language as Chu Hsi, quoting Ch'eng I; I have translated it in the same way in both cases. Professor Chan renders *hsin-fa* as "the central tradition," an interpretation which confirms its importance for both Ch'en and the Ch'eng-Chu school.

48. A close approximation of Chu's quotation. See p. 32 above.

49. Ch'en, *Pei-hsi tzu-i*, pp. 78–79 Tu-shu tzu-ti.

50. *Pei-hsi tzu-i*, pp. 89, 95; Chan, *Neo-Confucian Terms*, pp. 211, 213, 233.

51. Ts'ai Shen; T. Chung-mo, H. Chiu-feng, *Sung-jen so-yin*, p. 3783; Chan, *Men-jen*, p. 333; *Sung shih*, 434:1287; SYHA, 67:1.

Ts'ai Yuan-ting; T. Chi-t'ung, H. Mu-an, Hsi-shan. *Sung-jen so-yin*, p. 3809; Chan, *Men-jen*, pp. 331–32; *Sung shih*, 434:12875; SYHA, 62:1.

52. Ts'ai Shen, *Shu-ching chi-chuan*, preface, pp. 1b–2a. Hervouet, *Sung Bibliography*, pp. 22–23.

53. Chu Hsi, *Chung-yung chang-chü*, hsü, 2a (p. 39).

54. *Ibid.*, 1:28b–29a.

55. Huang Chen; T. Tung-fa, H. Yü-yüeh. From T'zu-ch'i, Chekiang. *Sung-jen so-yin*, p. 2870, *Sung shih*, 438:12991; SYHA, 86:1.

Fu Kuang; T. Han-ch'ing, H. Ch'ien-an, Ch'uan-t'ai. From Chekiang, Chia-hsing fu, Ch'ung-te hsien. *Sung-jen so-yin*, p. 3606; Chan, *Men-jen*, pp. 302–3, SYHA, 64:1.

56. Ts'ai Shen, *Shu-ching chi-chuan*, 1:18b–29a.

57. Cf. Benjamin Elman, "Philosophy *(I-li)* versus Philology *(K'ao-cheng)*: The *Jen-hsin Tao-hsin* Debate," p. 182. Elman takes this passage as referring to certain others who presented Ts'ai's commentary to the throne in such a way as to put undue emphasis on the "transmission of the mind." The editors of the *Ssu-k'u t'i-yao* (1:228–29) indicate that the presentation was made by Ts'ai's own son, Ts'ai Hang (c.s. 1229) during the Ch'un-yu period (1241–52) and Chan Hing-ho in Hervouet, *Sung Bibliography*, p. 23, says it took place about 1245. This timing is significant in regard to Elman's suggestion (p. 181) that in this passage Huang expressed the fear of the "consequences of an overemphasis on doctrines centering on studies of the mind *(hsin-hsüeh)* by court scholars such as Chen Te-hsiu." Chen had died in 1235, ten years before. Moreover there is strong countervailing evidence in both Chen's *Hsin-ching* and *Ta-hsüeh yen-i* that his understanding of the *hsin-fa* and *hsin-hsüeh* is the same as Ts'ai Shen's and Huang Chen's, i.e., that it is a method of world-ordering and nothing resembling the Ch'an transmission of the mind. Further, Huang identifies those who are at fault here with concentrating on the Mind of the Way, and equating the Mind with the Way. This would suggest a view similar to Lu Hsiang-shan and not Chen, who, if he differed at all from Chu Hsi, would have to be said to have overemphasized the *dangers* of the human mind rather than the equation of the mind with the Way. See my *Neo-Confucian Orthodoxy*, pp. 80–82, 99, 116. Huang Chen, *Huang shih jih-ch'ao*, in *Ssu-k'u ch'üan-shu chen-pen, erh chi*, 5:2a–3b Ta yü mo: Jen-hsin wei-wei.

58. *Huang shih jih-ch'ao*, 5:3b–4a.

59. *Huang shih jih-ch'ao*, 43:5b–6b, Yen-p'ing ta-wen.

60. Ch'en Ta-yü; T. Wen-hsien, H. Tung-chai. From Tu-ch'ang in modern Shantung province. He studied under Jao Lu, a follower of Huang Kan, and wrote the *Shang-shu chi-chuan hui-t'ung* (Comprehensive Explanation of the Collected Commentaries on the *Book of Shang*, which is no longer extant). *Sung jen so-yin*, p. 2541; SYHA, 83:2; Pu-i, 83:12. There were two scholars named Ch'en Ta-yü; the other, a follower of Yang Chien, received the *chin-*

shih degree in 1229. See SYHA, Pu-i, 74:66ab, and the comment of the Ssu-k'u editors in *Ssu-k'u ch'üan-shu tsung-mu t'i-yao*, 11:63, on the surviving work of the earlier Ch'en Ta-yü: *Shang-shu chi-chuan huo-wen*.

61. Cited in Ch'en Li, (Shang)-*Shu chi-chuan tsuan-shu*, 1:59a (v. 61, p. 231). Ch'en drew extensively on the writings of Chu Hsi, especially the *Yü-lü*, to supplement Ts'ai Shen's commentary. The comment of the *Ssu-k'u* editors, which prefaces this edition, emphasizes Ch'en's fidelity to Chu Hsi (v. 61 p. 202).

Since both the earlier and later Ch'en Ta-yü are said to have compiled collected commentaries on the *Shang-shu*, neither of which is extant, one cannot be sure which might have been quoted by Ch'en Li. However the passage in question does not appear in the extent *Shang-shu chi-chuan huo-wen* (*Wen-yüan ko Ssu-k'u* ed., A:38ab) of the earlier Ch'en Ta-yü. Here it is accepted by Ch'en Li as in essential harmony with the commentary he has drawn from "orthodox" sources. Thus if the question of authorship is not actually moot, it would seem that the later Ch'en Ta-yü, identified with the Jao Lu line of the Chu Hsi school, is the more likely source. This would also be consistent with the practice of the near contemporary of Ch'en Li, Tung Ting, who is in the same line of Huang Kan as the later Ch'en Ta-yü and whose collected commentary *Shang-shu chi-lu tsuan-chu*, cited the earlier Ch'en Ta-yü by his *hao* Fu-chai and the later by his *ming*, i.e., Ch'en shih Ta-yü, as is the case here. See *Ssu-k'u t'i-yao*, 11:63, *Shang-shu chi-chuan huo-wen*, and 11:67–68, *Shang-shu chi-lu tsuan-chu*. On Tung Ting (n.d.) see *Yüan-jen chuan-chi tzu-liao*, 1596; SYHA, 89:2b; SYHA, Pu-i, 89:9.

62. Ch'en Li; T. Shou Weng, H. Ting-yu from Hsiu-ning (modern Anhwei province). A classicist and devoted follower of Chu Hsi, who wrote commentaries on the ritual texts and Four Books as well as on the *Book of Documents*. *Yüan-jen so-yin*, p. 1301; *Yüan shih*, 189/4321; SYHA, 70:97; SYHA *Pu-i* 70:79a–92a.

63. Ch'en Li, *Shu-chi-chuan tsuan-shu*, 1:57a (61–230).

64. *Ibid*.

65. SYHA, 70:98, Shu-chuan tsuan-shu hsü.

66. SYHA *Pu-i* 70:86b, Jen-hsin wei-wei ssu-chü k'ou-i.

67. *Ibid*., 70:81b, *Chung-yung* k'ou-i.

68. *Ibid*., 70:82a, Preface to *T'ai-chi-t'u shuo*.

69. Hu Kuang et al., editors, *Lun-yü chi-chu ta-ch'üan*, 2:10b (p. 118), *Shih yu wu erh chih yü hsüeh chang*. In Genroku 4 (1691) ed., 2:14b–15a.

70. Lo Ta-ching (n.d.); T. Ching-lun, from Lu-ling in Kiangsi. *Sung-jen so-yin*, p. 4277; Hervouet, *Sung Bibliography*, pp. 314–15.

71. *Hsin-hsüeh ching-chuan*, a work no longer extant.

72. Lo Ta-ching, *Ho-lin yü-lu*, 18:3b–5b, Wen-chang hsing-li. See Hervouet, *Sung Bibliography*, pp. 314–15, where the entry for the *Ho-lin yü-lu* by Araki Toshikazu mentions only the less complete 16 ch. ed. available in China, and omits this more complete edition preserved in the Naikaku bunko.

73. See my *Neo-Confucian Orthodoxy*, pp. 17, 81, 150, 156; *Shushigaku taikei*, 10:8–11, article by Itō Tomoatsu.

74. *Neo-Confucian Orthodoxy*, pp. 67–69, 73–83, 177–80.

75. *Hsi-shan hsien-sheng Chen Wen-chung kung wen-chi* (Taipei: Commercial Press, KHCPTS ed., 1968), 42:750–51, Chiu-feng hsien-sheng Ts'ai chün mu-piao.

76. Chen Te-hsiu, *Hsin ching*, early Ming edition in the National Central Library, Taipei, p. 21b. The National Central Library also has the original Sung edition of 1242, with the same text, but the print is much less legible.

77. Hsiung Chieh, *Hsing-li ch'ün-shu, chü-chieh*, with commentary by Hsiung Kang, 1:16a (p. 54). On Hsiung Chieh see *Sung-jen so-yin*, p. 3622, and Chan, *Men-jen*, p. 289.

78. *Chen Hsi-shan wen-chi* (KHCPTS ed.), p. 448 (also SSGTK, 10:96), "Nan hsiung chou-hsüeh ssu hsien-sheng ssu-t'ang chi."

79. See Ri Taikei kenkyūkai, *Ri Taikei zenshū* (Tokyo, 1975), 2:260, for chart of the Learning of the Mind and for the views of Ch'eng Fu-hsin as cited by Yi T'oegye.

80. Ch'eng Fu-hsin, T. Tzu-chien, H. Lin-yin. *Yüan-jen so-yin*, p. 1429.

81. Also known as *Ssu-shu chang-t'u*. There are two extant versions known to me: 1) *Ssu-shu chang-t'u yin-k'uo tsung-yao*, 1337 ed. in two ts'e preserved in the National Central Library, Taipei; 1b) a hand-copied version of the same in the Shōheikō collection of the Naikaku bunko, Tokyo; and 2) *Ssu-shu chang-t'u tsuan-shih*, Te-hsin t'ang ed. of 1337 in 21 chüan with *Ssu-shu chang-t'u yin-k'uo tsung-yao* in 3 ch. in the Naikaku bunko. Unless otherwise noted, references herein are to this edition.

82. Ch'eng T'ung, ed., *Hsin-an hsüeh tzu-lu*, in *An-hui ts'ung shu*, 12:7a–10b.

83. *Ssu-shu chang-t'u*, 6a Fan li, Chung yung tao-t'ung chih ch'uan; chang-t'u shang 12b Lun hsin t'ung hsing-ching; Tsung yao chung 1b Sheng-hsien lun hsin chih yao; 7b Lun hsin t'ung hsing-ching.

84. Wing-tsit Chan appraises this work favorably for its careful scholarship in his "How T'oegye Understood Chu Hsi."

85. Yi T'oegye *I-hak t'ongnok*, 10:21b–22a (2:519).

86. For a fuller discussion of T'oegye's views of the Learning of the Mind and method of the mind as based on the Ch'eng-Chu concept and practice of reverence, see Sin Kuihyon, Sosan Chin Toksu ui Sinkyong kua T'oegye Yi Huang ui Sinhak [Chen Te-hsiu's *Hsin ching* and Yi Huang (T'oegye's) Learning of the Mind-and-Heart] in *T'oegye hakpo* (Seoul: T'oegye Study Institute, 1987), no. 53.

87. See my *Neo-Confucian Orthodoxy*, pp. 55, 59, 65, 148–49.

3. The New Learning of the Mind-and-Heart

1. *Sung shih*, 423:12638; *Yüan shih*, 190:4343; *Sung-yüan hsüeh-an* (Taipei: Ho-lo t'u-shu ch'u-pan she, n.d.), 87:50, 54. See also my "Chu Hsi's Aims as an Educator."

2. See Wing-tsit Chan, "Chu Hsi and Yüan Confucianism" in Hok-lam

Chan and W. T. de Bary, *Yüan Thought, Chinese Religion and Thought Under the Mongols*, p. 218. See also the discussion of David Gedalecia, "Wu Ch'eng and the Perpetuation of the Classical Heritage in the Yüan," in John D. Langlois Jr., ed., *China Under the Mongols*, p. 211.

3. See his "The Ch'eng-Chu School of the Early Ming," p. 43.
4. *Ibid.*, p. 43.
5. *Ibid.*, p. 42.
6. See Liu Ts'un-yan, "Taoist Self-Cultivation in Ming Thought," p. 309. Also biography by Julia Ching in *DMB*, p. 1302.
7. Ts'ao Tuan, *T'ung-shu shu-chieh*, A:47b.
8. Ts'ao Tuan, "Lu-ts'ui," in *Hsü Chung-chou ming-hsien wen-piao*, 1:18a.
9. "Lu-ts'ui" 1:24b–25a.
10. *Ibid.*, 1:25a. A slightly different wording is found in a handwritten copy of *Ts'ao Yüeh-ch'uan hsien-sheng chi*, "Ssu-shu hsiang-shuo hsü."
11. "Lu-ts'ui," 1:26b; see *Ts'ao Yüeh-ch'uan hsien-sheng chi*; preface to the *Ts'un-i lu*.
12. "Lu-ts'ui," 1:22b–23a.
13. Hsüeh Hsüan, *Tu-shu lu*, 8:4b.
14. *Ibid.*, 11:18a.
15. *Ibid.*, 8:4a. On Hsü and his "learning of the mind" see my *Neo-Confucian Orthodoxy*, pp. 20–38, 131–49.
16. Takeuchi Hiroyuki, in *Shushigaku taikei*, 10:42.
17. See Wing-tsit Chan, "Chu Hsi and Yüan Confucianism," p. 41. Chan sees this stress on reverence as a radical modification of Chu Hsi's order of learning and cultivation, and a "sharp departure from the orthodox Ch'eng-Chu position," but I believe this is said with respect to the direction of Hu's thought in the Ming context and should not be taken as indicating any fundamental break with Chu Hsi. To "abide in reverent seriousness and fathom principle (investigate things)" *(chü-ching, ch'iung-li)* had often been seen as basically complementary in the Chu Hsi school. See my *The Unfolding of Neo-Confucianism*, pp. 13–17.
18. Hu Chü-jen, *Chü-yeh lu*, No. 714, 8:30b.
19. *Chü-yeh lu*, 1:4a.
20. *Chü-yeh lu*, 1:4b–5a.
21. Chou Ch'i, T. T'ing-yu, H. Hsüeh t'ang, SYHA, Pu-i 44:119b–120a.
22. *Ssu-k'u ch'üan-shu tsung-mu t'i-yao*. (1928), vol. 3, p. 1928.
23. Chou Ch'i, *Tung-hsi jih-t'an lu*, 15:1a–19b.
24. Lou Liang; T. K'o-chen, H. I-chai. MS 282:7232; MJHA, 2:22; *DMB*, p. 989. Wu Yü-pi; T. Tzu-ch'uan, H. K'ang-chai. MS 282:7340; MJHA, 1:2; *DMB*, 1497. Theresa Kelleher, "Personal Reflections on the Pursuit of Sagehood: The Life and Journal of Wu Yü-pi (1392–1469)," Ph.D. dissertation, Columbia University; Ann Arbor: University Microfilms, 1982.
25. See Huang Tsung-hsi, MJHA, 10:55; Ch'ien Mu, *Wang Shou-jen*, p. 37; Tu Wei-ming, *Neo-Confucian Thought in Action, Wang Yang-ming's Youth (1472–1509)*, pp. 47–52; Julia Ching, *To Acquire Wisdom: The Way of Wang Yang-ming*, pp. 29, 41.

26. Ch'en Hsien-chang; T. Kung-pu, H. Pai-sha. MS 283:7261; MJHA, 5:48; *DMB*, p. 153. Jen Yu-wen, "Ch'en Hsien-chang's Philosophy of the Natural," in de Bary, ed., *Self and Society*, pp. 53–92; Paul Y. Jiang, *The Search for Mind*.

27. Hu Chü-jen; T. Shu-hsin, H. Ching-chai. MS 282:7232; MJHA, 2:12; *DMB*, p. 625.

28. Chan Jo-shui; T. Min-tse, H. Kan-ch'üan. MS 283:7266; MJHA, 37:79; *DMB*, p. 36.

29. See W. T. de Bary, "Individualism and Humanitarianism in Late Ming Thought," *Self and Society in Ming Thought*, pp. 151–71.

30. See Martina Deuchler, "Reject the False and Uphold the Straight: Attitudes Toward Heterodox Thought in Early Yi Korea."

31. See *Ch'uan-hsi lu*, *Wang Yang-ming ch'üan-shu*, 1:13; 2:49–50; 3:77, 102. Chan, *Instructions*, pp. 34, 129–30, 192–93, 253; Tu Wei-ming, *Neo-Confucian Thought in Action*, pp. 153–57, 160–63.

32. *Ch'üan-hsi lu*, 1:23, 2:63–64; Chan, *Instructions*, pp. 59–60, 162–64; Tu Wei-ming, *Neo-Confucian Thought in Action*, p. 50.

33. *Wang Yang-ming ch'üan-shu* I, *Wen-lu*, 3:190, Hsiang-shan wen-chi hsü.

34. *Ibid.* For a full translation, but somewhat different rendering of the preface see Ching, *Wisdom*, pp. 206–8.

35. *Ch'üan-shu* I, *Wen-lu*, 4:214, Chi-shan shu-yüan tsun-ching ko chi. A similar tribute (though, as here, not without some reservations) to Lu as the heir to Mencius is found in a letter of 1521. See *Ch'üan-shu* II, *Shu-lu*, 2:26; Yü Hsi Yüan-shan.

36. *Shu-ching*, Shun-tien; Legge, *Classics*, 3:44.

37. *Ch'üan-shu*, *Wen-lu*, 4:215–17.

38. *Ch'üan-shu*, *Wen-lu*, 1:123, Ta hsüeh wen.

39. Chan, *Instructions*, p. 271.

40. *Ch'üan-shu*, *Wen-lu*, 1:119.

41. Trans. adapted from Chan, *Instructions*, p. 274.

42. *Ch'üan-shu*, *Wen-lu*, 1:123; cf. Chan, *Instructions*, p. 280.

43. *Ch'üan-shu*, *Wen-lu*, 1:123.

44. Wang Chi, 1498–1583; T. Ju-chung, H., Lung-hsi. MS. 283:7274; *Ming-jen so-yin*, p. 70; MJHA, 12:1; *DMB*, p. 1351.

45. Wang Chi, *Lung-hsi chi*, 10:31b–32a. Fu Yen Chung-yü.

46. *Ibid.*, 10:32b.

47. Nieh Pao; T. Wen-wei, H. Shuang-chiang. MS 202:5336–7; MJHA, 17:84–96; *DMB*, p. 1096. Okada Takehiko, *Ōyōmei to Min-matsu no jugaku* (Tokyo: Meitoku, 1970), pp. 138–65.

48. Chan Jo-shui; T. Yüan-ming, H. Kan-ch'üan. On his life and thought see the biography by Chao-ying Fang, with note by Julia Ching, in *DMB*, pp. 36–42; Julia Ching, ed., *The Records of Ming Scholars*, pp. 202–4; Shiga Ichirō, *Tan Kansen no kenkyū*, and Shiga Ichirō, *Tan Kansen no gakusetsu*; Ann-ping Woo, "Chan Kan-ch'üan and the Continuing Neo-Confucian Discourse on

Mind and Principle," Ph.D. dissertation, Columbia University, 1984; Ann Arbor: University Microfilms, 1984.

49. MJHA, 37:87.

50. Chan, *Yüeh-yen*, No. 69, as edited in the Source Materials *(shiryō)* appended to Shiga Ichirō, *Tan Kansen no kenkyū*, 22:438.

51. MJHA, 37/91.

52. Chan, "Feng-chao chin-chiang chang shu," as quoted in Shiga Ichirō, *Tan Kansen no gakusetsu*, p. 196.

53. As found in Shiga, *Kenkyū*, 19:338, 353, 21:408–9.

54. Chan, ch. 22, Tsa chu, K'ung-men ch'uan-shou hsin-fa lun, in Shiga, *Kenkyū*, pp. 408–10.

55. Chan, ch. 20, Ching-yen chiang-chang, in Shiga, *Kenkyū*, 20:365–66.

56. Chan, ch. 19, Chin-chiang hou shu, in Shiga, *Kenkyū*, 19:339.

57. Chan, ch. 19, Tsai lun sheng-hsüeh shu, in Shiga, *Kenkyū*, 19:338.

58. Shiga, *Kenkyū*, 21:399.

59. MJHA, 37:98, Yü-lu.

60. MJHA, 37:101, Yü-lu.

61. MJHA, 27:86, Kan-ch'uan lun-hsüeh shu.

62. MJHA, 37:108.

63. J. Ching, *Records of Ming Scholars*, p. 25.

64. Lo Ch'in-shun; T. Yün-sheng, H. Cheng-an. MS 282:6236–38; MJHA, 47:34–64; *DMB*, pp. 972–74.

65. See Irene Bloom, "On the 'Abstraction' of Ming Thought: Some Concrete Evidence from the Philosophy of Lo Ch'in-shun," pp. 69–113.

66. Chang Shih; T. Ching-fu, H. Nan-hsien. *Sung-jen so-yin*, p. 2268; SS, 429:12770; SYHA, 50:1.

67. Lo Ch'in-shun, *K'un-chih chi*; Shang: 8a, Item 12: translation from Irene Bloom, *Knowledge Painfully Acquired.*

68. Lo Ch'in-shun, supplement to the *K'un-chih chi* in the Japanese edition. Fu lu 12a, Ta Huang. At the same time Lo rejects Chu Hsi's interpretation of the human mind and Mind of the Way.

69. Ch'en Chien; T. T'ing-chao, H. Ch'ing-lan. *DMB*, p. 148.

70. Ch'en Chien, *Hsüeh-pu t'ung-pien* (hereafter abbr. *T'ung-pien*), p. 3 T'i-kang. SSGTK, 10:534a (p. 375).

71. *T'ung-pien*, personal preface, p. 1, SSGTK, 10:532 (p. 369).

72. *T'ung-pien*, T'i kang, p. 2, SSGTK, 10:533b (p. 373). Itō Tomoatsu cites *Chü-yeh lu*, ch. 1, in the four-*chüan* edition as the source of the quotation from Hu. I have not found this in the editions available to me, but the same sense is conveyed in the TSCC ed., 1:3.

73. *T'ung-pien*, 11:179, Chung-pien chung; SSGTK, 10:540ab (p. 391).

74. *T'ung-pien*, 4:45–46, Hou-pien shang; SSGTK, 10:537a (p. 382).

75. *T'ung-pien*, 5:72–73, SSGTK, 10:537b (pp. 384–85). See also *Chu Tzu yü-lei* 126:4b (4823).

76. *T'ung-pien*, 5:73–74: SSGTK, 10:537b (p. 385).

77. *T'ung-pien*, 11:179–180, Chung-pien chung; SSGTK, 10:540ab (p. 391).

78. *T'ung-pien*, 11:181, Chung-pien chung; SSGTK, 10:540ab (p. 391).

79. *T'ung-pien*, 8:131, Hsü-pien chung; SSGTK, 10:539a (p. 388).

80. Chu, *Wen-chi*, 67:21b, Jen-shuo; 74:19a–23b Yü shan chiang-i; Chan, *Source Book*, pp. 596, 649.

81. *T'ung-pien*, 8:131; SSGTK, 10:539a (p. 388).

82. *Ibid.*

83. See my essay on "Neo-Confucian Individualism and Holism" in Donald Munro, ed., *Chinese Individualism and Holism*.

84. *T'ung-pien*, 9:156, Hsü-pien hsia; SSGTK, 10:539ab (p. 398).

85. See my *The Unfolding of Neo-Confucianism*, p. 188.

86. *Chu Tzu yü-lei*, 126:14a (4843). See also 4b (4823); 13a (484). *T'ung pien*, 10:163; SSGTK, 10:539b (p. 390).

87. Ch'en, *T'ung-pien*, 10:163–64; SSGTK, 10:539 (p. 391).

88. See his discussion of the reconstitution of the Way *(sheng-hsien chih t'ung)* as comparable to the reconstitution of the empire *(cheng-t'ung or ti-wang chih t'ung)* by great rulers of major dynasties. *T'ung pien*, 12:195, Chung pien hsia.

89. *T'ung-pien*, 10:181, Chung-pien hsü.

90. *T'ung-pien*, 12:189, Chung-pien hsia.

91. *T'ung-pien*, 12:10b, Chung-pien hsia.

92. Ku, *Jih chih lu*, 18:431. This statement is preceded by Ku's account of how Wang Yang-ming's views gained almost total, uncritical acceptance among scholars of the day, save for the challenge from Lo and Ch'en.

93. T'ang Po-yüan; T. Jen-ch'ing, H. Shu-tai (c.s. 1574). *DMB*, p. 1451; MS 282:7257, MJHA, 42:1. Araki Kengo, "Tō Hakugen no shingaku hiteiron," in *Yōmeigaku no kaiten to Bukkyō*.

94. *Ming Shen-tsung shih-lu*, 159:3 (p. 2922).

95. Ku, *Jih chih lu*, 18:431.

96. The *T'ang Shu-tai chi* is a rare work, to which I have not had direct access. I am grateful to Professor Lynn Struve, who has examined for me the copy in the *Kuang li-hsüeh pei-k'ao* edition in the University of Chicago Library, and reports that it contains no letter corresponding exactly to that quoted by Ku. Similar ideas are found in other letters, copies of which she has kindly made available to me.

97. The contents of the memorial are summarized by Araki Kengo in his "Tō Hakugen no shingaku hiteiron" (hereafter abbr. "Tō Hakugen") in *Yōmeigaku no kaiten to bukkyō*, p. 93–96.

98. *T'ang Shu-tai chi*, in *Kuang li-hsüeh pei-kao*, tse 42; chi: 14b; also in MJHA, 42:77.

99. *T'ang Shu-tai chi*, p. 16a.

100. Chan Jo-shui: T. Min-tse, H. Kan-ch'uan. MS 283:2266; MJHA, 37:79; *DMB*, p. 36. T'ang had studied under Lü Chin-shih (c.s. 1532), a disciple of Chan (see MJHA, 38:1).

101. Chan Jo-shui, "K'ung-men ch'uan-shou hsin-fa lun," as ed. by Shiga Ichirō in *Tan Kansen no kenkyū*, Shiryōhen, pp. 80, 408–10; see also MJHA 37:87, 89, 90, 101; 38:7–9, Araki, "Tō Hakugen," p. 98.

102. See Heinrich Busch in *DMB*, p. 743, and in his "Tunglin Shu-yüan and Its Political and Social Significance," *Monumenta Serica*, 14:113–14.

103. Wang Yang-ming, *Ch'uan-hsi lu*, 2: 42 Ta Ku Tung-chiao shu; Chan, *Instructions*, p. 112: "Mind is identical with principle. To learn means to learn this mind. To seek means to seek this mind." See also Chan, *Ch'üan-hsi lu hsiang-chu chi-p'ing*, pp. 187–88. The latter recounts an episode in which Ku speaks well of T'ang as a gentleman *(chün-tzu)*, even though the latter's criticism of Wang Yang-ming was couched in terms that were too extreme.

104. *Ibid.*, 17ab; MJHA, 42:79 Ta Ku Shu shih. . . .

105. *T'ang Shu-tai hsien-sheng chi*, 1:22ab, Shu Kuo Meng-chü. . . . MJHA, 42:82, Lun-hsüeh shu.

106. *Ibid.* and MJHA, 42:76, Tsui-ching t'ang chi-chieh.

107. *T'ang Shu-tai chi*, 1:22b; MJHA, 42:79–80, 82, Lun-hsüeh shu.

108. MJHA, 42:67 (Kan-ch'üan hsüeh-an 6:1).

109. *Jih chih lu*, 18:431.

110. *Ibid.*, 18:437–38.

111. *Ming shih*, 282:7257.

112. MJHA, 42:67.

113. MJHA, 42:67.

114. MJHA, Fan li, 1.

115. Teng Yüan-hsi; T. Ju-chi, H. Ch'ien-ku. MS 283:7291, MJHA, 24:44–50, *DMB*, p. 1280.

116. Tsou Shou-i; T. Hsien-chih, H. Tung-Kuo. MS 283:7268, MJHA, 16: *DMB*, p. 1310.

117. Teng Yüan-hsi, *Huang-Ming shu*, chuan 35–44.

118. *Huang-Ming shu*, 35:1ab.

119. *Huang-Ming shu*, 42:10b–12b.

120. *Huang-Ming shu*, 42:10b, 14ab.

121. *Huang-Ming shu*, 43:1a.

122. *Huang-Ming shu*, 44:24b.

123. *Huang-Ming shu*, 44:24b–25a.

124. *Huang-Ming shu*, 43:17a–22b; 44:1a–3b, 18b–22b.

125. Ch'en Lung-cheng; *DMB*, pp. 174–76; MS 258:6681–83; MJHA, 61:25.

126. Ch'en Lung-cheng *Chi-ting wai-shu*, 1:53b–55b.

127. As far as is known only the original 1606 edition of the *Huang-Ming shu* has survived the Ch'ing suppression of Teng's work. See Franke, p. 46, No. 2.1.2, *DMB*, p. 1281. This leads to the supposition that Ch'en's essay might have been the source of the *tao-hsüeh* category referred to in the *T'i-yao* rather than the *li-hsüeh* found in the original. *Ssu-k'u t'i-yao*, 50:1112.

128. *Ssu-k'u t'i-yao*, 50:1113.

129. Chang Huang; T. Pen-ch'ing, H. Tou-chin. MS 283:7292; MJHA, 24:50–56; *DMB*, pp. 83–84.

130. MS 283:7292.

131. Li Tsai, a student of Tsou Shou-i. MS 227; MJHA, 31:33; *DMB*, p. 876.

132. Nieh Pao. MS 202:5336; MJHA, 62:32; Hummel, *Eminent Chinese*, p. 532.

133. Liu Tsung-chou. MS 255:6531; MJHA, 62:32; *Eminent Chinese*, p. 532; and MJHA, 24:51. I wish to acknowledge the help of Wing-tsit Chan in clarifying the latter part of this passage.

134. MJHA, 24:52.

135. *Ibid.*, 24:56.

136. *T'u-shu pien; Ssu-k'u t'i-yao*, 136:2817; Franke, p. 313, No. 9.2.3.

137. *T'u-shu pien*, 77:65b.

138. *Ming-ju hsüeh-an*, 6:32:93.

139. Quoted in Morohashi, No. 10295:45, as defining *hsin-hsüeh*.

140. *Tuan-wen kung chi*, 6:8b–9a.

141. *Ibid.*, 6:9b–10b.

142. See Heinrich Busch, ''The Tunglin Shu-yüan and Its Political and Philosophical Significance,'' pp. 97–98.

4. The Learning of the Mind and Succession to the Way in the Early Ch'ing

1. There is a considerable literature on the subject but among recent works in English mention should be made of Benjamin Elman, *From Philosophy to Philology* and Edward Ch'ien, *Chiao Hung and the Restructuring of Neo-Confucianism in the Late Ming*.

2. Ch'ien Mu, *Chung-kuo chin san-pai nien hsüeh-shu shih*, p. 28.

3. Sun Ch'i-feng; T. Chi-t'ai, H. Hsia-feng. Chiang Fan, *Sung-hsüeh yüan-yüan chi*, 1:2–4. Hsü Shih-ch'ang, *Ch'ing-ju hsüeh-an* (hereafter abbr. CJHA), 1:1; Hummel, *Eminent Chinese*, p. 671, biography by Fang Chao-ying.

4. *Li-hsüeh tsung-ch'üan*, 23:38a–55a. In his section on Chang Huang, Sun quotes with warm approval the same passages on the Mind and Learning of the Mind, in Chang's *T'u-shu pien*, which I have discussed in the preceding.

5. See the biography by Hsü Shih-ch'ang appearing in the introductory matter for the *Li-hsüeh tsung-ch'üan*, p. 1b, or CJHA, 1:1.

6. See *Li-hsüeh tsung-ch'üan*, 23:46a.

7. *Ibid.*, Introduction (hsü) 2ab.

8. *Ibid.*, 4ab; see also preface of Chang Mu, p. 3ab.

9. *Li-hsüeh tsung-ch'üan*, 3ab.

10. *Li-hsüeh tsung-ch'üan, mu-lu*, 1a–2a, 7b–8a; Introduction, 9a.

11. *Li-hsüeh tsung-ch'üan*, 7ab.

12. *Ibid.*, 5b–6a.

13. *Ibid.*, 6b.

14. *Ibid.*, 7:6a, 24b–26b; 9:1b–2a.

15. Hsü Shih-ch'ang, CJHA, p. 2a.

16. *Li-hsüeh tsung-ch'üan, I-li*, 1b–2a.

17. *Ibid.*, I-li, 2a.

18. Huang Tsung-hsi, *Nan-lei wen-ting*, ch'ien chi, 1:16.

19. *P'o-hsieh lun*, 1a–b, in *Li-chou i-chu hui-k'an*, vol. 13.

20. Benjamin Elman, *From Philosophy to Philology*.

21. I have made a much fuller study of Lü's thought in a separate, as yet unpublished, paper entitled "Lü Liu-liang and the Return to Orthodoxy in the Early Ch'ing," on which the discussion here is based.

22. See Ch'ien Mu, *Hsüeh-shu-shih*, pp. 78–79.

23. Ch'en Ts'ung in Lü Liu-liang, *Ssu-shu chiang-i*, Mu-lu, 1:1b.

24. *Ibid.*, 1:1b–2a, comment on Ta-hsüeh chih tao; *Ssu-shu yü-lu*, 1:2a.

25. Sun Ch'i-feng, for instance. See pp. 125–126ff.

26. *Ssu-shu chiang-i*, comment on Tung ching an lu; *Yü-lu*, 1:7b–8a.

27. See my *Neo-Confucian Orthodoxy*, Part II.

28. *Ssu-shu chiang-i*, mu-lu, 5:6b; comment on *Analects* 2:4; *Yü-lu*, 14:8a.

29. *Ssu-shu chiang-i*, 5:6b; *Yü-lu*, 14:8ab.

30. *Ssu-shu chiang-i*, 4:2ab; comment on *Analects* 1; *Yü-lu*, 13:2a.

31. Chu, *Ta-hsüeh chang-chü*, ch. 1, p. 1.

32. Lü Liu-liang, *Ssu-shu chiang-i*, 42:2a; comment on *Mencius* "Chin ch'i hsin," *Yü-lu*, 45:1b–2a. See also *Ssu-shu chiang-i*, 42:18a.

33. Lü Liu-liang, *Ssu-shu chiang-i*, 42:1b.

34. *Ibid.*, 42:1b–2a.

35. Lü's *Yü-lu* was published in 1684; one quarter of Ku's *Jih-chih lu* was published in 1670 and the full thirty-two *chüan* edition in 1695.

36. On the Tung-lin aspects see Busch, "The Tunglin Shu-yüan," pp. 97–133. For Korea and Japan, see de Bary and Haboush, eds., *The Rise of Neo-Confucianism in Korea*, pp. 116–18, and my *Neo-Confucian Orthodoxy*, Part III.

37. It would be a digression to pursue these matters here. On the general point one may consult the article by Hellmut Wilhelm in Marius Jansen, ed., *Changing Japanese Attitudes Toward Modernization*, pp. 283–310.

38. Chang Lü-hsiang; T. K'ao-fu, H. Nien-chih. Hummel, *Eminent Chinese*, pp. 45–46; *DMB*, pp. 149, 1380; *Ch'ing hsüeh-an hsiao shih*, 1:5–15; *CJHA*, 5:1.

39. *Chang Yang-yüan ch'üan-chi; Pei-wang lu*, 4:2b.

40. See Okada Takehiko, "Chō Yōen to Riku Futei," p. 2.

41. *Ch'üan-chi, Pei-wang*, 2:16a.

42. *Ch'üan-chi, Pei-wang*, 3; 28a; see also 3:14b.

43. Ch'en Ch'üeh, T. Ch'ien-ch'u; Ch'ien Mu, *Hsüeh-shu shih*, 1:36–51; *CJHA*, 2:63.

44. *Ch'üan-chi, Pei-wang*, 2:11b.

45. *Ch'u-hsüeh pei-wang*, TSCC ed., Hsia: 15.

46. *Ch'üan-chi, Pei-wang*, 3:34a.

47. Okada, "Chō Yōen to Riku Futei," p. 9.

48. *Ch'üan-chi*, 5:2a–3a, Yü Ho Shang-yin.

49. *Ch'üan-chi, Pei-wang*, 3:16a.

50. Okada, "Chō Yōen to Riku Futei," pp. 4, 6.

51. *Ch'u hsüeh pei-wang*, shang:6–7; *Ch'üan-chi, Pei-wang*, 3:41a, 4:63b; *Pei-wang lu i*, 42:63b.

52. *Ch'üan-chi, Pei-wang*, 1:42a, 2:33ab.

53. *Ch'u-hsüeh pei-wang*, hsia; 13, 15.

54. *Ibid.*, 15; *Ch'üan-chi, Pei-wang*, 2:12b–13a.

55. E.g. *Ch'üan-chi, Pei-wang*, 2:46b, 3:2b, 4:2b, on Chen Te-hsiu; 2:40b on Hsüeh Hsüan; 2:22b on Wu Yü-pi.

56. Lü Liu-liang, *Ssu-shu chiang-i*, 38:8ab.

57. *Ch'üan-chi, Pei-wang*, 2:23b, 28b, 4:10b–11a.

58. *Ibid.*, 2:23b. In his *Pei-wang-lu i*, 1, there is a reference to "Hsiang-shan and Yang-ming" as examples of the continuing infiltration of Confucianism by Buddhism. *Ch'üan-chi*, 42:49A.

59. Lu Shih-i; T. Tao-wei, H. Fou-t'ing. Hummel, *Eminent Chinese*, pp. 548–49; *Ch'ing hsueh-an hsiao-shih*, 2:16–20; *CJHA*, 3:1; Okada, "Chō Yōen to Riku Futei," p. 16; Wei Cheng-t'ung, *Chung-kuo che-hsüeh tz'u-tien ta-ch'üan*, p. 700.

60. Okada, p. 15.

61. Lu Shih-i, *Ssu-pien lu chi-yao, ch'ien-chi, Ssu-k'u ch'üan-shu chen-pen, ssu chi*, 3:13a–14a. It should be noted that this is a selected condensation made from Lu's *Ssu-pien lu* by Chang Po-hsing and included in his *Cheng-i t'ang ch'üan-shu*. See the comment by the editors of the *Ssu-k'u ch'üan-shu tsung mu t'i-yao* prefaced to this edition.

62. *Ssu-pien lu chi-yao*, 29:1b.

63. See my *Neo-Confucian Orthodoxy and the Learning of the Mind-and-Heart*, pp. 67–69, 73–83, 88–89, 177–81.

64. Okada, "Chō Yōen to Riku Futei," p. 22.

65. Hummel, *Eminent Chinese*, p. 498, biography by Dean Wickes; Chiang Fan, *Sung-hsüeh yüan-yüan chi* (hereafter *Sung-hsüeh*), A:5–6, Hsü Shih-ch'ang, *Ch'ing-ju hsüeh-an*, 29:1a.

66. *CJHA*, 29:20a.

67. Chiang Fan, *Sung hsüeh*. A:5–6, *CJHA*, 29:20a.

68. *CJHA*, 29:1b.

69. *DMB*, p. 1010, biography by Julia Ching.

70. Li Yung, *Li Erh-ch'ü hsien-sheng ch'üan-chi* (hereafter abbr. *Ch'üan-chi*), Wang Hsin-ch'ing, ed. 7:3a, T'i-yung ch'üan-hsüeh; 15:10b, Shou shou chi-yao.

71. *Ch'üan chi*, 15:10b, Fu-p'ing ta-wen.

72. *CJHA*, 29:2a, 14b.

73. *CJHA*, 29:14b, Fu p'ing ta-wen.

74. *CJHA*, 29:2a.

75. *Ch'üan-chi*, 15:4b, Fu-p'ing ta-wen.

76. *Ch'üan-chi*, 1:1a, Hui-kuo tzu-hsin shuo.

77. *Ch'üan-chi*, 8:1a, Tu-shu tzu-te.

78. Li Yung, *Ssu-shu fan-shen lu* (hereafter abbr. *Fan-shen lu*), in *Li Erh-ch'ü hsien-sheng ch'üan-chi*, 1:8b–9a.

79. *Fan-shen lu*, 1:1a, 2:1a.

80. *CJHA*, 29:5b.

81. *Ibid.*

82. *CJHA*, 29:6b.

83. *Fan-shen lu*, 1:8a.

84. *Ch'üan-chi*, 4:4a, Ching chiang yao yu.

85. *Fan-shen lu*, 7:13b; 7:14a.

86. *CJHA*, 29:2a.

87. *Ch'üan-chi*, 2:3a, Hsüeh sui.

88. *Ch'üan-chi*, 1:4b–5a, Hui-kuo tzu-hsin shuo.

89. *Fan-shen lu*, 2:3a.

90. *Ch'üan-chi*, 2:4b, Hui-kuo tzu-hsin shuo.

91. Compare, for instance, their respective treatments of *ko-wu* in the *Great Learning* and *shen-tu* in the *Mean*, as seen in Li's *Ssu-shu fan-shen lu*, 1:4ab and 2:2b–3b, and in Lu's *Ssu-shu chiang-i*, 2:9b–10b, 17b–18b; 24:1ab, 7b–8a.

92. *Fan-shen lu*, 1:11a; *Ch'üan-chi*, 12:1b–2a; 15:1b, Fu p'ing ta-wen; *CJHA*, 29:13b.

93. *Fan-shen lu*, 2:4a.

94. *Ch'üan-chi*, 6:2a, Ch'uan-hsin lu.

95. *Ch'üan-chi*, 3:1a, Chang-chou . . . hui yü.

96. *Fan-shen lu*, 2:8a; *Ch'üan-chi*, 6:2a, Ch'uan-hsin lu; 12:2a, K'uang-shih yao-wu.

97. *CJHA*, 29:2b.

5. Orthodoxy Among the Mandarins

1. *Neo-Confucian Orthodoxy*, pp. 190–91.

2. Lu Lung-chi; T. Chia-shu, *Ch'ing hsüeh-an hsiao shih*, 1:1–5; Hummel, *Eminent Chinese*, pp. 547–48; Ch'an, "Hsing-li ching-i," pp. 551–52; *CJHA*, 10:1.

3. Yamanoi Yū, in SSGTK, 11:20–24.

4. The most commonly available edition of Lu's complete works, the late Ch'ing *Lu Tzu ch'üan-shu*, includes only an expurgated version. Editions of Lu's *Wen-chi* and *wai-chi* kept in such insititutions as the National Central Library of Taipei, the Jimbun kagaku kenkyūjo of Kyoto University, the Nai-kaku bunko of Tokyo, and so far as one can determine at present, the Peking Library, are all censored versions. I was able, however, to consult a restored version in the Library of Peking University, with handwritten notations taken from an original unexpurgated text in the possession of Ku Chieh-kang. This latter confirmed the extensive references to Lü Liu-liang and his ideas in Lu's writings, as well as in his *Discourses on the Four Books*, which in both form and content so resembled Lü's *Discourses*. Unfortunately, this problem was not taken into account in the study of T'ang Pin's philosophy and political thought made by Miura Shūichi, "Tō Hin to Riku Ryūki: Shinsho shidaibu no ningen rikai to keisei ishiki."

5. Lu Lung-chi, *San-yü t'ang wen-chi* (*Lu Tzu ch'üan-shu* ed.), 2:1ab.

6. Ibid., 2:1b–2a.

7. *Lu Tzu ch'üan-shu, Shun-yang chiang-i*, 1:6b–7a; 18b; 9:21b.

8. SSGTK, 11:200 (396), *San-yü t'ang jih-chi*, entry for 1678, 10 mo., 24th day.

9. *Lu Tzu ch'üan-shu, Ssu-shu chiang-i*, 1:1b.

10. Ibid., 2:1b–2a; and *Shun-yang chiang-i*, 2:1b.

11. SSGTK, 11:22, 188, 392; Benjamin Elman, "The *Jen-hsin Tao-hsin* Debate," p. 200–1.

12. Hellmut Wilhelm, "Chinese Confucianism on the Eve of the Great Encounter," p. 292.

13. *Ibid.*, p. 292.

14. *Ibid.*, p. 293.

15. T'ang Pin; T. K'ung-po, H. Ch'ien-an. Hummel, *Eminent Chinese*, pp. 709–10; Shimonaka Kunihiko, *Ajia rekishi daijiten*, 7:83a; *Ch'ing hsüeh-an hsiao shih*, 3:29–32; *CJHA*, 9:1. The brief sketch given here is based on the biographies prepared by Fang Chao-ying and Gotō Motomi respectively for the above-named compilations.

16. See Gotō and Fang as cited in note 15 and also Wing-tsit Chan, "The *Hsing-li ching-i* and the Early Ch'eng-Chu School in the Early Ch'ing," p. 554.

17. Wing-tsit Chan, "The *Hsing-li ching-i*, p. 554. It should be noted that Prof. Chan's concern here is to show how Chu Hsi's teachings emerged triumphant on their own merits and were not dependent on official favor for their success—which is not to say that such official efforts had no significance of their own.

18. T'ang Pin, *T'ang Tzu i-shu*, in *T'ang Wen-cheng kung ch'üan-chi*, T'ung-chih 9, 3:2b–3b, Li-hsüeh tsung-chuan hsü.

19. *Ibid.*, 3:4ab.

20. See Chan, "Hsing li ching-i," pp. 555–56.

21. *T'ang Tzu i-shu*, 3:52a, Ch'ien-ch'ing men tsou-tui chi for K'ang-hsi 22 (1683), 3rd month, 30th day.

22. *Ibid.*, 3:6a, Sun Ch'i-feng wen-lu hsü.

23. *T'ang Tzu i-shu*, 3:6b. Chi-shan Liu hsien-sheng wen-lu hsü.

24. *Ibid.*, 3:7a–9a. Chi-shan Liu hsien-sheng wen-lu hsü.

25. *T'ang Tzu i-shu, Yü lu*, 1:29a–30b, Hsüeh-yen.

26. See Huang Siu-chi, *Lu Hsiang-shan, A Twelfth Century Chinese Idealist Philosopher* (New Haven: American Oriental Society, 1944), pp. 69–70.

27. *T'ang Tzu i-shu*, chi, 3:56a.

28. *Ibid.*, 3:57a.

29. See esp. *T'ang Tzu i-shu*, 3:48ab, 61b–63a.

30. *T'ang Ch'ien-an chi*, 1:24–26, Yü Lu Chia-shu shu.

31. Li Kuang-ti; T. Chin-ch'ing H. Hou-an. *Ch'ing hsüeh-an hsiao-shih*, 6:113–18; *CJHA*, 40:1; SSGTK, 11:27–31; Hummel, *Eminent Chinese*, p. 473; Chan, "Hsing-li ching-i," pp. 546–47, 560–61.

32. See "Hsing-li ching-i," in *The Unfolding of Neo-Confucianism*, pp. 546–47.

33. *Ibid.*, pp. 547–48.

34. *Ibid.*, p. 568.

35. Li Kuang-ti, *Jung-t'sun ch'üan-chi*, 23:12b–13a.

36. *Chu Tzu ch'üan-shu*, Imp. edition of 1714, ch. 52–57.

37. Chan, "*Hsing-li ching-i*," p. 569.

38. Li Kuang-ti, *Chung-yung chang-tuan*, in *Ssu-shu chieh-i*, Tao kuang 5, 1:1a–3a.

39. *Jung-ts'un ch'üan-chi*, *Yü-lu*, ch. 18.

40. *Chu Tzu ch'üan-shu*, esp. ch. 52, 57.

41. Chan, "*Hsing-li ching-i*," p. 557, citing *Jung-ts'un ch'üan-chi*, 17:21a.

42. SSGTK, 11:411a (245), citing *Yü-lu*, 43.

43. *Yü-lu*, 20:6ab.

44. *Ch'üan-chi*, 17:20a–23b.

45. See Chan, *Hsing-li ching-i*, pp. 556–57.

46. *Ch'üan-chi*, 17:22b–23b.

47. Chan, "*Hsing-li ching-i*," p. 555.

48. *Ch'üan-chi*, 17:21a; SSGTK, 11:408b, 409a, 412a.

49. *Yü-lu*, 18:5b–6a; *Ch'üan-chi*, 17:22b–23a.

50. *Yü-lu*, 23:3b; Ōshima Akira, in SSGTK, 11:31.

51. *Ch'üan-chi*, 10:2b–3a; SSGTK, 11:405 (227). The preface to Li's *Yü-lu* reiterates the same view.

52. On this point see also *Ch'üan-chi*, 17:17a; SSGTK, 11:410 (241–43).

53. See my *Neo-Confucian Orthodoxy*, p. 52.

54. SSGTK, 11:410a, Memorial on Presentation of *Master Chu's Complete Works*; see also 407b–408a (233–34).

55. *Yü-lu*, 4, hsia lun, 17b–18a.

56. *Ibid.*, 4:18b.

57. *Chu Tzu ch'üan-shu*, 2:31a–46b.

58. *Yü-lu*, 24:6ab.

59. Chan, *Hsing-li ching-i*, pp. 571–72.

60. *K'ang-hsi yü-chih wen-chi*, 1st series, preface dated 1714, 18:14b–18b, 19:1a–3a, 8b–9b.

61. Chang Po-hsing; T. Hsiao-hsien, H. Ching-an, Shu-chai. *Ch'ing hsüeh-an hsiao-shih*, 2:21; CJHA, 12:1; Hummel, *Eminent Chinese*, pp. 51–52; H. Wilhelm, "Eve of the Great Encounter," pp. 291ff.

62. See *Cheng-i t'ang ch'üan-shu*, Hsü-chi, 4:10a–12b; TSCC ed., Hsü-chi, 4:216–17.

63. The favor shown to Li Yung (1627–1705) by the K'ang-hsi emperor may be taken as an example. Li was broadly catholic in his appreciation of Lu Hsiang-shan and Wang Yang-ming, along with Ch'eng-Chu. To more strict Chu Hsi schoolmen like Chang Po-hsing Li was an abomination, yet the Emperor himself seems to have had no qualms about this liberal tendency when he conferred special honors on Li. See Hummel, *Eminent Chinese*, pp. 498–99; *Ch'ing hsüeh-an hsiao-shih*, 4:62.

64. Chang does refer to it in his *Tao-t'ung lu*, but without going into its problematical nature, and in general he prefers the term *cheng-tsung*. *Cheng-i t'ang ch'üan-shu*, Hsü-chi, 4:12a; TSCC ed., p. 217.

65. Chang, *Cheng-i t'ang wen-chi*, TSCC ed., 8:104.

66. *Wen-chi*, 8:105.

67. *Wen-chi*, 8:105, Wen-hsüeh lu hsü. As far as I know there is no direct reference by Chang to Lü Liu-liang's undoubted influence on Lu Lung-chi, who is usually presented by him as a solitary champion of the Way. Whether later censorship, after the Tseng Ching affair, may have had some effect on the record of Chang's writings, as it did on Lü's, I have not so far been able to determine.

68. *Wen-chi*, 9:117, Lun hsüeh.

69. *Cheng-i t'ang hsü-chi*, 4:12a, Hsing-li cheng-tsung hsü.

70. *Cheng-i t'ang-ch'üan-shu*, mu-lu.

71. Chang Po-hsing, *K'un-hsüeh lu chi-ts'ui*, 1:17.

72. *Wen-chi*, 9:112.

73. Ch'en Chen-sheng; T. Hui-te and Sheng-fu. MS 282:7742; MJHA, 46:20–23; *Ming-jen so-yin*, p. 588. For his works see *Pu-i Ch'en hsien-sheng ts'un-kao; Cheng-i tang ch'üan-shu, Ch'en Pu-i wen-chi;* and *Ch'en Sheng-fu chi,* esp 1:6–9, 21–24.

74. *Shang-tsai yü-lu*, in *Chu Tzu i-shu*, 2:10a.

75. Chang, *Wen-chi*, 7:93–94, Ch'en Pu-i wen-chi hsü.

76. See Fang Chao-ying in Hummel, *Eminent Chinese*, pp. 747–49.

77. Chu Shih; T. Jo-chan, H. K'o-t'ing. Hummel, *Eminent Chinese*, p. 188–89; *CJHA*, 49:1.

78. Chang Po-hsing, *Wen-chi*, 9:117 Lun hsüeh; Araki Kengo, "Haku Ryo Ryūyō *Shisho kōgi* wo meguru jakkan no mondai."

79. See his memorial of presentation to the Yung-cheng Emperor in 1732, prefaced to Chu Shih, *Po Lü Liu-liang Ssu-shu chiang-i*, esp. 1:1b–2a.

80. Chu Shih, *Po Lü Liu-liang Ssu-shu chiang-i*, Ta-hsüeh:1a.

81. *Po Lü Liu-liang*, Ta hsüeh:1b–2a, 2b.

82. *Shang shu*, Chung hui chih kao; Legge, *Shoo King*, p. 182.

83. *Shih ching*, Ta-ya, Ta-ming; Legge, *She king*, p. 433.

84. *Analects* 2:4.

85. *Analects* 6:5.

86. *Mencius*, 4B:28; 7B:35, 2A:6.

87. *Po Lü Liu-liang*, Ta-hsüeh:5ab.

88. Chu, *Po Lü Liu-liang*, Ta-hsüeh:9b–10a, 24b–25a; Shang lun shang, 30b–31b; Hsia lun, 35b.

89. *Po lü Liu-liang*, Chung-yung, 7a–8a.

90. Ibid., 7a–8b.

6. Orthodoxy on the Eve of the Western Encounter

1. Liang Ch'i-ch'ao, *Ch'ing-tai hsüeh-shu kai-lun*. English translation published under the title of *Intellectual Trends in the Ch'ing Period*, p. 23.

2. Liang, *Intellectual Trends*, p. 78.

3. Hu Shih, *Tai Tung-yüan ti che-hsüeh*, p. 175.

4. So characterized in Fang Chao-ying's biography of Fang Pao in Hummel,

Eminent Chinese, p. 237. Fang Chao-ying was himself an excellent historian, and it was no particular prejudice of his but rather the common assumption of his "emancipated" generation that he gave vent to in such an opinion.

5. As shown for instance in Fang's extensive critique of Huang Tsung-hsi's *Nan-lei wen-ting (Ch'üan-chi;* tse 42) or his discussion of Buddhism in *Hsiang-kuo wei-yen* (tse 34, 35, 36), as well as in the *Han hsüeh shang-tui* itself.

6. Fang Tung-shu, *Han-hsüeh shang-tui,* 1900 (hereafter abbreviated *Shang-tui*).

7. *T'ung-ch'eng Fang Chih-chih hsien-sheng ch'üan-chi; K'ao-p'an chi wen-lu* (1848), 1:1a–13b; also in SSGTK, 11:430a, Pien-tao lun.

8. See the biographical and interpretive essay by Arita Kazuo in SSGTK, 11:36.

9. *K'ao-p'an chi wen-lu,* 4:31a–32b, Chung p'ien Chang Yang-yüan hsien-sheng nien-p'u.

10. Arita Kazuo, SSGTK, p. 36.

11. SSGTK, 11:424a (282), Han-hsüeh shang-tui hou hsü.

12. *Shang-tui,* 1:17b.

13. SSGTK, 11:424b (282), Han-hsüeh shang-tui hou hsü.

14. *Shang-tui,* 1:20a–22b.

15. SSGTK, 11:424b (283), Hou hsü.

16. *Shang-tui,* 1:15a–16b, 18ab.

17. *Shang-tui,* 1:15ab, 22ab.

18. *Ch'üan-chi,* tse 42, Pa Nan-lei wen-ting, 30a–31a.

19. *Ch'üan-chi, Shu-lin yang-chih,* A:37b–38a.

20. *T'ung-ch'eng Fang Chih-chih hsien-sheng ch'üan-chi, K'ao-p'an chi,* 1:1a–13b, Pien tao lun.

21. *K'ao-p'an chi,* 3:23b. Fang attributes this conception to "Master Tung" *(Tung Tzu),* but only the first sentence appears in *Han shu* 56 (Chung-hua ed., pp. 2518–19). The rest of the wording here I have been unable to locate in any of the extant writings of Tung or in the *Index du Tch'ouen Ts'ieou Fan Lou* (Peking: Centre Franco-Chinois d'études sinologiques, 1944), pp. 17–19, 94, 96–97. Wing-tsit Chan, in a personal communication, opines that the rest is Fang's own wording.

22. *K'ao-p'an chi,* 4:8a–10b, Ming-chi.

23. E.g., *Shang-tui,* 2B:10a, 11b, 47b, 48a; 3:9b.

24. *Shang-tui,* 1:1a–17a, esp. 9b–14b.

25. *Shang-tui,* 2A:6a.

26. *Shang-tui,* 1: Hsü li 1a.

27. *Ibid.,* 2A:1ab.

28. Fang does not hesitate to use the term in contexts where the distinction is made clear between Neo-Confucian and Buddhist *hsin-fa,* as in his analysis of the issues between Buddhism and Confucianism in *Hsiang-kuo wei-yen* (*Ch'üan-chi* tse 34), preface 8a and A:5a.

29. *Shang-tui,* 2A:2ab. See also SSGTK, 11:424a, Hou hsü.

30. *Shang-tui,* 2A:6a.

31. *Shang-tui,* 2A:2b–3a.

32. *Ibid.*, 2A:1b.

33. *Shang-tui*, 2A:3b, 4b; SSGTK, 11:432a–434b, Pien tao lun.

34. *Shang-tui*, 2A:3b.

35. Fang is well aware that Ku in the *Jih chih lu* makes much use of the writings or records of others, with only the briefest comment of his own (as in this case, less than one line). But the passage quoted here by Fang in 2A:5ab begins with the words "In my humble opinion," a standard opening formula used by commentators to mark the transition from quoted material to one's own comments, and Fang, reading the *Jih chih lu*, took this to be the start of Ku's comment, unaware that it too was quoted from the *Jih ch'ao* as the beginning of Huang's comment following his own quotations from Ts'ai Shen. Only by checking with Ts'ai Shen's original commentary, as well as Huang's *Jih ch'ao*, would one know where the commentary of one ends and the other begins, and so realize that the passage in question was not original with Ku. If Fang could be thus misled, it is understandable how Benjamin Elman, whether from reading *Jih-chih lu* or Fang's rejoinder, would have mistakenly attributed these opinions to Ku Yen-wu (see his "From Philosophy to Philology," pp. 203–4) rather than to Huang.

36. *Shang-tui*, 2A:6b–7a.

37. See also Fang, *Ch'üan-chi, Shu-lin yang-chih*, 2:25ab, Chu shu wu shih-yung.

38. SSGTK, 11:431a (303).

39. SSGTK, 11:36–37.

40. *K'ao-p'an chi wen lu*, 1:8b–10b (SSGTK, 11:432b–434b), Pien tao lun.

41. *Shang-tui*, 1:19a–22b, 2B:1a; 3:20a.

42. See also *Ssu-k'u ch'üan-shu tsung-mu t'i-yao*, 35:912–13, and *K'ao-p'an chi wen-lu*, 5:7b–11b, Shu Ch'ien Hsin-mei yang-hsin lu hou.

43. Fang underscores this in his preface to the *Han-hsüeh shang-tui*, 1b. As a major issue in Ch'ing thought, the subject is much more fully dealt with in Benjamin Elman, *From Philosophy to Philology: Intellectual and Social Aspects of Change in Late Imperial China.*

44. SSGTK, 11:427a (291).

45. *K'ao-p'an chi*, 4:32b–33b, Fang Wang-chi hsien-sheng nien-p'u hsü.

46. *Ibid.*, 427a (291), and Mao Hsing-lai, *Chin-ssu lu chi-chu*, 2:18a; Chan, *Things at Hand*, p. 52.

47. *Shang-tui*, 2B:10b–11a, 49ab.

48. So noted in the original editions of standard dictionaries such as *T'zu-hai* and *Tz'u-yüan*.

49. Referred to in my *Liberal Tradition in China*, pp. 37–40, 75–90.

50. For an extensive discussion of the problems of partisanship in late eighteenth–early nineteenth-century China, and the diverse factors and motivations at work, see James Polacheck, "The Inner Opium War," especially chapters 1, 2.

51. Elman, "From Philosophy to Philology" p. 203.

52. *K'ao-p'an chi wen-lu*, 4:32b–33b, Fang Wang-chi hsien-sheng nien-p'u hsü. Also SSGTK, 11:427ab.

53. *Shang-tui*, 3:20b. For this fundamental aim of Chu Hsi, see my *Liberal Tradition*, pp. 21–24.

54. *Shang-tui*, 2A:1b; 3:20b.

55. On this point see Elman, "From Philosophy to Philology," p. 202.

56. *Shang-tui*, 3:21b–22a.

57. *Lun-yü*, 1:1.

58. See also my *Liberal Tradition*, pp. 37–38. Fang also discusses the history of such discussion and the positive value of controversy as an essential element in scholarship and literature in a separate essay on Literary Debate found in *Ch'üan-chi, Shu lin yang chih*, B:1a–7b, Chu lin cheng-pien.

59. See Hamaguchi, "Hō Tōshu," p. 175a, citing the studies of Ōkubo Hideko in *Min-shin jidai shoin no kenkyū*, p. 337.

60. The point is discussed in Hamaguchi, "Hō Tōshu," pp. 170a–72b, and Elman, *From Philosophy to Philology*, pp. 242–45.

61. On the growing role of academies as research centers, see Elman, *From Philosophy to Philology*, pp. 136–37.

62. *K'ao-p'an chi wen-lu*, 1:33b–40b, and *I-te ch'üan ying lu*, Hsia: 13b–14a.

63. *Shang-tui*, 1:Chung hsü 3ab.

64. E.g., *Shang-tui*, 1:Hsü li 1b. However in *K'ao-p'an chi*, 7:18b, Hsin-chien T'ung-hsiang shu-yüan chi, Fang suggests criteria by which the Learning of the Mind might be adjudged proper or not.

65. See his discussion of the evolution of the term in *K'ao-p'an chi wen-lu*, 8:7b–8a, Pien-chih i-shou tseng Kan-sheng.

66. Polachek, "Inner Opium War," ch. 6, "The Ku Yen-wu Shrine Association."

67. T'ang Chien, *Ch'ing hsüeh-an hsiao shih*, 3/32.

68. Jerome Grieder, review of Elman's *From Philosophy to Philology*, p. 390.

69. See Fang, *Ch'üan-chi, Chu-lin yang-chih*, 2:25b.

Glossary

Araki Kengo 荒木見悟

Chan Jo-shui 湛若水
ch'an shih 禪師
Chang Heng-ch'ü 張橫渠
Chang Huang 章潢
Chang Lü-hsiang 張履祥
Chang Po-hsing 張伯行
Chang Shih 張栻
Chang Tsai 張載
Ch'ang Pi-te 昌彼得
Ch'en Ch'ang-fang 陳長方
Ch'en Chen-sheng 陳真晟
Ch'en Chien 陳建
Ch'en Ch'un 陳淳
Ch'en Ch'üeh (Ch'ien-ch'u) 陳確，
　乾初
Chen Hsi-shan 眞西山
Chen Te-hsiu 眞德秀
Ch'en Hsien-chang 陳獻章
Ch'en Li 陳櫟
Ch'en Lung-cheng 陳龍正
Ch'en Pai-sha 陳白沙
Ch'en Pu-i 陳布衣
Ch'en Ta-yu 陳大猷
Cheng Hsüan 鄭玄
cheng-hsüeh 正學

ch'eng 誠
Cheng ching 政經
Ch'eng Chü-fu 程鉅夫
Ch'eng Fu-hsin 程復心
Ch'eng Hao 程顥
Ch'eng I 程頤
Cheng-i t'ang ch'üan-shu 正誼堂
　全書
Ch'eng Min-cheng 程敏政
Ch'eng T'ung 程瞳
ch'eng-shen mo-tso 澄神默坐
Ch'eng-shih i-shu 程氏遺書
cheng-t'ung 正統
ch'i-pin 氣稟
ch'i so tsao chih shen 其所造之深
chia-kuei 家規
chiang-hsüeh 講學
chiang-hsüeh men-hu 講學門戶
chiang-i 講義
Ch'ien Ta-hsin 錢大昕
Ch'ien Te-hung 錢德洪
chih chih 致知
chih-fa 治法
chih liang-chih 致良知
chih-t'ung 治統
Chin-hsi yü-yao 近溪語要
Chin-ssu lu 近思錄

259

ching 敬

ching (quiescence) 靜

ching-hsüeh 經學

Ch'ing-ju hsüeh-an 清儒學案

ching-shih 經世

ching-shen 精神

Ch'iu Chün 邱濬

ch'iung-li 窮理

Chou Ch'i 周琦

Chou Ju-teng 周汝登

Chou Tun-i 周敦頤

chü-ching 居敬

chu-ching 主靜

Chu-hung 袾宏

chu-i 主一

Chu Shih 朱軾

Chu Tzu chia-li 朱子家禮

Chu Tzu ch'üan-shu 朱子全書

Chu Tzu ta-ch'üan 朱子大全

Chu Tzu yü-lei 朱子語類

Chü-yeh-lu 居業錄

ch'uan-hsin mi-chih 傳心密旨

ch'uan-tao cheng-t'ung 傳道正統

ch'uan-hsin 傳心

Ch'üan Tsu-wang 全祖望

chüeh 覺

chüeh-hsüeh 絕學

Daikanwa jiten 大漢和辭典

fa-shih 法師

Fang Tung-shu 方東樹

Fu Kuang 輔廣

Han-hsüeh shang-tui 漢學商兌

Han T'o-chou 韓侂冑

Hsieh Liang-tso 謝良佐

hsin 心

Hsin ching 心經

Hsin-an hsüeh-hsi lu 新安學繫錄

hsin-fa 心法

hsin-hsüeh 心學

hsin hsüeh (new teaching) 新學

hsin-shu 心術

hsin-tsung 心宗

Hsing-li ching-i 性理精義

Hsing-li cheng-tsung 性理正宗

hsing-li hsüeh 性理學

hsing shih-shih 行實事

hsiu-chi chih-jen 修己治人

Hsiung Chieh 熊節

Hsü Heng (Lu-chai) 許衡, 魯齋

Hsü Shih-ch'ang 徐世昌

hsüeh 學

Hsüeh Hsüan 薛瑄

Hsüeh-pu t'ung pien 學部通辨

Hsüeh-shu pien 學術辨

Hsüeh yen 學言

Hsüeh Ying-ch'i 薛應旂

hsün-ku 訓詁

Hsün Tzu 荀子

Hu Chü-jen 胡居仁

Huai-nan ko-wu 淮南格物

Huang Chen 黃震

Huang-Ch'ing ching-chieh 皇清經解

Huang Kan 黃榦

Huang-Ming shu 皇明書

Huang Shih-i 黃士毅

Huang Tsung-hsi 黃宗羲

Huang Yün-ch'i 黃筠谿

Hui-neng 慧能

Hung-fan 洪範

huo-jan kuan-t'ung 豁然貫通

i 義

i-kuan 一貫

i-li 義理

i-tao 翼道

I t'ung shu 易通書

jen 仁

jen-chu hsin-fa 人主心法

jen-hsin tao-hsin 人心道心

jen tao 人道

Jih chih lu 日知錄
jih yüeh lun-ch'ang wei shih-chi
　日月倫常爲實際
ju 儒
ju-lin 儒林
Juan Yüan 阮元

Kan-ch'üan 甘泉
kangaku 漢學
kang 綱
K'ang-hsi 康熙
Kao P'an-lung 高攀龍
k'ao-cheng 考證
ko-wu 格物
Ku Hsien-ch'eng 顧憲成
Ku Yen-wu 顧炎武
Kuan-chung 關中
Kuan-hsüeh 關學
Kuan Tzu 管子
k'uang 狂
K'un-chih chi 困知記
K'un-hsüeh chi 困學記
k'ung 空
kung-fu 工夫
K'ung-men ch'uan-shou hsin-fa
　孔門傳授心法

Li Chien-lo 李見羅
li-hsüeh 理學
Li-hsüeh tsung-ch'uan 理學宗傳
li-i fen-shu 理一分殊
Li Kuang-ti 李光地
Li Ts'ai 李材
Li T'ung 李侗
Li Yüan-kang 李元綱
Li Yung 李顒
liang-chih 良知
liang-hsin 良心
ling 靈
Liu Ch'i-shan 劉蕺山
Liu Tsung-chou 劉宗周
Lo Cheng-an 羅整菴

Lo Ch'in-shun 羅欽順
Lo Hung-hsien 羅洪先
Lo Ju-fang 羅汝芳
Lo Ta-ching 羅大經
Lo Ts'ung-yen 羅從彥
Lu Chia-shu 陸稼書
Lu Chiu-yüan 陸九淵
Lu Hsiang-shan 陸象山
Lu Lung-chi 陸隴其
Lu Shih-i 陸世儀
Lü Ching-yeh 呂涇野
Lü Liu-liang 呂留良
Lü Nan 呂柟
Lun-yü ta-ch'üan 論語大全

Ma Tuan-lin 馬端臨
ming-chiao 名教
ming ming-te 明明德
Ming-i tai-fang lu 明夷待訪錄
Ming-jen chuan-chi tzu-liao so-yin
　明人傳記資料索引
Ming-ju hsüeh-an 明儒學案
Ming-lun t'ang 明倫堂
Ming shih 明史
ming shih-li 明實理
ming-te 明德
Minmatsu shūkyō shisō kenkyū
　明末宗教思想研究
Morohashi Tetsuji 諸橋轍次
mo tso ch'ao-t'ing chih hua 黙佐朝
　廷治化
Mo Tzu 墨子

Nieh Pao 聶豹

Ou-yang Hsiu 歐陽修
Ou-yang Te 歐陽德

Pien-tao lun 辨道論
p'ien-ching 偏靜
p'ing-hsin erh lun, shih wei 平心
　而論, 實爲

po-hsüeh hung-tz'u 博學宏詞
P'o-hsieh lun 破邪論
Po Lü Liu-liang Ssu-shu chiang-i
　駁呂留良四書講義
pu-li wen-tzu 不立文字

San-yü-t'ang wen-chi 三魚堂文集
shen-tu 慎獨
Sheng-hsien tao-tung ch'uan-shou
　tsung hsü shuo 聖賢道統傳授
　總叙説
Sheng-hsien tao-t'ung 聖賢道統
sheng-hsüeh 聖學
Sheng-men shih-yeh t'u 聖門事業圖
Shiga Ichirō 志賀一郎
shih 識
shih-fei chih hsin 是非之心
shih-hsüeh 實學
shih shih ch'iu-shih 實事求是
Shih-Yu yüan-yüan 師友淵源
Shu-ching chi-chuan 書經集傳
Shun-yü ch'uan-hsin Chou-Ch'eng
　yen-hsing erh t'u 舜禹傳心周程
　言行二圖
Shushigaku taikei 朱子學大系
Sŏng-hak sipdo 聖學十圖
Ssu-shu chiang-i 四書講義
Ssu-shu fan-shen lu 四書反身錄
Ssu-k'u ch'üan-shu tsung-mu t'i-yao
　四庫全書總目提要
Ssu-pu ts'ung-k'an 四部叢刊
Ssu-shu fa-ming 四書發明
Ssu-shu t'u-shuo 四書圖説
ssu-wen 斯文
Sun Ch'i-feng 孫奇逢
sui-ch'u t'i-jen t'ien-li 隨處體認
　天理
Sun Pei-hai 孫北海
Sung-jen chuan-chi tzu-liao so-yin
　宋人傳記資料索引
Sung shih 宋史

Sung-Yüan hsüeh-an 宋元學案
Sung-Yüan hsüeh-an pu-i 補遺

ta-i 大意
Ta-hsüeh yen-i 大學衍義
Ta-hsüeh wen 大學問
tang 黨
T'ang Pin 湯斌
T'ang Po-yüan 唐伯元
tao-fa 道法
tao-hsüeh 道學
tao-t'ung 道統
tao wen-hsüeh 道問學
te-hsing 德性
Teng Yüan-hsi 鄧元錫
Ti-hsüeh lun 帝學論
t'i-jen t'ien-li 體認天理
ti-wang chih hsüeh 帝王之學
t'ien-li chih chieh-wen 天理之
　節文
t'ien-ming 天命
t'ien-ming chih hsing 天命之性
Tsa-hsüeh pien 雜學辨
Ts'ai Ching 蔡京
Ts'ai Chiu-feng 蔡九峰
Ts'ai Hang 蔡杭
Ts'ai Shen 蔡沈
Ts'ai Yüan-ting 蔡元定
Ts'ao Tuan 曹端
tse 則
Tseng Ching 曾靜
Tsou Shou-i 鄒守一
tsun te-hsing 尊德性
ts'un-hsin yao-fa 存心要法
ts'un shih-hsin 存實心
Tu Chu sui-pi hsü 讀朱隨筆序
Tu-shu lu 讀書錄
tu-shu jen 讀書人
T'ung-ch'eng 桐城
Tung Chung-shu 董仲舒
Tung-hsi jih-t'an lu 東西日談錄

Tung-lin 東林
tzu-te 自得
tz'u-ti 次第

Wang Chi 王畿
Wang Fu-chih 王夫之
Wang Ken 王艮
Wang-men tsung-chih 王門宗旨
Wang Shou-jen 王守仁
Wang Te-i 王德毅
Wang Tung 王東
Wang Yang-ming 王陽明
wei-hsüeh 偽學
wei-chi chih hsüeh 為己之學
Wei Chung-hsien 魏忠賢
Wei Liao-weng 魏了翁
Wen-chung Tzu 文中子
wen 文
Wen-hsien t'ung-k'ao 文獻通考
Wen-kung chia-li 文公家禮
wen-yüan 文苑
Wu-chu 無住

Wu Ch'eng 吳澄
wu-hsin 無心
wu-hsin yü shih 無心於事
wu-shih yü hsin 無事於心
wu-yü ku ching 無欲故靜
Wu Yü-pi 吳與弼

Yang Chien 楊簡
Yang Hsiung 揚雄
Yang Shih 楊時
Yao-chiang 姚江
Yao Nai 姚鼐
Yen Yüan 顏淵
Yen Sung 嚴嵩
Yi T'oegye 李退溪
yü-lu 語錄
yüan 元
Yüan-jen chuan-chi tzu-liao so-yin
　元人傳記資料索引
Yüan-tao 原道
Yung-cheng 雍正

Bibliography

WORKS CITED IN CHINESE, JAPANESE AND KOREAN

Araki Kengo 荒本見悟. *Minmatsu shūkyō shisō kenkyū* 明末宗教思想研究. Tokyo: Sōbunsha, 1979.

—— "Haku Ryo Ryūryō *Shisho kōgi* wo meguru jakkan no mondai" 駁呂留良四書講義をめぐる若干の問題. In *Yōmeigaku no kaiten to Bukkyō* 陽明学の開展と仏教, pp. 275–94. Tokyo: Kembun shuppansha, 1984.

Chan Jo-shui 湛若水. *K'ung-men ch'uan-shou hsin-fa lun* 孔門傳授心法論. In Shiga, *Tan Kansen*, Shiryōhen, pp. 408–10.

Chan Wing-tsit 陳榮捷. *Chu Tzu men-jen* 朱子門人. Taipei: Hsüeh-sheng, 1982.

—— Wang Yang-ming *Ch'uan-hsi lu hsiang-chu chi-p'ing* Taipei: Hsüeh-sheng, 1983. 王陽明傳習錄詳註集評.

Chang Huang 章潢. *T'u-shu pien* 圖書編. 1613 ed. In Kyoto University Jimbun kagaku kenkyūjo and Columbia University Starr Library.

Chang Lü-hsiang 張履祥. *Chang Yang-yüan ch'üan-chi* 張揚園全集. 1871 ed.

Ch'ang Pi-te 昌彼德. *Sung-jen chuan-chi tzu-liao so-yin* 宋人傳記資料索引. Taipei: T'ing-wen shu-chü, 1976.

Chang Po-hsing 張伯行. *Cheng-i t'ang ch'üan-shu* 正誼堂全書. 1866 ed.

—— *K'un-hsüeh lu chi-ts'ui* 困學錄集粹. TSCC ed. Also Item 56 in *Cheng-i t'ang ch'üan-shu*.

Ch'en Chen-sheng 陳眞晟. *Pu-i Ch'en hsien-sheng ts'un-kao* 布衣陳先生存稿. 1538 ed. 9 ch.

—— *Ch'en Sheng-fu hsien-sheng chi* 陳剩夫先生集. 4 ch. In *Cheng-i t'ang ch'üan-shu* and TSCC ed.

Ch'en Chien 陳建. *Hsüeh-pu t'ung-pien* 學蔀通辨. Taipei: Kuang-wen reprint, 1971.

Ch'en Ch'un 陳淳. *Pei-hsi tzu-i* 北溪字義. Beijing: Chung-hua, 1983.

Ch'en Li 陳櫟. *Shu-chi-chuan tsuan-shu* 書集傳纂疏. In *Wen-yüan ko ch'in-ting Ssu-k'u ch'üan-shu* 文淵閣欽定四庫全書.

Ch'en Lung-cheng 陳龍正. *Chi-t'ing wai-shu* 幾亭外書. Ming Ch'ung-chen 4 (1631) ed. In Naikaku bunko.

Ch'en Ta-yü 陳大禹. *Shang shu chi-chuan huo-wen* 尚書集傳或問. In *Wen-yüan ko ch'in-ting Ssu-k'u ch'üan-shu*.

Chen Te-hsiu 眞德秀. *Hsi-shan hsien-sheng Chen Wen-chung kung wen-chi* 西山先生眞文忠公文集. Taipei: Commercial Press KHCPTS ed., 1968.

—— *Hsin ching* 心經. Ming ed. In National Central Library, Taipei.

Ch'eng Fu-hsin 程復心. *Ssu-shu chang-t'u tsuan-shih* 四書章圖纂釋. Te-hsin t'ang ed. of 1337. In Naikaku bunko.

—— *Ssu-shu chang-t'u yin-k'uo tsung-yao* 四書章圖隱括總要. In National Central Library, Taipei. Hand copied version in Shōheikō collection of Naikaku bunko, Tokyo.

Ch'eng I 程頤. *Erh Ch'eng ch'üan-shu* 二程全書. 2 vols. with index. Kyoto: Chūbun shuppansha, 1979.

Ch'eng T'ung 程瞳, ed. *Hsin-an hsüeh-hsi lu* 新安學繫錄. In *Anhui ts'ung-shu* 安徽叢書.

Chia K'ai 甲凱. *Sung Ming hsin-hsüeh p'ing-shu* 宋明心學評述. Taiwan: Commercial Press, 1967.

Chiang Fan 江藩. *Sung-hsüeh yüan-yüan chi* 宋學淵源記. In *Ssu-ch'ao hsüeh-an*. Shanghai: Shih-chieh shu-chü, 1936.

Ch'ien Mu 錢穆. *Chu Tzu hsin hsüeh-an* 朱子新學案. Taipei: San-min shu-chü, 1971.

—— *Chung-kuo chin san-pai-nien hsüeh-shu shih* 中國近三百年學術史. Taipei: Taiwan Commercial Press reprint of 1937 edition, 1983.

—— *Wang Shou-jen* 王守仁. Shanghai: Commercial Press, 1934.

Ch'ien Ta-hsin 錢大昕. *Shih chia chai yang-hsin lu* 十駕齋養新錄. Kuang-su 2 (1876 ed.) Chekiang shu-chü.

Chou Ch'i 周琦. *Tung-hsi jih-t'an lu* 東溪日談錄. In *Ssu-k'u ch'üan-shu chen-pen*, erh chi. Taipei.

Chu Hsi 朱熹. *Chu Tzu i-shu* 朱子遺書. Taipei: I-wen yin-shu-kuan reprint of K'ang-hsi ed., 1969.

—— *Chu Tzu ta-ch'üan* 朱子大全. *SPPY ed.*

—— *Chu Tzu yü-lei* 朱子語類. cp. by Li Ching-te 黎靖德. Taipei: Cheng-chung, 1970.

—— *Chung-yung chang-chü* 中庸章句. See *Ssu-shu chi-chu*.

—— *Hsiao-hsüeh* 小學. In *Hsiao-hsüeh chi-chu*, 集註 SPPY ed.

—— *Hui-an hsien-sheng Chu Wen-kung wen-chi* 晦庵先生朱文公文集. Kyoto: Chūbun shuppansha, 1977.

—— *Ssu-shu chi-chu* 四書集註. Taipei: *Chung-kuo tzu-hsüeh ming-chu chi-ch'eng ed.* 中國子學名著集成, 1978.

—— *Ta-hsüeh chang-chü* 大學章句. See *Ssu-shu chi-chu.*

Chu Shih 朱軾. *Po Lü Liu-liang Ssu-shu chiang-i* 駁呂留良四書講義. 1731 ed., 8 ch.

Dai Nihon zoku zōkyō 大日本續藏経. Kyoto: 1905–12.

Fang Tung-shu 方東樹. *Han hsüeh shang-tui* 漢學商兌. 4 ch. Chekiang shu-chü, Kuang-hsü 26 (1900). ed.

—— *T'ung-ch'eng Fang chih-chih hsien-sheng ch'üan-chi* 桐城方植之先生全集.

Fung Yu-lan 馮友蘭. *Chung-kuo che-hsüeh shih* 中國哲學史. Beijing: Chung-hua, 1984.

Hamaguchi Fujio 濱口富士雄. "Hō Tōshu no kangaku hikan ni tsuite" 方東樹の漢学批判について. *Nihon Chūgoku gakkai hō*, No. 30 (1978), pp. 165–77.

Hihara Toshikuni 日原利国, ed. *Chūgoku shisō jiten* 中国思想辞典. Tokyo: Kembun shuppan, 1984.

Hsiung Chieh 熊節. *Hsing-li ch'ün-shu chü-chieh* 性理群書句解. Chūbun shuppansha KSKSSK reprint of Japanese 1668 ed., 3d series, No. 11.

Hsü Shih-ch'ang 徐世昌. *Ch'ing-ju hsüeh-an* 清儒學案. T'ientsin: 1938.

Hsüeh Hsüan 薛瑄. *Tu-shu lu* 讀書錄 in 53 ch. ed. of *Hsüeh Wen-ch'ing kung ch'üan-chi* 薛文清公全集. In Naikaku bunko, Tokyo [No. 299–87].

Hu Chü-jen 胡居仁. *Chü-yeh lu* 居業錄. In *Wen-yüan ko Ssu-k'u ch'üan-shu* ed. Taipei: Commercial Press, 1983.

Hu Kuang et al 胡廣. *Lun-yü chi-chu ta-ch'üan* 論語集註大全. CKTHMCCC ed. based on Ming edition of 1414 in National Central Library, Taipei. Also Genroku 4 (1691) ed. in Naikaku bunko (No. 277–41), Tokyo.

Hu Shih 胡適. *Tai Tung-yüan ti che-hsüeh* 戴東原的哲學. Peking: Jen-jen wen-k'u 人人文庫, 1926.

Huang Chen 黃震. *Huang shih jih-ch'ao* 黃氏日鈔. In *Ssu-k'u ch'üan-shu chen-pen*, erh chi.

Huang Kan 黃榦. *Mien-chai hsien-sheng Huang Wen-ssu kung wen-chi* 勉齋先生黃文肅公文集. Sung 40 ch ed., in Seikadō bunko, Tokyo.

Huang Tsung-hsi 黃宗羲. *Li Chou i-chu hui-k'an* 梨州遺箸彙刊. Hsieh Teng-ch'ang, ed. Shanghai: 1910.

—— *Ming-ju hsüeh-an* 明儒學案. Taipei: Commercial Press, Wan-yu wen-k'u ed., 1965.

—— *Nan-lei wen-ting* 南雷文定. Ch'ien chi TSCC ed.

Huang Tsung-hsi 黃宗羲 and Ch'üan Tsu-wang 全祖望. *Sung-Yüan hsüeh an* 宋元學案. Taipei: Ho-lo t'u-shu ch'u-pan she 河洛圖書出版社, 1975.

Ku Hsien-ch'eng 顧憲成. *Tuan-wen kung chi* 端文公集. Naikaku bunko ed. c. 1630.

Ku Yen-wu 顧炎武. *Jih chih lu chi-shih* 日知錄集釋. Kyoto: Chūbun shuppansha, 1978.

Li Kuang-ti 李光地. *Jung-ts'un ch'üan-chi* 榕村全集. Preface dated 1829.

—— *Ssu-shu chieh-i* 四書解義. 1825 ed.

Li Yüan-kang 李元綱. *Sheng-men shih-yeh t'u* 聖門事業圖. In *Pai-ch'uan hsüeh-hai* 百川學海.

Li Yung 李顒. *Li Erh-ch'ü hsien-sheng ch'üan-chi* 李二曲先生全集. Shanghai: Sao-yeh shan-fang 掃葉山房 ed., 1919.

Liang Ch'i-ch'ao 梁啓超. *Ch'ing-tai hsüeh-shu kai-lun* 清代學術概論. Shanghai: Commercial Press, 1927.

Lo Ch'in-shun 羅欽順. *K'un-chih chi* 困知記. Naikaku bunko ed. (Naikaku bunko kanseki mokuroku, p. 174.)

Lo Ju-fang 羅汝芳. *Chin-hsi yü-yao* 近溪語要. In *Lo Chin-hsi hsien-sheng ch'üan-chi* 羅近溪先生全集. Naikaku bunko 13 ch. ed.

Lo Ta-ching 羅大經. *Ho-lin yü-lu* 鶴林玉露. 18 chüan ed. of Kambun 2 (1662). Tokyo: Naikaku bunko.

Lu Lung-chi 陸隴其. *Lu Tzu ch'üan-shu* 陸子全書. Kuang-hsü 16 (1890) ed.

—— *San-yü t'ang chi* 三魚堂集. 1701 edition. In Beijing University Library with expurgations partially restored from unexpurgated edition in collection of Ku Chieh-kang.

Lu Shih-i 陸世儀. *Ssu-pien lu chi-yao* 思辨錄輯要. ch'ien-chi In *Ssu-k'u ch'üan-shu chen-pen ed.*, 4th series.

Lü Liu-liang 呂留良. *Ssu-shu chiang-i* 四書講義. 43 ch. ed. of 1686.

—— *Ssu-shu yü-lu* 四書語錄. In *T'ien-kai lou* 天蓋樓. 26-ch. ed. of 1684.

Ming Shen-tsung shih-lu 明神宗實錄. Taipei: Academia Sinica, 1962.

Ming-shih 明史. Chang T'ing-yü 張廷玉 et al., eds. Beijing: Chunghua, 1974.

Miura Shūichi 三浦秀一. "Tō Hin to Riku Ryūchi: Shinsho shidaibu no ningen rikai to keisei ishiki 湯斌と陸隴其: 清初士大夫の人間理解と 経世意識." *Bunka* (Tōhoku daigaku) (1984), 47 (1−2): 74−92.

Morohashi Tetsuji 諸橋轍次. *Dai kanwa jiten* 大漢和辞典. Tokyo: Taishūkan 大修館, 1960.

Morohashi Tetsuji, and Yasuoka Masahiro 安岡正篤. *Shushigaku taikei* 朱子学大系. Tokyo: Meitoku shuppansha, 明德出版社, 1974−82.

Okada Takehiko 岡田武彦. "Chō Yōen to Riku Futei" 張楊園と陸桴亭. In *Teoria*, no. 9, December 1965.

Ōkubo Hideko 大久保英子. *Min-Shin jidai shoin no kenkyū* 明清時代書院 の研究. Tokyo: Kokusho kankōkai 国書刊行会, 1976.

Shiga, Ichirō 志賀一郎. *Tan Kansen no kenkyū* 湛甘泉の研究. Tokyo: Fuma shobō, 1980.

—— *Tan Kansen no gakusetsu* 湛甘泉の学説. Tokyo: Fuma shobō, 1982.

Shimonaka Kunihiko 下中邦彦. *Ajia rekishi jiten* アジア歴史事典. Tokyo: Heibonsha, 1962.

Ssu-k'u ch'üan-shu tsung-mu t'i-yao 四庫全書總目提要. Chi Yün 紀昀 et al., eds. Shanghai; Commercial Press, 1933.

Sun Ch'i-feng 孫奇逢. *Li-hsüeh tsung-ch'uan* 理學宗傳. 26 ch. Taipei: I-wen yin-shu kuan, reprint of K'ang-hsi 5 (1666) ed., 1969.

Sung shih 宋史. T'o-t'o 脫脫 and Ou-yang Hsüan 歐陽玄, eds. Beijing: Chung-hua, 1977 ed.

Taishō shinshū daizōkyō 大正新修大藏経. Tokyo: 1914–22.

T'ang Chien 唐鑑. *Ch'ing hsüeh-an hsiao-shih* 清學案小識. In *Ssu-ch'ao hsüeh-an* 四朝學案. Shih-chieh shu-chü, 1936.

T'ang Pin 湯斌. *T'ang Ch'ien-an chi* 湯潛庵集, TSCC ed.

—— *T'ang Wen-cheng kung ch'üan-chi* 湯文正公全集. 1870 ed.

T'ang Po-yüan 唐伯元. *T'ang Shu-t'ai hsien-sheng chi* 唐睹臺先生集. In *Kuang li-hsüeh pei-k'ao* 廣理學備考, Wu-ching t'ang 五經堂 ed., 1702.

Teng Yüan-hsi 鄧元錫. *Huang-Ming shu* 皇明書. 1606 ed. In Kyoto University Jimbun kagaku kenkyūjo and Columbia University Starr Library.

Ts'ai Shen 蔡沈. *Shu-ching chi-chuan* 書經集傳. In *Wu-ching ssu-shu tu-pen* 五經四書讀本. Chia-ch'ing 10 (1805) ed.

Ts'ao Tuan 曹端. *Hsü Chung-chou ming-hsien wen-piao* 續中州名賢文表. K'ang-hsi 45 (1706) ed.

—— *Ts'ao Yüeh-ch'uan hsien-sheng chi* 曹月川先生集. K'ang-hsi 49 (1710) ed. in Naikaku bunko, Tokyo.

—— *T'ung-shu shu chieh* 通書述解. Ssu-k'u ch'üan-shu chen-pen, sixth series.

Tung Ting 董鼎. *Shang-shu chi-lu tsuan-chu* 尚書輯錄纂注 ed. *Wen-yüan ko Ssu-k'u ch'üan-shu*, Comm. Press ed. 61-631.

Tz'u hai 辭海. Shanghai, Chung-hua shu-chü 1937, revised edition, Hong Kong, 1937, Commercial Press, 1979–84.

Tz'u yüan 辭源. Shanghai: Commercial Press, 1926.

Uno Seiichi 宇野精一. *Shōgaku* 小学. Tokyo: Meiji shoin, 1965.

Wang Chi 王畿. *Lung-hsi chi* 龍溪集. Naikaku bunko copy of Wan-li 47 (1619) ed.

Wang Tzu-ts'ai 王梓材, and Feng Yün-hao 馮雲濠. *Sung-Yüan hsüeh-an pu-i* 宋元學案補遺. In *Ssu-ming ts'ung-shu* 四明叢書 ed.

Wang Yang-ming 王陽明. *Wang Yang-ming ch'üan-shu* 王陽明全書. Taipei: Cheng-chung shu-chü, 1953.

Wei Cheng-t'ung 韋政通. *Chung-kuo che-hsüeh tz'u-tien ta-ch'üan* 中國哲學辭典大全. Taipei: Shui-niu ch'u-pan-she 水牛出版社.

—— *Wen-yüan ko Ssu-k'u ch'üan-shu* 文淵閣四庫全書. Taipei: Commercial Press. 1983.

Yamanoi Yū 山井湧. "Riku Kasho" 陸稼書 in SSGTK XI, 20–24.

Yang Wan-li 楊萬里, Ch'eng-chai chi 誠齋集, SPTK ed.

Yi T'oegye 李退溪. I-hak t'ong-nok 理學通錄. In T'oegye chŏnsŏ 退溪全書. Seoul: Seng-kyun-kwan 成均館 ed. 1958.

—— T'oegye chŏnsŏ 退溪全書. In the edition published by the Ri Taikei kenkyūkai 李退溪研究会. Tokyo, 1975.

Yüan-jen chuan-chi tzu-liao so-yin 元人傳記資料索引. Wang Te-i 王德毅 et al., eds. Taipei: Hsin Wen-feng, 1979.

Yüan shih 元史. Sung Lien 宋濂 et al., eds. Beijing: Chung-hua, 1976.

WORKS CITED IN WESTERN LANGUAGES

Bloom, Irene. Knowledge Painfully Acquired: The K'un-chih chi by Lo Ch'in-shun. New York: Columbia University Press, 1987.

—— "On the 'Abstraction' of Ming Thought: Some Concrete Evidence from the Philosophy of Lo Ch'in-shun." In de Bary and Bloom, eds., Principle and Practicality, pp. 69–125.

Busch, Heinrich. "The Tunglin Shu-yüan and Its Political and Social Significance," Monumenta Serica (1949–55), vol. 14.

Chan, Hok-lam, Legitimation in Imperial China. Seattle: University of Washington Press, 1985.

Chan, Hok-lam and W. T. de Bary. Yüan Thought: Chinese Religion and Thought Under the Mongols. New York: Columbia University Press, 1982.

Chan, Wing-tsit. "The Ch'eng-Chu School of the Early Ming." In de Bary, ed., Self and Society in Ming Thought, pp. 29–52.

—— "Chu Hsi and Yüan Confucianism." In Chan and de Bary, Yüan Thought, pp. 197–232.

—— "The Hsing-li ching-i and the Ch'eng-Chu School in the Early Ching." In de Bary, ed., The Unfolding of Neo-Confucianism, pp. 543–572.

—— "How T'oegye Understood Chu Hsi." In W. T. de Bary and Ja-Hyun Kim Haboush, eds., The Rise of Neo-Confucianism in Korea, pp. New York: Columbia University Press, 1985.

—— Instructions on Things at Hand, New York: Columbia University Press, 1963.

—— Neo-Confucian Terms Explained: The Pei-hsi tzu-i by Ch'en Ch'un (1159-1223). New York: Columbia University Press, 1986.

—— Reflections on Things at Hand. Tr. of Chu Hsi's Chin-ssu lu. New York: Columbia University Press, 1967.

—— A Source Book in Chinese Philosophy. Princeton: Princeton University Press, 1963.

Ch'ien, Edward. *Chiao Hung and the Restructuring of Neo-Confucianism in the Late Ming*. New York: Columbia University Press, 1985.

Ching, Julia. *To Acquire Wisdom: The Way of Wang Yang-ming*. New York: Columbia University Press, 1976.

Ching, Julia, ed. *The Records of Ming Scholars*. Honolulu: University of Hawaii Press, 1987.

Davis, Richard L. "Historiography as Politics in Yang Wei-chen's 'Polemic on Legitimate Succession.'" *T'oung pao*, 69: 33–72.

de Bary, Wm. Theodore. *The Buddhist Tradition*. New York: Random House, 1969.

—— "Chu Hsi's Aims as an Educator." In W. T. de Bary and John Chaffee, eds. *Neo-Confucian Education: The Formative Stage*. Berkeley: University of California Press, 1988.

—— "Individualism and Humanitarianism in Late Ming Thought." In de Bary, ed., *Self and Society in Ming Thought*, pp. 145–248.

—— *The Liberal Tradition in China*. Hong Kong: Chinese University Press, 1982.

—— *Neo-Confucian Orthodoxy and the Learning of the Mind-and-Heart*. New York: Columbia University Press, 1981.

—— *Self and Society in Ming Thought*. New York: Columbia University Press, 1970.

—— *The Unfolding of Neo-Confucianism*. New York: Columbia University Press, 1975.

de Bary, W. T. and Irene Bloom, eds. *Principle and Practicality: Essays in Neo-Confucianism and Practical Learning*. New York: Columbia University Press, 1979.

de Bary, W. T., Wing-tsit Chan, and Burton Watson, eds. *Sources of Chinese Tradition*. New York: Columbia University Press, 1960.

de Bary, W. T. and Ja-Hyun Kim Haboush, eds. *The Rise of Neo-Confucianism in Korea*. New York: Columbia University Press, 1985.

Deuchler, Martina. "Reject the False and Uphold the Straight: Attitudes Toward Heterodox Thought in Early Yi Korea." In de Bary and Haboush, eds., *The Rise of Neo-Confucianism in Korea*, pp. 375–410.

Elman, Benjamin. *From Philosophy to Philology: Intellectual and Social Aspects of Change in Late Imperial China*. Cambridge: Harvard University Press, 1984.

—— "Philosophy (*I-li*) versus Philology (*K'ao-cheng*): The *Jen-hsin Tao-hsin* Debate." In *T'oung pao*, (1983), 69: 175–222.

Franke, Wolfgang. *An Introduction to the Sources of Ming History*. Kuala Lumpur/Singapore: University of Malaya Press, 1968.

Fung Yu-lan. *A History of Chinese Philosophy*. 2 vols. Derk Bodde, tr. Princeton: Princeton University Press, 1963.

Goodrich, L. Carrington and Chao-ying Fang, eds. *Dictionary of Ming Biography*. New York: Columbia University Press, 1976. (Abbreviated herein as *DMB*.)

Grieder, Jerome. Review of Benjamin Elman, *From Philosopy to Philology*. In *Journal of Asian Studies* (May 1987), 46(2): 388–390.

Hervouet, Yves, ed. *A Sung Bibliography*. Hong Kong: Chinese University Press, 1978; New York: Columbia University Press, 1979.

Hummel, Arthur W., ed. *Eminent Chinese of the Ch'ing Period*. Washington, D.C.: GPO, 1943.

Jansen, Marius, ed. *Changing Japanese Attitudes Toward Modernization*. Princeton: Princeton University Press, 1965.

Jen Yu-wen. "Ch'en Hsien-chang's Philosophy of the Natural." In de Bary, ed., *Self and Society in Ming Thought*, pp. 53–92.

Jiang, Paul Y. *The Search for Mind*. Singapore: Singapore University Press, 1980.

Kelleher, Theresa. "Personal Reflections on the Pursuit of Sagehood: The Life and Journal of Wu Yü-pi." Ph.D. dissertation, Columbia University. Ann Arbor. University Microfilms, 1982.

Langlois, John D., Jr., ed. *China Under the Mongols*. Princeton: Princeton University Press, 1981.

Legge, James. *The Chinese Classics*. 2d ed. rev. Oxford: Clarendon Press, 1892; rpt. Taipei, 1966.

Yi king. As reprinted in *I-Ching, Book of Changes*, ed. by Ch'u Chai with Winberg Chai. New Hyde Park, N.Y.: University Books, 1964.

Legge, James, tr. *The Shoo King*. See *The Chinese Classics*, vol. 1.

Liang Ch'i-ch'ao. *Intellectual Trends in the Ch'ing Period*. Immanuel Hsü, tr. Cambridge: Harvard University Press, 1959.

Liu T'sun-yan. "Taoist Self-Cultivation in Ming Thought." In de Bary, ed., *Self and Society in Ming Thought*, pp. 291–330.

Munro, Donald, ed. *Individualism and Holism: Studies in Confucian and Taoist Values*. Ann Arbor: University of Michigan Press, 1985.

Polachek, James. "The Inner Opium War." Ph.D. dissertation, University of California, Berkeley, 1982.

Tu, Wei-ming. *Neo-Confucian Thought in Action: Wang Yang-ming's Youth (1472–1509)*. Berkeley: University of California Press, 1976.

Wilhelm, Hellmut. "Chinese Confucianism on the Eve of the Great Encounter." In Marius Jansen, ed. *Changing Japanese Attitudes Toward Modernization*, Princeton: Princeton University Press, 1965.

Yampolsky, Philip. *The Platform Sutra of the Sixth Patriarch*. New York: Columbia University Press, 1967.

Yanagida Seizan. "The *Li-tai fa pao chi* and the Ch'an doctrine of Sudden Awakening." In Lewis Lancaster and Whalen Lai, eds., *Early Ch'an in China and Tibet*. Berkeley: Berkeley Buddhist Studies, 1983.

Index

"Abiding in reverence" (*chü-ching*), 145, 147
Academies (*shu-yüan*), 72, 73, 90, 203, 219, 224, 225
"Amended Version of the Lü Family Compact" (Chu Hsi), 141
Analects, 2, 7, 16, 33, 39, 45, 49, 74, 75, 78, 81, 137–39, 193, 211, 222, 223, 226
Anti-intellectualism, 103, 111, 122, 124
"Articles of the White Deer Grotto Academy" (Chu Hsi), 141, 223
Awakening (*chüeh*), 193

Bodhisattvahood, 4
Book of Documents (Shu-ching), 9, 40, 42, 46, 47, 104, 105, 209, 211, 222
Book of Shang (Shang-shu), 41, 42, 44, 49, 50, 75, 208, 209; commentary on the *Book of Shang*, 40, 44, 208; Great Plan (*Hung-fan*), 40
Book-learning, 27, 77, 90, 98, 100, 111, 115, 184, 201
Breakthrough to integral comprehension/ understanding (*huo-jan kuan-t'ung*), 8, 140, 145, 150, 161, 167, 214, 226, 232, 145, 226
Bright virtue (*ming-te*), 85, 113, 117, 135, 136, 139, 153-56, 196
Broad learning, 34, 111, 156, 203, 214, 215
Buddhahood, 4, 26, 137
Buddha-mind, 13, 21
Buddha-nature, 15, 19, 22, 140

Buddhism, 4-7, 9, 12, 13, 15-19, 21, 22, 29, 30, 37, 42-44, 50, 51, 74, 82, 97-103, 107, 112, 116, 120, 128, 133, 135, 139, 142, 149, 166, 167, 170-72, 179, 183, 186, 187, 197, 198, 203, 206-8, 210, 212, 213, 217, 220, 221, 224, 226, 231; Buddhist Learning of the Mind, 37, 136; examination of the mind, 13; Hinayana, 18; Mahayana, 18-20

Case Studies of Ch'ing Confucians (Ch'ing-ju hsüeh-an) (Hsü Shih-ch'ang), 152
Case Studies of Ming Confucians (Ming-ju hsüeh-an) (Huang Tsung-hsi), 104, 107, 108, 114, 129, 192
Catalogue of the Imperial Manuscript Library (Ssu-k'u ch'üan-shu tsung-mu), 77, 113-14, 130, 216
Chan, Wing-tsit, xv, 13, 72, 73, 85, 170, 176, 177, 180, 184
Chan Jo-shui (1466-1560), 79, 89, 105, 115, 119, 125, 146, 155
Ch'an Buddhism, 4, 6, 8, 13, 15-19, 21, 22, 29, 30, 42, 43, 50, 74, 82, 84, 94, 97-103, 110, 112, 113, 116, 128, 129, 131, 142-44, 147, 149, 150, 165-67, 172, 184, 190, 194, 195, 209, 210, 212-14, 217, 220, 221, 224, 226; Ch'an enlightenment, 150; Ch'an examination of the mind, 13; Ch'an Learning, 84, 101, 143; Ch'an meditation, 17, 166, 184, 190; Ch'an School (*Ch'an-tsung*), 149; word-

273

Other Works in the Columbia Asian Studies Series

NEO-CONFUCIAN STUDIES

Knowledge Painfully Acquired: The K'un-chih chi *by Lo Chi'in-shun,*
   ed. and tr. Irene Bloom   1987
To Become a Sage: The Ten Diagrams on Sage Learning by Yi T'oegye,
   ed. and tr. Michael C. Kalton   1988
A Heritage of Kings: One Man's Monarchy in the Confucian
   World, by JaHyun Kim Haboush   1988

INTRODUCTION TO ORIENTAL CIVILIZATIONS
WM. THEODORE DE BARY, EDITOR

Sources of Japanese Tradition   1958   Paperback ed., 2 vols., 1964
Sources of Indian Tradition   1958   Paperback ed., 2 vols., 1964
Sources of Indian Tradition   1988   Second edition, 2 vols.
Sources of Chinese Tradition   1960   Paperback ed., 2 vols., 1964

TRANSLATIONS FROM THE ORIENTAL CLASSICS

Major Plays of Chikamatsu, tr. Donald Keene   1961
Four Major Plays of Chikamatsu, tr. Donald Keene. Paperback text
   edition   1961
Records of the Grand Historian of China, translated from the Shih chi
   of Ssu-ma Ch'ien, tr. Burton Watson, 2 vols.   1961
Instructions for Practical Living and Other Neo-Confucian Writings by
   Wang Yang-ming, tr. Wing-tsit Chan   1963
Chuang Tzu: Basic Writings, tr. Burton Watson, paperback ed.
   only   1964
The Mahābhārata, tr. Chakravarthi V. Narasimhan. Also in paper-
   back ed.   1965
The Manyōshū, Nippon Gakujutsu Shinkōkai edition   1965
Su Tung-p'o: Selections from a Sung Dynasty Poet, tr. Burton Watson.
   Also in paperback ed.   1965
Bhartrihari: Poems, tr. Barbara Stoler Miller. Also in paper-
   back ed.   1967
Basic Writings of Mo Tzu, Hsün Tzu, and Han Fei Tzu, tr. Burton
   Watson. Also in separate paperback eds.   1967
The Awakening of Faith, Attributed to Aśvaghosha, tr. Yoshito
   S. Hakeda. Also in paperback ed.   1967
Reflections on Things at Hand: The Neo-Confucian Anthology, comp.
   Chu Hsi and Lü Tsu-ch'ien, tr. Wing-tsit Chan   1967
The Platform Sutra of the Sixth Patriarch, tr. Philip B. Yampolsky.
   Also in paperback ed.   1967
Essays in Idleness: The Tsurezuregusa of Kenkō, tr. Donald Keene.
   Also in paperback ed.   1967

The Pillow Book of Sei Shōnagon, tr. Ivan Morris, 2 vols.   1967

Two Plays of Ancient India: The Little Clay Cart and the Minister's Seal, tr. J. A. B. van Buitenen   1968

The Complete Works of Chuang Tzu, tr. Burton Watson   1968

The Romance of the Western Chamber (Hsi Hsiang chi), tr. S. I. Hsiung. Also in paperback ed.   1968

The Manyōshuū, Nippon Gakujutsu Shinkōkai edition. Paperback text edition.   1969

Records of the Historian: Chapters from the Shih chi of Ssu-ma Ch'ien. Paperback text edition, tr. Burton Watson   1969

Cold Mountain: 100 Poems by the T'ang Poet Han-shan, tr. Burton Watson. Also in paperback ed.   1970

Twenty Plays of the Nō Theatre, ed. Donald Keene. Also in paperback ed.   1970

Chushingura: The Treasury of Loyal Retainers, tr. Donald Keene. Also in paperback ed.   1971

The Zen Master Hakuin: Selected Writings, tr. Philip B. Yampolsky   1971

Chinese Rhyme-Prose: Poems in the Fu Form from the Han and Six Dynasties Periods, tr. Burton Watson. Also in paperback ed.   1971

Kūkai: Major Works, tr. Yoshito S. Hakeda. Also in paperback ed.   1972

The Old Man Who Does as He Pleases: Selections from the Poetry and Prose of Lu Yu, tr. Burton Watson   1973

The Lion's Roar of Queen Śrīmālā, tr. Alex and Hideko Wayman   1974

Courtier and Commoner in Ancient China: Selections from the History of the Former Han by Pan Ku, tr. Burton Watson. Also in paperback ed.   1974

Japanese Literature in Chinese, vol. I: *Poetry and Prose in Chinese by Japanese Writers of the Early Period,* tr. Burton Watson   1975

Japanese Literature in Chinese, vol. 2: *Poetry and Prose in Chinese by Japanese Writers of the Later Period,* tr. Burton Watson   1976

Scripture of the Lotus Blossom of the Fine Dharma, tr. Leon Hurvitz. Also in paperback ed.   1976

Love Song of the Dark Lord: Jayadeva's Gītagovinda, tr. Barbara Stoler Miller. Also in paperback ed. Cloth ed. includes critical text of the Sanskrit.   1977

Ryōkan: Zen Monk-Poet of Japan, tr. Burton Watson   1977

Calming the Mind and Discerning the Real: From the Lam rim chen mo of Tsonkhapa, tr. Alex Wayman   1978

The Hermit and the Love-Thief: Sanskrit Poems of Bhartrihari and Bilhana, tr. Barbara Stoler Miller   1978

The Lute: Kao Ming's p'i-p'a chi, tr. Jean Mulligan. Also in paperback ed.   1980

A Chronicle of Gods and Sovereigns: Jinnō Shōtōki of Kitabatake Chikafusa, tr. H. Paul Varley   1980

COMPANIONS TO ASIAN STUDIES

MODERN ASIAN LITERATURE SERIES

STUDIES IN ORIENTAL CULTURE

The Curse of the Father covers several difficult issues,
including depression and suicide.

Please remember that the diagnosis and treatment of depression and other psychiatric disorders requires trained medical professionals. The story told in these pages is designed to offer a fantastical story that shares Biblical insights about the battles some individuals face. The teaching therein should not be used as a substitute for seeking professional care for the diagnosis and treatment of any mental/psychiatric disorders. If you feel you are in crisis, or know someone who needs help, please call the National Suicide Prevention Lifeline. It is a free, 24-hour hotline, at 1.800.273.TALK (8255). Your call will be connected to the crisis center nearest to you. If you are in an emergency, call 911 or go to your nearest emergency room.

suicidepreventionlifeline.org

You are not alone.